Date Due

A Guide to
Small Business
Management:
Text and Cases

A. THOMAS HOLLINGSWORTH

University of South Carolina
School of Business Administration
Columbia, South Carolina

HERBERT H. HAND

Professor of Management
University of Management
University of South Carolina
and
Director, Small Business Development Center
of South Carolina

1979   W. B. SAUNDERS COMPANY   Philadelphia/London/Toronto

W. B. Saunders Company: West Washington Square
Philadelphia, Pa.   19105

1 St. Anne's Road
Eastbourne, East Sussex BN21 3UN, England

1 Goldthorne Avenue
Toronto, Ontario M8Z 5T9, Canada

Library of Congress Cataloging in Publication Data

Hollingsworth, Abner Thomas, 1939–

A guide to small business management.

1. Small business – Management.   2. New business
   enterprises – Management.   I. Hand, Herbert H., joint
   author.   II. Title.   III. Title: Small business
   management.

HD69.S6H578   658′.022   77–11336

ISBN 0–7216–4744–8

A Guide to Small Business Management: Text and Cases   ISBN   0-7216-4744-8

Last digit is the print number: 9   8   7   6   5   4   3   2   1

To Our Families

FOREWORD

Various definitions for a small business exist. The Small Business Administration utilizes maximum sizes in its definitions of small businesses. In the retailing sector, a business is small if its sales do not exceed $2 million to $7.5 million, with the definition varying based on the specific type of business. In the services sector, a business is small when its receipts are less than $2 million to $8 million, depending on the type of service business. In the wholesaling sector, a business is small if the sales do not exceed $9.5 million to $22 million, with the definition again varying based on the type of wholesaling business. In the manufacturing sector, the business is small if it employs less than 250 to 1500 employees, depending on the industry. In view of these definitions, over 95 per cent of all businesses in the United States may be classified as small.

When we pick up the newspaper or watch television or hear the stock market report, we essentially hear the "Fortune 500" companies. In many ways, the material success of the United States is associated with the General Motors, the United States Steels, the Gulf Oil Corporations, and other large firms. However, 19 out of 20 businesses in the United States are small, even though 80 per cent of the Gross National Product is contributed by the large firms. Therefore, small business is an extremely important element in our society.

The Committee for Economic Development formulated a definition of small business in 1947 that is still appropriate today; a small business must be characterized by a minimum of two of the following categories:

1. Management is independent and most often characterized by the managers being the owners. Independence, in this case, means independence from outside stockholder control over management decisions.
2. Equity capital is supplied by an individual or small group. This places a small business in contrast to companies

where equity stocks are traded on a stock exchange or as an over-the-counter stock.

3. The operations are essentially local. One interpretation of this is that "local" may vary with whether the business is service, retailing, wholesaling, or manufacturing. However, "local" usually means that the employees and owners live in the same general area. For wholesaling and manufacturing businesses, particularly, markets may be elsewhere, but production or warehousing functions would usually be in one location.

4. The business must be small compared to the largest competitors. For example, at one time, American Motors was considered to be a small manufacturer because of the ratio of its sales to those of General Motors.

The preceding definitions of small business present general guidelines. Almost all new ventures are small, whether they are service, retail, wholesale, or manufacturing businesses. From a practical viewpoint, the definition of "small" varies among small-businessmen themselves. No doubt, some individuals in the retail sector may consider their business to be large when sales reach $200,000. Most entrepreneurs intuitively know when their business is no longer small. Presumably, they will know by changes in their accustomed method of operation or the way the business must be restructured or reorganized. An important, but often unstated, definition of the small business is that the small-businessman must be in direct control of the operation. While this definition lacks the neatness and precision of both the Small Business Administration and Committee for Economic Development definitions, it does capture the reality of the small business.

It is the aim of the Small Business Administration to aid, both financially and managerially, the small firms. The Small Business Institute (SBI) has been a significant step in offering managerial assistance to the small firm, as well as giving college students excellent business training. A number of the cases in this text are a direct result of the SBI Program.

LINCOLN A. SIMON
Chief of Management Advisory Services
Small Business Administration
Washington, DC

PREFACE

Many individuals are operating or considering operating their own small business. The decision to enter the area of small business is a major one for most people. It affects your life, family, resources, friends, and ego.

While the decision is a major one, it can be fun. This is particularly true when you have gathered the necessary information to make a truly rational decision for yourself.

The purpose of the text is to assist you in initiating and operating your own small business. The book does not *detail* every aspect of the small business, but it does cover all aspects and assists the reader in finding more information about them.

There has been a great deal of work done in the area of small business, but much of it is, at best, anecdotal and difficult to apply. We have tried to exclude these aspects. In its place, an attempt has been made to bring together various pragmatic guidelines that, if followed, will lead to success in small business. The book is directed at students who are interested in initiating a business of their own or entering an existing small business, and at small-businessmen and women who want to improve their present business performance.

We have kept the material both succinct and straightforward without sacrificing completeness. The reader should be able to answer the following questions through the use of this text: First; "Do I really want to be a successful small-business owner?" Second; "What are the things that I must do to initiate and attain success in the small-business area?"

The book is divided into three sections. Section I, The Entrepreneur and the Process of Small Business, consists of two chapters. Chapter 1 discusses entrepreneurs and the characteristics that make them successful at various stages in their businesses' life cycles. It also provides a self-test, by which you may assess your own characteristics relative to success in small business. Chapter 2 describes a model for analysis of the small firm.

Section II, Initiating the New Firm, outlines the various aspects of starting the new firm. The Business Plan is the keystone of the section and each chapter contributes to the formulation of the plan.

Section III, Managing the Small Business, covers those functions which must be performed if a firm is to be successful.

The large number of cases provided in the text allows the reader to gain first-hand knowledge of the myriad opportunities and problems facing the small business. We feel that in order to comprehend the concepts described in the first three sections of the text, these concepts must be applied. The cases serve this purpose by allowing you to see how concepts have been applied, both correctly and incorrectly. The cases have been selected to give you as broad a view as possible of the area of small business.

A series of checklists have been provided in Appendix I. We feel that these can be utilized as guidelines by small-business owners. Such checklists are only worthwhile if utilized prior to a decision, and we would suggest that you carefully review each one.

Appendix II covers the various facets of the legal environment facing the small-business owner. It also offers an appraisal of the various forms of legal structure that can be utilized by small businesses.

We would like to thank the following persons for their helpful suggestions in the preparation of this book:

Narendra Bhandari—University of Baltimore
C. Edward Cavert—Northern Virginia Community College
Benjamin Compaine—Knowledge Industry Reports
Roger Collons—Drexel University
Richard L. Howe—Orange Coast College
Richard Lorentz—University of Wisconsin, Eau Claire
Frank Paine—University of Maryland
Roderick D. Powers—Iowa State University
Joseph C. Schabacker—Arizona State University
Leonard T. Schira—Western Kentucky University
Dennis H. Tootelian—California State University, Sacramento

CONTENTS

I. THE ENTREPRENEUR AND THE PROCESS OF SMALL BUSINESS   1

Chapter 1

AREAS OF OPPORTUNITY FOR SMALL BUSINESS AND CHARACTERISTICS OF OWNERS   3

Chapter 2

THE SMALL BUSINESS AS A PROCESS   19

II. INITIATING THE NEW FIRM   31

Chapter 3

THE BUSINESS PLAN: KEYSTONE OF THE FIRM   33

Chapter 4

FINANCING THE SMALL BUSINESS   41

Chapter 5

SALES PROGRAMS FOR SMALL BUSINESSES   51

Chapter 6

SITE AND LOCATION ANALYSIS FOR THE SMALL BUSINESS   66

Chapter 7

PREPARATION OF PRO FORMA STATEMENTS   84

III. MANAGING THE SMALL BUSINESS   95

"THE MAN WHO MANAGED HIS BUSINESS BY EAR"
(A Case and MBO Exercise)   97

Chapter 8
THE MANAGEMENT OF THE SMALL BUSINESS   109

Chapter 9
RECORDS FOR THE SMALL BUSINESS   128

Chapter 10
THE FUTURE: COPING WITH CHANGE AND UNCERTAINTY   141

APPENDIX I
CHECKLISTS FOR SMALL-BUSINESS OWNERS   145
    A. Checklist for Starting a Business   145
    B. Checklist for Evaluating a Franchise   154
    C. Checklist for Buying a Business   162
    D. Checklist for Location Analysis   163
    E. Checklist for Site Analysis   163
    F. Checklist for Marketing Analysis   167
    G. Checklist for Promotional Advertising (newspaper)   169
    H. Checklist for Interior Layout Arrangements   171

APPENDIX II
THE LEGAL ASPECTS OF SMALL BUSINESS   173

CASES   216
  1. Student Enterprises   216
  2. Edgar Speer   225
  3. The Case of the Missing Time   239
  4. Expressway Lumber Company   245
  5. Star Tool and Machine Company, Incorporated   251
  6. The Wheel, Incorporated   263
  7. Fu Chow House   274
  8. The Richard Tracy Detective Agency   280
  9. S.T.'s Chopper Shop   291
10. Repair, Renovation, Rejuvenation:
    Auto-restorations Incorporated   300
11. Harris Tire and Retreading Company   313
12. Sports 1999   324
13. Lundberg's Superette and Package Store   335
14. The Sports Center   342
15. The Last Dinosaur: A Craftsman in Thought and Deed   346
16. Sunny Days Nursing Home   356

17. Industrial Door, Incorporated   370
18. Max's Exxon Service Station   383
19. American Hydraulic Paper Cutter, Incorporated   392
20. Barnes Lumber Company   402
21. J.W. Adams Company   412
22. Harten House Motor Inn and Restaurant   423

Index   424

THE ENTREPRENEUR AND THE PROCESS OF SMALL BUSINESS

This section deals with the characteristics common to entrepreneurs and the opportunities available to them. Chapter 1 defines the characteristics most often associated with successful entrepreneurs and offers a check list for evaluating yourself against such characteristics. This chapter also explores a number of opportunities available to small business.

Chapter 2 looks at small business as a process. A succinct decision model is provided to allow analysis of cases, both on-going concerns and new ventures. Careful attention to this model will enhance the probability of success in business for potential entrepreneurs.

CHAPTER 1

AREAS OF OPPORTUNITY FOR SMALL BUSINESS AND CHARACTERISTICS OF SMALL-BUSINESS OWNERS

INTRODUCTION

This chapter provides insight into the various opportunities available to the small-business owner. It also examines these owners in terms of the characteristics most often associated with them at various stages in the life cycle of the company. A self-analysis checklist will help you determine your readiness for entering a small business.

WHAT SMALL BUSINESSES OFFER THE BEST CHANCES FOR SUCCESS?

The six categories discussed in this chapter represent the fields in which businesses are most likely to be successful. A balanced and practical view of opportunities and risks for potential entrepreneurs is presented. After reading this section, you may have the impression that only the less attractive opportunities are left for small businesses. This is, in part, true. However, within these areas exist many worthwhile opportunities that have a huge potential for success.

THE SMALL-BUSINESS OWNER AS A TECHNOLOGICAL INNOVATOR

One of the assumptions of economic theory is that the small business can attain economic success if it is the first in the field with a new product or a technological breakthrough or service. This appears obvious to the casual observer. However, several cautions are necessary when considering the technological innovator. Almost all technologically oriented small businesses are located in the vicinity of technological centers. For example, the Route 128 research complex near Boston is composed primarily of technological innovators. Many outstanding educational institutions and research centers are located in the area. The technological innovators utilize both the abundance of written technical reports and researchers from these institutions. In many ways, this type of small business is restricted to specific locations, such as Boston, Washington, D.C., and Los Angeles. The second caution is that small businesses generally gain access to those aspects of technological innovation that the large corporations elect not to use. Therefore, the profit potential and profit stability are probably too low for the larger concerns to consider. The third caution regarding technological innovation is that there exists a heavy reliance on federal government support for the financing of the ventures through grants and research contracts. One reason for this is that the risk level is so high that commercial lending institutions generally prefer more conservative ventures. The disadvantage of a heavy reliance on government assistance is that little financial continuity exists for the company, as most funding of this type does not exceed one year.

Nevertheless, opportunities do exist for technological entrepreneurs. The opportunities are limited to specific geographical areas, the risks are high, and the financing is either difficult to obtain or sporadic. Many entrepreneurs are attached to this field because of the huge potential for profit. Companies that had small beginnings, like IBM, Xerox, and Texas Instruments, are not soon forgotten. However, many technological businesses fail because their owners rely too much on technology and not enough on management expertise.

THE SMALL BUSINESS OWNER WHO PERFORMS A SPECIAL SERVICE

A second niche that small businesses often fill is that of providing a specialized service. Quite often, large manufacturers find it either unmanageable or infeasible to perform certain services for their own companies. From the viewpoint of the large corporation, this is the make-or-buy decision. Generally, if the large corporation can buy the item or service at a lower cost than it can make it, it will buy the item or service from another company, often a small business.

The large company's decision is considerably more complex than may appear from the above statement. For example, how are costs computed? At one time, the American Institute of Certified Public Accountants supported over 25 acceptable methods of calculating cost. Most of the variations of cost calculation revolve around the amount of overhead to include in cost. Since large companies vary considerably in not only their method of cost calculations but also the amount of overhead, it is apparent that some present more profitable opportunities than others for small businesses. Unfortunately, the method of learning this is from experience. A second consideration of the large corporation is that of making it easier for themselves. Some products or services are inherently more difficult to deal with. In such cases, the large company may well be able to produce the product or perform the service more cheaply, but the problems associated with it just aren't worth the trouble. This also presents an opportunity for small business.

Note that both basic conditions under which small businesses can find a market providing a specialized service have their limitations. Under the first condition, margins are likely to be low. Under the second condition, the job is likely to be distasteful. However, many entrepreneurs have done remarkably well here financially because of the relatively few small businesses willing to compete.

SMALL BUSINESS IN WHICH INDIVIDUAL ATTENTION IS REQUIRED

Many businesses exist that require a great deal of personalized attention to clients. The most obvious examples of such businesses are those operated by doctors, lawyers, psychologists, and family counselors. Many of us do not think of our physician's office as a small business, but it is. Businesses operated by barbers, beauticians, and funeral directors also fall into this category. Of course, poorly paid personal service areas are least attractive to large corporations. In areas such as medicine and funeral directing, we see large corporations moving in to compete. The reason is obvious. When huge profit potential exists, the large corporations are interested. In such cases, the small business tends to either expand or be pushed out. One example is the Kaiser Permanente Health Maintenance Organization in California. Medical costs have soared in the past decade. Kaiser provides an individualized service, comparable to those of private physicians, at a lower cost to the patient. This isolated instance of large corporation competition points up the need for a small business to be continually aware of the environment in which it competes. Even though one's business may be extremely profitable today, it may be gone tomorrow if its competitive position is not constantly evaluated.

SMALL BUSINESS FOR WHICH ONLY A LOCAL MARKET EXISTS

Most of the large corporations choose not to compete for a product or service where only a local market exists. For example, much of the textile industry is concentrated in the Carolinas. Textile mills have some very specific needs in their production methods. Bobbin carts are used almost exclusively by the textile industry. Consequently, a group of small businesses manufacturing bobbin carts have flourished in this area. No large manufacturers compete in this local market. Similarly, service businesses prosper which supply specialized housekeeping services to the textile mills. Distributorships have grown that supply very specialized tools to the textile industry. Opportunities for small business exist in every part of the country where a local market exists.

As a general rule, the more local the market, the greater the opportunity for small business. In South Florida a large local market exists for the care and cultivation of subtropical plants, though as a percentage of the national market for house plants, it is very small. Consequently, the market is dominated by local small businesses: large business is geared to mass production *and* mass distribution, so a local market is generally not acceptable for the large corporation. Since almost all small businesses are local, it is worthwhile for aspiring entrepreneurs to view carefully the local potentials for either complete lack of competition or ineffective competition. Quite often, a few well thought out questions and some careful observations can produce a worthwhile venture.

SMALL BUSINESS OPPORTUNITIES WHEN THE MARKET IS SMALL

The most common type of opportunity exists when the market is small. Of course, the definition of "small" varies greatly among persons, among types of businesses, and by locality. A market may be small for a number of reasons. A business often fails because the market is *so* small that even one company cannot survive. Craftsmen of various types often fall into this category. For example, in Case 15, *The Last Dinosaur,* a businessman who specialized in elegant, handcrafted, handfinished hardwood kitchen cabinets had an extremely difficult time once the local market for $6000 kitchen cabinets was saturated. The same can be true of silversmiths. A relatively tiny market may exist in certain locales for handcrafted silver items.

A market may be small from the viewpoint of the large companies, but quite adequate to fulfill the needs of numerous small businesses. Major oil companies sell many types of petroleum products. Often they elect to have company-owned and -operated service stations for gasoline sales, while they concurrently distribute heating oils through agents or jobbers who have one or two truck operations, since the market for heating oil may be small compared with the market for gasoline. More commonly, a large corporation elects not to compete when the market is small in relation to the effort required to operate the business.

This is quite different from the limited market of the silversmith. Recently a man who panned for gold in a played-out commercial gold area appeared on television. He stated that he made $15,000 to $20,000 a year. This small businessman indicated that "the company left because hit just twarn't worth the effort." Many people feel that most small businesses fall into this category.

SMALL BUSINESS OPPORTUNITIES IN FRANCHISING

Franchising has been utilized as a method of distribution for more than fifty years. A franchise usually consists of a continuing relationship between franchisor and franchisee. Although the franchisee operates the firm as an independent business, certain procedures must be followed. These include payment of fees to the franchisor as well as the use of specified items. These procedures are spelled out in the initial contract, and a potential entrepreneur should be aware of any limitations.

The obvious advantage with an established franchisor is that much of the preliminary research has been completed. The results of such research are available to the franchisee through written materials, and training courses such as McDonald's "Hamburger U."

For the potential entrepreneur the major disadvantage is a loss of control. After a large initial investment, the entrepreneur may still find that the franchise agreement is very similar to simply working for another organization. You share in the mistakes of the franchise as well as the successes.

These points must be evaluated carefully in investigating the franchise option. Checklist B in Appendix I illustrates a number of other aspects that should be weighed carefully before signing a franchise contract.

SUMMARY OF AREAS WHERE THE CHANCES OF SUCCESS ARE GREATEST

The six preceding categories are not mutually exclusive. The term "market niche" usually represents some combination of the various categories. Small businesses offer tremendous potential for being independent, doing something new and different, getting away from the bureaucracy, and conceivably generating a substantially greater income.

EXPERIENCE—A NECESSARY QUALIFICATION

The small-business owner must know what specific needs are characteristic of a particular business. Essentially, this is a matter of experience. Every business has needs that are peculiar to it, the "tricks of the trade." The chances of success in a specific business are diminished substantially if the owner has had no previous experience in that business. For example, in the service station business, cash and inventory control are critical problems. Gas pump attendants have been known to pocket a cash sale or to take a set of spark plugs home for their own cars. Since most service stations are open between ninety and one hundred hours a week, it is almost impossible for the owner to be on duty all the time. Therefore, the prospective owner must have experience in both cash and inventory control if the station is to succeed.

This example points out two abilities required of small-business owners: first, that they recognize some of the major problems associated with a specific business; second, that they implement practical methods to control these problems. Experience is an excellent teacher; basic points are remembered because of the trauma associated with a bad experience. Consider the M.B.A. graduate from Stanford University who decided to enter the service station business. He was wise enough to apprentice himself to the business for a year. His level of education was unknown to his various employers during the year. He pumped gas, he changed tires, he developed some mechanical skills, he learned the language of the service station business and, most importantly, he carefully observed everything that happened. At the end of the year, this bright and energetic young man opened his own service station. At last report, he was netting over $50,000 a year—substantially better than he would have done with a large corporation.

Other methods exist to gain information for deciding what is needed for success in a specific business. Commercial loan officers in banks are a particularly good source of information. Bankers are usually well informed and can supply information to aspiring small-business owners about various types of businesses. However, bankers are usually conservative in their advice, and should be so evaluated. Another source is a supplier for the specific business. Suppliers are not only potential credit-granting sources of funds for a business, but they can also provide valuable insights into that business which is their *specialty*. Suppliers tend to be optimistic in attitude.

It is a good practice to balance off several sources of information. For example, you might compare your own experience in a business to a banker's opinion and again to the supplier's thoughts. Each of these sources will provide different bits of information for your particular decision. The end result of this process should be a well-defined list of those things which must be done if you are to succeed in your business.

WHAT CHARACTERISTICS DOES THE SMALL-BUSINESS OWNER HAVE?

Many efforts have been made in the past to categorize those individuals who become small-business owners. Such attempts have been relatively unsuccessful. The lack of success in identifying the characteristics associated with successful small-business owners is probably due, in great part, to the range of roles that the small-business owner must fulfill in the life cycle of a specific company. Figure 1–1 gives some indication of the shape of the life cycle curve in relation to the roles of small-business owners.

While little evidence of a factual nature exists to substantiate the role characteristics associated here with the five portions of the life cycle curve, many individuals have speculated about such characteristics.

For example, some general characteristics of the small-business owner, thought to be associated with successful accomplishment in any of the five phases, are a high level of motivation,

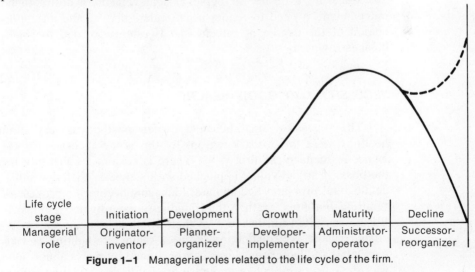

Life cycle stage	Initiation	Development	Growth	Maturity	Decline
Managerial role	Originator-inventor	Planner-organizer	Developer-implementer	Administrator-operator	Successor-reorganizer

Figure 1–1   Managerial roles related to the life cycle of the firm.

---

1. Source: Carroll V. Kroeger, "Managerial Development in the Small Firm," *California Management Review*, Vol. XVIII, No. 1, 1974 p. 42

good health, total commitment, and self-discipline. Characteristics often associated with the originator-inventor (entrepreneur) stage are a willingness to take risks, self-confidence, and a degree of specialization. Those characteristics often associated with the planner-organizer stage are the ability to define objectives and to make decisions ("the buck stops here"), a commitment to getting results, and the ability to test reality. The characteristics often associated with the developer-implementer and administrator-operator stages are the abilities to select, motivate, and develop people, and to be a generalist. The following sections will expand on each of these concepts to develop your understanding of the needs of a company through various stages of the life cycle of its owner(s).

GENERAL CHARACTERISTICS

NECESSITY FOR HIGH LEVELS OF MOTIVATION

Much has been written about the high level of achievement need in small-business owners, the urge to achieve just for the sake of achieving. One of the most appropriate ways to set achievement motivation in operation for the small-business owner is profit. Unfortunately, a substantial amount of theoretical material has been written about motives other than profit. This tends to cloud the fact that the small business ceases to exist when it ceases to make a profit. Long-term survival depends on making a profit in the short run. Other motives thought to be important at this stage are a desire for personal achievement, a desire to be independent, a need to render a particular service, and an appreciation of the degree of esteem that is often accorded to small-business owners.

NECESSITY FOR GOOD HEALTH

The successful small-business owner must be in very good health. One of the primary reasons for this is the necessity for the owner to manage the firm daily. There is seldom a substitute for the boss. If an individual is plagued with sickness, then decisions, details, and problems accumulate. Managing becomes a process of "putting out fires" rather than guiding a coordinated company. Businesses often fail because of their continual "management by crisis." There is a distinction between major fire-fighting and effectively handling crises. Fires can be avoided; crises cannot. One way the entrepreneur can minimize fire-fighting is by being actively on the job every day. Therefore good health is critical.

A less apparent aspect of health is the decrease in mental

alertness and initiative that results when a person's health is less than perfect. The entrepreneur may be physically at work every day, but may be mentally working at substantially less than one hundred per cent. Another aspect of good health is its energy level. Successful small-business owners have tremendous amounts of energy. The need for maintenance of good health, a continuing problem for entrepreneurs, is critical in the start-up phase, and continues throughout the life of the business.

TOTAL COMMITMENT

How would you feel if you heard that an article appeared recently that indicated that large corporations no longer expect *total* commitment; that is, a ten-hour working day would now be acceptable instead of a twelve? You should study your reaction to that question in terms of your own lifestyle.

The first few years are critical in a small business. Depending on the type of business, the small-business owner may be able to get by with something less than total commitment after this critical period. However, small businesses are full of crises. You have to solve problems even when you would rather be doing other things. The variety and intensity of the crises are great for those who compete in small business. You must not only be capable of recognizing the crises, but also be ready to intervene with total commitment and see the crises through to successful resolutions. This is not meant to imply that you can show a lack of commitment at other times, but rather that you must make a herculean effort when crises do occur.

Total commitment also extends to a need for the complete support of your family. It is extremely difficult to succeed in a small business if your family does not give their whole-hearted support. The sacrifices may be financial, they may call for a willingness to give up family time, and they may simply entail acceptance of your irritability. Commitment includes the entire family.

SELF-DISCIPLINE

Self-discipline is vital to all small-business owners. They must be able to contain their impulses, particularly when the business is just starting. If the business becomes moderately successful, the entrepreneur may feel a need to indulge in status symbols like expensive cars or highly enjoyable business trips that are only marginally useful.

The owner should be aware of the timing of cash flows. Several cases in this book deal with small-business owners who received cash inflows at irregular intervals each month, but failed to match them against end-of-the-month bills. Each month they came up short and couldn't meet all of their obligations. Self-discipline is needed to keep your money from "burning a hole in your pocket."

ORIGINATOR-INVENTOR (ENTREPRENEUR) ROLE CHARACTERISTICS

Entrepreneurs are individuals who create some sort of innovative economic activity that did not previously exist. They provide goods and services through new businesses or by attempting to revitalize existing businesses. Entrepreneurs share some common characteristics when they begin a venture: enthusiasm, a concern for people, integrity, and a commitment to their firm. They perceive the world optimistically. As one successful entrepreneur states: "Success comes to those who see the glass as half-full, not half-empty." True entrepreneurs are more than small-business owners. They build a firm and are constantly seeking new outlets for their energies. It is common for these individuals to be involved with several innovative activities simultaneously.

Entrepreneurs also have a facility for dealing with people on a face-to-face basis. They have a product to sell—themselves—and they do it well. They sell themselves to potential investors, employees, and customers. It is their personal promise to deliver which insures a sale. Such individuals are capable of imparting their enthusiasm to those with whom they come in contact; they spread a contagious feeling of success to those around them. Their organizations reflect this optimism.

Most entrepreneurs have a high degree of integrity. Their word becomes a bond, a personal commitment. This allows the flexibility needed for success and the ability to hire others who supplement the entrepreneur's weak points. They, too, are fully committed to their enterprise. The entrepreneur's philosophy is that success is nothing more than picking an opportunity and then working it.

Entrepreneurs are aware of the many opportunities available. They perceive the entire world as a source of opportunities. Their major problem is selecting one and finding the time to exploit that opportunity. If they face a single problem, it is the fact that they cannot take advantage of all the opportunities open to them. The entrepreneur's commitment is both psychological and financial. In many cases entrepreneurs have a great deal of difficulty separating their personal resources from those of the firm. The entrepreneur's office is everywhere. As one entrepreneur puts it: "When I drink coffee, the Board's in session."

The entrepreneur initiates the firm and maintains it. However, if the firm is to survive, the owner must supplement entrepreneurial enthusiasm with managerial skills to handle routine activity. Thus, the successful small-business owner is both an entrepreneur and a manager. The entrepreneurial side of this owner is innovative with respect to the external environment and tends to initiate many projects. The managerial side must constantly act as the mediator between what the entrepreneur wants to do and what can actually be done. To be successful, both of these aspects must be present, since one complements the other. For example, the entrepreneur does not worry about disasters until they are imminent. The manager begins planning for contingencies; the entrepreneur ends with such plans. The latter works best under a high degree of pressure whereas the former attempts to reduce ambiguity and pressure. In actual practice, few small-business owners completely fulfill both roles.

WILLINGNESS TO TAKE RISKS

Their high failure rate attests to the fact that small businesses are faced with many dangers. Many of the thoughts associated with an entrepreneur's willingness to take risks will be taken up in a subsequent section entitled "The buck stops here." From a practical standpoint, it is difficult to separate making a decision from accepting a risk. However, a characteristic of entrepreneurs is their willingness to accept these risks. Clearly, many individuals in large firms are willing to assume *no* risks. At the other extreme are individuals who will wager on anything. They make decisions based on nothing but a hunch. Obviously neither of these individuals will last long in a small business. Somewhere between the two extremes are people who can make decisions when the odds are unknown, but can be estimated by incomplete information. True entrepreneurs are reasonably sure that the risk can be taken. They are confident that their commitment, their decision-making ability, their health, their mental attitude, their energy level, and their profit motivation will carry them through.

SELF-CONFIDENCE

Do you really believe that your firm can survive and prosper? Entrepreneurs often don't like to consider the possibility of failure. Rather, they feel that the opportunity is greater than the problem. They are confident that everything will work and that they have the personal resources to make it happen. This is a feeling that permeates the *successful* firm. When this happens, almost everyone connected with the company feels successful. This self-confidence is also reflected in the entrepreneur's ability to objectively appraise feedback, both positive and negative. Successful entrepreneurs have the ability to improve their businesses by applying this feedback. Typically, they don't rationalize away poor performance. Successful entrepreneurs accept responsibility and don't lay the blame for their problems on others.

PLANNER-ORGANIZER CHARACTERISTICS

PERSONAL OBJECTIVES

Are personal and company objectives well-defined? If not, take time to analyze them thoroughly. Make up a dream list. Once objectives are specified, consider whether they can be realized through business ownership. For instance, high aspirations and a need for independence can probably be realized through your own business. However, if one of your objectives is to accumulate money, working for someone else may offer better returns. Recently, a student investigated the possibility of opening his own restaurant. Since he could project earnings for himself of only $15,000 the first year, he decided to take another job. His monetary objectives outweighed his need for independence, and he was realistic enough to face this fact.

"THE BUCK STOPS HERE"

To operate an effective small business, the ability and willingness to make decisions is an absolute necessity. Much lip service is given to decision-making and decision-making techniques, as though they were rote processes. They are not. Few individuals have both the ability and the willingness to make decisions. Almost all of the important decisions, especially those that deal with the future, have one major problem: there is *never* enough information. Effective entrepreneurs must be able to make major decisions with less information at their disposal than they would like. Those who put off making a decision until they have "enough" information either never make the decision or make it too late to be effective. Many successful entrepreneurs indicate that they willingly make decisions with inadequate information, but with the full knowledge that they must make the decision work.

The successful small-business owner must be able to make timely decisions. Typically very little delegation of authority is found in a small business. As a result, the small-business owner's day is filled with both large and small decisions. It becomes appropriate to delegate many of the small decisions as the business grows. However, change occurs slowly and often the owner continues to make all decisions, tending to limit the growth potential of the firm.

ORIENTATION TO RESULTS

Some people often complain that they have been very busy but never seem to accomplish anything. Such people fail to realize that activity is not the key; results are. The world does not reward attempts; it rewards success. Too often, individuals confuse what they are doing with what they are attempting to do. For the small-business owner, such an attitude may result in failure. The entrepreneur must engage in productive work—not busy work—if the firm is to be successful.

ABILITY TO TEST REALITY

Entrepreneurs have to reassess and reevaluate their actions constantly. One example of potential failure is the small-business owner who has never formally appraised the market, but can tell you all about it. Recently, an individual was starting a business to sell solar heating units to homeowners. When asked why he felt that it was a good business venture, he replied, "with electric and gas prices increasing, it can't miss." He went on to say, "The high initial costs for solar units will be overcome in less than twelve years at current costs for gas and electricity." One fact he had not appraised was the local real estate market. Homes in the more expensive areas, where he planned to market his product, changed owners on the average of once every three years. The high cost of the solar heating units, added to the normal sale price, was perceived by buyers to make the resale price of the house uncompetitive. Given the turnover, homeowners could not recover their initial investment. This did not produce a good forecast for the business and he hasn't sold one unit yet. He failed to test the market and distorted reality to fit his perceptions. This will neither make an entrepreneur effective nor a firm successful. Again, it was an attempt but not a successful one.

An awareness of the environment, both within the company and outside it, is extremely important to the success of an entrepreneur. Entrepreneurs must be effective reality-testers. They must be aware of both the market and the means for servicing it.

DEVELOPER-IMPLEMENTER AND ADMINISTRATOR-OPERATOR CHARACTERISTICS

SELECTING, MOTIVATING, AND DEVELOPING PEOPLE

At this stage, the small-business owner needs excellent skills in selecting and developing people. Successful small-business owners often select individuals who complement their own style. A very active, sales-oriented individual often selects an operating manager for the firm who is his opposite. The operating manager may be highly detail-oriented and able to run the day-to-day operations. This allows the owner to pursue outside sales without constant concern about the daily details. The owner should also be proficient at motivating people. Closely associated with this, small-business owners should be highly capable of distributing rewards. They must infuse those around them with enthusiasm. Such individuals need to be surrounded by people who share their enthusiasm. "I would rather have one individual working *with* me than ten working *for* me" is an often repeated phrase. Since small-business owners need to concentrate on success and optimism, they do not like to have people around them who are pessimistic or who constantly look at the possibilities for failure. If the individual can't be motivated, that person will not work long for the business.

Administrators also learn to motivate people outside their business. They motivate bankers and investors to lend them money and motivate customers to buy their products or services. Why can one individual walk into a bank with a well-formulated business plan and not get a loan while another gets money on signature alone? As a number of lenders have stated: "You can feel success." This is the successful entrepreneur-manager's trademark.

GENERALIST VERSUS SPECIALIST

Small-business owners are not always highly skilled technically, but they usually possess a minimum level of expertise in their field. This expertise allows them to operate the business even though they may not necessarily be the most technically proficient individual in the company. An individual can operate a service station without being the best mechanic at the station. The entrepreneurial function here is attracting auto repair trade; someone else can service the cars. However, the service station entrepreneur must have the minimum expertise to judge the abilities of the mechanics and to hire people to service the trade attracted to the station.

A generalist's approach is an important ingredient at this stage in the life cycle of a business. The small-business owner must be able to handle any sort of problem that arises. The owner of a small apartment complex recently related that in his two years of ownership, he and his wife had learned to repair everything from clogged toilets to minor air conditioning problems. These skills were frequently learned during off hours when no other assistance was available: evenings, weekends, and holidays. During the early phases of a business, it is important that small-business owners are competent and possess the self-confidence to handle most problems. As the business progresses and becomes more successful, it may be of benefit to consider hiring specialists in technical areas.

SELF-EVALUATION FOR SMALL-BUSINESS OWNERS

There are a number of tests that purport to measure entrepreneurial potential. They ask questions related to subjects as diverse as your need for independence, your marital status, your sex, your sports interest, and your planning ability. However, in reviewing most of these approaches, it has been found that few of them attempt to predict success: only activity.

The following self-appraisal form refers to those areas that are important to success and can be controlled or affected by the individual.

If the statement is *rarely* true of you, score 1.
If the statement is *usually* true of you, score 2.
If the statement is almost *always* true of you, score 3.

Score

1. I have firmly established my personal objectives. _____
2. My personality is the type that fits my business. _____
3. I tend to get things accomplished within reasonable time constraints. _____
4. I can change my objectives as my markets dictate. _____
5. I have common sense. _____
6. I would like to achieve something worthwhile. _____
7. I enjoy being responsible for getting things accomplished. _____
8. I like to operate alone and make decisions on my own. _____
9. Risky situations do not pose an unusual threat to me. _____
10. I can deal with uncertainty. _____
11. I can take and use negative comments from others. _____
12. I can sell myself and my business. _____
13. There is little chance for me to fail. _____
14. I have the energy needed to accomplish the task. _____
15. I am truly excited about the business. _____
16. I have a record of good health and miss little work because of sickness. _____
17. My business does not violate my social status. _____
18. My family is firmly committed to long hours and hard effort in regard to the business. _____
19. I get the job done with little wasted time. _____
20. I can select individuals to assist me in my weak areas. _____
21. I am able to get people working *with* me. _____
22. I have a high level of self-discipline. _____
23. I can appraise the world in a realistic manner. _____
24. I have the skill and experience necessary for my business. _____

A score of 60 to 72 is good, 48 to 58 is fair, and under 48 is poor. It should be apparent that a high score is not a guarantee of success; many other factors must also be given consideration. However, if you have been both honest and objective in your answers, you may gain some insight into the degree your personal characteristics may affect the success of your business. A low score should certainly make you reconsider whether or not you want to own a small business.

SUMMARY

The purpose of this chapter was to provide an overview of several important aspects of small business. The three topical subdivisions of this chapter—opportunity areas for small businesses, experience in a small business, and characteristics of small business owners—provide a framework for the reader to begin a self-evaluation with respect to starting a small business. Statistics indicate that over 400,000 small businesses fail in the United States each year and that 80 per cent of all small businesses fail within the first five years of operation. One of the underlying premises of this chapter is that your chance of failure can be reduced substantially by carefully applying the material in this chapter to your specific situation.

STUDY QUESTIONS

1. What portion of businesses in your community would be considered small?

2. Locate four businesses in your community, two of which are doing well, two of which are doing badly. Explain why you think they are operating as they are.

3. In your experience, do you feel that the small-business owners you know would agree with the concepts in this chapter? Would they "pass" the entrepreneur test?

REFERENCES AND SUGGESTED READINGS

Broom, H. N., and J. G. Longenecker. *Small Business Management*, 4th ed., Cincinnati: South-Western Publishing Co., 1975.

Checklist for Going Into Business, Small Marketer's Aid No. 71. Washington, D.C.: Small Business Administration, 1976.

Hermans, Hubert J. M. "A questionnaire measure of achievement motivation," *Journal of Applied Psychology*, Vol. 54, No. 4, 1970, pp. 353–363.

Hornaday, J. A., and J. Abound. "Characteristics of successful entrepreneurs," *Personnel Psychology*, Vol. 24, No. 2, 1971, pp. 141–153.

How To Analyze Your Own Business, Management Aid No. 46. Washington, D.C.: Small Business Administration, 1971.

J. K. Lasser Tax Institute, ed. Bernard Griessman. *How to Run A Small Business*. New York: McGraw-Hill Book Co., 1974.

Kroeger, Carroll V. "Managerial development in the small firm," *California Management Review*, Vol. XVII, No. 1, 1974, pp. 41–47.

Kuehn, W. H. *The Pitfalls in Managing A Small Business*. New York: Dun and Bradstreet, 1973.

"Opening your own business: a personal appraisal," *Small Business Reporter*, Vol. 7, No. 7. San Francisco: Bank of America, 1971.

Problems in Managing A Family Owned Business, Management Aid No. 208. Washington, D.C.: Small Business Administration, 1976.

Schrage, H. "The R+D entrepreneur: profile of success," *Harvard Business Review*, Nov.-Dec. 1965, pp. 56–69.

CHAPTER 2

THE SMALL BUSINESS AS A PROCESS

INTRODUCTION

Studying small business is as difficult as agreeing on its definition. Success in small business is often possible by doing relatively simple tasks, but by doing them exceedingly well. On the other hand, a great number of jobs must be done. Failure to deal effectively with any one of the many tasks may lead to failure of the business itself. Since top-level management in a small business is often one person (or a very few people), that person must not only perform the simple tasks well, but must also have, or develop, the ability to view the entire business objectively. This chapter will provide a framework for doing this.

Figure 2–1 is a synthesis of the material in this book. The value of viewing a small business as a process is that basic relationships are defined, omitting attention to a specific area is less likely, and a systems perspective is provided. Any attempt to present a total process will be incomplete; however, Figure 2–1 is a starting point for developing specific plans for a particular business. "Small business as a process" attempts to interject logic into the decisions necessary for small businesses. As this model indicates, numerous questions must be answered, and an appropriate sequence for answering these questions is suggested. Certainly, interpretation varies for different businesses, however, the basic framework is applicable to the majority of small-business situations. The chance for success in the small business can be improved if the process in Figure 2–1 is honestly and thoroughly analyzed in light of the characteristics, questions and activities represented. As knowledge about a specific business increases, you should be able to modify and expand the process to provide a meaningful framework for analysis of that business.

Figure 2–1 may be used several ways. First, it may be used in the analysis of cases. A case is a picture of a business situation

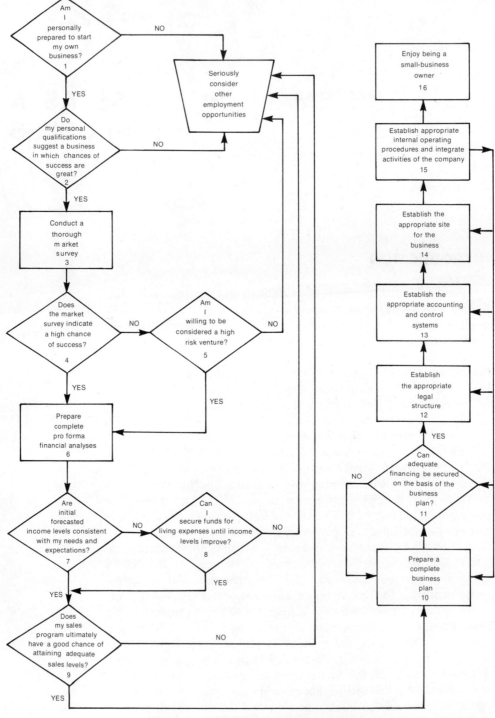

Figure 2–1 Small business as a process.

at a given point in time. "Small business as a process" may be used to detect weaknesses, flaws, or omissions by the owners in small business cases. Once the problems are defined, recommendations to deal with them can be enumerated. In making recommendations for any part of the process, care must be exercised to evaluate the impact of that change on other parts of the business. For example, a change in the sales program costs money. If a recommendation is made to hire a super-star salesperson, a number of other questions surface in the business process. Can the company afford to hire a super-star? Will a person of that caliber be attracted to the company? How does one control a super-star salesperson on whom the company may become dependent?

Figure 2–1 may also be used to assist in an individual's decision to become an entrepreneur. Inasmuch as this decision will be a critical decision in your life, a serious effort should be made to answer adequately all the questions presented in the figure.

A third way Figure 2–1 may be used is to analyze a small business currently in operation. The procedure is similar; however, the stage suggesting other employment opportunities is not usable unless dissolution of the business is actively being considered. In this instance, emphasis must be placed on recommendations and an active implementation procedure.

USE OF THE SMALL BUSINESS AS A PROCESS CHART

The balance of this chapter is devoted to an analysis of Figure 2–1. While an attempt will be made to clearly state its use, the reader should remember that flexibility and creativity are hallmarks of successful entrepreneurs and should be remembered when using "Small business as a process." Checklists A and C in Appendix I should also be used with all segments of this figure.

AM I PERSONALLY PREPARED TO START A BUSINESS OF MY OWN?

The first block of the chart deals with the critical personal qualifications that the key individual (or individuals) possesses. Since decisions regarding the various qualifications are often subjective, an analysis of this critical area is often omitted. This is a serious error, since all succeeding questions are based on the answer to this question. In conducting a self-analysis prior to starting your own business, honesty is essential. Since our perception of ourselves is often distorted, it is also wise to secure separate appraisals by your spouse, parents, friends, professors, business associates, doctors, and ministers. If you are using the figure to conduct a case analysis, it is necessary to look for clues to the personal characteristics of the individuals in the case.

Information regarding this decision can be derived from the self-evaluation checklist in the previous chapter. One of the most critical personal characteristics is the high level of motivation needed to achieve outstanding results. This could be represented by high academic grades or by positions of leadership in student organizations, service clubs, professional organizations, or voluntary organizations. Success in previous jobs, awards received for excellence in an occupation, a high previous salary level, and outstanding recommendations from former customers or clients also point to a high aspiration level. Many indications of an individual's motivation to achieve may be found if an honest assessment is made.

The second basic area of personal preparation is that of commitment. How is commitment measured? Certainly, the most important aspects of this area are confidence in the business and the amount of time devoted to the business. Very few small businesses succeed when the commitment of the owner is so low that the business is only a part-time job. A second level of measuring commitment is gauged by the number of hours in a week the owner is willing to spend working. If the owner expects a 40-hour week, the owner's commitment is not strong enough to withstand the rigors of small business. A third level of commitment might be reflected by the time at which an individual arrives for work.

A third basic area of personal preparation is exploration of the existence or non-existence of both technical and managerial skills. These characteristics are discussed in depth in several chapters of this book. However, once again it is necessary to determine to what extent an individual possesses these skills.

A fourth area is health. Without adequate health or with impaired physical or mental abilities, the chance for success is substantially reduced. An individual who lacks stamina is physically unable to make a total commitment to the firm.

Several other personal qualifications necessary for success will be found in Chapter 1. A composite profile of the key individual or individuals must be constructed out of all these characteristics to arrive at a "yes or no" decision regarding personal qualifications. As the model indicates, if a negative decision is reached on the personal qualifications section, it is better to consider being someone else's employee rather than risk ending in the portion of those small businesses that fail.

DO MY PERSONAL QUALIFICATIONS SUGGEST A BUSINESS IN WHICH MY CHANCES OF SUCCESS ARE HIGH?

Block 2 is the forthright process of taking the answers from Block 1 and applying them to selecting a specific business. Of paramount importance is the availability of technical skills on the part of the potential entrepreneur. In its simplest form, does the individual have some worthwhile experience or background that suggests a viable business? So often, people enter a small business on the basis of statements such as "I think I'd like that business," or "I think I could do well in the such and such field," or "Everyone seems to be doing very well in the so and so business," or "I have always been interested in _____, and it is a logical business for me to enter."

Interest or opportunity is not enough. It is necessary to have some real experience in the specific business. Go to work for a business similar to the one you are considering for a few months, learn the specific problems in that business, learn what it takes to sell or to not sell that product, learn what the customers like, what type and quantity of service is required to excel, what types of employees are available in the industry, and what an employee must do to make the business succeed for the owner. The list of questions you come up with may be very long. Make use of your apprenticeship, no matter how long or short, to ask these questions. Catalog the answers and appraise for yourself whether or not they are accurate. The end product of the question posed in Block 2 is "Do I *really* know what it takes to succeed in this business?"

If you are interested in a franchise, refer to Checklist B in Appendix I.

CONDUCT A THOROUGH MARKET SURVEY

Block 3 is explained in the next chapter and in Checklist F of Appendix I. It is useful to note at this point that the type of market survey suggested varies not only with whether a business is being started from scratch, being purchased from another owner, or a franchise, but also with the *type* of business — retail, wholesale, service, or manufacturing — within each of these three categories. Regardless of the classification of the market survey, the basic questions to be answered are:

1. What is the market for my potential product?
2. What type and quality of competition exist in my potential market?
3. What sort of technology or technological change will affect my product in the future?
4. What is occurring in the national, state, and local economies that will affect my business?
5. How will changing social or political norms affect my business?

An analysis of Block 3 may be diagrammed:

Estimate demand for my product

Evaluate type and quality of
competition

Evaluate national, state, and
local economies with regard to
my product

MARKET
SURVEY

The market survey should clearly point out both significant opportunities for success and significant problems to be overcome. Many times the success or failure of a small business is based on the thoroughness of the market survey. This step is often completely eliminated, leaving the aspiring small business in an unfavorable position. If the market doesn't exist, the best salesperson in the world won't be able to sell the product.

DOES THE MARKET SURVEY INDICATE A HIGH CHANCE OF SUCCESS?

Block 4 requires a decision. Are you willing to stake your reputation, physical resources, financial resources, and family's goodwill on the results of the market survey? How high do the chances of success have to be before you make the commitment?

Some general observations are appropriate for this decision. Many would-be entrepreneurs reach this point and decide against going into a business of their own. Many individuals plainly prefer the security of a salaried job. A person will often talk about going into business; however, only a fraction of those who talk about it are willing to do so.

A second observation is that no business has zero risk involved with it; in fact, as stated earlier, over 400,000 small businesses fail in the United States every year. It is anticipated that the risk can be reduced by adhering to some variation of "Small business as a process." All aspiring small-business owners must make a decision regarding their acceptable risk level. If you are seriously considering the decision to the extent that it keeps you awake at night or occupies all of your thoughts during the day, then you should reevaluate your desire to be in business for yourself. Seriously consider how well you handle the stress involved in taking risks.

Individuals who conduct market surveys often look at the results of their surveys as though the projection is real. Any market survey has a very large number of "*if*" statements. These *if* statements are often stated in a forthright manner. However, the *if* statements are not always articulated. An aspiring entrepreneur must be aware of the assumptions underlying the market survey. The more clearly the assumptions are stated, the clearer the chances for success and failure become.

Perfect information does not exist. Every entrepreneur must be willing to make the decision of Block 4 with less than perfect information. If you are unwilling to do this, you should consider an occupation in which your job is more structured. Unfortunately, many people have the impression that the decision-making tools and techniques described here are based on certainty and are tools for eliminating risk. The entrepreneur must readily accept uncertain and incomplete information and make the best decision possible with it.

PREPARE COMPLETE PRO FORMA FINANCIAL ANALYSES

Block 6 requires the preparation of complete pro forma financial analyses. Pro forma statements are the projection of the past into the future and are capsulized in the form of a profit and loss statement, a balance sheet, and a cash flow statement. Many small businesses do *not* routinely complete pro forma statements. Certainly, there is less justification for their use once the business is operating successfully. However, during the initiation of a business, pro forma statements are critical, since these projections may be used to locate trouble spots before they occur. The importance of estimating your future financial condition is covered in Chapter 4.

If the trouble spots can be located early, corrective action can be taken before a major error occurs. For example, if the projected sales volume is barely sufficient to attain a profit, you know that a major effort must be expended in selling your product in order to survive. Similarly, the completion of pro forma statements should be a well-defined objective. If this objective is attained, you know in advance what your financial condition will be. If it is not, you may estimate your financial condition from what you have. During critical phases of your business' initiation, the time and effort spent on pro forma statements can provide very favorable returns.

ARE INITIAL FORECASTED INCOME LEVELS CONSISTENT WITH MY NEEDS AND EXPECTATIONS?

Many small businesses fail because the initial income level is insufficient to meet the living expenses of the owner, who is unaware of this condition until it is too late to rectify it. It is apparent that Block 7 is a direct result of Block 6. Implicit in the question posed in Block 7 is the need to project personal expenses during times when the business is not returning enough income to support the owner. Most prospective entrepreneurs and their families are willing to accept a low standard of living in the formative years of their business in return for an improved lifestyle later.

Owners may, however, start withdrawing capital, not profit, from their business. Once this process starts, it is usually irreversible. As working capital is withdrawn for living expenses, fewer and fewer dollars are available for financing inventories and accounts receivable. The cash position of the company deteriorates, sales decline, the company becomes delinquent on its accounts payable, trade credit dries up, and the business becomes a failure statistic. Your business needs you and your capital most during the start-up process, and you must make arrangements to supplement your income during this period.

DOES MY SALES PROGRAM ULTIMATELY HAVE A GOOD CHANCE OF ATTAINING ADEQUATE INCOME?

A very successful entrepreneur once said, "Nothing happens until a sale is made!" The lifeblood of any business is the ability to sell its product or services. Owners of marginal businesses typically make comments such as, "If I'm patient, people will recognize the quality of my product or service," or "I have a product or service that is not really amenable to selling," or "What we stress is efficient production methods," or "We sell through advertising alone." Sales are developed by face-to-face contact with your customer, dogged determination in selling, and persevering in the face of a "no."

The question to be answered in Block 9 is, "Can you be reasonably certain that your expenditures and activities in selling are sufficient and are going to produce sales?" Entrepreneurs often make the mistake of thinking that there is no cost associated with sales except for such obvious expenses as advertising. The key individual in all organizations is the salesperson — not the order-taker, but the salesperson. Evaluate the question posed in Block 9 while making a hard-nosed analysis of your potential company. Can you *sell* your product and do you want to? Remember, "Nothing happens until a sale is made." Refer to Checklist G in Appendix I for a further analysis.

PREPARE A COMPLETE BUSINESS PLAN

At this point, a substantial amount of work has occurred, and many decisions have been made. All of the work preceding the preparation of a workable business plan is crucial to its effectiveness. Preparation of a carefully thought out plan is detailed in Chapter 3. The preparation of a thorough business plan serves two basic purposes. First, it provides a vehicle to transmit information to persons outside the company, such as bankers, who can supply working capital; investors, who can supply equity capital; and suppliers, who can supply trade credit. A thorough business plan also formalizes your thoughts regarding the company's internal management, providing guidelines to coordinate your efforts.

CAN ADEQUATE FINANCING BE SECURED ON THE BASIS OF THE BUSINESS PLAN?

Financing — short-term, long-term, trade credit — can generally be secured if all the work specified above has been accomplished. However, consideration must be given to the level of risk associated with the business venture. Often, entrepreneurs are willing to accept a much higher level of risk than those who are being asked to commit money. Various suppliers of financial resources also have differing opinions of what constitutes "acceptable risk." In particular, banks and insurance companies have relatively low levels of acceptable risk. Block 11 of Figure 2–1 implies a continuum of these differing opinions. A very conservative commercial bank would prefer a low risk venture. The individuals who are willing to gamble on a high risk business if the potential returns are also high are on the other end of the continuum. Potential returns may be measured not only in the prospective return on invested capital, but also in acquisition of equity shares if the business succeeds.

Assuming a thorough preparation of Blocks 1 through 10, securing adequate financing is a question of finding a source of capital to whom the risk level is acceptable when consistent with the risk inherent in the specific business. Of course, the lower the risk level, the greater the availability of financing. This is not to say that high risk businesses should not be considered — they have always been within the domain of small business. The high risk entrepreneur simply has to look longer and harder for external funds. Financing can usually be secured if the questions and activities in Blocks 1 through 10 have been properly completed.

DECISION PROCESS BLOCKS 12 THROUGH 15

The details of how to complete the activities in Blocks 12 through 15 are found in Chapters 7 through 11. The information necessary for successful implementation of any business may be found in these chapters. The activities and questions found in

Blocks 1 through 11 are generally more challenging to potential entrepreneurs. However, Blocks 12 through 15 constitute a vital link in effectively operating your business. Since many of these activities are less exciting than those preceding, small-business owners often tend to give them lower priority. This is a serious mistake, since the chances of any business continuing are improved by completing the routine functions: establishing internal operating procedures, appropriate accounting procedures, appropriate control methods, and an appropriate management style. Also, refer to Checklist H for help with Block 15 and Checklists D and E for Block 14. All are found in Appendix I and will enhance your analysis.

OPEN YOUR DOOR FOR BUSINESS

You wouldn't be human if you didn't have *some* reservations as you begin your new business. The successful entrepreneur always asks penetrating questions. If he doesn't, someone else will, and that someone may be your new competitor. Remember, few people are willing to make the effort to be truly successful. If you are willing to make the effort to be successful, and if you have established a sound basis for that success, you will be successful.

The real key to continuing success in business is maintaining a balance among *all* the activities required in the business. The small business may be unique in this respect. Regardless of the type of business, the effective owner must coordinate all activities within the firm. Decisions must be made that balance the results of the sales, finance, and operations of the business. For example, it is a waste of effort if a successful marketing strategy is completed while the company's operations are unable to deliver the product or service in the way the salesperson described it to the customer. The business is being run poorly if operations are unable to keep the cost of the product or service low enough to be competitive in the market. The business venture is hardly worthwhile if the sales people are attaining sales at such a competitive price that even the best production department in the world would be unable to produce a satisfactory product and still turn a profit.

The small business must cultivate many information sources in order to integrate activities in the company effectively. As one successful entrepreneur said, "I have to be everywhere all of the time." Information sources include present and former customers, employee suggestions and complaints, trade shows, the activities of your competitors, and organizations such as the local chamber of commerce. Perhaps the best information source is a keen power of observation for your own business. How do your employees handle a customer on the phone? What happens when a customer comes into the store, plant, or office? Are your premises clean, attractive, and orderly? Are your employees appropriately dressed? How is a customer handled when the product or service requested is not available? Is your operating equipment in good condition? Can you rely on your equipment to deliver the product when the customer wants it? Is your accounting system giving you the information you need at the proper time? Does your accounting system provide adequate information for controlling all the activities of the business? Does your legal structure give you proper liability and tax protection in light of changing business conditions? Is your location still appropriate in view of a changing business environment?

The basic point is that the successful entrepreneur must not only have sources of information and be keenly observant, but must also be able to evaluate all of this information. These evaluations should lead to decisions regarding any needed changes in the company. The continued survival of the company relies solely on this process.

STUDY QUESTIONS

1. As a start in the application of Chapter 2, apply the "process" to Case 19, American Hydraulic Paper Cutter, Incorporated.

2. After completing Question 1, what modifications should be made in Figure 2–1 in its application to this specific case? What additional information would have been useful? How would this additional information have been used? Would your conclusions have been substantially changed if you had the additional information?

3. What do you feel would be the typical reaction of a small-business owner to the process in Figure 2–1. Why?

REFERENCES AND SUGGESTED READINGS

Broom, H. N., and J. G. Longenecker. *Small Business Management,* 4th ed., Cincinnati: South-Western Publishing Co., 1975.
Checklist for Going into Small Business, Small Marketer's Aid No. 71. Washington, D. C.: Small Business Administration, 1976.
How to Analyze Your Own Business, Management Aid No. 46. Washington, D. C.: Small Business Administration, 1971.
J. K. Lasser Tax Institute, ed. Bernard Griessman. *How to Run a Small Business,* New York: McGraw-Hill Book Co., 1974.
Kuehn, W. H. *The Pitfalls in Managing a Small Business,* New York: Dun and Bradstreet, 1973.
"Opening your own business: a personal appraisal," *Small Business Reporter,* Vol. 7, No. 7. San Francisco: Bank of America, 1971.
Problems in Managing a Family Owned Business, Management Aid No. 208. Washington, D. C.: Small Business Administration, 1976.

INITIATING THE NEW FIRM

This section deals with the various aspects of initiating your own firm. Since this can be done many ways, such areas as evaluating and buying a going concern and franchising are covered, as well as simply starting with an idea.

Chapter 3 discusses the business plan and market survey. Financing the business is covered in Chapter 4. The sales program is covered in Chapter 5, and locating the business in Chapter 6. The preparation of pro forma statements is discussed in Chapter 7.

This section should give the reader an indication of the various programs needed to initiate a successful small business.

CHAPTER **3**

THE BUSINESS PLAN: KEYSTONE OF THE NEW FIRM

INTRODUCTION

Entrepreneurs are often reluctant to commit a business plan to writing. One reason for this is that they perceive time as such a precious commodity. A real need must exist in order to convince the entrepreneur that it is necessary to work on the business plan when the same time could be spent selling products, handling a customer complaint, or setting up a delivery schedule. Another reason for not taking the time to develop a business plan is that conditions may change so rapidly that written plans are rapidly outdated. The entrepreneur often believes it easier, quicker, and more effective to adapt than to make a commitment on paper that may make the firm less flexible. However, a business plan can be a useful tool for the owner and key people in the company, by providing information and guidelines for current and future decisions — without hampering needed flexibility.

Another reason for a business plan is to provide adequate information to those who may supply financing. The need for financing occurs at various times in the life of the business: on starting the business, prior to an expansion, at seasonal peaks and valleys, and when the business is in financial trouble. At these times, some variation of a business plan is required to obtain financing. A similarity exists between the two reasons for the plan. In each case, the plan makes all facets of the business explicit.

The business plan, therefore, is the keystone of the firm. It is both a reference for judging the progress of the firm and a marketing document. While allowing flexibility, the plan gives constant direction to the firm.

THE BUSINESS PLAN

The basic business plan has two major components: a general outline of the firm providing a history of the business, including its marketing aspects, and a detailed financial information section.

The general outline of the business section would include:

1a. information about the owners and other key people in the company,

1b. a statement indicating what these people do in the company,

1c. information regarding the market for the products or services,

1d. information regarding the products or services themselves, and

1e. information regarding the market strategy.

If the business has been in operation for several years, this information is of an historical nature. If the company is to be started in the future, the information is projected or estimated.

The financial information section would include:

2a. statements for the past 3 to 5 years if the company has been in business for that length of time,

2b. a statement of the legal form of the company, that is, a proprietorship, a partnership, or a corporation,

2c. personal financial statements of the owners,

2d. projected financial statements for the business, and

2e. a list of suppliers and customers.

PART I OF THE BUSINESS PLAN

KEY PEOPLE

The information needed for item 1a is discussed in Chapter 1. The business plan should include basic information such as full name, age, past experience, specific accomplishments, and special skills. Often, information about the owners is sufficient. However, if other key people are in the company, similar information should be included about them. For example, a sales manager or the person in charge of producing the goods or rendering services may have skills critical to the success of the company.

This section should also include a description of the job performed in the company by each individual described. The job description assists in the internal management of the company by providing a vehicle for defining responsibilities within the company. The technique for writing job descriptions is discussed in Chapter 8.

MARKET SURVEY

The existence of a market and an evaluation of competition are critical to the success of a business. The market survey, therefore, is very important to the validity of the business plan. Commercial loan officers are always instructed to probe this aspect of the plan to determine how realistically the market survey has been completed.

The purpose of a market survey is to determine if a market exists for your particular company's products. A market survey is necessary for those starting a new business, for those buying an existing business, and for those operating an existing business. Typically, a market survey is thought of as a one-time proposition; however, it should be an on-going activity of the small business.

The market survey should answer four basic questions:

1. Who are the customers for the products?
2. What size is the market for the products?
3. What are the characteristics of the market for the products?
4. What is the nature of the competition for the products?

Who are the customers for our products?

Determination of the existence of a market is the initial step. For example, how does one decide whether a market exists for a sporting goods store? One begins by consulting the most recent census information. Census information is generally available from the local Chamber of Commerce and is always available directly from the U.S. Department of Commerce. This source of data includes items such as number of households, age, per capita income, race, and home ownership of the population within a town or city. Census data may be updated with information from the "Annual Survey of Buying Power" published by *Sales Management Magazine*. The entrepreneur combines the census areas from which the company will draw customers. Is the population of the area composed of the age groups that will buy the specific sporting merchandise to be offered for sale? Are income levels sufficient to support the purchase of recreation items? In conjunction with the census data, a check of the community or area recreation facilities is advisable, in order to note which age groups are involved in various sports. What sports are most popular in the area? What percentage of the population appears to play each sport? Are the facilities used seven days a week or just on the weekends? How many hours a day are they used for each sport? Do leagues for various sports exist? The acquisition of such information in a systematic way provides a good estimate of a market for sporting goods.

What size is the market for our products?

The second step is to compute an average family income for the area the business is to serve. Estimates of the percentage of family income spent on sporting goods are available from several sources.[1] To calculate an example, if 2000 households are in the area to be served by the sporting goods store, if the average income per household is $16,000, and if 2 per cent of that income is spent on sporting goods, then the market estimate for the area would be $640,000 in total sales per year.

What are the characteristics of the market for the products?

Two primary characteristics need to be considered in evaluating this portion of the market survey. First, which components of our products are seasonal? In the sporting goods example, baseball, basketball, football, and soccer are seasonal sports. Depending on the information acquired in earlier parts of the survey, estimates are made of sales for each of the seasonal items. This information subsequently becomes important in projecting income statements and cash flow statements, as well as in making purchases of inventory. Suppliers are often helpful in estimating the seasonal aspects of a business.

The second characteristic is the influence of variables in the economy on the business. What effect would a recession have on the sporting goods business? The answer to such a question is difficult. However, the previously gathered census data will supply clues. If the business area in question is populated essentially by professional, managerial, and government-employed heads of households, the business will be relatively unaffected by a recession. On the other hand, if the area is populated by production workers in industries susceptible to recessions, huge fluctuations in sales are probable. Again, this information is useful for projecting income and cash flow statements.

Competition for the products

A market survey should always include an assessment of the competition in the area — all businesses striving for the same sales dollar. In appraising this, an area map should be used to record the location of competitors. Some subjective estimate should be made of the size and quality of the competitor with special acknowledgement of the competitor's managerial capabilities, aggressiveness, pricing structure, and reputation. How crowded are the facilities of the competitors? What type and qual-

---

[1] For example, see Nelson, R. L., *The Selection of Retail Location*, F. W. Dodge Corporation, 1958, Chapter 14.

ity of product or service do they give? What sort of dollar volume do the competitors appear to be generating? Are the current competitors highly successful, or are they just barely surviving, and why? Would your entry expand the market or would your share come out of someone else's business? Is the market so attractive that large competitors or discount stores will enter the area? What specific things are the current competition not doing that you can do well?

The aspiring entrepreneur must be able to generate meaningful and relevant questions that are appropriate to the success of the business. Decisions must be made and some subjective risks estimated. Often small businesses are opened without the benefit of a good evaluation of the competition. In some situations, no competition may exist. You are then confronted with the genuine question of whether a fantastic opportunity exists or whether there is simply no market.

A related concern is how the current competition is doing financially. What is the failure rate in the area for your particular type of business? Does a high failure rate necessarily mean "keep out?" Does a lack of failures necessarily mean "open up?" Certainly, a series of failures is a danger signal, but the causes of the failures are important to ascertain. Bankers usually give advice about local competitive conditions. Interviews with those who have failed are often helpful if you are capable of carefully evaluating not only what is said but the person saying it, as well. In some cases, interviews with former customers provide insight into the reasons for failure. High failure rates can be due to a multitude of factors. If the failures are due to a lack of a market or an inadequate market compared with the number of competitors, you have no chance of success. If the volume is there, but the failures are due to inadequate management, you have sufficient reason to continue the investigation.

While the above information is difficult to acquire, it does represent an important aspect of the market survey. The fact that the information is difficult to obtain should not deter the entrepreneur from making the estimates. The assessment of competition is really a comparison of your abilities and skills with those of your competitors.

The market survey, as noted, is an integral segment of the business plan. The omission of this segment has resulted in the failure of many firms. A valid market survey is certainly the first step to success for the small business.

The market survey should clearly specify the products or services sold by the company. The pro forma statements (cash, income statement, and balance sheet) should explicitly cover each of the products. For simplicity, Chapter 7 assumes one product. In practice, projections are made for each product and subsequently combined into totals.

Chapter 5, which gives information on the possible products and services, also covers the sales program necessary to sell the company's product. In the business plan, specific recognition should be given to different sales programs for various products within the company.

PART II OF THE BUSINESS PLAN

FINANCIAL STATEMENTS

Financial statements for the past three to five years are appropriate for inclusion in the business plan. Financial statements form a portion of the business plan, whether the plan is to be used for internal purposes or for securing financing. In either situation, the reader of the plan is able to inspect the financial trends and developments, projected or actual, within the business. Historical financial statements are used to predict the future, assuming that all portions of the general outline, or history, of the company remain the same.

A statement of the legal form must be prepared for lenders because of the liability and financial relationships covered by each form. These forms are explained in detail in Appendix II. Corporations are designed to protect the financial assets of their stock-owners. For this reason, a corporation generally gives a lender to the corporation less protection than other forms of ownership.

For these reasons, lenders often require the personal financial statements of the owners of the corporation. If the company assets are deemed inadequate by the potential lender, owners of small businesses will often be asked to pledge their personal assets, in addition to those of the company. Often, the pledge of personal assets requires the consent of one's spouse, since joint ownership of personal assets is not unusual.

The fourth part of the financial information section shown above is the pro forma financial data. Chapter 7 deals with this subject in detail. Pro forma statements are normally consistent with the preceding years' financial statements. If the pro forma projections show substantial changes from the preceding years, some justification must be spelled out in the company component of the business plan. These projected financial statements are very important in plans for either a new business or the purchase of an existing company. The importance of this type of statement is due to the increased risk levels associated with both of these options. Careful preparation of the projected cash flow statement, the projected income statement, and the projected balance sheet provides benefits both for the internal management of the company and for securing financing.

The last portion of the financial information section of the business plan is a list of suppliers and customers. This information is used primarily by potential lenders. Suppliers are contacted by the lenders with regard to the financial status of the company's account with them. Often, customers are contacted regarding the quality, value, and adequacy of the product or service supplied by the company. When there are few customers, a detailed analysis of each should be provided in the list.

SUMMARY

The business plan should be an impressive document, since it represents the business more than any other single document. The plan integrates all aspects of the business into a comprehensive operating entity. Lack of planning is a major reason for the failure of the small firm.

To paraphrase an old saying, "A man with no destination may take any road." The business plan is a vehicle for establishing meaningful goals for the company and for subsequently providing the supporting structure and strategy to attain those goals. Few small-business problems of a major nature exist that cannot be managed effectively by using the material specified in the first seven chapters of this book.

The main points of the business plan are:

1. An abstract containing the basic aspects of the plan and the business;
2. The objectives of the firm; where you intend to go, your products and services;
3. The market survey; do you have a viable plan? Can you deliver to the market?
4. The manufacturing processes; how are you going to make your product or locate your services?
5. Pro forma financial statements; a summary of your financial "haves" and "have nots";
6. Analysis of the statements; assuring investors of your worth;
7. Your personal finances;
8. Your legal structure;
9. A summary of your personnel's qualifications: who are you, and why will you make it in business?

STUDY QUESTIONS

1. In your experience, what type of market survey is usually performed by a small-business owner?

2. Why is a market survey a key ingredient for success?

3. Why is the business plan important? What parts are the most important?

4. Why does the market survey provide the key to the business plan?

REFERENCES AND SUGGESTED READINGS

"Annual survey of buying power," *Sales and Marketing Management,* New York: Bill Publishing Co., July (each year).

Baumbeck, Clifford M., Kenneth Lawyer, and Pearce C. Kelley. *How to Organize and Operate a Small Business,* 5th ed., Englewood Cliffs, N. J.: Prentice-Hall, Inc., 1973.

Breaking the Barriers to Small Business Planning, Management Aid No. 179. Washington, D. C.: Small Business Administration, 1976.

Brockhous, W. L. "How to develop a plan for securing venture capital," *Business Horizons,* June, 1976, pp. 66–72.

Business Plan for Small Construction Firms, Management Aid No. 221. Washington, D.C.: Small Business Administration, 1974.

Business Plan for Small Manufacturers, Management Aid No. 218. Washington, D.C.: Small Business Administration, 1974.

Carson, Deane, ed. *The Vital Majority,* Washington, D.C.: Small Business Administration, 1973.

Cooper, Arnold C. "Small companies can pioneer new products," *Harvard Business Review,* September–October, 1966, pp. 77–84.

Dible, D. M. *Winning the Money Game,* Santa Clara, California: The Entrepreneur Press, 1974.

"Financing small business," *Small Business Reporter,* San Francisco: Bank of America, Vol. 13, No. 7, 1976.

Goeldner, C. R., and Laura M. Dirks. "Business facts: where to find them," *MSU Business Topics,* Summer, 1976, pp. 23–36.

Mancuso, J. R. "How a business plan is read," *Business Horizons,* August, 1974, pp. 33–42.

National Directories for Use in Marketing, Small Business Bibliography No. 13. Washington, D.C.: Small Business Administration, 1971.

Nelson, R. L. The Selection of Retail Location, New York: F. W. Dodge Corporation, 1958.

Nicholas, Ted. *How to Form Your Own Corporation for Under $50.00,* Wilmington, Delaware: Enterprise Publishing Co., 1972.

Profile Your Customers to Expand Industrial Sales. Management Aid No. 192. Washington, D.C.: Small Business Administration, 1971.

Sales Potential and Market Shares, Small Marketer's Aid No. 112. Washington, D.C.: Small Business Administration, 1973.

Small Store Planning for Growth, Small Business Management Series No. 33. Washington, D.C.: Small Business Administration, 1966.

Stanford, M. J. "Forecasting for new enterprises: why and how," *Journal of Small Business Management,* Vol. 12, No. 1, June, 1974, pp. 36–41.

Statistics and Maps for National Market Analysis, Small Business Bibliography No. 12. Washington, D.C.: Small Business Administration, 1972.

"Steps to starting a business," *Small Business Reporter,* San Francisco: Bank of America, Vol. 10, No. 10, 1972.

Using Census Data in Small Plant Marketing, Management Aid No. 187. Washington, D.C.: Small Business Administration, 1974.

Waite, F. G. "How sound planning helps a new business succeed," *Nation's Business,* 1976, pp. 61–64.

CHAPTER 4

FINANCING THE SMALL BUSINESS

Two of the most severe problems faced by the typical small business are the lack of equity capital and the inability to secure debt financing or credit. This chapter is concerned with the various methods which a small-business owner can use to acquire either the capital itself or the use of capital.

FINANCING THE SMALL BUSINESS

The financing of a small business is accomplished with some combination of equity capital and debt capital. Equity and ownership are synonymous. The small-business owner is often short of equity capital and is forced to resort to extensive use of debt capital. Therefore, to secure equity capital without going into debt, it is necessary to give up some part of the ownership of the company. The attitudes of small-business owners vary substantially with respect to the degree of ownership to be relinquished in order to acquire equity capital. Some feel that they must own 100 per cent of the company, some demand controlling interest, and others are willing to accept control by others. Differing legal structures provide means by which equity is divided among one or more persons. The primary advantage of equity capital is that it is not necessary to repay it. Because of this, the more equity capital a company has, the more financially solvent a company is considered to be.

It is a common practice for a supplier of debt capital to request the option of converting debt capital into equity capital as payment for the willingness to supply debt capital. The supplier of debt capital attempts to protect his investment in two ways: through foreclosure in the event of financial difficulty, and acquisition of ownership if the company prospers.

Debt capital comes in a number of forms. One variation requires periodic, usually monthly, payment of interest with complete repayment of the principal at maturity. More common, however, is the payment of a constant amount that includes both principal and interest. Debt financing, if possible, should be arranged so that cash outflows coincide with projected cash inflows, as discussed in Chapter 7. Depending on the industry and economic conditions, as well as the specific small business and its equity position, various combinations of debt financing will be available to the entrepreneur. The small-business owner must determine which sources of debt financing are available and select those forms that are most beneficial to the company.

Table 4–1 lists a vast range of financing alternatives available to the small business.

Just as immense variations exist in the definition of small business, huge variations in methods of financing small business also exist. Many of the financing alternatives found in Table 4–1, such as floating a stock issue through a security dealer, would not be acceptable for the average small-business owner. However, numerous equity and debt financing methods are appropriate for even the smallest of businesses.

The balance of this chapter will focus on those methods of financing that are both most common and most appropriate to the small business. The first section will deal with the primary sources of equity financing; the second section will cover the primary sources of debt financing.

SOURCES OF EQUITY FINANCING

Sources of equity financing for small business are often few and far between. The four most common sources are discussed in descending order of their availability. Note that some equity sources may also be sources of debt financing.

OWNERS AND ORIGINATORS OF THE COMPANY

The primary source of equity for a small business is funds supplied by the owners of the company. It is often mandatory for a small-business owner to have a large proportion of personal assets invested in the business — either directly or indirectly.

Direct investments include buying shares of the corporation stock, or providing funds for the operation of either a proprietorship or a partnership. Another important form of direct investment is returning net profit to the company. The temptation to withdraw all profits is great, but it is wise to overcome this temptation and keep profits in the firm to provide for additional working capital. Owners also supply capital through debt financing.

Table 4–1 SOURCES OF DEBT AND EQUITY FINANCING FOR SMALL BUSINESSES

Lender or Investor	Debt	Equity
Closed-end investment companies		✓
Colleges, universities, and other endowed institutions		✓
Commercial banks	✓	
Commercial finance companies	✓	
Consumer finance companies	✓	
Corporate venture capital departments or subsidiaries	✓	✓
Credit unions	✓	
Customers	✓	✓
Economic Development Administration	✓	
Employees	✓	✓
Equipment manufacturers	✓	
Factoring companies	✓	
Family investment companies	✓	✓
Financial consultants, finders, and other intermediaries	✓	✓
Founders	✓	✓
Industrial banks	✓	
Insurance companies	✓	✓
Investment advisers		✓
Investment bankers	✓	✓
Investment clubs		✓
Leasing companies	✓	
Mutual funds		✓
Mutual Savings banks	✓	
Parent companies	✓	✓
Pension funds		✓
Private individual investors		✓
Private investment partnerships		✓
Privately owned venture capital corporations		✓
Relatives and friends	✓	✓
Sales finance companies	✓	
Savings and loan associations	✓	
Securities dealers		✓
Self-underwriting		✓
Small Business Administration	✓	
Small business investments companies	✓	✓
State and local industrial development commissions	✓	
Tax-exempt foundations and charitable trusts		✓
Trade suppliers	✓	
Trust companies and bank trust departments		✓
Veterans Administration	✓	

From Donald M. Dible. "Debt versus Equity Financing," in *Winning The Money Game,* Donald M. Dible, editor. Santa Clara, California: The Entrepreneur Press, 1974, page 284.

RELATIVES AND FRIENDS

Relatives and friends will occasionally make an investment in the company. The advantage of this source of equity is the relative ease and informality of securing funds. One disadvantage is that the investment may include the requirement that a son or a brother-in-law be hired as a part of the deal. This person may either be incompetent or lack the necessary skills for the position.

Once the family is on the payroll, it is extremely difficult to remove it. A second disadvantage is that friends and relatives may feel they have the right to constantly advise the founder of the company. Because of the leverage these individuals have as friends and relatives, this is often a difficult situation. The third disadvantage is that long-term ill will may occur if the business fails or is not as successful as the friends and relatives think it should be.

In short, relatives and friends are often good sources of equity capital, but there are disadvantages as well as advantages. Quite often, however, no other alternative for acquiring equity capital exists. In this case, careful thought must be given to the various terms and conditions so the equity is acquired in a business like manner.

WEALTHY INDIVIDUAL INVESTORS

Because of the structure of the federal income tax laws, a small business may be an attractive investment for wealthy individuals. For example, many physicians, dentists, attorneys, and corporate executives are in a 70 per cent marginal tax bracket. This means that if they invest their money in corporate bonds at 8 per cent, their return after taxes will be only 30 per cent of the 8 per cent rate, or about 2.4 per cent. By investing in a small business, the investor's return is taxed at the capital gains rate of 25 per cent when the stock is sold — a substantial improvement in return. The Internal Revenue Code (Section 1244) provides that gains in small businesses may be taxed at the capital gains rate, and that up to $50,000 in capital losses may be deducted in one tax year. For an individual in the 70 per cent tax bracket, the real losses are only $15,000 because of the tax shelter, and if the stock appreciates, there will be a net gain. Thorough study of Section 1244 of the Internal Revenue Code is recommended if the small-business owner is considering this alternative.

CUSTOMERS

Occasionally a potential or actual customer will provide either equity or debt capital. Equity capital may be provided either to encourage more competition for items which the customer buys in large quantities, or to develop a supplier who can provide services to the customer at a lower cost. The customer who provides capital to the small business often requires substantial discounts for the merchandise. The customer can provide debt capital in several ways to a small business: by loan guarantees, by making a loan directly to the small business, by leasing or lending specialized equipment, and by making payments for the merchandise as it is constructed.

In situations in which the customer provides equity or debt capital, the small business is often placed in the position of relying on a small number of large accounts. If the small-business owner elects to follow this option, it is advisable to construct pro forma statements carefully, with explicit consideration of seasonal and cyclical swings in the demand for the products of the customer. The changes in cash flow may not be detrimental to the customer who supplied the funds, but they could be to a small business that is not as well-financed.

SOURCES OF DEBT FINANCING

Some sources of equity financing may also be sources of debt financing. However, the reverse situation is seldom true. Suppliers of debt financing typically perform this function to generate a profit, and generally have little ownership interest in companies to which debt financing is supplied.

OWNERS OR ORIGINATORS OF THE COMPANY

Owners may be a source of debt financing by guaranteeing loans to their own business. A guarantee to a lender is provided by offering some non-company asset as collateral for a loan. In some cases, an owner may lend the company money directly. Such a transaction presents several problems. If the company has several owners, a competitive interest rate must be negotiated. If a loan from a financial institution is outstanding, it is usually necessary to subordinate the owner's loan to that of the financial institution. Loans to the company should be clearly noted as business propositions and not as attempts to acquire additional equity. Often, the owner makes an indirect investment in a small business by leasing plant, office, property, or equipment to the company. The lease benefits the owner by providing a return on an existing asset and may provide tax benefits.

COMMERCIAL BANKS

Commercial banks are in business to supply debt financing. A large portion of a commercial bank's business is with small businesses. Commercial banks provide three distinct types of loans: working capital loans, term loans, and longer term real estate loans.

Working capital loans are normally extended to provide the

small business with the cash necessary to take care of seasonal peaks, to take large trade discounts, or to meet any unusual cash needs of a less than twelve-month duration. Generally, working capital loans should be self-liquidating; that is, cash inflows that occur at a later date should cover the amount of the loan plus interest plus an additional profit. Commercial bankers need assurance of both the financial strength of the company (usually a balance sheet), and the adequacy of the cash flows to cover the loan (usually a cash flow statement).

Term loans range in length from one to five years. Typically, the loans are for the purchase of a fixed asset of a durable nature that will produce revenue for the company. The commercial banker wants assurances that sales will materialize over these longer periods of time. Sales agreements, sales contracts, and the number of customers purchasing the item on a continuing basis are assurances that would be satisfactory. If the asset is such that the resale value is low, commercial bankers will be more concerned with assurances of adequate and continued sales volume.

Real estate loans by commercial banks are another type of term loan made to small businesses. From the commercial bankers' viewpoint, real estate loans are secure if accurate appraisals are done. Industrial and commercial land appraisal is more volatile than other types of real estate. Commercial bankers, therefore, tend to require a substantial down payment.

Relations with commercial bankers are very important. Establishing good working relationships with your bankers is an important part of being a small-business owner. It is important to take the time to talk to your bankers periodically, even when you don't need money. Let them know how your business is progressing. It is particularly important to give bankers plenty of notice when applying for a loan. They are generally unimpressed by the obvious lack of planning that precipitates a request for an immediate loan.

Banks do not supply equity capital. By the same line of thought, banks do not supply "start-up" capital. Bankers will consider working capital loans and term loans when the equity position of the company is great enough to afford financial protection. However, the banker generally assumes that the small-business owner will provide equity capital for the business from any of the sources specified in preceding sections of this chapter.

TRADE CREDITORS

Trade creditors can be an important source of debt financing. An extension of trade credit terms can be anywhere from a few days to several months, but it must be earned. Trade credit is easier to acquire than debt financing from a commercial bank because margins are higher for trade creditors. Credit terms vary with the type of business. In some situations, creditors will give more liberal credit terms to a business owner if the owner's needs are specified. In order to move seasonal goods, a creditor will often grant extended billing terms. The small-business owner is also advised to establish good credit ratings with trade creditors. Trade creditors, like commercial bankers, are much more likely to extend lenient credit terms if accounts have been paid promptly in the past. Trade creditors, like other suppliers of equity and debt financing, will occasionally make direct loans or guarantee a loan for a small business.

SALES FINANCE COMPANIES

The purpose of sales finance companies is to provide the installment plan for the customer of the small business when the funds of the business are inadequate for the job. Typically, installments for such items of high unit value as furniture, appliances, automobiles, boats, jewelry, air conditioners, stereo systems, and tires are covered.

The sales finance company can relieve the small business of almost all duties related to the credit function. Generally, the sales finance company approves or disapproves the credit application and payments are made by the customer directly to the finance company. Variations in the procedure are common — one finance company may handle all of the credit accounts of the small business; several finance companies may handle all of the accounts of the small business; or the small business may handle some accounts and use one or more finance companies to handle the balance. Commercial banks often have a department that handles sales financing and sometimes the business owner feels obligated to grant these installment sales to his bank as well as to several finance companies.

Finance companies perform other functions for the small-business owner, including floor planning in which the finance company owns the merchandise but stores it in the display room of the small business. In addition, finance companies often lend money to small businesses on inventories, on accounts receivable, and for equipment.

Sales finance companies can provide a large amount of debt financing. Depending on the type of business, it is possible for the small-business owner to have a relatively small amount of capital invested in the inventories and accounts receivable. The costs of sales financing should be explored in depth and incorporated into the pro forma statements discussed in Chapter 7. Factors, or factoring companies, provide a similar, but slightly different, form of debt financing.

COMMERCIAL FINANCE COMPANIES

Commercial finance companies are similar to sales finance companies. The basic difference is that the customer pays his account directly to the small business and is usually unaware of the financing transactions. Funds are provided to the small business in exchange for pledging the accounts receivable. On expensive items, sales may be pledged for a specified period of time. Commercial financing is a method in which the financial burden of accounts receivable is removed from the small business. Commercial finance companies provide large sums of money for working capital to small businesses, and also provide funds for inventory financing, leasing of equipment, and field warehousing.

LEASING

Since leasing does not require a capital outlay, it is an attractive alternative for small businesses that are short of cash. Equipment leasing is a very specialized field and requires an in-depth knowledge of specific industries. Usually, leasing companies specialize in only one sector, such as fleet leasing of tank trucks. Leasing is generally more expensive than borrowing funds from other debt financing sources. The advantage of leasing is that all lease expense is tax-deductible.

MANUFACTURERS OF ORIGINAL EQUIPMENT

Manufacturers of equipment often provide either financing or leasing of the product they sell. With the advent of high technology items, this has become more prevalent. For example, many small businesses now use a mini-computer. Since this investment represents a substantial outlay to the typical small business, the manufacturer will often provide financing for the computer. One advantage of this method is that the business owner may claim as a tax-deductible expense both the depreciation and the interest, as well as acquiring equity in the equipment. This method may be contrasted with leasing, in which no equity in the equipment is acquired.

THE SMALL BUSINESS ADMINISTRATION

The Small Business Administration is a keystone in the small-business community. The SBA is important because it not only provides a focus for presenting the problems of the small-business owner, but provides financial and management assistance directly to the small business as well. In order to qualify for a Small Business Administration loan, the company must meet the SBA definition of small business as specified in the Foreword of this text.

Several basic loans are made by the Small Business Administration. These loans are important to small businesses throughout the United States because the SBA often supplies funds which the small business is unable to secure through normal financial channels. Loan officers within the SBA evaluate each loan application for the benefit of the small-business owner, as well as evaluating the loan's chance of being repaid. Often, the loan officer will refer the small-business owner to the Management Assistance Division for help of a non-financial nature.

Direct Loans. If two or more lending institutions refuse to grant a loan to a small business, the SBA may make a direct loan if the amount does not exceed $150,000. The loan applicant must demonstrate an ability to repay the loan, as well as other company liabilities, out of profits acquired within the term of the loan. Normally, projected cash flow and projected income statements are required. Business construction loans may have terms up to fifteen years, working capital loans may have a maturity up to six years, and other loans have maturities up to ten years.

Economic Opportunity Loans. These loans are granted to economically disadvantaged groups as well as to Vietnam veterans. An E.O.L. is a direct loan.

Disaster Relief Loan. The SBA provides loans to small businesses that are destroyed or severely damaged by disasters such as floods, tornadoes, or hurricanes. The Disaster Relief loan is another form of direct loan.

Participation Loans. The majority of the loans made by the SBA are participation loans. A participation loan also requires that the applicant have been rejected for a loan by at least two commercial lending institutions. The SBA participates in the loan by either:

> guaranteeing up to 90 per cent or $350,000 of a bank loan, whichever is less. The commercial bank provides the cash and the SBA provides the guarantee; or
> providing $150,000 as the SBA's contribution (participation) in the loan with the bank.

Congress appropriates a specific budget each year for the loan program of the SBA. To serve the financial needs of more small businesses, the SBA attempts to write more participation loans than direct loans.

In summary, the Small Business Administration provides a needed service to the small-business community. Financial assistance (debt financing) is made available to those who could not otherwise qualify for loans or leases. The success of many small businesses in the United States today is due to the ability of the

Small Business Administration to provide both financial and managerial assistance. Disadvantages associated with Small Business Administration loans are the longer lead time required to secure a loan than through a commercial bank, the effect of collateral requirements on trade credit, and the additional paperwork required by most governmental agencies. The SBA has recently attempted to streamline some of the paperwork bothersome to commercial banks in the past.

SUMMARY

Numerous methods exist for the acquisition of equity or debt financing for small businesses. Table 4–1 specified forty different sources of funds. The majority of this chapter discussed the eleven most common methods which small businesses use to acquire funds. The task of the small-business owner in financing the business is to select those combinations of methods of financing that are available to the company, most appropriate to the company, and represent the least cost to the company.

STUDY QUESTIONS

1. How can small-business owners raise equity capital?

2. What are some problems associated with different sources of equity capital?

3. What do you think are the criteria utilized by a banker to grant loans to small businesses?

4. How can a small-business owner establish initial credit? How can credit be reestablished if difficulties have arisen?

REFERENCES AND SUGGESTED READINGS

A Handbook of Small Business Finance, Small Business Management Series No. 15. Washington, D.C.: Small Business Administration, 1975.

Dible, Donald M. Up Your Own Organization, Santa Clara, California: Entrepreneur Press, 1971.

Dible, Donald M. Winning the Money Game, Santa Clara, California: Entrepreneur Press, 1974.

InterBusiness Financing: Economic Implications for Small Business, Small Business Research Series No. 3. Washington, D.C.: Small Business Administration, 1962.

Rubel, Stanley M. Guide to Venture Capital Sources, 3rd ed., Chicago: Capital Publishing Corporation, 1974.

The ABC's of Borrowing, Management Aid No. 170. Washington, D.C.: Small Business Administration, 1976.

Wayne, William. How to Succeed in Business When the Chips Are Down, New York: McGraw-Hill Book Company, 1972.

CHAPTER 5

SALES PROGRAMS FOR SMALL BUSINESS

INTRODUCTION

Sales for the products, goods, or services of any small business can be broken down into two basic categories: residual sales and generated sales. Residual sales occur simply because a particular type of business exists at a particular location at a particular time. These are sales that would occur with no sales promotion. Generated sales occur because the small business has taken some overt action to promote the business. It is misleading to consider one category independent of the other. The categories should be considered a package. However, for a clear explanation some differentiation is necessary.

Within the residual sales category, factors such as the results discussed in the "Market survey" section of Chapter 3 should be considered. Other factors that should be considered include site location, the comparative attractiveness of the product (such as Burger-King versus Joe's Drive-in), and the previous reputation of the company. Often the small business relies too heavily on residual sales. In many cases, this level of sales is too low to support a profitable business. In the vast majority of businesses, promotion of some type is necessary to acquire generated sales.

TYPES OF GOODS TO BE SOLD

To understand more fully the promotion techniques available to the small business for the generation of sales, it is necessary to define the various types of goods sold by small businesses. The following discussion concerns the four types of goods sold, as well as the promotion conditions generally associated with each.

The first three types of goods to be discussed are categorized by each individual in the marketplace. For example, one individual may consider a camera to be a specialty good while another may consider it to be a shopping good. Whatever the decision, the categories serve as a basic tool for selecting promotion methods.

SPECIALTY GOODS

Specialty goods are items of merchandise that have a distinctive quality to a specific buyer. Often these items are of high monetary value. Even though prices are generally comparatively high for specialty goods, the buyer places more emphasis on the product's distinctive characteristics than on price. Quite often, specific brand preferences are associated with a specialty good. The buyer has decided, in advance, that a specific product is desired and is willing to search for it. For example, some men will buy only Brooks Brothers suits, which are not sold through most men's clothing stores. These men will often travel great distances to meet a sales representative from Brooks Brothers. Another example is the person purchasing a high-fidelity stereo system, who is convinced that a certain stereo speaker is superior to any other brand and consequently searches for a business that carries this brand.

Several promotional techniques are associated with specialty goods. Advertising may be directed to much wider portions of the trading locale, with emphasis on brand and location rather than price. Area newspapers, radio, and television may be appropriate because the buyer of specialty goods will seek out the seller. The use of price-cutting is generally not effective in attracting this kind of buyer, because the specialty buyer places emphasis on the specific characteristics of the product. The place of purchase needs to be designed so as to induce the customer to feel like a discriminating buyer. The premises must be extremely well kept, neat, and comfortable. A stereo retailer may have a sound-proof room with plush easy-chairs, thick carpets on the floor, and iced tea for customers.

A fourth consideration is that the buyer is concerned with both expert installation and special services, and thinks that only this seller offers these. The merchandise must be delivered carefully and politely, and special installation problems should be expedited by the seller. The buyer often wishes to have a special modification to the purchase which the seller should be prepared to render.

CONVENIENCE GOODS

Convenience goods are merchandise which the buyer wishes to buy with the least possible effort. Since speed is important, price often isn't. "Shopping around" is generally unacceptable to the buyer of these goods. In contrast to specialty goods, convenience goods are generally both low in value and constantly used by the buyer. Convenience goods are often purchased on an impulse or emergency basis, rather than a planned basis. Examples of products that are placed in the convenience category are antifreeze, proprietary and prescription drugs, gasoline, milk, and soft drinks.

Several promotional techniques are associated with convenience goods. The display of convenience goods as impulse items is important. Often, at Thanksgiving, a supermarket will place a display of cranberry sauce in the middle of an aisle, and cigarettes and candy bars are almost always near the cash register. Well-trained sales people are not as necessary as they are for specialty goods. The price is low, and the buyer knows the item is a staple; thus a major sales effort by an individual is unnecessary. It is undesirable for a store specializing in convenience goods to be located near a competitor. For example, the convenience grocery store is seldom located near a supermarket. Buyers are only willing to pay a higher price for a gallon of milk if they can save driving several miles to the supermarket or save waiting in a long line at the supermarket. A wide range of selections for a product is not as important as having one generally acceptable brand. For example, a buyer will usually accept whatever brand of aspirin is available rather than make the effort to go to another store. The final consideration is that stores specializing in convenience goods can often be open long hours and still be profitable since buyers are not generally price conscious and profit margins are relatively high.

SHOPPING GOODS

Shopping goods are those the buyer wishes to compare with similar items. Comparison can be made in terms of price, quality, service, and fashion, or any combination of these four characteristics. Comparison shopping is important because the items shopped for are usually high in value and purchased infrequently. Buyers in this category attempt to balance off the relative advantages of price, quality, service, and fashion. Once the buyer is convinced of the best balance for a product, a sale will occur. Automobiles, television sets, and home furniture are examples of shopping goods.

There are several promotional considerations associated with shopping goods. Location near competitors is advantageous, as this permits the customer to compare easily. If buyers wish to comparison shop and your business is not near the competition, they will probably not frequent your store. The salespeople must be trained both to recognize that customers are comparison shopping and to guide customers in determining the value of the company's product over that of the competitors'. Skilled salespeople are needed and must be paid accordingly.

INDUSTRIAL GOODS

Industrial goods are those goods sold to other businesses. These products are either resold by the next business, used directly in the manufacture of another product, or used indirectly to support the manufacture of another product. Industrial goods cover a wide variety of products: capital items such as buildings and expensive equipment; less expensive capital equipment such as office machines and hand tools; farm products that will be reprocessed into a different product, such as tomatoes into tomato soup; natural resources such as coal, oil, gasoline, and lumber; component parts that become a portion of a new product; and supplies that contribute to the manufacture of a product but do not become a portion of the product itself, such as the fuel oil used to heat a plant or typing paper.

As opposed to the case in the preceding three sections, the seller of industrial goods usually goes to the buyer's office for the sale. Therefore, analysis of buyer behavior in your store is clearly inappropriate; rather, it is necessary to recognize attributes characterizing industrial goods sales. First, buyers of industrial goods, usually called purchasing agents, are generally well-informed regarding the technical aspects of both your product and your competitor's. Purchases are based primarily on the ability of the product to perform rather than the ability of the sales personnel or an extensive promotion. Industrial goods buyers often have specifications to which the seller is expected to conform.

Industrial goods buyers are price conscious when presented with comparable quality — particularly when economic conditions are unfavorable. Industrial goods are either of high unit value or the total sale is large. The small business should exercise care not to be too dependent on a small number of large accounts. The small business is often in a precarious position in this market because the middleman is often eliminated or bypassed by the middleman's supplier. Finally, buyers of industrial goods often require installation, extensive service after the installation, and continuing technical advice.

PROMOTION OF GOODS TO BE SOLD

In view of the information presented in the previous sections on specialty goods, convenience goods, shopping goods, and industrial goods, the direct and indirect promotion methods available to the small business will be discussed. In appraising promotion methods, it is necessary to consider the specific businesses and products sold by the business, to relate the promotional conditions to the specific product, and to apply the method most appropriate to both the product and the promotional conditions.

Several different methods of promotion exist. Since most businesses primarily use personal selling, advertising, and customer relations, the emphasis will be on these. Depending both on the types of goods sold by your particular business and the particular segment of the buying public you wish to attract, various promotion methods should be selected. For example, if you are in the camera business and wish to attract the specialty goods buyer, you would select different promotion methods than if you wished to attract the shopping goods buyer.

PERSONAL SELLING

Personal selling is an under-rated attribute of small businesses that has several facets. The first is prospecting; that is, finding prospective customers. Every business owner that utilizes personal selling should work diligently to develop a plan for acquiring prospects. For example, a heating oil distributor found deed transfers at the county court house to be the quickest way to reach new homeowners. A tire distributor maintains a record of every new automobile purchased in the county. Prospecting methods vary with the type of business. The entrepreneur is limited only by imagination.

The second facet of personal selling is familiarizing the potential customer with your product. The heating oil distributor sends a salesperson to the current residence of the buyer of the new home. The potential customers are made aware of the product before they even have need for it. The tire distributor sends a personalized letter to purchasers of new cars about twenty-four months after each car was purchased. Many methods exist and each small business must adopt the method that appears to be most appropriate to its situation.

The third facet of personal selling is actually making the sale. Often personal characteristics of the individual affect the ability to close the sale. A sales representative with a pleasing and accommodating personality, who is well-dressed and well-groomed, possesses an initial advantage. Once the buyer's attention has been caught by this first impression, it must be held by thorough product knowledge. Product knowledge should permit the salesperson to make comparisons with the competition, if necessary. A thorough knowledge of pricing structure for the business and of the characteristics linked with different prices are associated with product knowledge. The good salesperson must also be adept at filling the specific needs of the buyer through the company. For example, the difference in product quality among competitors is not always distinguishable, but the buyer may be interested in speed of delivery, a specific modification of the product, or credit terms. The salesperson must serve as the interface between the needs of the customer and the capabilities of the small business, promising neither too much nor too little.

ADVERTISING

Advertising includes radio, television, newspapers, the Yellow Pages, billboards, specialties or novelties, and direct mail.

Mass media advertising (such as radio, television, and newspapers) generally gives more coverage than most small businesses require. If a business operates in a small portion of a metropolitan area, the bulk of the advertising dollars spent on the media are missing the prospective buyers. If the small business services most of the area covered by the media, it is worthwhile to give consideration to this form of advertising. The Yellow Pages are primarily for companies selling shopping goods or those companies in which the primary contact is made by the customer. Billboards are often useful for a small business because the message of the billboard is essentially localized, and can be placed near the specific business. Small businesses tend to use specialties or novelties. The forms of specialties are virtually endless, ranging from pencils, to T-shirts, to matchbooks, to calendars. The advantage of specialties is that they are placed directly in the hands of the consumer and have a relatively low cost for each unit that actually reaches a prospective buyer. Direct mail is used perhaps most often by small businesses. The cost of direct mail varies with the degree of personalization in the mailed material. Direct mail has the same advantages as the use of specialties: it allows selective coverage, is relatively inexpensive, and can be adapted to various types and sizes of market.

HOW EFFECTIVE IS ADVERTISING?

Considering the millions of dollars spent on advertising by small businesses, very little effort is made to evaluate the effectiveness of advertising. Such an evaluation is an extremely difficult task but some effort should be made. Since most methods of evaluating the effects of advertising are short-term methods, perhaps a small-business owner is well advised to consider advertising programs of which the impact is also short-term. Institutional advertising may be best left to the larger corporations. This is possible, in part, through cooperative advertising programs with suppliers.

Some ways to measure advertising effectiveness are:

1. the use of coupons which the buyers must bring to the business to receive a specific benefit,
2. advertising one specific item for a specified time period,
3. withholding a specific advertising method for a week or month and comparing the differences,
4. perhaps best, simply asking customers why they are buying a particular product at a particular time, either verbally or with a very short questionnaire. If it is done verbally, tabulation sheets should be maintained to summarize results.

Advertising arouses much debate. Sellers of advertising often indicate that they really don't know how effective it is, but that the small business can't take the chance of not using it. However, if substantial sums of money are spent for advertising, an evaluation of its effectiveness must be made. A small business would not hire a salesperson and subsequently never inspect that employee's record of sales. Advertising should be no different. Checklist G in Appendix I provides a method of evaluating newspaper advertising, which can be applied to any type of advertising.

CUSTOMER RELATIONS

Customer relations is the total experience of customers with a specific small business. Word-of-mouth advertising results from customer relations and can be either good or bad. Customer relations are developed over a period of several years. Often small businesses are unaware of the tremendous impact that their daily customer relations have on future business. Customer relations are as important as personal selling and advertising. This is particularly true if your market is very localized or if the buyers of your product have contact through trade associations. The day-to-day operation of a small business is a powerful sales tool for the future. A rude employee, an unfulfilled promise, an uncorrected error today may cost you a surprising large number of future sales. Future sales rest heavily on efficient daily operations.

OTHER PROMOTION METHODS

The small business may gain assistance from large corporations with many types of advertising. Assistance may be in the form of cooperative advertising, the use of newspaper advertising mats, the knowledge and experience of sales representatives, use of special displays, loans of specialized equipment, engineering and other technical assistance, and the use of standardized accounting or inventory control systems. The small business should carefully consider all available offerings from its suppliers and evaluate their probable impact on sales.

Other promotion methods include special sales, publicity, customer services, and in-store displays.

PRICING

Every product sold by a small business has a price. Price is the common denominator of business transactions. Price, therefore, is a part of all sales programs. Pricing, like almost all areas of selling the product, is a subjective and intuitive area of decision.

To the buyer, price may be viewed as an equation[1] where

Price = List price less: Quantity discounts
                          Seasonal discounts
                          Cash discounts
           less: Trade-in allowances
                  Damaged goods allowance

According to this, the buyer views list price as only a starting point in determination of a final price. This theory will not apply to all small-business pricing structures, but will vary with the characteristics of a particular business. Large corporations often have rigid policies with respect to these aspects of pricing. Some large companies will not accept trade-in allowances on merchandise, and some do not give a cash discount. If the policies of large competitors are known, small businesses can compete more effectively by offering these discounts or allowances.

The value expected by the buyer must also be considered. The buyer will expect not only the physical product, but will also have some perception of the service to be received, the degree to which the company will guarantee the quality of the product, the ease with which the product will be served if defective, worn out, or damaged, packaging of the product, credit terms available, and whether trading stamps or premiums are given.

Pricing is an extremely complex process. The entrepreneur should carefully consider all aspects of pricing before actually making the pricing decision. The following sections deal with the types of pricing most often used by small businesses. A great number of pricing methods exist owing to the complexity of determining a fair price from the viewpoint of the buyer. The discussion of price in the paragraph above should serve as a framework for evaluating each pricing method for a specific small business and its products.

---

[1] Based on material in E. J. McCarthy. *Basic Marketing,* 5th ed. Homewood, Illinois: Richard D. Irwin, Inc., 1975.

Bait pricing is illegal in interstate commerce and unethical in all situations. However, it is mentioned here to verify its presence. Bait pricing is the practice of advertising a very low price for a product, but making it extremely difficult for the consumer to buy at that price once in the place of business. The salesperson attempts to switch the buyer to a more expensive product.

Bid pricing is used by small businesses when a separate price must be established for each job. The basic problem in bid pricing is the determination of the appropriate variable costs, overhead costs, and profit to be applied to each job. Since other businesses are bidding against your company, the rote application of standard overhead costs and profit should be avoided. Insight and experience are necessary to successfully manage the pricing function in a company of this type.

Markup pricing is one of the common methods used by retailers and wholesalers. The markup is a specified percentage above cost. Markups are normally determined on the basis of industry tradition or trade discounts. Some small businesses apply different markups to different products, while others mark all items in the line up by the same percentage. Recently, more emphasis has been placed on variable markups to reduce the number of slow-moving items for small businesses. Trade associations supply information of this type to small-business owners.

Manufacturers and wholesalers often use **freight absorption pricing** to penetrate a new market. By absorbing the freight on a product, the company may expand its market beyond those areas closest to the plant or warehouse. Freight absorption pricing reduces the profit margin in the hope that increased volume will increase total profits.

Full line pricing is used by businesses carrying a complete line of products. The pricing strategy will depend on the managerial view of the entire line of products. In an expensive clothing store aimed at one market, all the prices will be high. In a grocery store carrying varying grades of vegetables aimed at several market levels, the prices will not be related, but will be based on the grade of vegetable.

Introductory pricing is a temporary measure to capture the customer's attention. This is distinct from bait pricing because the company sells at the stated price to develop new customers. The intent of the entrepreneur is to raise prices once the company has gained a foothold in the market. The disadvantage of this method is that a price war may result if established competitors meet the introductory pricing levels.

Leader pricing is commonly practiced in retail stores when items with high sales appeal are priced slightly above wholesale cost. These price leaders are genuine bargains which have the sole purpose of attracting customers into the store. Generally, leader pricing is used for items that customers buy in small amounts at one time.

Prestige prices imply a quality or status product. For the truly prestigious product, a decrease in price may lead to a decrease in sales. Products such as this are uncommon, but examples do exist, such as the Rolls-Royce automobile.

Price lining is the practice of establishing three or four levels of prices for a broad range of merchandise. Men's neckties are often priced at $5.00, $7.50, and $10.00, with no prices between the three lines of price.

Price skimming is the practice of obtaining sales at comparatively high prices in the process of introducing a new product or service. As the market is skimmed, businesses will usually begin to decrease their prices slowly to continue generating additional sales.

CONSUMER CREDIT

Credit is certainly an item that must be considered as part of a small business sales program. Not extending credit may lose customers for a business; however, granting credit too easily may cause a large number of bad debts. This section deals with the variables that should be considered in deciding the level of consumer credit to be offered.

ADEQUACY OF WORKING CAPITAL

Many small businesses have a shortage of working capital. Poorly defined credit policies and a lack of awareness of the capital accounts receivable often contribute to the working capital shortage. A method of evaluating the working capital needs of a particular business is to refer to industry averages, looking, for example, in the *Annual Statement Studies* of Robert Morris Associates. The industry averages show the percentage of total assets in accounts receivable and the number of days that accounts receivable remained uncollected. These data become a basis for estimating how much working capital a business should commit to consumer credit.

BUSINESS AND CONSUMER CREDIT CONSIDERATIONS

It is impossible to generalize about the necessity of consumer credit in a specific business. Generally, however, products with a short life span, those which are perishable, and those with a small profit margin are not sold on credit. Many of the exceptions are due to the business' lack of financial acumen, to the presence of competitors who offer credit to those to whom it is not normally given, or to the desire of a business to gain a competitive advantage.

In many cases the occupation or income level of customers tends to dictate the decision whether or not to grant consumer credit. Individuals with high incomes, stable employment, and stable living patterns normally are good credit risks. Often, individuals in agricultural businesses require consumer credit until their crops are harvested. Each business' credit policy must be evaluated on the nature of the clients the business serves.

CREDIT CARDS

It is estimated that one out of seven persons has a major credit card. Translated into family groups, about one out of three people has access to a major credit card.

There are five advantages to allowing the use of credit cards: first, credit buyers typically buy more than cash buyers; credit losses are minimal on credit card sales since the credit card company assumes the account receivable without recourse; third, cash flows and cash planning are likely to be improved because the small business is paid promptly and regularly by the credit card company; credit card holders are more likely to shop at businesses where their credit has, in effect, been approved in advance by the credit card company; and finally, the costs of a credit department in the business are either eliminated or minimized.

Offsetting the advantages are the costs of using the credit card system which include a percentage of the sale, a rental charge for the use of the imprinting machine, a one-time fee to join the credit card organization, and advertising fees.

ESTABLISHING A CREDIT DEPARTMENT

This area is extremely important to the small business since it directly affects the cash flow of the firm. The attitude, tact, and thoroughness of the person handling consumer credit may mean the difference between success and failure.

Three basic types of consumer credit accounts are applicable to the small business. The open account permits the consumer to charge purchases throughout the month; at the end of the month, the customer is billed and is expected to pay the account in full. Cycle billing is used when the number of accounts becomes large. Cycle billing is the distribution of billing dates throughout the month, depending on the first letter of the customer's last name.

Budget accounts are the second basic form of consumer credit. Budget accounts are designed primarily for the purchase of expensive items for which it is difficult to complete full payment under an open account. Normally, budget accounts are ninety days in duration and are not charged interest unless the terms of the agreement are violated. Down payments may or may not be required.

Installment accounts are longer in duration than budget accounts. Often, installment accounts are opened for periods of up to three or four years. Typically, the consumer makes a substantial down payment, and the balance plus a charge for the credit is divided over the months of the contract. The down payment is, in some cases, an older item that is traded in. Interest rates are usually about 1 per cent a month. Installment generally requires that a chattel mortgage be issued so that the seller has the option of repossessing the merchandise in the event of customer default. With the chattel mortgage, the buyer acquires title to the purchase only after the entire account is paid.

PROCEDURES FOR EXTENDING CONSUMER CREDIT

Small businesses should follow well-defined procedures in deciding whether or not to extend credit. Credit losses are inevitable — but how much loss is acceptable? Establishing good credit procedures will assist in reducing these losses. The three basic categories of consumer credit discussed above require varying amounts of the credit manager's time and attention. However, regardless of the category of consumer credit, common procedures exist to establish and monitor the account. These procedures are outlined below.

CREDIT APPLICATION

A credit application should be designed that contains all of the pertinent information about a potential customer. The application form should be maintained in a permanent record where it can be referred to as needed and updated when appropriate. The basic purpose of the application is to provide positive identification of the customer. Items to be included are: name of applicant, spouse's name, applicant's current address, previous addresses, age, present employer, past employers, approximate income, information on whether the current residence is owned or rented, active and inactive credit references, and bank references.

A complete application form allows the applicant to be positively identified for further credit checks by either the credit bureau or other business references. A permanent file is created which may be used to analyze both good and bad credit decisions.

In the event that credit is extended and the customer leaves the area, a substantial amount of information exists to trace the individual, and if the applicant is rejected for credit, a permanent record exists for future reference.

THE CREDIT CHECK

Most retail and service businesses use a local credit bureau. Several types of report are available from credit bureaus. The two most common are the in-file report and the revised report. The in-file report is essentially the credit file as it has existed since the last revision. Often, but not always, a credit bureau updates the in-file reports with publicly recorded information such as chattel mortgages, lawsuits, receiverships, and bankruptcies. The in-file is less extensive than the revised report.

The revised report includes a check of current credit references that the applicant supplied on the credit application mentioned above. Normally, the credit check will be handled on the telephone with the information recorded in a space provided on the credit application. This then becomes a portion of the business record system. For an additional charge, the credit bureau will mail the business a written copy of the report. Credit bureaus normally charge a monthly fee plus an additional charge for each report received.

THE FOUR "C"s

The four "C"s of credit investigation are character, capacity, collateral, and conditions. Character deals with personal characteristics of the credit applicant such as reputation, desire to pay bills, personal conduct and honesty. Capacity is the applicant's ability to pay the debt at the agreed time. The credit check normally supplies adequate information to judge capacity, by evaluating stability of employment, income levels, and fixed payment levels. Collateral is the net worth of some possession of the applicant. Normally an estimate of this net worth may be made from the credit check through a series of educated guesses. How close is the amount of the house mortgage to the estimated value of the applicant's home? What size mortgage does the applicant take on an automobile compared with the value of the car? How large are the applicant's savings accounts? Condition is the state of the economy for the area in which the applicant lives and works. It is possible for the economy to be generally good, but for the applicant's industry to be in a slump.

After evaluating the applicant, the small business must make the final decision: Credit or no credit.

INFORM THE APPLICANT

The applicant must be informed of the decision. If the applicant is accepted, it is a good opportunity to create some good will for the company. If the applicant is rejected for credit, tact is required. Individuals who are borderline credit cases are generally very sensitive about a credit rejection. At any rate, a well rehearsed procedure for informing the applicant of a "no" may convert the individual into a cash customer. Normally, credit management is not considered to be a sales tool, but it is, and the method by which the applicant is informed of the decision can be an excellent sales tool if it is carefully planned. This is one area in which small businesses may be substantially superior to large, impersonal businesses.

FOLLOW-UP

A periodic check on the condition of the accounts receivable is necessary, particularly in the small firm. Each account should be checked to determine whether the credit conditions of the sale are being met.

If the terms of the sale are for forty-eight hours of credit, then the small business should not wait thirty days to determine whether a delinquency procedure is needed. One delinquency procedure is mailing a standard printed notice within a few days after the account becomes delinquent. Often, companies have a series of notices, sometimes color-coded to match the degree of delinquency. Standard notices are often followed by a personal letter, a telephone call, or both. The final steps are repossession or turning the account over to either an attorney or a collection agency. The small-business owner should have a general idea of expected credit losses for the particular business. The National Cash Register Corporation has compiled bad debt–loss ratios in a booklet entitled "Expenses in retail businesses." If a company exceeds the averages, its owner should re-examine the entire procedure for extending consumer credit.

SUMMARY — SALES PROGRAMS FOR SMALL BUSINESSES

To establish a meaningful sales program for a small business, excellent product knowledge is required. This product knowledge should enable the small business to categorize the market by the type of goods to be sold — specialty goods, convenience goods, shopping goods, or industrial goods. The promotion considerations associated with each of the goods should be studied. At that point, methods of promotion and pricing of the goods should be established, as well as the credit procedure. Each of the steps follows a logical order. However, the entrepreneur must use a substantial amount of insight to make these basic decisions.

STUDY QUESTIONS

1. Give examples of locally marketed specialty, convenience, and shopping goods. How is each different from the others? Do all retailers handle the products in the same manner? Why or why not?

2. How do industrial goods differ from retail goods?

3. What are the criteria associated with a successful salesperson?

4. How do you think a small-business owner measures the effect of advertising?

5. Explain why stores may price identical goods differently.

REFERENCES AND SUGGESTED READINGS

Advertising – Retail Store, Small Business Bibliography No. 20. Washington, D.C.: Small Business Administration, 1971.

Assail, Henry, and C. E. Wilson. "Integrating consumer and in-store research to evaluate sales results," *Journal of Marketing,* Vol. 36, April, 1972, pp. 40–45.

Broom, H. N., and J. G. Longenecker. *Small Business Management,* 4th ed., Cincinnati: South-Western Publishing Co., 1975.

Building Customer Confidence in Your Service Shop, Small Marketer's Aid No. 128. Washington, D.C.: Small Business Administration, 1972.

Building Good Customer Relations, Small Marketer's Aid No. 120. Washington, D.C.: Small Business Administration, 1974.

Expand Overseas Sales With Commerce Department Help, Management Aid No. 199. Washington, D.C.: Small Business Administration, 1971.

Granger, C. W. J., and A. Billson. "Consumers' attitude toward package size and price," *Journal of Marketing Research,* Vol. 9, August, 1972, pp. 239–248.

Manufacturers' Sales Representation, Small Business Bibliography No. 67. Washington, D.C.: Small Business Administration, 1971.

National Mailing-list Houses, Small Business Bilbiography No. 29. Washington, D.C.: Small Business Administration, 1971.

Parsons, Leonard J., and W. Bailey Price. "Adaptive pricing by a retailer," *Journal of Marketing Records,* Vol. 9, May, 1972, pp. 127–133.

Salaverry, Mimi. "Advertising," *Small Business Reporter,* Vol. 9, No. 1, 1969, pp. 1–16.

Sales Management for Manufacturers, Small Business Bibliography No. 71. Washington, D.C.: Small Business Administration, 1969.

Selling by Mail Order, Small Business Bibliography No. 3. Washington, D.C.: Small Business Administration, 1972.

Steinhoff, Dan. *Small Business Management Fundamentals,* New York: McGraw-Hill Book Co., 1974.

CHAPTER 6

SITE AND LOCATION ANALYSIS FOR THE SMALL BUSINESS

INTRODUCTION

Chapter 3 discusses the market survey as part of the business plan. The market survey determines the existence of a market for the products or services to be sold. It provides basic information which gives the small-business owner signals whether or not to proceed further with the analysis. This chapter not only substantiates the preliminary findings of the market survey, but also provides additional related information for selecting a specific site and location for the business. A portion of this analysis uses an alternate method to ascertain the market for a company's products or services. For more information on location analysis, you should refer to Checklists D and E in Appendix I.

Locating small businesses has become more complicated over the years. This is partly due to increased population, the movement to the suburbs, and the subsequent development of community, neighborhood, and regional shopping centers. In addition, small-business owners have the options of locating in industrial parks, unrestricted raw land, central business districts, neighborhoods, or business strips somewhere between the others. Location analysis is an imprecise science. Not surprisingly, one of the prime causes of small-business failure appears to be an inadequate location.

The need to select a location for business occurs infrequently and so a maximum effort should be made for this important step. Essentially, this step is taken when a new business is started, when a business in operation is being expanded, when a lease is cancelled, or when a lease expires. Less frequently, the owner pays off a lease or sells property in a poor location so that the business can be moved — an important decision.

A distinction should be made between *location* and *site*. "Location" refers to the region of the country, state, trading area, county, or city in which the business is to be located. "Site" refers to a specific address within the location category: Store A-26 in the Tri-County Shopping Center; 200 Main Street. Several warnings are worth considering. A location should not be selected *solely* because it is the native area of the prospective business owner; it should be selected objectively. However, since most small businesses are not located objectively, it is wise to consult an independent expert who is capable of giving such location and site advice. A site should not be chosen simply because it is available — it may be available because the last business failed at that site.

While a technical difference exists between location and site, it is difficult to keep this distinction in application. For this reason, the terms will be used synonymously for the balance of this chapter.

Location analysis is important to small manufacturing firms, wholesalers, retailers, and service firms. Each of the four categories of small business will be considered here, but the emphasis will be placed on retail location analysis.

RETAIL LOCATION ANALYSIS

In order to survive, most retail businesses rely on potential customers walking into their store. The location of a retailer is important in attracting these potential customers. It is not the only factor, but it is the one most difficult to change once the store is open. Eight factors — trading area, business climate, competition, visibility and accessibility, aesthetics, site history, hours of operation, and some general site evaluations — should be considered before deciding on a location.

TRADING AREA

The concept of trading area is important in identifying possible retail locations. This concept centers on people, the potential customers and, therefore, the key to any business. It is essential to find out how many people live in the area under consideration, how they spend their money, and what their shopping habits are. Chapter 5 presented information about marketing in small business which should be kept in mind while making an analysis of a trading area. Retail sales in an area are closely related both to the number of people in the area and to the purchasing power of these people. The total purchasing power of an area is indicated by the number of people employed in the area, payrolls of local industries, social security payments to the elderly, and by bank deposit data. The distribution of wealth in any area is another factor influencing sales, and retailers should be aware of it. These variables were discussed in Chapter 3, in which a projected share of the market was estimated in terms of dollar volume.

BUSINESS CLIMATE

The health, stability, and growth potential of a trading area are related to the number, type, and character of businesses, organizations, and industries within the area; to the existing legislation related to licensing and taxation; to the relationship between retailers and financial institutions in the community; and to the support of various state agencies.

Local industry is significant in providing stable and assured income to an area. Small businesses are indirectly affected by any type of economic disturbance in the larger industries. When manufacturers in an area are *not* diversified, the community enjoys prosperity when demand for the products is good, but must endure hardship when demand slacks off. The machine tool industry, the aerospace and aircraft industries, and the automobile industry provide examples of this situation. Areas that possess diversified industries remain stable because these industries weather cycles in the economy better.

State and local legislation on taxation and licensing policies can also affect location choice. Variations in tax rates among cities, counties, and states can make one location more attractive than another. Fair-trade laws and unfair trade-practice acts should be reviewed. Laws affecting hours of operation and Sunday openings should be compared among alternate locations. Frequently, entrepreneurs find they must secure loans to finance expansions, seasonal inventories, renovations, and equipment replacements. Having a good financial relationship with a banker who understands the retailer's problems becomes an asset of great value.

Evaluating the business climate of a community is similar to evaluating a company before purchasing stock. Locating a small business in a community is an investment in that community and as much information as possible should be gathered about the area in order to make a wise decision.

COMPETITION

When vying for a share of the market, an accurate assessment of the competition is necessary. This assessment should include the number, estimated size, and perceived quality of established competition. Furthermore, complete information would include historic data on each firm, its financial strength, its management and personnel abilities, its progressiveness, and its pricing structure. Such information is difficult to acquire, but of great value. By organizing these data sources, you can deduce the specific and general characteristics of your competition. This information must also be weighed during the location decision process.

Depending on the type of business, vacancies in nearby buildings may present a competition problem. The hazard associated with such a situation is that competitors may seek to place either a non-compatible business or one competing for the same market at such a location, thereby reducing the profitability of a retailer already situated. A developer may be able to inform the small-business owner of the possibility of such an occurrence. To defend against this, the retailer may seek control of such locations, either directly or indirectly, so that only compatible businesses may be grouped together. For this reason, shopping centers often define the "mix" of businesses to be included in the property. Locating in business strips, or other areas where competition cannot be controlled, increases the risk.

The retailer should be aware, however, that all specialty retailers do not compete with each other, even if they sell the same goods. A grouping of stores, taken cumulatively, may have an assortment of goods in one store that complements items sold in the others.[1] This cumulative attraction is the goal of shopping center developers who plan a tenant mix to maximize their investment's ability to draw crowds, and to improve their chance of success. Cumulative attraction exists between both similar units and complementary units. A row of automobile dealers is an example of similar units with desirable locations close to one another. Specialty apparel owners like to locate near department stores, counting on shoppers who like to wander among stores. Complementary units are highly compatible, generating larger flows of traffic through *each* of the stores. The location, character, size, and type of chief competitors require close study by the entrepreneur before deciding on a location. This analysis should offer a balanced approach which not only recognizes that compatible stores can increase sales, but also that stores which are too different will repel customers from the market area. A children's clothing store placed next to a liquor store may be disaster.

ACCESSIBILITY AND VISIBILITY

The rising cost or lack of public transportation, the change in consumer shopping habits to one-stop shopping, and the increased

---

[1]For an analysis of types of businesses that complement each other, see Richard Nelson, *The Selection of Retail Locations,* F. W. Dodge Corporation, 1958, Chapter 7.

use of the automobile for shopping trips are trends that focus attention on the accessibility of location. Downtown areas often have more difficulty attracting customers because of their congestion, distance from the suburbs, and lack of adequate parking. Shopping centers, in contrast, offer free and easily accessible parking and are usually closer to shoppers' homes.

Accessibility depends on the street networks and public transportation routes. Highways, interstate freeways, and streets that offer wide roads, where driving is safe and the flow of traffic is steady, are good routes to and from shopping areas. The proximity of residential areas is significant in determining accessibility. Accessibility is often measured in driving *time* rather than miles. People will normally take the path of least resistance, shopping near their homes rather than spending time on the road.

Occasionally, a location is unsatisfactory because its appearance is unsatisfactory. The location may have experienced either failure or marginal success, even though other factors are advantageous. Remodeling your business re-creates the public's image of it. Locations have a life cycle, usually consisting of an abrupt climb, a limited peak, and a steep decline. Remodeling may even be an alternative to changing the location of a business currently in operation.

AESTHETIC FACTORS

Certain aesthetic factors may detract from a site — unusually high noise levels, junkyards, garbage dumps, hospitals, bars, poor parking, poor sidewalks, poor roads, smoke, dust, vacant buildings, cheap movie houses, and buildings in need of repair. The reputation of an area is an important consideration. However, these factors would not be negative for all types of business. Both flower shops and gift shops thrive close to hospitals. In locating a retail business, the specific nature of the business must be considered in conjunction with aesthetic factors.

SITE HISTORY

The history of the site is an important consideration. Knowing the identity of previous occupants and their line of business is vital to a prospective new business. Why did they leave? This information is available from the owner of the site, local merchants, neighbors, or the real estate broker. The reputation and the type of goods sold on the site previously add to or detract from the site's potential. A site where two fast food concerns previously failed has a definite disadvantage if the prospective business is another fast food restaurant. In fact, if a previous business was similar to the one being considered, the reason for past failure is vital information. Was it poor management or simply that the area could not support that type of business? Another negative situation is a quality clothing store locating where a discount store has previously been located.

HOURS OF OPERATION

Stores located together should have the same basic hours of operation to attract the greatest possible number of customers, so a potential entrepreneur must consider the hours of nearby stores. The entrepreneur may be considering opening a bookstore between a laundromat and a drug store, both of which will have longer hours of operation than the bookstore owner may have planned. Customers expect businesses located together to have similar hours of operation.

GENERAL FACTORS

Other factors which must be considered when selecting a retail location are plans for street or highway changes, access to interstate highways, and the attitude of the trading area population toward a specific type of business.

LOCATION ANALYSIS FOR WHOLESALERS

Location analysis for wholesalers is less complex than for retailers. The type of analysis depends on whether the wholesaler sells directly from the warehouse or at the customer's place of business. Plumbing or heating wholesalers are usually visited at the warehouse by both tradesmen and retail customers. Preportioned food wholesalers, in contrast, seldom have customers at their place of business. Thus, the location, type, and decor of the building must be appropriate to the specific type of wholesaling. However, whether customers want rapid delivery or prefer to pick up goods at the warehouse, a location central to the customers is desirable, either to provide convenience or to reduce delivery costs.

Wholesalers buy in large quantities and sell in smaller quantities. Both incoming and outgoing access must therefore be considered in the choice of a location. Care in designing or selecting a building may result in substantial savings several years in the future. In the event that a warehouse is being built, compliance with zoning regulations must be maintained. Practically all cities now specify areas acceptable for wholesaling operations.

LOCATION ANALYSIS FOR MANUFACTURERS

Location analysis is also critical for manufacturers. A smaller number of failures exist because of poor location for manufacturing plants than for retail stores or wholesale houses, because manufacturers generally have more expertise and are better funded than the retailer. A comparative analysis of potential manufacturing locations should include:

1. proximity to the market to be served;
2. the availability of a labor supply with adequate skills, the degree of competition for the labor market, the prevailing and anticipated wage rates, and the extent of unionization;
3. the availability and adequacy of raw materials to be used in the production process (proximity to the market is normally more important here, except when extensive waste occurs in converting the raw materials to a finished product, or when the raw materials are perishable);
4. transportation facilities for both incoming raw materials and outgoing finished products (obviously, a great deal of variation exists due to the nature of the finished products, the nature of raw materials, and the demands the customers put on the manufacturer);
5. availability of suppliers to support the manufacturing operation;
6. availability and rate structure of utilities (this factor depends on the quantity of water, natural gas, electricity, and distillate required in the manufacture; utilities are often a major portion of the cost of goods sold and should be considered carefully);
7. political attitudes of the state, county, area, and municipality toward manufacture (This encompasses many factors, including the level of taxation, ordinances on the operation of manufacturing plants, and the availability of community services, such as police and fire protection, sewage systems, and hospitals.);
8. quality of life, including such factors as the quality of education and neighborhoods, the availability of cultural activities and facilities, the availability of recreational facilities, and climate; and
9. site availability, supporting services costs, zoning restrictions, and construction expertise and costs.

Assistance is available from state development boards, and from development sections of commercial banks, railroads, and utilities.

LOCATION ANALYSIS FOR SERVICE FIRMS

As in the preceding three categories, the location of a service business is critical to its success. The Small Business Administration has compiled an excellent checklist for evaluating the site for a service business. This segment of their report states:

In the service business, your sales potential will depend on the area you serve. That is, how many customers in this area will need your services? Will your customers be industrial, commercial, consumer, or all of these?

When picking a site to locate your business, consider the nature of your service. If you pick up and deliver, you will want a site where the travel time will be low and you may later install a radio dispatch system. Or, if the customer must come to your place of business, the site must be conveniently located and easy to find.

You must pick the site that offers the best possibilities of being profitable. The following considerations will help you think through this problem.

In selecting an area to serve, consider the following:

–population and its growth potential
–income, age, occupation of population
–number of competitive services in and around your proposed location
–local ordinances and zoning regulations
–type of trading area (commercial, industrial, residential, seasonal)

For additional help in choosing an area, you might try the local chamber of commerce and the manufacturer and distributor of any equipment and supplies you will be using.

You will want to consider the next list of questions in picking the specific site for your business.

Will the customer come to your place of business?
How much space do you need?
Will you want to expand later on?
Do you need any special features required in lighting, heating, ventilation?
Is parking available?
Is public transportation available?
Is the location conducive to drop-in customers?
Will you pick up and deliver?
Will travel time be excessive?
Will you prorate travel time to service call?
Would a location close to an expressway or main artery cut down on travel time?
If you choose a remote location, will savings in rent offset the inconvenience?
If you choose a remote location, will you have to pay as much as you save in rent for advertising to make your service known?
If you choose a remote location, will the customer be able to readily locate your business?
Will supply of labor be adequate and the necessary skills available?
What are the zoning regulations of the area?
Will there be adequate fire and police protection?

Will crime insurance be needed and be available at a reasonable rate?[2]

INFORMATION SOURCES FOR LOCATION ANALYSIS

There are many sources of information, but those listed here are readily available to most individuals.

STANDARD METROPOLITAN STATISTICAL AREA

The SMSA is a population classification published every ten years by the U.S. Department of Commerce. The SMSA represents a city and its suburbs and includes data such as the population and its age, composition, personal income, and employment, and the amount of trade in the area. A total of 218 items are included. Specific "Census tracts" within each SMSA may be identified in order to zero in on specific site locations.

The SMSA contains maps of the various census tracts, such as Figure 6–1. A proposed location has been marked by a circled "X" on Tract 205.03. In this case, the entire tract is the trading area of a proposed business because of such boundaries as the Saluda River on the southwest side of the tract and an interstate highway on the northeast side. If actual or possible competition exists within the trading area, it is appropriate to mark it on the tract at this time.

Figure 6–2, also taken from the SMSA, contains information regarding the population in tract 205.03. Note that in 1969 there were 1225 families and unrelated individuals living in Tract 205.03 and that the mean income was $14,007.

SALES AND MARKETING MANAGEMENT MAGAZINE

Sales and Marketing Management is published monthly. Each year, the July issue is devoted to the "Survey of buying power," which contains data on the population and its income levels, and on specific categories of retail sales for major population centers in the United States. The "Survey of buying power" may be used annually to update the information presented in the SMSA.

---

[2]Small Business Administration. *Business Plan For Small Service Firms,* Washington, D.C.: U.S. Government Printing Office, p. 5, 1973.

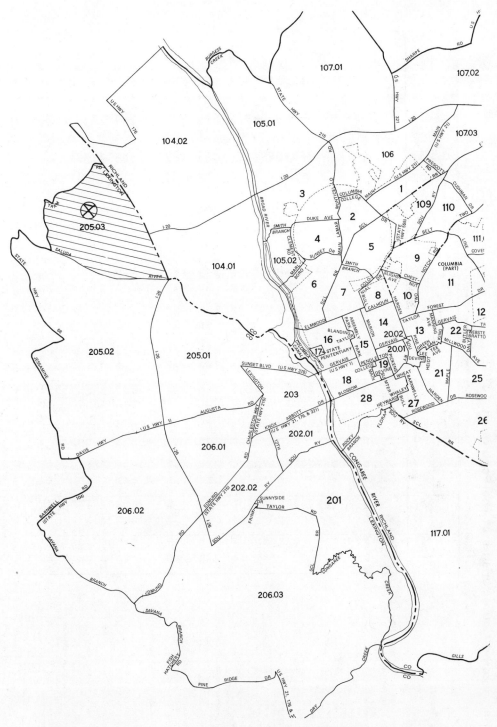

Figure 6-1 Census tract map. (From Census Tracts of South Carolina, Standard Metropolitan Statistical Area; Washington, D.C.: U.S. Department of Commerce, Bureau of the Census, 1970.)

Table P-4.   Income Characteristics of the Population: 1970

[Data based on sample, see text. For minimum base for derived figures (percent, median, etc.) and meaning of symbols, see text]

Census Tracts	Total SMSA	Lexington County	Richland County Total	Columbia	Balance	Tract 0201	Tract 0202.01	Tract 0202.02	Tract 0203	Tract 0205.01	Tract 0205.02	Tract 0205.03	Tract 0206.01	Tract 0206.02
INCOME IN 1969 OF FAMILIES AND UNRELATED INDIVIDUALS														
All families	72 454	23 339	49 115	20 682	28 433	952	792	710	1 014	2 436	821	1 062	1 388	1 081
Less than $1,000	2 416	535	1 881	1 007	874	18	–	11	30	25	16	–	19	8
$1,000 to $1,999	2 973	997	1 976	1 031	945	21	21	19	30	97	15	24	24	11
$2,000 to $2,999	3 215	910	2 305	1 242	1 063	37	19	33	81	78	16	11	42	13
$3,000 to $3,999	4 007	1 260	2 747	1 385	1 362	56	30	48	73	146	30	28	77	16
$4,000 to $4,999	4 307	1 351	2 956	1 493	1 463	33	59	29	115	143	20	4	60	51
$5,000 to $5,999	5 338	1 745	3 593	1 660	1 933	25	53	34	77	182	84	21	164	66
$6,000 to $6,999	5 347	1 683	3 664	1 648	2 016	95	58	61	94	163	50	20	99	51
$7,000 to $7,999	5 308	1 764	3 544	1 429	2 115	96	69	56	63	218	59	30	112	95
$8,000 to $8,999	5 377	884	3 493	1 355	2 138	124	96	46	54	200	83	52	175	102
$9,000 to $9,999	4 551	679	2 872	1 064	1 808	95	51	60	99	130	61	60	116	105
$10,000 to $11,999	8 739	3 219	5 520	2 009	3 511	193	94	133	62	305	203	129	211	216
$12,000 to $14,999	9 118	3 182	5 936	2 054	3 882	126	96	107	93	291	98	251	208	220
$15,000 to $24,999	9 198	2 728	6 470	2 287	4 183	33	120	69	132	414	76	354	77	106
$25,000 to $49,999	2 185	361	1 824	834	990	–	26	–	6	33	10	62	–	21
$50,000 or more	375	41	334	184	150	–	–	4	5	11	–	16	4	–
Median income	$8 617	$8 756	$8 542	$7 612	$9 170	$8 766	$8 906	$9 300	$7 111	$8 830	$9 615	$13 817	$8 554	$10 208
Mean income	$9 840	$9 375	$10 061	$9 562	$10 424	$8 596	$10 636	$9 037	$8 657	$10 077	$9 657	$14 879	$8 650	$10 478
Families and unrelated individuals	118 451	27 299	91 152	57 241	33 911	1 058	989	806	1 337	2 966	1 008	1 225	1 639	1 293
Median income	$5 599	$7 895	$4 855	$3 095	$9 181	$8 371	$8 033	$8 674	$5 948	$7 843	$8 458	$13 189	$7 879	$9 205
Mean income	$7 102	$8 494	$6 686	$5 095	$9 371	$8 061	$9 159	$8 447	$7 408	$8 897	$8 596	$14 007	$7 786	$9 077
Unrelated individuals	45 997	3 960	42 037	36 559	5 478	106	197	96	323	530	187	163	251	212
Median income	$1 882	$2 097	$1 865	$1 777	$2 809	$3 000	$2 233	$2 500	$2 559	$2 623	$3 146	$6 328	$2 109	$1 146
Mean income	$2 790	$3 302	$2 742	$2 568	$3 905	$3 255	$3 219	$4 084	$3 488	$3 473	$3 942	$8 320	$3 009	$1 933
TYPE OF INCOME IN 1969 OF FAMILIES														
All families	72 454	23 339	49 115	20 682	28 433	952	792	710	1 014	2 436	821	1 062	1 388	1 081
With wage or salary income	65 076	21 059	44 017	17 904	26 113	930	721	677	908	2 272	739	1 033	247	1 030
Mean wage or salary income	$9 094	$8 987	$9 146	$8 575	$9 536	$8 433	$9 711	$8 683	$7 969	$9 332	$9 437	$13 348	$8 408	$9 679
With nonfarm self-employment income	6 929	2 494	4 435	1 735	2 700	20	84	49	115	226	85	158	130	106
Mean nonfarm self-employment income	$8 894	$6 348	$10 326	$11 570	$9 527	…	$8 451	$5 621	$3 720	$7 830	$5 456	$7 842	$5 567	$7 503
With farm self-employment income	1 231	672	559	162	397	–	15	4	–	24	5	15	6	11
Mean farm self-employment income	$1 747	$1 565	$1 966	$2 953	$1 564	–	$125	$84	$227	$214	$80	$52	$233	$111
With Social Security income	10 463	3 452	7 011	3 799	3 212	106	125	84	227	214	80	52	233	111
Mean Social Security income	$1 435	$1 374	$1 465	$1 497	$1 427	$1 295	$1 568	$1 936	$1 673	$1 396	$1 388	$1 266	$1 573	$1 595
With public assistance or public welfare income	2 073	506	1 567	902	665	33	17	16	17	52	–	52	17	7
Mean public assistance or public welfare income	$738	$730	$761	$761	$687	$738	$241	$53	$895	$895	$200	$266	$307	$291
With other income	18 097	4 746	13 351	6 279	7 072	123	241	53	224	641	200	461	307	291
Mean other income	$2 256	$1 590	$2 492	$2 756	$2 258	$859	$2 056	$1 263	$3 218	$1 920	$1 769	$1 538	$1 314	$1 266

Figure 6–2   Census tract data. (From Census Tracts of South Carolina, Standard Metropolitan Statistical Area; Washington, D.C.: U.S. Department of Commerce, Bureau of the Census, 1970.)

LOCAL CHAMBERS OF COMMERCE

Chambers of commerce may have the SMSA information, census tracts, and census maps. In addition, chamber of commerce representatives can give valuable information on the direction and growth of the area, zoning maps, location of major shopping centers, discount stores, and other shopping districts.

OTHER LOCAL SOURCES OF INFORMATION

The public utility companies serving an area usually have representatives in their commercial department who have information on past site histories and growth of the area, and who make predictions of future growth. Utility representatives can be particularly informative about local industrial development. A retailer would find them an excellent source of information.

City, county, or regional planning boards and area newspapers usually also have departments which compile, or have access to, data pertaining to present and future development.

HIGHWAY DEPARTMENTS

City, county, and state highway departments are excellent sources of information. This information may be used to determine if there are plans to widen a highway near the planned site. Many retail businesses have opened a few months prior to a major highway change that resulted in traffic dislocation, noise, dirt, and lost parking spaces. City reclamation projects also cause these problems. These factors may combine to result in disaster at the cash register. On the other hand, knowledge of planned highway construction is invaluable for determining future traffic flows. The highway department may also have traffic counts on the roads near potential locations.

THE SMALL BUSINESS ADMINISTRATION

The SBA has many booklets on locating and managing a small business. Table 6–1 illustrates the type of information available from the Small Business Administration.

THE TELEPHONE COMPANY

The local telephone directory is an important source of information because it lists the competition. Table 6–1 indicates that it takes a population of about 13,500 people to support a florist

Table 6-1 NUMBER OF INHABITANTS IN AREAS SERVED BY STORES, BY SELECTED BUSINESS (NATIONAL AVERAGES)

Kind of business	Number of inhabitants per store	Kind of business	Number of inhabitants per store
Food stores		*Building material, hardware, and farm equipment dealers*	
Grocery stores	1,534	Lumber and other building	
Meat and fish (seafood) markets	17,876	materials dealers	8,124
Candy, nut, and confectionery stores	31,409	Paint, glass, and wallpaper stores	22,454
Retail bakeries	12,563	Hardware stores	10,206
Dairy products stores	41,587	Farm equipment dealers	14,793
Eating, drinking places		*Automotive dealers*	
Restaurants, lunchrooms, caterers	1,583	Motor vehicle dealers— new and used cars	6,000
Cafeterias	19,341	Motor vehicle dealers— used cars only	17,160
Refreshment places	3,622		
Drinking places (alcoholic beverages)	2,414	Tire, battery, and accessory dealers	8,764
		Boat dealers	61,526
General merchandise		Household trailer dealers	44,746
Variety stores	10,373	Gasoline service stations	1,195
General merchandise stores	9,837		
		Miscellaneous	
Apparel and accessory stores		Antique and secondhand stores	17,169
Women's ready-to-wear stores	7,102	Book and stationery stores	28,584
Women's accessory and specialty stores	25,824	Drug stores	4,268
		Florists	13,531
Men's and boy's clothing and furnishing stores	11,832	Fuel oil dealers	25,425
		Garden supply stores	65,118
Family clothing stores	16,890	Gift, novelty, and souvenir shops	26,313
Shoe stores	9,350		
		Hay, grain, and feed stores	16,978
Furniture, home furnishings, and equipment stores		Hobby, toy, and game shops	61,430
		Jewelry stores	13,495
Furniture stores	7,210	Liquefied petroleum gas (bottled gas) dealers	32,803
Floor covering stores	29,543		
Drapery, curtain, and upholstery stores	62,460	Liquor stores	6,359
		Mail order houses	44,554
Household appliance stores	12,585	Merchandising machine operators	44,067
Radio and television stores	20,346		
Record shops	112,144	Optical goods stores	62,878
Musical instrument stores	46,332	Sporting goods stores	27,063

From Wendell O. Metcalf. *Starting and Managing a Small Business of Your Own,* Washington, D.C.: Small Business Administration, 1973, p. 27; taken from Bureau of the Census, U.S. Department of Commerce. "Number of establishments with payroll from 1967 Census of Retail Trade; Number of inhabitants residing in the United States (excluding Armed Forces overseas), as of July 1, 1967."

shop. A city of 120,000 can therefore support about eight or nine florists. A simple count of the number of existing businesses and a check on the total population, along with projected growth figures can help to determine whether or not an area has the potential to support another business of a specific type. The telephone directory may also be used to locate the number and types of institutions in an area. A bicycle shop may want to locate near a university. The directory tells where the university is and whether other bike shops are already located nearby.

BANKERS

Bankers know the area, its past history, and its future. They also know what competition the new business will face. They are an excellent source of information. Bankers are discussed extensively in other parts of this book, but they are noted again here to emphasize their importance.

SUPPLIERS

Potential suppliers are excellent sources of information regarding specific businesses. Suppliers were also discussed in other portions of this book and are noted here only for emphasis.

OPERATING EXPENSE INFORMATION

Deducing the cost of doing business is an integral part of location analysis. The end result of any location analysis is to determine whether an acceptable profit can be made at a specific location. Many industry sources exist to supply expense information. A few examples of such suppliers are *Decorating Retailer,* the Beauty and Barber Supply Institute, the National Automobile Dealers Association, the National Retail Hardware Association, *Lilly Digest* (for pharmacies), the National Restaurant Association, and the National Sporting Goods Association. In addition, several excellent general sources exist, including *Expenses in Retail Business* (published by National Cash Register), and *Annual Statement Studies* (published by Robert Morris Associates).

LOCATION ANALYSIS PROBLEM

PROBLEM INTRODUCTION

An aspiring entrepreneur must, at some point, get as many facts together as possible and make a decision. How to make a decision to buy or start a small business, by carefully utilizing available information, is illustrated here. This problem concerns a pharmacy. A pharmacy was chosen because pharmacies have a unique blend of characteristics. Tough competition exists for independent drug stores from discount drug stores. Drug stores may or may not be owned by a pharmacist; that is, some specialized skill may or may not be necessary. Drug stores have a wide option of marketing and pricing alternatives. Location of a drug store is important. The merchandise in a drug store is composed of all the various types of goods discussed in Chapter 5. Sales can be cash, charge, or a combination.

Evaluating the profitability of a specific location is a difficult task, filled with many uncertainties. One of the characteristics of entrepreneurs discussed in Chapter 1 is the ability to deal with uncertain situations. There is *never* "enough information that is accurate enough" when opening or buying a business. This statement is true for this current analysis. Inadequate and conflicting information for the problem will be presented. The small-business owner must select the information that will be used, and proceed. Different small-business owners will make different decisions, when presented with identical information. As you study the problem in this chapter, place yourself in the position of actually making such decisions.

Dun and Bradstreet indicates that inadequate sales revenue is a major cause for retail business failures; the location simply can not or does not support the business. However, estimating potential sales is possible. If a small-business owner plans to spend thousands of dollars to open a business, it is wise to make every effort to insure that the business will be profitable.

First it is necessary to determine the magnitude and characteristics of the population in the trading area of the proposed business. Census tracts, discussed in the section on Standard Metropolitan Statistical Areas, are one of the best ways to estimate population.

LOCATING A DRUG STORE

Assume that we wish to locate a pharmacy at the "X" in Figure 6–1, in Census Tract 205.03. Figure 6–2 specifies that the mean income in Tract 205.03 was $14,007 in 1969. To simplify the problem, the 1969 information will not be updated. However, updates may be made with the "Annual survey of buying power" which has been discussed previously.

Our analysis of the competition indicated that no pharmacies exist at the present time in Tract 205.03. Two supermarkets exist, however, and both of them have an extensive array of drug store items, but neither sells prescriptions. In addition, a third supermarket is under construction and it can be assumed that it will also carry drug store items. Figure 6–2 also indicates that 1062 families live in Tract 205.03. Assuming about four persons per family, and including the 163 unrelated individuals, we would estimate that about 4411 persons live in the trading area. Table 6–1 specifies that about 4268 persons are necessary to support one drug store. The Chamber of Commerce and the Regional Planning Center project an average growth rate of 15 per cent per year for the next five years. It appears, so far, that a drug store may be justified in Tract 205.03.

A sales estimate should be obtained next. Nelson indicates that the average family spends 2.25 per cent of its income in drug-stores.[3] It is, therefore, estimated that each family will spend $315.16 each year for drug items. Total revenues for drug items for each year are estimated at $386,071 by multiplying estimated family purchases by the number of families in the tract. If more than one tract were covered by the trading area, it would be necessary to estimate the amount of the additional tracts within the trading area and perform the same calculation on that fraction of the tracts' population and income. If the trading area crosses natural boundaries, such as the river adjacent to the tracts, and if it is obvious that a portion of the population has no access to the business, the area cut off from the business is not included. Given the competition for the total estimated drug sales of $386,071, we will conservatively estimate that the proposed pharmacy itself will have approximately $225,000 in sales per year. Table 6–2 indicates three different sources of operating expense information.

As you can readily observe, some differences exist among the information sources. Two report owners' salaries and one does

---

[3]Nelson, R. L. *The Selection of Retail Location,* New York: McGraw-Hill, 1958, Chapter 14, Other sources include "Personal consumption expenditures by product," U.S. Bureau of the Census, *Statistical Abstract of the United States: 1976* (97th edition), Washington, D.C., 1976; and "Annual costs of budgets," *Handbook of Labor Statistics: 1976,* U.S. Department of Labor, Bureau of Labor Statistics, Bulletin 1905, Washington, D.C., 1976.

Table 6–2 OPERATING RATIO ESTIMATES FOR DRUG STORES FROM SEVERAL SOURCES

Assets	Source A (%)	Source B (%) $10,000–50,000	Source C (%) under $250,000
Sales	100.00	100.00	100.00
Cost of sales	63.5	63.15	67.40
Gross margin	36.5	36.85	32.60
Owner's salary	9.3	4.16	
All other expenses	23.3	21.98	30.10
Profit before taxes	3.9	2.75	2.60*

*Source C does not report owner's salary; however, it is assumed that owner's salary is included.

not. One source appears to be inconsistent because the various percentages come nowhere close to balancing. Two sources define the dollar amount of the assets of the drug store, one does not. Some information is better than none, but its validity must be questioned constantly. To estimate the potential income, Source A was chosen primarily because it was a reputable trade source of information. On the basis of the sales estimate of $225,000, Source A indicates a potential salary of $20,925 plus $8775 of additional income before taxes. Debt repayment would necessarily come from either the owner's salary, the profit remaining after taxes, or the depreciation allowances which reduce taxes and create a positive cash flow.

Assuming the potential profit is acceptable, the next step is to prepare pro forma statements for the first few months, quarters, or years.

PROBLEM SUMMARY

This problem illustrates the information available to the small-business owner and shows how to utilize the data to determine whether or not to initiate a small firm. It is up to you to determine whether the profit warrants your efforts and risks.

SUMMARY

In effect, selecting a location is both a beginning and an ongoing process. Small-business owners must be aware of the factors and relationships that influence their businesses. They must also be able to deal effectively with them. In practice, the location decision is often an irreversible decision. Great care should, therefore, be exercised in selecting a location. With thought, adequate information, and careful planning, the chance of finding an acceptable location can be greatly increased.

STUDY QUESTIONS

1. Evaluate the site of a business in your community. Is it congruent with the criteria in this chapter?

2. What types of business normally locate in close proximity? What types do not?

3. What are the criteria a small-business owner should follow in determining whether to buy, lease, or rent facilities?

4. Do you feel that there are any firms in your community that do not have a population base to warrant their existence? Why?

REFERENCES AND SUGGESTED READINGS

Annual Lilly Digest, Indianapolis, Indiana: Eli Lilly Company, 1977.

Annual Statement Studies, 1976 edition, Philadelphia: Robert Morris Associates, 1976.

"Annual survey of buying power," *Sales and Marketing Management,* New York: Bill Publishing Company, July (each year).

Duncan, Delbert J., Charles F. Phillips, and Stanley C. Hollander. *Modern Retailing Management,* 8th ed., Homewood, Ill.: Richard D. Irwin, Inc., 1972. 1972.

Expenses in Retail Business, Dayton, Ohio: National Cash Register Company, 1977.

Handbook of Labor Statistics: 1976, Bulletin 1905. Washington, D.C.: Bureau of Labor Statistics, U.S. Department of Labor, 1976.

Hartley, Robert F. *Retailing: Challenge and Opportunity,* Boston: Houghton-Mifflin Company, 1975.

Hicks, Clifford M. *An Introduction to Business,* New York: Holt, Rinehart, and Winston, 1948.

"Income Expenditures and Wealth," *Statistical Abstract of the United States: 1976,* Washington, D.C.: Bureau of the Census, Department of Commerce, 1976.

Kerin, Roger A., and Michael Harvey. "Evaluation of retail store locations through profitability analysis," *Journal of Small Business Management,* January, 1975, pp. 41–45.

Lewison, Dale M. "Some theoretical developments in the evaluation of retail trade area adequacy," *Center Paper #16,* College of Business Administration, University of South Carolina, Columbia: October, 1976.

Lewison, Dale M., and Nelson R. Nunnally. "Retail site evaluation and selection: new models or same old approaches?" *Center Paper #17,* College of Business Administration, University of South Carolina, Columbia: May, 1975.

Life *Study of Consumer Expenditures,* Volumes 1–7, Time Incorporated, 1957.

Lowry, James R., "Using a traffic study to select a retail site," Small Marketer's Aid #152, Washington, D.C.: Small Business Administration, May, 1973.

Metcalf, Wendell O. *Starting and Managing A Small Business of Your Own,* Washington, D.C.: Small Business Administration, 1973.

Nelson, R. L. *The Selection of Retail Location,* F. W. Dodge Corporation, New York, 1958.

"Number of establishments with payroll," *Census of Retail Trade,* Washington, D.C.: Bureau of the Census, Department of Commerce, 1967.

Tracts of South Carolina, Standard Metropolitan Statistical Area, Washington, D.C.: Bureau of the Census, U.S. Department of Commerce, 1970.

Zaloudek, Robert F. "Practical location analysis in new market areas," *Stores,* November, 1971, p. 15, ff.

CHAPTER 7

PREPARATION OF PRO FORMA STATEMENTS

INTRODUCTION

Pro forma statement is another name for a budget. The purpose of doing either pro forma statements or budgets is to permit the entrepreneur to formulate estimates for critical areas of the business, including sales by product, expenses by product, and overhead expenses.

The budget serves several useful purposes for the small business. First, a meaningful estimate of both profit and cash position is made for the month, quarter, or year. It is difficult to overemphasize the importance of preparing pro forma statements for this purpose. The reasons small businesses fail are that they don't make a profit, they run out of cash, or both. Usually, both of these disasters come as a surprise to the entrepreneur. The purpose of the budget is to remove unpleasant surprises whenever possible.

The second basic advantage of the budget is that it provides a sound framework for making future decisions. For example, if you know your business is not going to be profitable next month, you can take the necessary actions now to remedy the situation. Is sales volume going to be inadequate? If so, start enumerating alternatives to change that situation. Have expenses gotten out of control? If so, start cutting expenses. Has overhead gotten too high?

The point is, if you are aware of the probable future, you can take steps to make corrections. If you are unaware of the future, lack of action may lead to closing your business inadvertently. The same reasoning applies to the value of projecting the cash position of the company for the next month, quarter, or year. One additional justification for cash budgeting is that when you run out of cash, your business either slows down or stops. Employees seldom work without being paid. Suppliers get nervous if their invoices are not paid and trade credit begins to disappear, making your cash position worse. Various governmental agencies can and do shut down businesses for not paying income taxes, social security taxes, or unemployment compensation taxes. While a small business may be unprofitable for short periods of time without danger of closing, no business can run out of cash without dire consequences.

The preparation of pro forma statements is both difficult and time consuming. In some cases, the preparation of budgets is opposed because of the excuse that no one can predict the future. However, many small-business owners are extremely accurate in predicting the near-term future. Those who take the time and effort to do so are effectively eliminating unpleasant financial surprises.

Pro forma statements, like market surveys, should be prepared on a continuing basis. When a small business is functioning smoothly and the company is profitable, pro forma statements are often forgotten. However, budgets are mandatory in such critical periods as starting a new business, buying an existing business, or managing a small business that is in financial trouble.

CONDITIONS AFFECTING THE PREPARATION OF PRO FORMA STATEMENTS

The procedures for preparing a budget are essentially the same, whether on a monthly, quarterly, or annual basis. Budget considerations do vary between starting a new business, buying an existing business, and operating an ongoing business.

BUDGETS FOR STARTING A NEW BUSINESS

Pro forma statements for a new business are the most difficult to prepare because there is no past financial information. Sales estimates can be made from the information sources mentioned in Chapter 3, that is, census data, suppliers, and previous experience. Expense data can be estimated from information provided by trade suppliers, Robert Morris Associates' *Annual Statement Studies,* the Bank of America brochures on various businesses, and the Small Business Administration studies on specific businesses. Overhead expenses can be estimated from such local sources as utility companies (gas, electricity, water) and real estate companies (dollars per square foot to lease a building). It is important to be as thorough as possible in estimating the sales, expenses, and overhead. Since the greatest errors in estimates will occur in the first few months, it is worthwhile to make three estimates: an optimistic estimate, an average estimate, and a pessimistic estimate. By carefully combining these estimates, the potential small-business owner can establish some reasonably accurate upper and lower estimates. Numerous combinations exist. Your combination might be a pessimistic sales forecast with an average expense prediction and a high overhead prediction. As experience is acquired in the business, the need for pessimistic and optimistic projections decreases, and estimates become closer to actual results.

BUDGETS FOR BUYING AN EXISTING BUSINESS

Completing pro forma statements when buying an existing business is not as difficult as when starting a new business, since previous years' financial statements are available from which to make projections. However, several areas should be given careful consideration, a number of which are listed in Checklist C, Appendix I.

First, the buyer should be certain that the past financial statements of the company are accurate. Two methods exist to verify financial statements. The first method is to have the financial statements certified by the Certified Public Accountant who is responsible for the records of the company. In purchasing a business, statements prepared without audit have little credibility. In the event that the C.P.A. refuses to certify the statements or if a C.P.A. is not responsible for the company's accounting records, it is advisable to compare the company's income statement with the previous owner's Federal Income Tax return. Agreement between the two documents is reasonable assurance of the validity of the company's financial statements.

An analysis of expenses should also be undertaken. Many times a business is for sale because it has been poorly managed in the past. A careful appraisal may indicate expenses that can be reduced under a more efficient owner. Sales levels should be scrutinized carefully. Often, a business up for sale has not had an aggressive sales force. It may be possible to increase sales levels substantially. Again, Robert Morris Associates' *Annual Statement Studies,* Bank of America brochures, and S.B.A. publications may be helpful in determining whether various sales ratios are appropriate for a particular business. Is the cost of goods sold adequate as a percentage of sales? Are sales expenses low or high as a percentage of sales, compared to industry averages? Simply check against the industry norms.

Once the preceding analyses have been completed, preparation of a pro forma income statement, balance sheet, and cash flow statement may begin.

BUDGETS FOR MANAGING AN ONGOING BUSINESS

Budgets in this category are simplest in concept because the small-business owner is aware of the accuracy of the financial statements. The results may be difficult to use. If salaries in your company are discovered to be out of line, it is difficult to cut your own salary, release a long-time employee, or cut back the shop hours without changing some well-established patterns. This is always painful. Because you have been intimately associated with the business, it becomes extremely difficult to budget either a lower or a higher figure. This is true even when the survival of the company is at stake. However, assuming that this can be overcome, the budgeting process is similar to the conditions specified in the two sections above.

PREPARATION OF PRO FORMA STATEMENTS

Three types of pro forma statement are important: the income statement, the cash position statement, and the balance sheet. The following example in this chapter includes samples of all three types of projection.

The projections start with a study of the current balance sheet, shown in Table 7–1. When a company has been in business for several years or when an existing company is being purchased, the balance sheet will be more complicated. However, for understanding the construction and mechanics of budgeting, this statement is sufficient.

The balance sheet, as of December 31, 1978, indicates that the H Cubed Drug Store has $5000 in cash and that the owner's equity is $9831. The company is in a poor cash position because its accounts payable is much larger than the total of cash and accounts receivable.

In addition to a current balance sheet, several other important schedules and information must be estimated. They are:

1. Sales projections by month — the following sales forecasts are made:
    December — actual sales were $12,000
    January — estimated sales are $25,000
    February — estimated sales are $19,000
    March — estimated sales are $21,000
    April — estimated sales are $18,000

2. For purposes of this example, it is estimated that 65 per cent of sales are cash; the remaining 35 per cent are paid by the tenth of the month following purchase; and there are no bad debts.

Table 7–1 H CUBED DRUG STORE
Balance Sheet
December 31, 1978

Assets		
Current assets		
Cash	$ 5,000	
Accounts receivable	4,200	
Inventory	30,353	
Total current assets		$39,553
Fixed assets		
equipment, fixtures, and other	$10,000	
less depreciation	1,000	
Net fixed assets		9,000
Total assets		$48,553
Liabilities & Equity		
Current liabilities		
Accounts payable	$23,722	
Total current liabilities		$23,722
Long-term liabilities		
Small Business Administration loan	$15,000	
Total long-term liabilities		$15,000
Owner's equity	$ 9,831	
		$ 9,831
Total liabilities and stockholders' equity		$48,553

3. The average cost of merchandise sold is 61.41 per cent of the sales dollar; if an item sells for $10, it cost the H Cubed Company about $6.14 to purchase it.

4. The inventory policy of the company is to maintain a basic inventory of $15,000 in merchandise plus the merchandise equivalent to the cost of the goods to be sold in the following month. For example, the sales forecast for January is $25,000. The inventory on hand at the *end* of December would be computed:

Basic inventory	$15,000	
January estimated sales ($25,000) multiplied by the average cost of merchandise (61.41%)	15,353	
Ending inventory 12/31/78		$30,353

5. Suppliers request payment for *all* purchases made during a given month by the tenth of the following month.

6. All employees in the company are salaried and are paid on the fifteenth day and the last day of each month.

In order to concurrently prepare monthly projected cash balances and a quarterly projected income statement, the schedules and calculations presented in Table 7–2 are necessary.

Note that all of the data in Schedules A, B, and C are projected or estimated, with the exception of December's, which were known. Arrows specify that credit sales in a specific month (schedule A) are cash inflows in the following month (schedule B), and that the ending inventory in a specific month is the beginning inventory for the following month (schedule C). Table 7–2 also estimates the purchases in Schedule C. Recall that all purchases in a given month must be paid by the tenth of the following month; the $23,722 worth of merchandise purchased in December must be paid for by January tenth.

Table 7–3 is pro forma or projected cash flow statement. The statement estimates the company's cash balance as of the first day of each month. Note that previously constructed Schedules B and

Table 7–2 SALES, COLLECTIONS, AND PURCHASES PROJECTED SCHEDULES

	December	January	February	March	April
Schedule A: Sales					
Sales forecast	$12,000	$25,000	$19,000	$21,000	$18,000
Cash from sales (65%)	7,800	16,250	12,350	13,650	11,700
Credit sales (35%)	4,200	8,750	6,650	7,350	6,300
Schedule B: Collections					
Cash sales this month		$16,250	$12,350	$13,650	$11,700
Balance of last month's credit sales		4,200	8,750	6,650	7,350
Total collections		$20,450	$21,100	$20,300	$19,050
Schedule C: Purchases					
Ending Inventory*	$30,353	$26,668	$27,896	$26,054	
Cost of goods sold†	7,369	15,352	11,668	12,896	
Total	$37,722	$42,020	$39,564	$38,950	
Less beginning inventory	14,000	30,353	26,668	27,896	
Purchases necessary	$23,722	$11,667	$12,896	$11,054	

*Basic inventory of $15,000 plus 61.41 per cent of next month's sales
†61.41 per cent of the current month's sales

Table 7–3 H CUBED DRUG STORE: PROJECTED STATEMENT OF CASH RECEIPTS AND DISBURSEMENTS FOR THE THREE MONTHS ENDING MARCH 31, 1979

	January	February	March
Cash receipts:			
Beginning cash balance	$ 5,000	$ 678	$ 513
Cash receipts (Schedule B)	20,450	21,100	20,300
Total cash available	$25,450	$21,778	$20,813
Cash disbursements:			
Purchases (Schedule C)	$23,722	$11,667	$12,896
Salaries	2,800	2,600	2,500
Rent	800	800	800
Utilities	600	600	600
Insurance	400	200	200
Miscellaneous	1,450	358	644
Interest expense		40	338
Total disbursements	$29,772	$16,265	$17,978
Projected cash balance	($ 4,322)	$ 5,513	$ 2,835
Working capital loan (9½%) (repayment)	$ 5,000	($ 5,000)	
Adjusted cash balance	$ 678	$ 513	$ 2,835

C are used in the preparation of this statement. Items such as salaries, rent, depreciation, insurance, and interest are known with a reasonable degree of certainty. Items such as utilities and miscellaneous expenses must be estimated. For purposes of simplifying the illustration, 24.2 per cent of sales was used as an estimate of expenses.

Table 7–3 shows that the total cash available is the sum of all estimated and known cash inflows to the company in a specific month. Total disbursements is the sum of all estimated and known cash outflows from the company in a specific month. Note that in January, a cash deficit of $4322 is projected. On the basis of this projection, the company elected to secure a working capital loan in the amount of $5000 to cover the cash shortage, projecting repayment of this loan in February. In actual practice, the small business would probably attempt to borrow a larger amount because of the uncertainties associated with several of the projections. However, in this example, a cash deficit of $4322 is incurred in January (before obtaining the loan); February leaves the company with a cash balance of $513 after repaying the January working capital loan; March improves H Cubed's position substantially with an estimated cash balance of $2835.

Whether for a new company, for purchase of an existing company, or for analysis of a company currently in operation, bankers tend to be impressed with careful, methodical cash budgets. On the basis of work such as this, it is likely that the company's bank will extend a small loan to the company even though the financial statements indicate that the company has had financial problems in the past.

The third document to be prepared in the budgeting process is the projected income statement, Table 7–4. The various sources of information are noted in the right-hand column. Note that the estimated net profit before taxes for the quarter is $8,854. Even though the company is profitable for the quarter, Table 7–3 indicates that the company had projected short-term cash flow problems. The example points up the need for both a cash flow statement and an income statement. Lack of attention to either of these documents is a serious omission for the small business.

The final document to be prepared is the projected balance sheet in Table 7–5, which is prepared from the preceding documents and in which several items should be noted. First, comparing the December 31, 1978 and the March 31, 1979 balance sheets, there is a decrease in the cash account, a substantial increase in the owner's equity account (since the company generated a profit), and a continued excess of current liabilities over current assets.

An assessment of the financial state of the company on the basis of the projected statements demonstrates that the company is becoming profitable, but is still in a precarious cash position. Continued preparation of pro forma statements is still needed.

Table 7–4 H CUBED DRUG STORE
PROJECTED INCOME STATEMENT
MARCH 31, 1979

			Source of Information
Sales		$65,000	Schedule A
Cost of goods sold		39,916	Schedule C
Gross margin		$25,084	
Operating expenses			
Salaries	$7,900		Table 7–3
Rent	2,400		Table 7–3
Utilities	1,800		Table 7–3
Depreciation*	500		
Insurance	800		Table 7–3
All other expenses	2,452		Table 7–3
Total operating expenses		15,852	
Profit before interest and taxes		$9,232	
Interest expense, SBA			
loan at 9%	$ 338		
Working capital loan			
(9½% in January)	40		
Total interest expense		378	
Net profit before taxes		$8,854	

*Note depreciation is not a cash disbursement.

Table 7-5 H CUBED DRUG STORE
PROJECTED BALANCE SHEET
MARCH 31, 1979

Assets

Current Assets:		
Cash (Table 7-3)	$ 2,835	
Accounts Receivable (Schedule A)	7,350	
Inventory (Schedule C)	26,054	
Total Current Assets		$36,239
Fixed Assets:		
Equipment, fixtures, and other	$10,000	
less depreciation (Table 7-4)	1,500	
Net Fixed Assets		$ 8,500
Total Assets		$44,739

Liabilities & Equity

Current Liabilities:		
Accounts Payable (Schedule C)	$11,054	
Total Current Liabilities		$11,054
Long-Term Liabilities		
Small Business Administration loan	$15,000	
Total Long-Term Liabilities		$15,000
Owner's Equity	$18,685	
		$18,685
Total Liabilities and Stockholders' Equity		$44,739

SUMMARY

An example and discussion of projected budget statements has been presented in this chapter. This example may be modified for use in any small business. Conditions will differ: Some businesses have 100 per cent cash sales, some are 100 per cent credit business; a wide variety of credit terms exist for payment of a company's purchases; inventory policies differ among companies; periodic loan repayments are often mandatory. Variations in a particular company's policies and conditions may be accommodated within the technique illustrated in this chapter.

The material in this chapter is complex; so is operating a small business. You are advised to go over this material several times to understand fully the procedures and mechanics of budgeting for a small business. Financing is usually difficult for a small business to obtain. One reason is that small businesses generally need to improve substantially their budgeting skills in order to discuss financial needs intelligently with suppliers of money.

Budgeting, when well done, reduces financial surprises. Businesses run on money, and the entrepreneur is advised to develop all possible financial skills, with special emphasis on pro forma statements.

STUDY QUESTIONS

1. Recalculate the problem in Chapter 7. Change the January sales from $25,000 to $16,000 and the cash sales from 65 per cent to 80 per cent. What changes occur in the cash flow statement, the income statement, and the balance sheet?

2. What policies can be established for the H Cubed Drug Store that will improve its cash position? How will these policies affect sales?

3. Do you feel that the H Cubed Drug Store would be granted a working capital loan? Why or why not?

REFERENCES AND SUGGESTED READINGS

Controlling Cash in Small Retail and Service Firms, Small Marketers Aid No. 110, Washington, D.C.: Small Business Administration, August, 1976.

Horngren, Charles T. *Accounting For Management Control,* 3rd ed., Englewood, N.J.: Prentice-Hall, 1974.

Is Your Cash Supply Adequate? Management Aids for Small Manufacturers No. 174. Washington, D.C.: Small Business Administration, October, 1976.

Sound Cash Management and Borrowing, Small Marketing Aid No. 147, Washington, D.C.: Small Business Administration, January, 1972.

MANAGING THE SMALL BUSINESS

This section illustrates the managerial aspects of operating a small business, with the case: "The man who managed his business 'by ear'." This case will be used throughout the section to demonstrate various concepts related to Bill Brady, the small-business owner.

Chapter 8 presents the management by objective (MBO) process and the various managerial aspects needed for Bill Brady to set, measure, and accomplish his objectives.

Chapter 9 discusses the records needed for a small-business owner to manage a firm effectively. Chapter 10 is a summary both of this text and of the various means by which the concepts in this book can be applied to minimize the risks facing a small-business owner.

THE MAN WHO MANAGED HIS BUSINESS "BY EAR"

"Listen, Jack," said Bill Brady to his new accountant, Jack Larkin, "selling is what counts in business."

"It certainly does, Bill," Larkin said, "but what about profits? You can't grow without profits."

"Get sales and get the right price and the profits come naturally," Brady emphasized.

"Unless your costs run away with profits. You have to keep track of where your income is going," Larkin argued.

"Cost controls in my business are a waste of time and money," Bill insisted. "I manage my business by ear. And my business shows a profit every year."

Larkin shook his head. "Of course you can't make a profit without a sale. But your profit would be higher if your costs were in line. And I'll prove it to you."

Bill Brady and his wife, Mary, were partners in Brady's, a store selling dry goods and general merchandise in a small town in northern Wisconsin. Sales of Bill's business had been increasing and Bill intended to expand even further. But he wanted to be sure he was on solid ground. So he had turned the store's figures for the past year over to Jack Larkin, and asked Jack to "take over the books and advise me."

"In selling, you're tops," continued Larkin, "but your take from the business isn't as good as it might be. You were telling me the other day you wanted to add a line of men's and women's casual clothes. What are you going to use to finance the new merchandise, to build the new shelves?"

"New shelves?" Bill exclaimed. "Why, I'm thinking of building a new alcove. That window over there is coming out. The landlord has enough footage to his lot line for me to construct a nice alcove."

From *How to Build Profits by Controlling Costs*, New York: Dun and Bradstreet, 1969, pp. 3–19. Printed by permission.

"How are you going to finance the construction? It's going to cost you a lot of money."

"I figure $4500 with fixtures."

"How are you going to get the money?"

"The bank. You know my credit is good. I've had a loan at the bank every year since the store began. And I always pay back promptly."

"Plus interest."

"Right. Interest is part of my monthly costs. For a while, I'll have two loans to pay."

"I don't doubt the bank will help you out again. But do you realize, Bill, you might have been able to avoid interest charges and finance the expansion out of earnings?"

"Where have I gone wrong, Jack?"

"With the additional sales you are pulling in, you should also be piling up bigger profits. But apparently you're not. Some of your profits are getting away through holes in your cost management policy. Tell you what, I'll analyze your costs and financial condition from the figures you and your wife gave me for your income tax returns. And I'll also jot down typical operating ratios and a few typical financial ratios on dry goods and general merchandise stores. Then we can compare your results with others in your line. Let's make a date for next Wednesday, OK?"

The next Wednesday, Jack Larkin returned with this analysis of Brady's operations for the year ending December 31, 197–. The income statement he showed to his client, Bill Brady, is shown on the opposite page.

Jack started his analysis, "Not too much we can do about sales. They're already moving in the right direction. But we do need to take a good, hard look at expenses. In your business, it seems to me, there are two ways to build profits. First, you can continue to increase sales while you hold merchandise costs and expenses in line. Another way is to hold sales and gross profit margins about even while you reduce expenses. There are other ways to boost profits but they don't apply to your case at the moment. As I look at your income statement I see you get a good sales volume."

"We tried for $160,000 this year and hit $187,770, thanks to our expanded credit accounts."

"Next, comparing your gross margin with that of a typical store in your line, I see yours was 32.9 per cent or 3.9 per cent better than the 29.0 per cent typical gross margin. Your buying and pricing is right and apparently you keep mark-downs well under control."

"What do those arrows mean in front of the ratios for my store, Jack?"

"I put them there to emphasize your costs are higher than

				Operating Ratios of Brady's (%)	Typical Operating Ratios for the Line (%)*
Net Sales			$187,770	100	100
Inventory Jan. 1, 197–		$ 30,601			
Purchases	$122,698				
Less Purchase Disc	766				
	121,932	121,932			
		152,533			
Less inventory Dec. 31, 197–		26,540			
Cost of Goods Sold		125,993	125,993	67.1	71.0
Gross Margin			61,777	32.9	29.0
Partners' Compensation			10,149	↓ 5.4	6.7
Employees' Wages			19,838	↑ 10.5	9.6
Occupancy Expense			8,358	↑ 4.5	3.9
Advertising			4,910	↑ 2.6	1.5
Bad Debt Losses			3,193	↑ 1.7	0.0
Buying Expense			2,751	↑ 1.5	0.4
Depreciation, Fixtures			1,879	↑ 1.0	0.8
All Other Expenses			9,388	↑ 5.0	4.0
Total Expense			60,466	↑ 32.2	26.9
Net Profit Before Income Tax			1,311	↓ 0.7	2.1
Gross Margin			61,777	32.9	29.0
Inventory Turnover				4.4 times	2.6 times

*Based on performance of stores grouped by credit policy with credit sales 25% or more of total sales.

usual for your line. Your expenses ran 32.2 per cent of net sales, 5.3 per cent more than the typical store. I have here for comparison typical ratios based on a recent analysis made of the cost of doing business for dry goods and general merchandise stores. Now, Bill, here's how better control of costs might have increased your profits. Supposing you had held expenses to 26.9 per cent, the level of the typical store. Your total expenses would have been only $50,510. And your net profit before taxes would have been increased from $1311 to $11,267. That's enough to build an alcove, install the fixtures, and buy a good part of the new merchandise you'd need to fill the shelves."

"Gosh, if I only had that $10,000 extra profit! I see only two arrows pointing downward . . . the one for Mary's and my salary and the one for net profit."

"That's where your lack of cost control makes you take a licking, Bill. Before we analyze costs any further, let's see what you and Mary get out of all your effort. Look at partners' compensation: yours is only 5.4 per cent, whereas the average for your line of business is 6.7 per cent. And look at net profit of $1311 before income tax; 0.7 per cent against a typical net profit of 2.1 per cent. Compensation and net profit represent your take from the business. And your take is well below average."

"That has me puzzled. Jack. I know we're selling more than ever before but I've never been so pinched for funds. Mary and I decided two years ago we'd have to draw a smaller salary until the expansion program was completed. But each year our take has been less and less."

"You're not alone, Bill. Lots of businessmen today face the same problem of holding costs in a more profitable ratio to net sales."

"What can I do about it? For all Mary and I do in this store we deserve at least the usual cut from the melon."

"From what I've seen of your business so far, Bill, you deserve more than the average. You have a very nice operation here. I can see you building your alcove in a short time and possibly opening a branch in Brookview in a few years. And perhaps with no further loans from the bank. Just from earnings kept in the business."

"Now you're talking my language, Jack. Yes, I see myself expanding into Brookview, too."

"But not before you get costs under control."

"Where do I begin?"

"You said you had budgeted sales at $160,000. Did you also budget costs?"

"No. We just tried to keep them as small as possible."

"We'll have to organize budgeting and record keeping better than that! I suggest we examine each item of your income statement. That way we can see where we can build profits, where we can reduce costs.

NET SALES

"Let's begin at the beginning with **net sales.** Your sales are increasing. But are you sure you are doing all you can to build sales even more? Could your clerks benefit from training to make them more effective sales people? Your talent, Bill, is selling. Why not pass along more of your successful selling techniques to the rest of your sales force? And have you considered setting up a prize incentive system or a bonus plan for your sales clerks?

GROSS MARGIN

"You have a better than average **gross margin.** That's all in your favor. If we can find new ways to reduce merchandise costs further, you have that much more money for yourself and to cover operating expenses. With competition so keen today, it's important to buy from the right supplier who'll deliver quickly and who offers advantageous terms on special quantity purchases. And do you earn all discounts offered?"

"Sometimes. I would all the time if I had the money. Right now, I have to count heavily on turnover to pay my bills. January is my worst month for sales. If some of my receivables come in more slowly than usual I may not have the cash to discount."

"Yet, if you took advantage of every possible discount, you'd reduce cost of goods and build gross margin.

"Now, Bill, before we take up each expense, I want to get this straight: it would be a mistake to assume we should try to reduce each and every cost item. In fact it may pay you to increase some of them. Control of costs is relative and results from a more profitable balance of individual costs. Perhaps you should actually spend more for such items as employees' incentives and advertising. Let's take a look now at your operating costs for last year. Some of these, such as rent, are fixed, though the rest of your occupancy expense may vary. Others, such as buying expenses, are wholly variable. Fixed costs, as a per cent of sales, can be reduced only by increasing net sales; the variable and semi-variable costs you can possibly reduce by limiting selectively the dollar amount spent. First of all, **partners' compensation.**"

"We don't want to cut that!"

EMPLOYEES' WAGES

"Of course not, Bill. But take **employees' wages.** Can you reduce anything there?"

"There may be a way. Alma Haine in the bedding section says she wants to retire April 1. Maybe I could get along without a replacement for Alma by shifting some personnel."

"That might cut the amount of dollars you pay out in wages. But let's look at this another way, Bill. You pay about $19,800 in wages. Dividing annual sales by that figure gives you about $9.50 in sales for every dollar of wages."

"Do you think I could increase that amount?"

"With training of your sales help, yes. You might step it up to eleven or twelve dollars per dollar of wages. One way of doing that is to be sure your employees are the best you can hire for the wages you and your competitors pay. That means knowing your local labor market and persuading the best people to come to you. It means checking their experience and their references carefully. And training them.

OCCUPANCY EXPENSE

"Next, let's look at your **occupancy expense.** The rent you pay is only $4800 a year. That's not bad for such a big place right on Main Street."

"No, it isn't, Jack, but to keep this old place together and looking right is expensive. Modernization, repair, and mainte- nance, according to our lease, is up to me. That's where the rest of the $8358 goes . . . into keeping the place cool in sum- mer, warm in winter, and well-lighted."

"Perhaps you can cut down heating bills by checking loose window sashes, sealing storm windows with masking tape, and building a winter vestibule around the front door. That will trap some of the cold air. You face North."

"And a little East, right in the line of the winds that come down the valley. Yes, I've been thinking about recaulking some of the windows."

"And how about your use of electricity? Your conditioner can be turned off before closing time during the summer; the coolness will continue for a while. In winter, most of your cus- tomers will come in wearing coats. You can keep your heat at a level lower than your home and still be comfortable. With a hot water system you have a residual heating effect, too. You can afford to cut the heat long before closing. At night a re- duced temperature is sufficient; in the morning you can raise it again. I notice, too, you have an old, corrugated iron ceil- ing."

"It came with the building. If it were my own building I would re-cover the ceiling with insulating tile. But it's too big a project. The iron will last a few more decades."

"But you might consider changing the color from gloomy blue-gray. That ceiling absorbs light rather than reflects it. It probably is the reason you have so much auxiliary lighting in this store. The globes you have here just don't create enough light."

"I've put the biggest bulbs into them, too."

"You can get the most illumination per dollar from fluo- rescent lighting. Your relatively expensive bulbs and dark paint are among the many small costs which have built up your high occupancy expense."

BUYING EXPENSE

"Let's look now at **buying expense.** Who does the buying for Brady's?"

"Mary and I do it. Sometimes we take the station wagon down as far as Chicago to bring back merchandise. I find it pays on smaller items, particularly apparel."

"How much do you estimate it costs to make the trip in gas, food, and hotel expenses? You must stay at least one night in the city. How many trips do you make each year?"

"Too much and too many. I pick up merchandise every two weeks or so. Mary reads the trade papers and keeps track of what merchandise is moving. So I go to get it. And I pick up reorders sometimes, too. Don't want to lose any sales because I don't have the merchandise."

"That's a good policy. You carry rather small inventories for the volume you transact."

"Sure, I let my suppliers pay for storage."

"That's OK. But maybe the money you spend on your buying trips is more than you might spend if you estimated inventory needs more carefully in the first place. Too little inventory can lose you sales as well as increase buying and shipping expenses. The cheaper methods of transportation are usually the slowest but you won't have to pay a premium for speed if you plan your purchases accurately."

ADVERTISING

"Now, about **advertising**," Jack continued.

"That's the great unknown around here. I know I pay a lot of money for advertising and I don't know if I'm getting the results I should."

"How about your newspaper advertising?"

"Sometimes a customer comes in with my ad for a sale in his hand. I guess the space I buy does me a lot of good. It's hard to count results, though.

"Mary also mails post cards to our credit customers."

"That's advertising, too, Bill. But to control advertising expenses you should find out which effort brings the best response. Then concentrate your spending there. Tell me, how do you make your promotions get interest and action?"

"Last November I built two revolving Christmas trees: tall, green pyramids with shelves. Mary filled them with costume jewelry, perfumes, and other bright, interesting gifts. They were priced about right for the gift you'd want to give an aunt who has everything. Mary persuaded me to let the newspaper run a drawing of the trees in my usual space. We did very well with that idea. But it was expensive."

"Why not use more of the free displays your suppliers are always ready to put in? You can be selective and choose the material which best fits your store's merchandising plans. And have you thought about cooperative advertising with your suppliers or community advertising with some of the other merchants in town?"

"No, I haven't, Jack. But it's a good idea. I'll do something about that as soon as I can."

"You might tell Mary, too, to look into the postage she pays for her mailings. No need to use first class mail in most cases. Personalized letters generally are more effective than post cards. A letter sent third class bulk mail costs less than post cards or a first class letter. I gather you do quite a lot of advertising by mail."

"There are more than 2000 on our customer list, Jack."

"That could mean a considerable savings each time you mail third class instead of post card or first class."

"And we mail ten or a dozen times a year. I'll tell Mary about third class mail. We might be able to save a few hundred dollars that way."

DEPRECIATION AND OTHER EXPENSES

"Now, Bill, let's take depreciation and other expenses. I've written off $1879 as this year's depreciation on fixtures. I've lumped together such things as insurance, breakage, pilferage, spoilage of display merchandise, and maintenance expense. Some of these other expenses are unavoidable. Some things are bound to spoil, for example. On the other hand, **breakage** can be brought within reasonable bounds by being sure shelves are stocked neatly and securely and by encouraging all the store personnel to handle inventory more carefully. You're fairly well set up here for guarding against **pilferage.** There are only a few doors customers can use. If you, your wife, and your clerks keep an eye out for shoplifters, you can cut down the amount of inventory loss. You can't avoid some **spoilage** of dresses and goods by long exposure on display racks or in the window. But you can give faded goods away, once they're cleaned, to a needy family or to a charity bazaar. That builds goodwill and puts the material to use. And quantities of slow-moving merchandise which might spoil or discolor on the shelves can be moved by a well-timed sale. For **insurance** you ought to consult your agent about variable coverage. You keep your inventory low . . . that's a help. But your off-season coverage may still be too high.

BAD DEBT LOSSES

"And finally, Bill, your **bad debt losses.** A store loses money through bad debts because credit is not extended carefully enough in the first place and, secondly, because it may lack a well-defined, effective collection policy. Over half your sales, Bill, are on credit terms. You must select your credit customers carefully. Be sure you have full identification, name, address, and bank reference. And follow through on these references."

"Mary can do that for me."

"Even then, a few of your carefully screened accounts may delay. You'll save yourself time and money by clearly defining your credit and collection policy when a customer opens a credit account. And then be sure to send him a monthly statement on time. Your card or revolving file will tell you when an account is running past due. Then you can send a tactful reminder, such as a duplicate bill or prompt note. Some stores freeze further credits until an account pays up; others are adding a one-half per cent a month carrying charge on all credit accounts. They make this charge refundable if the account pays within thirty days."

"That sounds like a good idea, Jack."

"We have now considered the major items on your **income statement** from net sales to net profit before taxes. Step by step I've suggested some ways to reduce certain of your expenses in order to bring them closer to typical operating ratios for your line. It's up to you, now, to reduce these costs throughout the year. Such a program of control will pay off for you in greater profits, a greater take for you and Mary from your business."

"I'm all for that."

"And now I'd like to show you how your **balance sheet** can point the way to sound management, control of costs, and greater profits. Whatever you do as manager of your business shows up in your balance sheet, too. And it is even more apparent when you compare balance sheet items over a period of years. Take your problem of credit granting which we were talking about a moment ago. That shows up on your balance sheet in the left-hand column as the amount carried in accounts receivable.

Cash in Bank	$19,138	Accounts Payable		$29,973
Accounts Receivable	26,083	Owing Bank (due within year)		3,240
Merchandise	26,540			
Total Current Assets	71,761	Total Current Liabilities		33,213
		Owing Bank (due in more than		
Fixtures & Equip.	9,411	one year)		2,700
(Reserve for		**Net Worth Dec. 31, 197–**	46,819	
Depreciation of 2.542)		**Plus Reinvested Earnings**	850	
		to Dec. 31, 197–	47,669	
Station Wagon	2,000			
Deposits	410	**Net Worth Dec. 31, 197–**		47,669
Total	83,582	**Total**		83,582

"When I listed your assets and liabilities as of December 31, 1978, I also summarized your statements for the three past years.

	December 31, 197–	December 31, 197–	December 31, 197–
Current Assets	$46,440	$51,617	$71,761
Current Liabilities	6,471	12,201	33,213
Other Assets	6,143	7,552	11,821
Tangible Net Worth	45,319	46,819	47,669
Net Working Capital	39,969	39,416	38,548
Net Sales	**92,651**	**115,660**	**187,770**
Net Profit (before taxes)	2,463 (2.7%)	1,953 (1.7%)	1,311 (0.7%)

"You have accounts receivable of $26,083 listed on your balance sheet. And they are included in the $71,761 of current assets listed in the comparative figures. See how fast your assets and liabilities have increased during the past three years? But your net worth and working capital have not. Also, your sales are up but your profits are not keeping pace."

"It's my apparel department, Jack. The volume in apparel has more than tripled since I started to sell on credit. The people around here are prospering. So I encourage them to buy on thirty-day credit."

"And they apparently do, judging from the size of your receivables. Tell me, how are the collections coming in?"

"Fair. Most of my customers mean well, though."

"Mean well but apparently they're slow. It looks like you have too much of your money in receivables. What's your collection period?"

"Come again?"

"What's your collection period?"

"You're way out beyond me, Jack. You'll have to tell me."

"All right, I will. Let's see how much you carry as receivables. $26,083. And what's the split of your annual sales between cash and credit?"

"That I can answer. Mary has been keeping track for me. Let's see. This book has it. No, it's the other one. Here we are. You'll have to check the book for totals, Jack."

"Total sales on open account: $105,725; cash: $82,045. Dividing $105,725 by 365 days in a year you have net credit sales per day of $289.82. Then dividing your receivables ($26,083) by $289.82 gives you a collection period of about ninety days.

"As a general rule of thumb, the collection period of any business selling merchandise on open-book account should be no more than one-third greater than net selling terms. In this case, since your open account selling terms are net thirty days, you should have a collection period of no longer than forty days. *Yours is more than twice that long.* By letting receivables slow down this way, you encourage accounts to delay.

"And the longer they delay, the bigger are the chances they won't pay at all. Your income statement showed a bad debt loss of $3193, more than twice your net profit. You ought to determine immediately the age of each of your accounts.

"Now," Jack continued, "there are a few other things your balance sheet can tell us. Dun and Bradstreet sent me these financial ratios, which are comparisons of various items on your balance sheet and income statement. Collection period is a ratio we've already discussed. Here are five other important ratios . . . I've figured yours and put beside them, for comparison, typical ratios for the line."

	Financial Ratios of Brady's	Typical Financial Ratios for the Line
I. Current assets to current debt	↓ 2.2 times	3.49 times
II. Net profit on tangible net worth	↓ 2.7%	9.20%
III. Net sales to tangible net worth	↑ 3.9 times	3.19 times
IV. Net sales to net working capital	↑ 4.9 times	3.83 times
V. Current debt to tangible net worth	↑ 69.7%	36.10%

"I see you've used arrows again."

"Yes, they show four things: your current ratio of assets to liabilities is low, only 2.2 times; your profit is low in comparison with your investment; you turn over your net worth and net working capital faster than usual; and your debt is heavier than the debt typically carried by businesses in your line.

"Your long collection period is a symptom of your heavy receivables. Your large debt, as shown by the ratio of current debt to tangible net worth, can affect your credit standing and your position with the suppliers who can offer you the best service and merchandise. Suppose a manufacturer, closing out a line, offered you a substantial discount on an attractive group of dresses if you could pay cash. Could you take advantage of the offer without special financing? I doubt it, Bill.

"You said January was your dullest month for sales. I've taken that into consideration. Here's roughly what you'll have coming in and going out between now, January 3, and the end of the month.

EXPECTED CASH FOR JANUARY		MUST PAY IN JANUARY	
Cash on hand and in the bank	$19,100	Bills	$30,000
Cash income	12,500	Owing bank	270
(including expected sales		(monthly amount)	
for cash and collection of		Expenses	4,230
receivables)		(including partner's draw-	
		ings, wages, advertising,	
		occupancy, other)	
	$31,600		$34,500

"It looks to me as if you're not going to have enough cash at the end of January to pay everything due then."

"Some of those bills are due March 1. I'd say only about $27,000 of that $30,000 is due by February 1."

"It's still going to be tight for you, Bill. Your best bet is to concentrate this month on collecting past due accounts. Then you'll have the cash to meet your bills. And you might be able to earn more discounts and take advantage of some manufacturers' January clearance sales for cash.

"So you see, Bill, how your balance sheet has given us a way to help you build profits by controlling costs. We traced the effect of heavy receivables on your cash position. I've shown you a way to keep track each month of your expected cash intake and outgo. Many progressive business people project their cash position months in advance. Then they follow through with positive action. This control results in sufficient cash to cover normal costs and gives the business owner money to use when advantageous buying opportunities come along.

"Let's look into the months ahead, Bill. By way of summary, here's what you should do to build your profits by controlling costs:

1. keep your sales moving up as you have been;
2. Watch your average gross margin — keep control of markdowns; earn discounts when offered;
3. cut down variable operating expenses wherever possible;
4. go ahead with a collection clean-up campaign;
5. be more selective about extending new credit;
6. keep accurate records — study them frequently to see how well you've kept costs in line, and call me whenever you have a question or a problem."

"That does it, Jack. The alcove will have to wait until I put the business I already have in order. The way Mary and I work we deserve to enjoy all the profits we can earn."

"I couldn't agree with you more."

"Jack, you're the best investment I'll make this year. I just didn't realize mere figures could tell me so quickly where I was goofing in the management of my business."

CHAPTER 8

MANAGEMENT OF THE SMALL BUSINESS

INTRODUCTION

Since it is the small-business owner who must insure that his firm operates efficiently, this chapter will illustrate managerial practices that can help him accomplish this. The focal point of the chapter will be the determination, measurement, and accomplishment of Bill Brady's objectives from "The Man Who Managed His Business by Ear."

Objectives for each small business, even those in the same type of business, will vary, according to the personality of the owner. However, it is imperative that objectives be established. There must be definitive, measurable objectives by which the progress of the business can be ascertained over time.

This chapter will specifically discuss these aspects of management: management by objectives (MBO), planning, controlling, organizing, delegating, motivating, leading, and the personnel function — selecting, training, appraising performance, job descriptions, job evaluation, and wage rates.

MANAGEMENT BY OBJECTIVES

Management by objectives (MBO) is a goal- or result-oriented method of management that establishes goals, determines how these goals are to be attained, and appraises results on predetermined dates. An MBO program provides a systematic process through which superiors and subordinates participate in decision making. It entails establishing specific performance objectives, specifying definitive measures for them, and attributing costs and revenues to each one. It also provides a set of dates at which time progress toward attaining objectives is to be evaluated. MBO establishes clear objectives, provides feedback on performance, and utilizes each individual's judgment, discretion, and self-control to attain high levels of performance.

The alternative to managing by objectives is to manage without them, certainly not an efficient means of operation, since there can be no coordination of resource utilization. The following aspects of management are all related to MBO, and Bill Brady's objectives will be used to illustrate this relationship.

These objectives represent the basic guidelines for Bill's business and completely define both the opportunities he will exploit and the ones he will not. This will keep him from trying too much, too soon, as in the case of his firm's expansion. The objectives, therefore, form the basis for the total operation of the firm. Bill must also insure that the goals are correct and that all the business resources, including the owner's time and talents, are totally committed to the attainment of these goals.

The MBO program must take both costs and profits into consideration. Not all objectives, however, are measurable in terms of costs and profits and therefore a number of intangible measures must also be specified. These subjective goals are best measured with monthly reviews and with as many intangible measures as feasible.[1]

This is a very brief description of an MBO program; however, the reader should be able to gain a complete understanding of the concepts by carefully perusing the objectives established for Bill Brady in Figure 8–1 and by noting how Bill's objectives become the basis for all his managerial decisions.

PLANNING

Lack of sound planning is often cited as one of the major causes of failure in the small firm. Planning is particularly critical in the small firm since a small firm lacks extensive resources. A mistake in an entrepreneur's plan may cause immediate disaster, since the business is unable to cope effectively with short-run financial problems. There is no disaster fund to cushion problems.

Small-business owners constantly state that they have no time to plan. Instead, they manage by crisis, putting out small fires as they occur. Admittedly, this is more fun for them than planning to avoid crises. The small-business owner has a limited amount of time and as the firm expands, this resource diminishes. Therefore, during the initiation phase, it is imperative that planning become habitual. There are enough unavoidable contingencies to provide excitement without fostering avoidable ones.

Another obvious reason for "front-end" planning is its low

---

[1]Herbert H. Hand and A. Thomas Hollingsworth. "Tailoring MBO to Hospitals," *Business Horizons,* February, 1975, pp. 50–51.

cost to the potential small-business owner. The initial business plan requires a great deal of time and effort, but very few financial resources. It also forces the planner to evaluate personal characteristics as actual strengths or weaknesses for the particular business. Thus, weaknesses can be strengthened beforehand, not during the initial operation phase when time will not be as readily available.

A plan establishes the basic objectives of the firm, determines how these objectives can be attained considering various aspects of the environment, and determines the amount of resources necessary. In Bill's case, his firm's objectives also reflect his personal objectives. Bill's objectives clearly show the direction of his firm but they do not represent his total plan. For instance, he needs a financial plan to cover his expansion. All aspects of the business plan are covered in Chapter 3, and apply to the new concern as well as the ongoing one. Formulation of objectives and constant reference to them are important to the business. It is the best method to utilize resources.

A note of caution: paradoxically, a little success may lead to failure. As a business experiences success in its first few years, there may be a tendency not to plan as carefully as in the beginning. Controls therefore become loose and before realizing it, the business owner finds that the business is no longer on a sound basis. A constant re-evaluation of objectives will predict problems before they become serious. For instance, Bill has an objective to insure that his personnel are the best for the wages paid. This objective insures that he will constantly be evaluating and improving his personnel. This means that they will be courteous and able to advise customers. Without such an objective, salespeople could become surly and poorly informed about Bill's products. Ultimately this would be reflected in decreased sales, but by monitoring his salespeople, Bill can prevent the problem from occurring.

FORECASTING

Forecasting is an important aspect of the planning process and is covered in Chapters 2 and 6. Forecasting provides the small-business owner with an idea of what resources are required, when they will be required, and how many will be needed. For the new firm, forecasting is difficult since there are no past figures to project into the future. However, lenders are very interested in the techniques businesses use to ascertain their objectives, and careful thought should be given to using the methods discussed below.

A number of methods for gathering data are applicable both to the initiation of a new business and to the operations of an

OBJECTIVES WORKSHEET

Individual's name: Bill Brady

Supervisor's name: The small business environment

Objectives	Measures	Time frame for review	Review comments
Sales objective: increase sales by 10%, by training sales people and by establishing a sales incentive program.	Has this occurred?	quarterly	
Gross margin objective: take advantage of all trade discounts.	Number of discounts *not* utilized.	monthly	
Personnel objective: insure that each employee is the best for the wage paid.	Actual sales by employees; amount of training given; results of reference check; personal judgement.	monthly	
Store improvement objectives: repaint the ceiling; caulk windows; minimize heating and cooling costs.	Has the ceiling been painted? the windows caulked? heating and cooling costs reduced? employees rewarded for reducing these costs?	monthly	
Inventory objective: carefully evaluate the cost of carrying inventories against the cost of trips for buying.	Has the comparison been made? Is this information utilized to change buying procedures?	quarterly	

Objective	Evaluation question	Timing		
Advertising objective: evaluate each mode of advertising in a cost/benefit analysis.	Are all modes of advertising being evaluated? all mailing lists current? Are effective checks randomly made?	as needed		
Internal operations objective: minimize shoplifting, insurance costs, and displays of "spoiled" merchandise.	Comparative analysis: are these decreasing? How much "spoiled" merchandise is on the shelves?	monthly		
Bad debt objectives: decrease bad debts by 10%; clean up overdue credit accounts.	Has bad debt decreased by 10%? Are overdue accounts being cleared?	quarterly (bad debts) monthly (overdue credit)		
Collection period objective: reduce the collection period to 40 days, by aging accounts receivable to determine problem accounts.	Has this been done?			
Ratio objectives: increase current ratio; increase profit relative to investment; maintain a high ratio of net sales to both net worth and working capital; decrease debt to net worth ratio.	Have these been accomplished?	yearly		

Figure 8–1 Objectives worksheet for Bill Brady's dry goods store.

ongoing firm. Talking to wholesalers may give you some idea about how competitive products are moving. You may also look at census data to determine probable demand. The owner of one restaurant began his business planning by checking his trading area's growth projection through the telephone company. He also stopped in at a number of local firms to talk about where people went for lunch. He then checked prices to calculate the average expenditure.

In another instance, two individuals were interested in expanding their auto-supply business by adding another store. They selected an area of small towns and simply drove up and down every street in town noting competition and general economic conditions. They also acquired the vehicle registrations for the counties under consideration. A visit to local chambers of commerce provided population figures, economic estimates, and maps of the towns. They also had a rough census, a count of all garages and gas stations, a count of all auto-repair facilities, and a count of all their potential competitors. They then acquired industry projections and percentages and compared them with their rough counts. As a result, they decided to locate in a specific area of one small town and to offer services untried by competitors.

These are two examples of ingenuity in forecasting. Every avenue of data collection should be utilized during this phase. As noted, the cost of gathering this information is far exceeded by the benefits it can provide in the planning process. The two examples above prove this; both businesses are highly successful. These examples demonstrate that difficulty in forecasting is not an excuse for not planning. The planning process has to be completed if there is to be any hope for success.

STRATEGY

Strategy formulation results from the planning process. Strategy is the means of implementing the various objectives of your plan. The strategy of a firm must be congruent with its resources. For example, Bill Brady's objective of hiring the best personnel possible is qualified by "at the wage paid." It would be unreasonable to hire marketing executives and pay them extremely high salaries since his firm has neither the resources nor the need to do this.

A firm's strategy must constantly be evaluated in terms of its owner's objectives. Bill may minimize shoplifting by displaying all merchandise behind counters; however, his customers may resent this in a dry goods store. This could reduce sales to a greater extent than the savings realized through the reduction of shoplifting.

The planning process is important to all small businesses, new and old. Once plans are formulated and objectives, measures, and time frames established, a set of controls must be implemented to insure the attainment of the objectives.

CONTROLLING THE SMALL BUSINESS

The control process begins after time frames have been set. Actual results are compared with projected results to determine the level to which objectives have been attained. For example, Bill has an objective to take advantage of all trade discounts. It is measured by whether he did or did not do this. If not, then the control process continues by suggesting remedial actions. In this case, such remedial action consists of a better planned cash flow and more attention to payment dates. The latter can be established by some sort of visual posting system to make Bill aware, at all times, of the important discount dates. If there are no discrepancies between actual and planned objective attainment, the control process begins again. It is a continuous process of monetary objective attainment.

Quality control is another control problem for the small business and is discussed in Chapter 9. Quality is certainly seen in Bill's objective to improve the internal environment of his firm.

A third control problem facing the small business is crime. 1974 saw a loss in excess of 20.3 billion dollars to American business through crime, and small business is 35 times more likely to be a victim of crime than the firm grossing 5 million dollars or more.[2] There are a number of measures to prevent burglary, such as secure locks and window latches, alarm systems, and night lights. Insurance should cover losses fully. Don't invite burglary. Keep your cash elsewhere, or deposit it daily; don't keep it on the premises for extended periods.

Armed robbery is always a threat. Again, control your cash, and don't invite trouble by keeping large amounts of money. If you are robbed, remember that you and your employees and customers can't be replaced.

As noted in Bill's objectives, the shoplifter always poses a problem for the retailer. To lessen the threat of shoplifting, Bill should carefully place small items where they can be watched. Mirrors and a watchful group of clerks can also reduce shoplifting. Price tags on merchandise should also be tamperproof.

Dishonest employees also pose a problem, and again, layout is important. Make sure that both shoppers and employees can be observed. Patterns tend to develop with dishonest employees, and being kept in sight makes them vulnerable to disclosure. Bill should make random trips through the store and observe his em-

---

[2]"Crime prevention for small business," *Small Business Reporter,* Bank of America. Vol. 13, No. 1, 1975.

ployees. Keeping keys secure is also important. Only those who need keys should have them.

ORGANIZING THE SMALL FIRM

During the initial phase of the small business, there is no need to set up distinct functional areas with individuals in charge of each area. Bill would not find this feasible. However, an organization chart, showing each person's position, should be prepared to insure that everyone in the firm knows to whom they are responsible, and to minimize conflicts in even the small firm.

In order to define fully your business there should be a functional chart, even if it is just for the owner's reference. Many times, small-business owners contend, "I don't need an organization chart. I know everything about the firm," or, "Organization charts are useless since they really don't represent a true picture of the firm." In response to the first comment: *you* might be aware of all aspects of the business, but others in your firm are not. The organization chart is a viable tool for communicating these aspects to others concerned with your firm: employees, investors, and partners. Also, the organization chart should be compared with your strategy and objectives to determine whether you are in fact organized and intend to be organized properly to accomplish your objectives.

In response to the second comment, the organization chart is a map of the firm at a particular time. You would not leave New York to drive to Houston without a map. The organization chart is an organization's map. You would not depend on a 1942 road map for your trip nor should you depend on an outdated organization chart.

When exploring possible business opportunities for a firm, the first criterion is whether the opportunity is within the parameters of the firm's objectives. The second criterion is whether the firm has the personnel to accomplish or to exploit the opportunity. Many small businesses remain small because of their lack of personnel. The owner-entrepreneur-manager-generalist is often finally stretched too far and the business either ceases to grow or begins to fail because it cannot meet client expectations. The organization chart is your guide to determining whether you are adequately staffed to take advantage of special opportunities.

This chart can also assist the small-business owner in applying a simple job evaluation analysis. By observing those activities that require the majority of time, job evaluation formats can be prepared. Since time is a small-business owner's most important and scarcest resource, the jobs that would free the most time for the owner are the most important to the firm. The second criterion for job evaluation is to supplement your firm's skill level. This

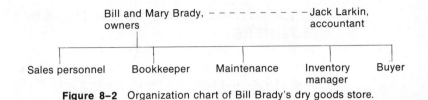

Figure 8-2 Organization chart of Bill Brady's dry goods store.

may take precedence when acquiring the skill is the major factor in short-run survival. Bill acquired Joe Larkin, an accountant, to assist his business in an area that Bill found time-consuming and in which he was not well trained.

An organization chart for Bill's operation is shown in Figure 8-2. Although everyone reports to Bill, they are not necessarily all of equal importance to the firm. Some may be required to be more skilled or highly trained than others, hence the need for job evaluation.

JOB EVALUATION

Figure 8-3 demonstrates a simple job evaluation format based on Bill's organization chart. Since the jobs are ranked by their importance to the firm, the salary allocations should reflect this. In this particular case, the salaries do decrease as the job rank decreases; however, a small-business owner may need to pay higher wages than specified because of a "tight" labor market for various classifications.

A small business may also have individuals who are overpaid relative to the local labor market because of their experience with the firm. When this is the case, they are "red circled" and although their pay remains the same, when one of them leaves a position, a lower wage is paid to the replacement.

The process of job evaluation should give the small-business owner confidence that employees are being rewarded in keeping with their contribution to the firm.

Rank	Comparative annual salary
Buyer	$ X X X X X X
Retail salesperson I	X X X X
Bookkeeper	X X X
Retail salesperson II	X X X
Inventory manager	X X
Maintenance	X

Figure 8-3 Job evaluation format for Bill Brady's dry goods store.

DELEGATING ACTIVITIES IN THE SMALL BUSINESS

The organization chart should provide the basis for delegation. Time, as previously mentioned, is one of the small-business owner's scarcest resources, and delegation can be a primary factor in time management. Delegation is the process of assigning routine duties to subordinates to free the owner from time-consuming activities.

All business owners are busy, yet not all are successful. Some owners are busy performing activities which would be better delegated. These activities should be delegated either because they require expertise that the owner does not have, or because they are routine. The first is the reason Bill Brady hired Jim Larkin; the second is the reason Bill hires salespeople.

Each business owner should establish a time utilization inventory, and use it for a few days. A basic form is shown in Figure 8–4. In the first column, times are shown in 30-minute intervals, a choice of increment that can be condensed or expanded. Activities should specify exactly what was done in the time listed. Start your time inventory from when you awaken and take it to when you go home in the evening. Leave the comments section blank — no judgments should be made during this stage.

After activities have been recorded for two days, they should be labeled, by degree of urgency, as urgent, highly important, important, necessary, or unnecessary, and by asking, "Could it have been performed by someone else?" "Was each activity completed?" and "Are these activities consistent with the objectives established for the firm?" The last is the most important question, for if the activities are inconsistent with the objectives of the firm, there is a serious problem. Perhaps the real personal objectives of the owner have not been identified, or perhaps the objectives of the firm are simply being ignored.

In Bill's case, assume that he has completed the time analysis inventory, and that it shows he has spent most of his time talking to salespeople from outside his business, making cash sales, and keeping inventory records. It is obvious that these are not the most important aspects of the firm, as shown in his objectives. He will have to discipline himself to train salespeople, take advantage of discounts, and evaluate advertising. Another problem is that some aspects of Bill's venture may be more interesting to him than other aspects. For instance, his buying trips may be interesting, but they are likely made too often to be profitable. Again, you must evaluate your own time utilization and determine the proper level of delegation. The form in Figure 8–4 is only one of many methods for performing this assessment.

As part of the delegation process, coordination must occur. Coordination is the process of arranging the resources of the firm to attain the maximum uses of such resources. In Bill's case, he must coordinate his sales and advertising efforts, with his training

Time period	Activity	Degree of urgency
8:00 – 8:29		
8:30 – 8:59		
9:00 – 9:29		
9:30 – 9:59		
and so on		

Figure 8–4.   Time analysis, diagnostic.

of salespeople, with the arrival of inventory for sale. If these all happen at completely different times, Bill might advertise merchandise that is not in stock or that employees are unaware is in stock. This will not enhance his chances of making sales.

MOTIVATION IN THE SMALL BUSINESS

The most important asset that any small business has is its human resources. This may consist of the owners and their families or a number of hired employees. In any case, these are the individuals who make the sales, provide the service, or manufacture the product. Their efforts determine the degree of success in the small business and they must be properly motivated.

The initial step in the motivation process is to insure that all employees have definite objectives and measures. These objectives may be communicated by job descriptions, discussed later in this chapter, or by more complex methods, such as Bill Brady's objectives. Even if some of the employees are family members, they must have objectives. After objectives have been established for all the members of an organization, they must be reviewed to insure that all the objectives of the firm are being accomplished. All the activities needed to accomplish your final goals must be performed either by yourself or by your employees.

As an example, Bill's salespeople certainly wish to increase sales by 10 per cent and they can also assist in decreasing the level of bad debts. These are two objectives. Obviously, there are others that would be covered in a job description for sales personnel.

Focusing on these two objectives, the second step in the motivation process is to reward salespeople for attaining their objectives. Definitive goals — a dollar amount of sales — must be established and a percentage paid to the individual if the goal is met or exceeded. Employees should also be rewarded if they assist in reducing bad debts by carefully assessing all credit requests that they receive. Any such program must be monitored to insure that salespeople do not become overzealous; bad debts could be reduced to zero if *no* credit is given. Again, careful control is needed.

The motivation process ties goal attainment to rewards. Employees can see and benefit from their actions when they have concrete objectives and measures and are subsequently rewarded for attaining them.

THE LEADERSHIP FUNCTION IN THE SMALL BUSINESS

Some businesses subsist, while others grow. Some businesses barely survive, while others continually expand. Management leadership makes the difference. There are five traits associated with good management.[3]

Perception. Effective managers have the ability to continually look for new methods, products, or approaches. They listen carefully to everyone connected with the business, and translate comments into actions. They always investigate reasons for both new and lost customers.

Boldness. Successful managers are doers. They make no excuses, and they don't blame others. They take risks and live with their uncertainty.

Persistence. The effective manager keeps trying until the right combination occurs. The same mistakes are not made twice.

Persuasion. Again, managers are the business. They must persuade others who are involved with a business to gain their support, and so, to be successful.

Ethics. Your business should provide something to society, and you have to set a high moral standard. People with situational ethics, that is, people who rationalize their actions by hiding behind changing situations, are soon recognized. Once your ethics are shown to be questionable, your ability to persuade is severely hampered. This will certainly detract from your success.

As a leader you must make decisions for your business and you must be responsive to feedback, both good and bad. The successful business owner listens objectively, decides rationally, and rarely argues to protect an ego.

---

[3]Schabacker, Joseph C., ed. *Strengthening Small Business Management,* Washington, D.C.: The Small Business Administration, 1971, p. 144.

THE PERSONNEL FUNCTION IN THE SMALL BUSINESS

The aspects of the personnel function discussed in this section include selection and hiring, training, appraisals, job descriptions, job evaluations, and wage rates.

JOB DESCRIPTIONS

The written job description covers the specific duties and work to be accomplished for a particular position. It also lists qualifications and any special aspects needed in potential job seekers. It may also include personal characteristics preferred by the business owner. For the new firm, initial job descriptions will cover a variety of activities. As the firm grows, and more employees are hired, the job descriptions will become more specific. However, during the initial phase, the small firm offers built-in job enrichment and a friendly, personal attitude which is attractive to many employees.

The organization chart can be used to formulate job descriptions. In the early stages of a business, one job may cover a number of the functions shown on the organization chart.

An example of a job description for one of Bill Brady's salespeople is shown in Figure 8–5. As stated before, this job description forms the basis for a number of objectives for this individual. However, other specific objectives may need to be established for motivation.

Job Summary: Waits on customers, makes sales, has knowledge of all merchandise, and assists retail salesperson II as needed.

Basic Qualifications:
1. bondable
2. high school education
3. handle basic math
4. be able to work evenings and Saturdays
5. two years' experience in retail sales

Characteristic Duties and Responsibilities:
1. waits on customers in a pleasant manner
2. closes sales with customers as quickly as possible
3. makes change, and records charges
4. wraps or bags articles as required
5. restocks shelves as necessary
6. takes phone orders as necessary
7. reports to Mr. Brady
8. monitors possible shoplifting
9. assists in supervising retail salesperson II when necessary

Figure 8–5 Job description: Retail salesperson I.

PERFORMANCE APPRAISAL

The performance appraisal function should be continuous in the small firm. As noted above, goals should be established. After this is accomplished, each employee should receive feedback relative to performance. This is a significant part of the motivational process.

Although informal feedback is a good method for appraising performance, a formal appraisal should also be conducted at least semi-annually. This review may consist of going over past objectives and accomplishments, and setting new objectives. This is also a good method for planning employee performance.

Figure 8–6 is a sample performance appraisal form. Being an example, it would require significant modification before it could be utilized as a valid measure of performance. However, it does demonstrate the format and some considerations in the performance appraisal process.

TRAINING

Training salespeople is one of Bill's objectives. To train his salespeople effectively, Bill must know specifically what is to be in his training program. His personnel should know the products, be able to communicate such knowledge effectively to customers, and be able to close a sale. This training can be done on-the-job in most cases. However, if a new employee has never made change or used a cash register, Bill may have to do some training prior to putting that individual into the store.

Training should have specific objectives and measurable results.

SELECTION

Selecting and hiring individuals for the small business is the final area to be covered in this section on personnel. The initial step in the process is analyzing the job description carefully, and listing those qualifications and characteristics you feel are important to the job. These should include previous experience, education, and licenses. You may also determine whether testing is a viable method of determining a candidate's potential; however, there are some possible legal ramifications to testing. Testing is especially applicable when manual skills are necessary for efficient job performance. This would apply to Bill, since a prospective employee must have a knowledge of basic math to make change, an integral part of a salesperson's job. Bill could use a

Name_____

Date_____

Evaluator_____

The above individual should be appraised as objectively as possible, on these criteria:

	satisfactory				*poor*
Customer relations	1	2	3	4	5
Personal appearance	1	2	3	4	5
Judgment	1	2	3	4	5
Job knowledge	1	2	3	4	5
General performance	1	2	3	4	5

Evaluator's comments_____

_____

Employee's comments_____

_____

I certify that this evaluation has been discussed with me. I understand that my signature does not constitute agreement.

Employee_____   Date_____
                    Signature

Evaluator_____   Date_____
                    Signature

Figure 8-6. Performance appraisal: Retail salesperson I.

basic math test to determine these qualifications. However, tests that do not relate directly to the job must be used with care.

The Equal Employment Opportunity Commission was established by the Civil Rights Acts of 1964, and has been involved in disputes concerning fair employment practices. Since the Griggs versus Duke Power Company decision, firms may not use tests unless they are validly and reliably tied to particular job descriptions. Therefore, you must take care, in all phases of your selection process, to insure that the entire process relates an individual's qualifications to those required on the job. This care includes interviewing, which is considered a test.

Bill now has his job description and a basic math test. He should also have an application form. There are a number of standardized forms available in stationery stores and they can be used to obtain the necessary demographic information: age, marital status, address, and so on. The most important aspect of the forms is a list of references. Before making any decisions, references should be checked. Although written references are advised, recent freedom of information decisions by the courts have caused individuals to become hesitant to give completely candid references in writing. This is particularly true in such highly subjective areas as poor attitude. Phone calls to a few people listed as references may be advantageous to acquire both a true feel for the reference and perhaps a great deal more information about your candidate.

Finally, check for gaps in employment. Sometimes individuals purposely forget to include previous employers who may not give them a good reference. Again phone calls to those listed may, in many cases, aid in filling in the blanks.

APPLICANTS

Bill must now begin to seek applicants for his sales position. Personal contacts are helpful in finding talented and dependable employees. When you begin your business, you may be able to bring some of your former colleagues to your organization. University professors may know some area students who want part-time work.

The classified ads in the "help wanted" section of local newspapers and other local publications are a possible source of candidates.

Employment agencies, both state and private, are also a source of applicants. The state agencies may or may not perform a detailed screening of applicants, depending on their staff and the state's unemployment levels. Private agencies will pre-screen. However, unlike state agencies, they charge a fee, to be paid by either the employee or the employer.

Schools, particularly vocational schools or two year colleges, provide a pool of individuals from which to choose. This is a free service, and gives you some knowledge of an interviewee's basic qualifications and ability to learn.

Your suppliers are also good sources of potential employees. In many cases they will be aware of a person's entry into the job market before that person is. They may tell you that an individual is unhappy at present, and would welcome a good offer. Suppliers and salespeople are also good judges of capabilities and can give you a good idea of an individual's potential.

Businesses similar to your own are closely related to this last source. Ethics come under consideration when hiring your competitor's personnel, but this *is* a source of employees.

INTERVIEWING

After screening applicants by using the application form, references, and the test, Bill is ready for the interviews. An interview should give Bill a chance to judge the applicant's ability to meet people and exchange information, an important ability for a sales job.

Two aspects of the interview must be stressed: It is the candidate's first exposure to the firm, and snap judgments are not always correct.

Since this is the first time the candidate views the potential work situation, honesty is imperative. Give the candidate a true picture of both yourself and your operations. Don't pretend to have an ideal situation. If you do, your new employee will find out later that you don't, and leave. This wastes time and money and can be avoided, in many cases, during the initial interview.

Personnel consultants agree that decisions to hire or not are usually made at some point early in the interview, probably too early. Don't jump to conclusions. Take your time. If it becomes evident that an individual doesn't fit, politely but firmly dismiss that person. You may be able to suggest some alternative employment. If the applicant seems like a good prospect make an offer. Now is the time to make the decision.

If the applicant declines your offer, find out why. The answer may aid you in future interviews and it could bring to light some misconceptions that are affecting the applicant's decision. In any event, the effort will be worthwhile.

SUMMARY

This chapter has discussed the organizational aspects of managing the small business. Bill Brady's objectives were used to illustrate many of the management concepts. Planning, coordinating, controlling, organizing, delegating, motivating, and leading were discussed. The personnel function was discussed, and the hiring process traced from job description to interviewing.

The following questions should help you analyze your operating or potential firm with regard to the concepts introduced in this chapter. There are no definitively right or wrong answers, but you should consider a "no" answer carefully, to determine whether you have neglected a basic part of your firm's management.

Rate your firm by the following questions:

1. Are measurable objectives for the firm fully described?
2. Have you fully described the type of business in which you are involved?
3. Do you have a complete description of your control systems: records, responsibilities set-up, measurable objectives, and time frames?
4. Do you have an up-to-date organization chart? Is it logical; that is, are like activities appropriately grouped?
5. Is everyone aware of the organization chart? Does everyone use it? If not, should it or should they be changed?
6. Do you have an organization chart for the next five years?
7. Are job descriptions available on all jobs?
8. Has a simple job evaluation and wage study been performed?
9. Have you recently done a time utilization analysis of yourself? Your key subordinates?
10. Do you have a list of your key personnel and their qualifications? Do these conform to their job description? Do these conform to their specific objectives?
11. Do you constantly seek outside information regarding your business: from customers? from friends? from suppliers?
12. Are you fully utilizing the educational facilities in your area?
13. Are your facilities and controls established to make your firm more efficient?
14. Are your wages a reflection of job evaluations and job descriptions?
15. Do you have written plans and procedures for reviewing your organization periodically?

STUDY QUESTIONS

1. Why is MBO particularly important to the owner of a small business?

2. Why is performance appraisal important to both the motivational and leadership functions of the small-business owner?

3. Why is a job evaluation system important to small business?

4. Why is time utilization important to small-business owners?

REFERENCES AND SUGGESTED READINGS

Anderson, R. E. "An OSHA checklist: is your plant in compliance?" *Industrial Relations*, July–August 1972, pp. 14–25.

Crites, Sherman E. "Of men and money: the problem of the small business," *Management Accounting*, April 1970, Vol. 101, pp. 14–16.

Goety, Billy E. "Management of risk in small new enterprises," *Society for the Advancement of Management Journal*, January 1973, pp. 21–27.

Hanan, Mack. "Venturing corporations — think small to stay strong," *Harvard Business Review*, May–June 1976, pp. 139–148.

Komives, John L. "Opportunities and problems of managers of small businesses," *Society for the Advancement of Management Journal*, October 1971, Vol. 36, pp. 73–76.

Kroeger, Carrol V. "Managerial development in the small firm" *California Management Review*, Fall 1974, Vol. 17, No. 1, pp. 41–47.

Markland, Robert E. "Can computers help the small businessman?" *Journal of Systems Management*, April 1972, pp. 27–30.

McConkey, Dale D. "Ecological problems facing small business," *Journal of Small Business Management*, Fall 1972, Vol. 10, pp. 1–6.

McKee, Wayne, W. "Small business can be computerized," *Management Accounting*, April 1972, pp. 49–52.

Newman, Louis E. "Advice for small company presidents," *Harvard Business Review*, November–December 1959, pp. 121–128.

Sandoval, Hilary. "The magic of good management," *Journal of Small Business Management*, Winter 1971, Vol. 9, pp. 6–7.

Schabacker, Joseph C. "So now you're president . . . says L. T. White," *Journal of Small Business Management*, Winter 1971, Vol. 9, pp. 21–25.

Steinmetz, Lawrence L. "Critical stages of small business growth," *Business Horizons*, February 1969, pp. 29–36.

CHAPTER 9

RECORDS FOR THE SMALL BUSINESS

INTRODUCTION

To determine whether objectives have been met, certain records must be maintained by the small business. Jack Larkin has demonstrated to Bill Brady the importance of controlling costs in relation to sales. Bill has become aware that he has concentrated primarily on selling rather than on cost effectiveness. Inadequate records are a sign of poor management in the small firm. Again, the level to which objectives have been accomplished cannot be ascertained unless adequate records are kept as indicators.

TYPES OF GENERAL RECORDS

The initial decision for any business is to determine the types of records that will be kept as part of the business. Chapter 7 discusses the pro forma statements, or budgets, that should be maintained. These include a balance sheet, sales projections by month, a collections schedule, purchases, cash receipts and disbursements, and an income statement.

Several other records must also be maintained, including depreciation schedules, inventory records, tax withholding records, FICA records, employment tax records, and other state and local records.

This chapter discusses these records and how they affect the small business.

MAINTENANCE OF THE RECORDS

There are three alternatives for where the business' records will be created and maintained: within the firm itself, through a

Certified Public Accountant, or through a public accountant. The choice depends on the abilities and time available in the firm.

The new owner may have to learn all the necessary forms, both state and federal, fill out these forms, and spend time updating the resulting files. This takes time away from the business. But one advantage is that the owner is constantly aware of the various aspects of the firm, especially if the firm is small and just getting started. Decisions can be made immediately without waiting for someone else to provide the information. The owner must determine if this time can be spent more profitably in the business. If so, another alternative must be used to maintain the records.

The two remaining ways to keep accurate and timely records are to use either public accountants or Certified Public Accountants. Individual states vary as to precisely how an accountant is defined; there are regulatory states and permissive states. The regulatory states specify the categories of licensed accountants within the state and the degree to which each category is required to pass licensing examinations. Within a regulatory state, both Certified Public Accountant and public accountant, accounting practitioner, or similar titles exist. The term Certified Public Accountant is consistent throughout all states. All C.P.A.'s are licensed by the State Board of Accountancy and, by virtue of their extensive knowledge, are permitted to render judgments on financial statements. Even in regulatory states, public accountants are not normally required to pass a qualifying examination. However, they are required to be licensed. In the permissive states, C.P.A.'s are, again, licensed by the State Board of Accountancy. However, public accountants need not either pass a qualifying examination or be licensed.

The small-business owner, when selecting an accountant, must recognize that a great deal of consistency exists among C.P.A.'s by virtue of their having passed the same qualifying examination. However, C.P.A. firms differ in their orientation. Some firms deal mainly with large firms, while others deal with all sizes of businesses. Some independent C.P.A.'s deal only with specialty groups such as professional associations. In any case, before selecting a C.P.A., the small-business owner should check with friends and other people in similar businesses to determine the best C.P.A. for the business.

Public accountants do not have the same licensing requirements, and so consistency of quality may be a problem. In many cases, they are strictly bookkeepers and offer little managerial advice. They usually charge less than C.P.A.'s.

Again the choice depends upon the needs of the business and its owner. The complexity of the business and the projected growth will have a bearing on the decision. If the finances are highly complicated, as in a firm involved in both construction and manufacturing, in which depreciation and changing land values must be evaluated, then a C.P.A. is certainly the first choice. If the finances are not complex, as in the case of an individual who builds one home at a time, a public accountant or bookkeeper should be sufficient.

SETTING UP ACCOUNTING CLASSIFICATIONS

For your accounting records to be useful in the management of your business, the various accounting classifications must be selected carefully. Often the new business owner does not take an active part in establishing the record keeping procedures. This procedure is often delegated to the person or firm designated to maintain the records. It must be recognized that the two basic objectives of accounting records are to provide profit information for the owners and various government agencies, and to provide information with which to manage the business effectively.

Too often, emphasis is placed solely on the first objective. However, in view of both objectives, the business owner will find it beneficial in the long run to participate actively in establishing the accounting classifications. The starting point in such a process is a review of typical financial statement formats for similar businesses.[1] The classifications within the accounting systems should then be tailored to your specific business. Bill Brady would find it worthwhile to expand his objective of increasing sales by 10 per cent and focus on increasing sales of the more profitable items. It is possible to divide Bill's products into three classifications: A, B, and C. These are general classifications and will vary according to the type of business, but this example demonstrates the concept.

Classification A would consist of items utilizing little storage area, hence small items, but of both high cost and high margin. Jewelry fits into this classification, as do some cosmetics. Classification B items would consist of fairly expensive specialty clothing utilizing more store area than A items, but their cost would be lower and their margins also lower. Women's dress blouses and men's dress shirts are examples of this classification. Finally, classification C would consist of high volume items requiring large store areas and having low margins. Sweat shirts and work clothes fit into this classification. Since Bill's firm sells several product classifications, it is beneficial to know, for each product classification:

1. the actual sales less allowances for each product or service;

---

[1]For example, see James, Marjorie D., ed. *Portfolio of Accounting Systems for Small and Medium-sized Businesses,* Prentice Hall, Englewood Cliffs, N.J., 1968.

2. the direct cost of goods sold for each product or service;
3. the gross profit for each product or service; and
4. those overhead expenses that cannot be directly allocated to any product or service; that is, those expenses which essentially continue regardless of the level of sales.

An example of such an income statement is shown in Table 9–1 and can be compared to Bill Brady's statement on page 99.

This example is certainly oversimplified but it illustrates the need to place your products into accounting classifications so that proper decisions can be made regarding item profitability. Bill's sales efforts should be concentrated on A items, and C items should be evaluated to determine if they are really necessary to his business.

One problem in setting up accounting classifications is the extent to which sales are broken down by products or services. Obviously, the greater the breakdown, the more costly it is to keep the financial records. The additional cost is offset by the greater amount of information developed with which to make decisions about the company. The owner's knowledge of the business is an asset in setting up the accounting classifications. Previous sections of this book have noted the need for experience in any given business. This experience will certainly be reflected in the record keeping system.

The second problem in establishing accounting classifications is the extent to which variable or direct costs, and fixed or overhead costs can be differentiated. Previous experience becomes important to this judgment. Referring to the income statement example in Figure 9–1, it is apparent that the more accurately the direct or variable expenses are defined, the more accurate the profit by product classification will be. The objective in setting up these accounting classifications should be to insure that as many

Table 9–1 ACCOUNTING CLASSIFICATIONS

		A		B		C
Net sales		$37,554		$56,331		$93,885
Inventory Jan. 1, 197–	12,240		10,710		7,651	
Purchase less discount	12,193		30,483		79,256	
	24,433		41,193		86,907	
Less inventory Dec. 31, 197–	14,679		9,572		2,288	
Cost of goods sold		9,754		31,621		84,619
Gross margin		27,800		24,710		9,266
Total expenses (all other expenses allocated evenly)		20,155		20,155		20,155
Net profit before taxes		$ 7,645		$ 4,555		$(–10,889)

variable expenses as possible are defined and subsequently removed from the overhead expenses category. The method of defining variable expenses will vary from business to business, as well as from individual to individual. It is important that criteria for defining variable costs are established that are meaningful to the business and individual. One definition of direct or variable expense is that the particular expense varies directly with the number of units sold. In Bill's case, his purchases are directly related to his sales, and so, are variable. However, employees or salespeople are needed all the time and their wages are a fixed overhead item. The cost is there whether they make a sale or not. This, then, is a fixed cost, or overhead.

A decision must be made regarding the propriety of the cost criteria in a number of such situations in establishing accounting classifications. The higher the percentage of expenses that can be classified as either variable or direct, the greater the amount of information the owner will have on which to base decisions. The more information, the more likely the small business is to be efficiently managed.

TIMING OF FINANCIAL INFORMATION

A related question regards the timeliness of the information received from the financial records. If financial statements are prepared once a year, much of the information is out of date. Information received in January is of little use for making a decision in the preceding March. The frequency of financial statements will vary to some extent with the type of business and the degree to which the business is seasonal or fashion oriented. However, most business owners err on the side of not having statements prepared often enough. The advantages of having monthly statements are that you have current profit and management control information, and that you can develop excellent records over time by which you can compare your results. For example, you can compare cost of goods sold as a per cent of sales for January of 1980 with January of 1978. If January, 1978, was acceptable and CGS has increased as a percentage of sales, the change should be investigated. Setting up an accounting system is extremely important. The small-business owner should take an active part in defining this system.

BILL'S OBJECTIVES AND PRODUCT CLASSIFICATIONS

The account classifications will help Bill measure his objectives for sales, gross margin, inventory, advertising, and internal operations. Again, the measures are important to an effective MBO program.

The sales and gross margin objective measures are obvious; objectives for inventory will be covered later in this chapter. The advertising objective can be accomplished by concentrating ads on the A classification items, or at least by drawing people into the store to buy those items. In internal operations, the A and B classifications should be protected from pilferage. These items should also be prominently displayed since they are high margin items.

INCOME AND EXPENSE REPORTING — CASH OR ACCRUAL

Two basic methods exist to report the income and expenses of the business. The cash basis method of reporting specifies that income and expenses are reported for tax purposes in the year that payment is actually received or that the expense is actually paid. For example, if the company taxes are paid on a calendar year basis and a sale is made in September, 1978, but not collected until February, 1979, the income is reported in 1979. The same procedure applies to payment of any expense associated with the business. A number of small service firms utilize this method.

The second method of reporting, the accrual basis method, is more common. This method specifies that income and expenses are reported for tax purposes as they are earned or incurred, as opposed to when they are received or paid out. Taxes are paid in 1978 on a sale made in September of that year even though payment will not be received until the next tax year. Again, the same procedure applies to expenses incurred in one taxable year but not paid until a succeeding taxable year. It is generally felt that the accrual basis provides the owner with both a more stable financial report and one more representative of the actual condition of the company.

DEPRECIATION SCHEDULES

Depreciation is the method used by the Internal Revenue Service to permit an annual expense deduction for assets with a life expectancy greater than one year. Depreciation is a non-cash expense with the sole function of reducing taxes. Numerous methods exist for calculating the annual amount of depreciation. The purpose of having different methods of depreciation is to attempt to provide equity to a wide range of businesses by writing off fixed assets such as machinery, cars, and buildings. If you have an established business in a stable industry, you choose a depreciation method that permits equal annual deductions over the estimated life of the asset. If you are in a business in which changes in technology or market are rapid, you choose an accelerated depreciation method to write off the asset as rapidly as possible. If you are starting a business in which you do not expect to generate a profit for several years, you probably prefer a depreciation schedule that permits greater deductions in later years when the expense will be more beneficial from a tax standpoint. If yours is a rapidly growing company in which you can predict working capital shortages, you may wish to avail yourself of special provisions in the tax laws that permit extraordinarily large first-year depreciation schedules.

Regardless of the depreciation method used, however, only the value of the asset minus its salvage value can be depreciated and subsequently considered expense. The depreciation method merely determines the timing of the depreciation expenses. The basic information necessary to establish a depreciation schedule is the cost or market value of an asset, its useful life, corresponding to guidelines established by the I.R.S., its estimated salvage value, and the depreciation method. You will need to check with the I.R.S. if you are keeping your own books. If you are using a C.P.A. or an accountant you will be supplied such information.

SINGLE OR DOUBLE ENTRY BOOKKEEPING

In many ways, the question of single or double entry bookkeeping is academic. If the services of a professional accountant are utilized, you will need a double entry system, which has proved its value over centuries of use. The primary advantages of double entry bookkeeping are that it provides a system with great accuracy, and that it is reliable in the event of outside audit or dishonest employees. However, the single entry system is used in many businesses. Its primary advantages are its simplicity and the small amount of time it requires. A single entry system is generally used in a simple business, in a strictly one-person business, or in a business just getting started. Most office supply stores and trade associations maintain supplies of forms for single entry systems for a wide variety of businesses.

INVENTORY VALUATION

The method by which business inventories are valued affects the size of the profit and, subsequently, the amount of taxes paid. Careful consideration should be given to the valuation method,

Table 9-2 PROFIT CALCULATION

	Sales	Beginning Inventory	Purchases	1500 Units Ending Inventory			Profit	Taxes (50%)
II. Cost method (a) LIFO	$15,000	$ 4,000	$16,000	1000 @ $4.00 500 @ $8.00			$ 3,000	$ 1,500
(b) FIFO	$15,000	$ 4,000	$16,000	1500 @ $8.00			$ 7,000	$ 3,500
				Cost	Market	Lower of cost or market		
II. Lower of cost or market	$15,000	$ 4,000	$16,000	$12,000	$10,500	$10,500	$ 5,500	$ 2,750

since I.R.S. permission is required to switch once you have decided on a particular method.

The I.R.S. approves both the cost method and lower of cost or market method of inventory valuation. In the event that the cost method is chosen, either LIFO (last in — first out) or FIFO (first in — first out) may be used to place a dollar value on the inventory. In the event that the lower of cost or market method is chosen, the dollar value is obtained from a comparison of the actual cost with an estimate of its current market value. These methods are demonstrated in Table 9–2.

Table 9–2 illustrates how inventory valuation is directly related to profit calculation, and to taxes. Assume a beginning inventory of 1000 units valued at $4000 from both the cost and market valuation. Purchases during the year totaled 2000 units at $8.00 a unit. Sales volume during the year was 1500 units at $10.00 a unit. Inventory at year end was 1500 units. The market value at year end was $7.00 a unit. Table 9–2 portrays in a simple manner how the inventory valuation method influences profit and taxes.

The inventory valuation method obviously affects the amount of taxes paid in a specific tax year. The decision on inventory valuation method should be carefully considered with respect to both the specific business involved and the advice of a professional accountant.

SPECIFIC TYPES OF ACCOUNTING RECORDS AND FORMS NEEDED FOR MBO

THE BALANCE SHEET

Bill Brady's balance sheet illustrates his financial position as of December 31, 197–. This balance sheet was used by Jack to calculate the financial ratios on page 105. The first ratio, current assets to current debt, is one test of solvency or a measure of the business assets that are available to meet all debts due within one year. The low ratio indicates that Bill may have difficulty acquiring short-term financing.

The second ratio, net profit to tangible net worth, indicates how well invested capital is being utilized in the firm. Again the ratio is low, demonstrating that net worth is not being utilized to its full extent. Costs are affecting the level of net profit and should be of concern to Bill.

The third ratio, net sales to tangible net worth, demonstrates that sales are high relative to the industry. Referring to the second ratio, this reemphasizes the fact that costs are too high and that Bill is not taking advantage of his higher sales in terms of profit.

The fourth ratio, net sales to net working capital, denotes how well the working capital of the firm is utilized. In Bill's case, the ratio is high, signifying that he is doing well in terms of utilizing his working capital or cash. However, it is not so high that he is vulnerable to creditors.

The fifth ratio, current debt to tangible net worth, measures what Bill owes relative to what he owns. The larger this ratio, the more creditors have invested in the business. In this case, Bill's large debt could hinder his ability to borrow and so take advantage of cash sales by his wholesalers.

All of these ratios are related to Bill's ratio objective. He can now ascertain the variables he must consider in attaining this objective. This will assist Bill in making MBO work.

SALES PROJECTION BY MONTH

Bill needs this projection to assist him in meeting and measuring his sales objective: increasing sales by 10 per cent. He should also refer to his product classifications to insure that he is concentrating on the most profitable sales and not simply sales for the sake of sales.

COLLECTIONS SCHEDULE

Bill needs this schedule so that he can age his accounts receivable and discontinue credit on his slow-paying customers. He should also contact individuals as soon as they pass the safe collections period. This will assist Bill in accomplishing his bad debt and collections objective.

PURCHASE SCHEDULE

This schedule is necessary to insure that Bill fully utilize both trade credit and trade discounts to meet his gross margin objective. Trade credit is used to purchase inventories for resale as well as supplies of an expendable nature to be used in the operation of Bill's business. Trade credit is represented on Bill's balance sheet as accounts payable. In many instances, trade credit can provide large proportions of the funds needed to operate the business. For Bill to qualify for trade credit, his ratios must be in line with that of the industry.

Once Bill qualifies for trade credit, a wide variety of terms are available. Examples of a few are:

Terms of Sale	Explanation
1/10	1 per cent discount for payment in ten days — no other conditions;
1/10, n/30	1 per cent discount for payment in ten days — if not paid in ten days, entire invoice must be paid within 30 days with no discount;
E.O.M.	The company will be billed at the end of a specific month for all purchases made during that month;
3/10, n/30, R.O.G.	3 per cent discount for payment within ten days — entire invoice to be paid within 30 days; however, both the discount terms and the net terms start upon the receipt of the goods — not on the date of sale;
1/10, n/30, E.O.M.	1 per cent discount for payment within 10 days — entire invoice to be paid within 30 days; however, both the discount terms and the net terms begin at the end of the month in which the sale was made.

Bill's objective is to avail himself of as much credit as possible. He now realizes that good credit terms are given to good credit risks, and will work to make himself a good risk.

CASH RECEIPTS AND DISBURSEMENTS

As shown in Chapter 7, this statement demonstrates the cash flows in and out of the business. Without this statement, Bill is unaware of whether he can expand or take advantage of discounts. To fulfill his gross margin objective, he must utilize this statement to determine the number of discounts he has missed.

INCOME STATEMENT

Bill's income statement, broken down by product classifications, was shown in Table 9–1. He certainly needs this to maximize both sales and profits, as has been discussed.

TAX FORMS

There are a number of Federal Income Tax forms that must be completed by the small business. The Internal Revenue Service has prepared a "Mr. Businessman's Kit" which contains "Circular 'E' — employer's tax guide" to explain, and assist you in preparing these tax payments. In handling these taxes, it should be remembered that these monies are *not* to be used as working capital. The kit will also explain how you can get a federal identification number.

Forms exist covering state sales taxes, state income tax, unemployment insurance tax, and worker's compensation, as well as forms covering inventory and property taxes, and business licenses. These state taxes vary, and your accountant will be of assistance to you in determining the forms applicable to your business. If you have decided not to use an accountant, your state tax office will be able to assist you.

INVENTORY RECORDS

Inventory costs are important to Bill. He must weigh his buying trips against inventory carrying costs. Inventory policies vary by type of business. For a manufacturer, a high level of raw materials and goods-in-process inventory is costly. However, if raw materials are scarce and some orders are prepaid, then these inventory costs are worthwhile. All inventory decisions are specific to a business firm. A note of caution: make sure that *you* make such decisions. Salespeople for suppliers like to have you carry larger and larger inventories of their goods. The owner of a small grocery store recently related that he had fourteen cases of gallon jars of olives stored in front of his shelves. When asked why, he replied that he had no room for them in his storage area. Why then had he purchased them? Because they were a good buy. How many jars had been sold in the last six months? Two. This store owner is carrying someone else's inventory and not making the decision himself. Bill must take care that *he* does not overcommit himself to fashion sensitive inventory, since it can lose its value very quickly.

Inventory costs vary, depending on the business. Basically, they are: opportunity costs in terms of money and space, losses due to spoilage and obsolescence, the cost of insuring merchandise, and losses due to out-of-stock items.

Inventory control systems range from very simple to highly complex. The majority of small-business owners use perpetual inventories, supplemented with the usual controls and a periodic year end count. There are various methods of inventory control with a perpetual system; the two most common are bin cards and sales tickets. By checking the updated ledger and the bin cards, the retailer can check how much of a particular item is in stock. Reorders usually occur when visual inspections warrant them.

A monthly count of items is needed to control pilferage in the small business. This count should concentrate on costly items, and the ABC classification inventory system allows the owner to do this.

Table 9-1 demonstrates the importance of these classifications to Bill. His A products are small and very expensive, his B products are less expensive, and his C products are the least expensive, bulky items. Products in the A category certainly take up less space than the others, yet for Bill they have the highest profit. Bill's trade, however, is based on being a full-line store (A, B, and C products), so he cannot simply drop *all* C items or he would lose his customers. But, he should consider the need for each C item.

In a manufacturing firm, a few items — 10 to 20 per cent — account for a high percentage — 60 per cent — of the value of inventory. These are A items. Fifty to 60 per cent of the items in the inventory may account for only 20 per cent of the value of the inventory. These are C items. The B items are those that fall in between. The C items obviously do not require the stringent controls that A and B items do, since they do not compose the major proportion of the inventory investment. However, A and B items should be carefully controlled through perpetual inventories.

The other items in inventory that require careful attention are mainstay items. Processes may depend on them or your customers may depend on being able to get them from you. In either case, careful attention to these items is needed regardless of their dollar value. Poor inventory control can be very costly if you cannot provide the item that your customer requests. Therefore, having too little invested in inventory can be as unprofitable as having too much invested. Again, Bill must carry all three types of item to realize his profit on his A products.

QUALITY AND COSTS

Quality records are always necessary for the small business. They represent a cost to the business: too high a quality level may increase not sales, but costs. A child's plastic, $1.98 toy, manufactured to exact specifications, is an example of too high quality. Too low a quality level will lose customers quickly, when they do not receive what they have paid for.

A manufacturer must meet quality expectations which are usually explicit. A service firm's quality can be judged by results: does or doesn't the service work? Retailing is not as easily measured; quality in products is subjective. Most small stores are consistent in the quality of their merchandise. Thus, customers tend to identify the small firm with a particular quality level, and each store maintains its own personality.

Records must be maintained by retailers like Bill to check on the quality of their merchandise. This can be done by analyzing complaints for each product. Quality of customer service must also be observed. Chapter 8 explains the relationships between management and quality.

SUMMARY

This chapter has described the various records that must be maintained to insure that the business is managed efficiently. The need for these records was demonstrated by using the case of "The man who managed his business by ear," and by detailing the objectives Bill Brady should draw from the case. Quality has also been shown to be an important aspect of the records system.

STUDY QUESTIONS

1. What do you feel are the three most important records to the manager of a small business? Explain your reasons.

2. Explain how an ABC type of inventory system differs among retailing, wholesaling, and manufacturing firms. How is it similar?

3. Do the records discussed in this chapter completely measure Bill Brady's financial objectives? If not, what other records are needed?

REFERENCES AND SUGGESTED READINGS

"Beating the cash crisis," *Small Business Reporter,* 1975, pp. 1–8.

Berg, Charles J. "Cutting overhead," *Journal of Systems Management,* February 1972, pp. 24–27.

Deardem, John. "Profit-planning accounting for small firms," *Harvard Business Review,* March-April 1963, pp. 32–42.

Etzel, Michael J. "How much does credit cost the small merchant?" *Journal of Retailing,* Summer 1971, Vol. 47, No. 2, pp. 52–92.

Grablowsky, Bernie J. "Management of accounts receivable by small business," *Journal of Small Business Management,* October, 1976, pp. 23–28.

Jones, Dorothy, ed. "Avoiding management pitfalls," *Small Business Reporter,* 1973, Vol. 11, No. 5, pp. 1–15.

Jones, Gardner M., and Saber A. Awad. "The use of accounting techniques in small firms," *Management Accounting,* February, 1972, pp. 41–44.

Welsh, John A., and Jerry F. White. "Keeping score in business: an accounting primer for entrepreneurs," *Journal of Small Business Management,* October, 1976, pp. 29–40.

CHAPTER 10

THE FUTURE: COPING WITH CHANGE AND UNCERTAINTY

INTRODUCTION

Small businesses have been an integral part of American society since its inception. They have allowed individuals the freedom to enter, expand, or leave their own businesses. They have also allowed them the opportunity to fail.

Small businesses, particularly in service areas and areas requiring specialized services, have been able to do a more effective job than large firms. Small businesses have also provided a plethora of new ideas and materials for our economy. The small-business owner, in many cases, will take the risk that a larger firm will not. The practice of discovering competitive niches and exploiting them has insured the survival of the small firm. However, as you have seen, many small ventures fail.

This chapter is devoted to specifying for you a number of the risks facing the small-business owner and how, by referring to the material in the text, such risks can be minimized. Remember the major asset that you can use to minimize risk in a small business is *SOUND MANAGEMENT*.

RISKS FOR SMALL BUSINESSES

Basically, risks facing the small business are the same as those facing any organization; however, for most small firms, these risks are magnified.

The Loss of a Competitive Niche. A competitor will attempt to gain your competitive niche if the niche becomes profitable enough. You may find that you are competing with the larger firms when the profit margin warrants their entry.

Changes in Demand. The tastes of the consuming public are difficult to predict. Demand is altered by a number of uncertain factors. For instance, during our intense energy shortage, demand for locking gas caps rose sharply. One gas station owner in a metropolitan area was able to sell four cases of caps that were in storage since 1945. Keeping this inventory did not force the station out of business since it was only a small part of the total inventory; however, a single-product firm may be severely damaged when faced with a decline in demand for that product.

Damage to the Business. This category covers such areas as natural disasters, stealing, employee theft, vandalism, and carelessness.

Shoplifting and employee pilferage are constant problems. Winds, storms, tornadoes, rain, hail, and lightning are all damaging disasters. Many instances of damage are simply the result of carelessness. Glasses are dropped, equipment is broken, and displays are ruined. These things may happen as a result of customer, employee, or your own carelessness.

Out-of-date Management. Managerial obsolescence is a constant problem facing the small-business owner, particularly in businesses that change rapidly. Managers can become dated in both managerial techniques and the technical aspects of their business.

Death of Key Individuals. A number of organizations grow in size, but remain a "one person company." The majority of contacts and operating procedures are all vested in a single individual. Should something happen to this "key" person, the firm would suffer irreparable damage, perhaps even termination.

Improper Financial Planning. This has been noted by almost everyone concerned with small businesses as a primary problem. An inability to predict cash flows and cash requirements can create serious problems. This is particularly true when there is no large "buffer" of cash in the firm.

Liability of the Business. The risk always exists that a legal action will be taken against the firm. Such suits may range from EEO violations against employees, to customers who feel that you have failed to fulfill their contracts. Suits may be brought by former employees because they did not receive a fair accounting of all that was due them when leaving the business. In *all* these cases you need competent legal advice since any of them may have to be settled by the court.

These are the major risks facing a small business. They are not all-inclusive, but they do represent major areas of risk which you must minimize to insure that your business is successful.

MINIMIZING RISK

The Loss of a Competitive Niche. This risk can be minimized by constantly looking for new niches to keep your business as vigorous as it was at initiation. You should also welcome competition; it keeps you sharp. However, you must keep abreast of your competitors and insure that you are still offering better goods and services.

Chapter 5 will assist you in updating your sales objectives. Chapter 6 insures that you keep both site and location in mind while planning. A good location now may not suffice in five years. Chapter 7 helps insure that you keep your budget in mind all the time. Finally, careful reviews of your MBO program, as demonstrated in Chapter 8, should predict risks before they become problems.

Changes in Demand. To minimize this problem, you must be constantly aware of what is occurring in your market. A constant reevaluation of the factors of the business plan, reviewed in Chapter 3, is extremely important. Remember how you determined your initial forecasts and keep doing them. Do not deny reality. If demand for your product is changing, change with it; don't say that the change doesn't exist.

Damage to the Business. The effect of crime on business is discussed in Chapter 8. Remember that the layout in a retail store is an important control and that control systems such as check-out lists are important in controlling inventories in all types of firms.

Insurance is the key protection for disasters. Don't become insurance-poor but remember that, because of inflation, you may not be able to replace your assets at their initial cost. A yearly reevaluation of insurance is a necessity to minimize this risk.

Out-Of-Date Management. There is no guaranteed method to avoid your own obsolescence; however, there are precautions that you can take. Subscribe to and read at least two journals in your particular field. Subscribe to and read a management journal aimed at the operating manager. Finally, you should attend one meeting a year that will put you in contact with individuals in your business. From one meeting, you can get a multitude of ideas. The sales displays always prevalent at such meetings are also innovative. Go to learn and you will.

Death of Key Individuals. There are two ways of protecting your business from the traumatic experience of losing a key individual. First, your firm should be organized to allow an orderly succession of management. As shown in Chapter 8, there should be someone who can move into every position to insure that the basic functions are routinely performed. Job descriptions are also an aid.

Second, key individuals should be insured. This gives your firm funds to recruit a new individual.

Improper Financial Planning. Chapter 7 provides the key to minimizing this risk. It is imperative that carefully formulated pro forma statements are established and utilized.

Liability of the Business. Careful attention to current regulations is needed in this area. Also, insurance can be a hedge against a number of these risks. Don't forget that being right and proving it may take a large amount of your time. Don't hesitate to compromise when necessary.

SUMMARY AND CONCLUSIONS

This book is directed at assisting you in attaining success in your business. Use it for that purpose. Refer back to the text material and the checklists as you make your many decisions. Above all, remember: the key to success is you and your ability and desire to manage your business effectively.

REFERENCES AND SUGGESTED READINGS

Carrington, James H., and Jeanne M. Aurello. "Survival tactics for the small business," *Business Horizons,* February, 1976, pp. 13–24.

Charlesworth, Harold K. "The uncertain future of small business: can this picture be changed?" *MSU Business Topics,* Spring, 1970, pp. 13–20.

Donham, Paul. "Whither small business?" *Harvard Business Review,* March–April, 1957, pp. 23–31.

Goetz, Billy E. "Management of risk in small new enterprises," *S.A.M. Advanced Management Journal,* January, 1973, pp. 21–27.

Golde, Robert A. "Practical planning for small businesses," *Harvard Business Review,* Vol. 42, No. 5, September–October, 1964, pp. 147–161.

"Meeting the competition of giants," *Harvard Business Review,* Vol. 45, May–June, 1967, pp. 172–184.

Wheelwright, Steven C. "Strategic planning in the small business," *Business Horizons,* August 1971, pp. 51–58.

Woodward, Herbert N, "Management strategies for small companies," *Harvard Business Review,* January–February, 1976, pp. 113–121.

APPENDIX I

Checklists for small–business owners

Checklists are extremely useful to managers. They do not provide complete answers to all decision problems, but they do offer decision-making guidelines. Checklists demonstrate a number of alternatives that, while they may be rejected, at least should be considered.

The following checklists are guides to the successful initiation and management of small firms. The checklists bring up many questions, but experience demonstrates that these questions must be answered if a business is to be successful. Most importantly, a checklist provides a structure to point out potential problems before they occur.

The following checklists have been constructed on the experiences of small businesses. Checklist A covers items that should be carefully considered when contemplating the initiation of a business venture. Checklist B provides guidelines for evaluating a potential franchise operation. Checklist C gives general factors to consider when buying an ongoing firm. Checklist D provides bases for evaluating possible locations for a business, and Checklist E provides guidelines for site analysis. Checklist F provides aid in evaluating the potential market for your output. Checklist G allows an evaluation of advertising. Checklist H covers interior layout.

These checklists should be utilized carefully both during the initiation phase of your business and also, periodically, during the life of your business.

CHECKLIST A

This checklist contains the items that individuals should consider before beginning a new firm. There is no set number of "yes" answers that guarantees success; however, there should certainly be a large number of "yeses" relative to "nos."

CHECKLIST FOR STARTING A BUSINESS

check if
answer
Are you the type?   is "yes"

Have you rated your personal qualifications using a
scale similar to that presented in Chapter 1 of this
book?   _____

Have you had some objective evaluators rate you on
such scales?   _____

Have you carefully considered your weak points
and taken steps to improve them or to find an associate whose strong points will compensate for them?   _____

What business should you choose?

Have you written a summary of your background and
experience to help you in making this decision?   _____

Have you considered your hobbies and what you like
to do?   _____

Does anyone want the services you can perform?   _____

Have you studied surveys and sought advice and
counsel to find out what fields of business may be expected to expand?   _____

Have you considered working for someone else to
gain more experience?   _____

What are your chances for success?

Are general business conditions good?   _____

Are business conditions good in the city and neigh-
hood where you plan to locate?   _____

Are current conditions good in the line of business
you plan to start?   _____

What will be your return on investment?

Do you know the typical return on investment in the
line of business you plan to start?   _____

Have you determined how much you will have to in-
vest in your business?   _____

Source: Wendell O. Metcalf. *Starting and Managing a Small Business of Your Own,* Washington, D.C.: 1973. Small Business Administration, pp. 87–94.

check if
answer
is "yes"

Are you satisfied that the rate of return on the money you invest in the business will be greater than the rate you would probably receive if you invested the money elsehwere? _____

How much money will you need?

Have you filled out worksheets similar to those shown at the end of this checklist? _____

In filling out the worksheets have you taken care not to overestimate income? _____

Have you obtained quoted prices for equipment and supplies you will need? _____

Do you know the costs of goods which must be in your inventory? _____

Have you estimated expenses only after checking rents, wage scales, utility rates, and other pertinent costs in the area where you plan to locate? _____

Have you found what percentage of your estimated sales your projected inventory and expense items are and compared each percentage with the typical percentage for your line of business? _____

Have you added an additional amount of money to your estimates to allow for unexpected contingencies? _____

Where can you get the money?

Have you decided how much money of your own you can put into the business? _____

Do you know how much credit you can get from your suppliers—the people you will buy from? _____

Do you know where you can borrow the rest of the money you need to start your business? _____

Have you selected a progressive bank with the credit services you may need? _____

Have you talked to a banker about your plans? _____

Does the banker have an interested, helpful attitude toward your problems? _____

Should you share ownership with others?

If you need a partner with money or know-how that you don't have, do you know someone who will fit— someone you can get along with? _____

check if
answer
is "yes"

Do you know the good and bad points about going it alone, having a partner, and incorporating your business?

Have you talked to a lawyer about this? _____

Where should you locate?

Have you studied the make-up of the population in the city or town where you plan to locate? _____

Do you know what kind of people will want to buy what you plan to sell? _____

Do people like that live in the area where you want to locate? _____

Have you checked the number, type, and size of competitors in the area? _____

Does the area need another business like the one you plan to open? _____

Are employees available? _____

Have you checked and found adequate: utilities, parking facilities, police and fire protection, available housing, schools, and other cultural and community activities? _____

Do you consider costs of the location reasonable in terms of taxes and average rents? _____

Is there sufficient opportunity for growth and expansion? _____

Have you checked the relative merits of the various shopping areas within the city, including shopping centers? _____

In selecting the actual site, have you compared it with others by using a score sheet similar to the one shown in Chapter 6? _____

Have you had a lawyer check the lease and zoning? _____

Should you buy a going business?

Have you considered the advantages and disadvantages of buying a going business? _____

Have you compared what it would cost to equip and stock a new business with the price asked for the business you are considering buying? _____

How much should you pay for it?

Have you estimated sales and profits of the going business for the next few years? _____

check if
answer
is "yes"

Are your projected profits satisfactory? _____

Have you looked at past financial statements of the business to find the return on investment, sales, and profit trends? _____

Have you verified the owner's claims about the business with reports from an independent accountant's analysis of the figures? _____

Is the inventory you will purchase a good buy? _____

Are equipment and fixtures fairly valued? _____

If you plan to buy the accounts receivable, are they worth the asking price? _____

Have you been careful in your appraisal of the company's good will? _____

Are you prepared to assume the company's liabilities and are the creditors agreeable? _____

Have you learned why the present owner wants to sell? _____

Have you found out about the present owner's reputation with employees and suppliers? _____

Have you consulted a lawyer to be sure that the title is good? _____

Has your lawyer checked to find out if there is any lien against the assets you are buying? _____

Has your lawyer drawn up an agreement covering all essential points, including a seller's warranty for your protection against false statements? _____

Should you invest in a franchise?

Have you considered how the advantages and disadvantages of franchising apply to you? _____

Have you made a thorough search to find the right franchise opportunity? _____

Have you evaluated the franchise by answering the questions in Checklist B? _____

Have you worked out plans for buying?

Have you estimated what share of the market you think you can get? _____

Do you know how much or how many of each item of merchandise you will buy to open your business? _____

Have you found suppliers who will sell you what you need at a good price? _____

Do you have a plan for finding out what your customers want? _____

Have you set up a model stock assortment to follow in your buying? _____

Have you worked out stock control plans to avoid over-stocks, under-stocks, and out-of-stocks? _____

Do you plan to buy most of your stock from a few suppliers rather than a little from many, so that those you buy from will want to help you succeed? _____

How will you price your products and services?

Have you decided upon your price ranges? _____

Do you know how to figure what you should charge to cover your costs? _____

Do you know what your competitors charge? _____

What selling methods will you use?

Have you studied the selling and sales promotion methods of competitors? _____

Have you studied why customers buy your type of product or service? _____

Have you thought about why you like to buy from some sales people while others turn you off? _____

Have you decided what your methods of selling will be? _____

Have you outlined your sales promotion policy? _____

How will you select and train personnel?

If you need to hire someone to help you, do you know where to look? _____

Do you know what kind of person you need? _____

Have you written a job description for each person you will need? _____

Do you know the prevailing wage scales? _____

Do you have a plan for training new employees? _____

Will you continue training through good supervision? _____

What other management problems will you face?

Do you plan to sell for credit? _____

If you do, do you have the extra capital necessary to carry accounts receivable? _____

Have you made a policy for returned goods? _____

Have you planned how you will make deliveries? _____

check if
answer
is "yes"

Have you considered other policies that must be made in your particular business? _____

Have you made a plan to guide yourself in making the best use of your time and effort? _____

What records will you keep?

Have you planned a system of records that will keep track of your income and expenses, what you owe other people, and what other people owe you? _____

Have you worked out a way to keep track of your inventory so that you will always have enough on hand for your customers but not more than you can sell? _____

Have you planned your method for keeping payroll records and taking care of tax reports and payments? _____

Do you know what financial statements you should prepare? _____

Do you know how to use these financial statements? _____

Have you obtained standard operating ratios for your type of business, which you plan to use as guides? _____

Do you know an accountant who will help you with your records and financial statements? _____

What laws will affect you?

Have you checked with the proper authorities to find out what, if any, licenses to do business are necessary? _____

Do you know what police and health regulations apply to your business? _____

Will your operations be subject to interstate commerce regulations? _____

If so, do you know to which ones? _____

Have you received advice from your lawyer regarding your responsibilities under federal and state laws and local ordinances? _____

How will you handle taxes and insurance?

Have you worked out a system for handling the withholding tax for your employees? _____

Have you worked out a system for handling sales taxes? Excise taxes? _____

Have you planned an adequate record system for the efficient preparation of income tax forms? _____

Have you prepared a worksheet for meeting tax obligations?

Have you talked with an insurance agent about what kinds of insurance you will need, and how much it will cost?   ⎯⎯⎯⎯⎯

Will you set measurable goals for yourself?

Have you set goals and sub-goals for yourself?   ⎯⎯⎯⎯⎯

Have you specified dates when each goal is to be achieved?   ⎯⎯⎯⎯⎯

Are these realistic goals; that is, will they challenge you, but at the same time not call for unreasonable accomplishment?   ⎯⎯⎯⎯⎯

Are the goals specific, so you can measure performance?   ⎯⎯⎯⎯⎯

Have you developed a business plan, as shown in Chapter 3?   ⎯⎯⎯⎯⎯

Have you allowed for obstacles?   ⎯⎯⎯⎯⎯

Will you keep up to date?

Have you made plans to keep up with improvements in your trade or industry?   ⎯⎯⎯⎯⎯

Have you prepared a business plan, which will be amended as circumstances demand?   ⎯⎯⎯⎯⎯

WORKSHEET 1

Estimated monthly expenses		Your estimate of how much cash you need to start your business (See Column 3)	What to put in Column 2 (These figures are typical for one kind of business; you will have to decide how many months to allow for in your business)
Item	Your estimnate of monthly expenses based on sales of $ ___ per year		
	Column 1	Column 2	Column 3
Salary of owner-manager	$	$	2 times Column 1
All other salaries and wages			2 times Column 1
Rent			3 times Column 1
Advertising			3 times Column 1
Delivery expense			3 times Column 1
Supplies			3 times Column 1
Telephone and telegraph			3 times Column 1
Other utilities			3 times Column 1
Insurance			Payment required by insurance company
Taxes, including Social Security			4 times Column 1
Interest			3 times Column 1
Maintenance			3 times Column 1
Legal and other professional fees			3 times Column 1
Starting costs you only have to pay once			**Leave Column 2 blank**
Fixtures and equipment			Fill in worksheet 2 and put the total here
Decorating and remodeling			Talk it over with a contractor
Installation of fixtures and equipment			Talk to suppliers from whom you buy these
Starting inventory			Suppliers will probably help you estimate this
Deposits with public utilities			Find out from utility companies
Legal and other professional fees			Lawyer, accountant, and so on
Licenses and permits			Find out from city offices what you need
Advertising and promotion for opening			Estimate what you will use
Accounts receivable			What you need to buy more stock until credit customers pay
Cash			For unexpected expenses or losses, special purchases, and so on
Other			Make a separate list and enter total
Total estimated cash you need to start with		$	Add up all the numbers in Column 2

WORKSHEET 2

List of furniture, fixtures, and equipment

Leave out or add items to suit your business. Use separate sheets to list exactly what you need for each of these items.	If you plan to pay cash in full, enter the full amount below and in the last column.	If you are going to pay by installments, fill out the columns below. Enter in the last column your downpayment plus at least one installment.			Estimate of the cash you need for furniture, fixtures, and equipment.
		Price	Down-payment	Amount of each installment	
Counters	$	$	$	$	$
Storage shelves, cabinets					
Display stands, shelves, tables					
Cash register					
Safe					
Window display fixtures					
Special lighting					
Outside sign					
Delivery equipment, if needed					
Total furniture, fixtures, and equipment (Enter this figure also in Worksheet 1 under "Starting costs you only have to pay once."					$

* Source: "Checklist For Going Into Business," Small Marketers Aid No. 71, Washington, D.C.: Small Business Administration, 1972.

CHECKLIST B

This checklist must be carefully evaluated before you make any contractual commitments to a franchise company. There are a number of excellent franchises available that offer marketing and managerial assistance to the franchisee. There are also a number of companies that fail to provide these services. This checklist will alert the user to potential problem areas with a particular franchise.

CHECKLIST FOR EVALUATING A FRANCHISE

FRANCHISE INDEX/PROFILE

General

1. Is the product or service: *yes*   *no*
   a. considered reputable?   _____   _____
   b. part of a growing market?   _____   _____
   c. needed in your area?   _____   _____
   d. of interest to you?   _____   _____

Source: C. R. Stigelman. *Franchise Index/Profile,* Small Business Management Series, No. 35, Washington, D.C.: Small Business Administration, 1973, pp. 31–41.

	yes	no

e. safe,   _____ _____

   protected,   _____ _____

   covered by guarantee?   _____ _____

f. connected with a well-known
   personality, a sound franchise without
   a well-known personality?   _____ _____

2. Is the franchise:

  a. local?   _____ _____

     regional?   _____ _____

     national?   _____ _____

     international?   _____ _____

  b. full-time?   _____ _____

     part-time?   _____ _____

     possibly full-time in the future?   _____ _____

3. Existing franchises

  a. What date was the company founded and what date was the first franchise awarded? Company founded? _____
First franchise awarded? _____

  b. Number of franchises currently in operation or under construction. _____ Information on those to contact:

     Franchise 1: owner _____

                 address _____

                 _____

                 telephone _____

                 date started _____

     Franchise 2: owner _____

                 address _____

                 _____

                 telephone _____

                 date started _____

     Franchise 3: owner _____

                 address _____

                 _____

                 telephone _____

                 date started _____

     Franchise 4: owner _____

                 address _____

                 _____

                 telephone _____

                 date started _____

  d. How many franchises are planned for the next twelve months (not including those awarded and not yet in operation)? _____

4. Why have franchises failed?

  a. How many franchises have failed? _____ How many of these have been in the last two years? _____

  b. Why have franchises failed?

Franchisor reasons: _____

_____

Better Business Bureau reasons: _____

_____

Franchisee reasons: _____

_____

_____

5. Franchise in local market area
   a. Has a franchise ever been awarded in this area? _____
   If so, and if it is still in operation:
   owner _____
   address _____
   telephone _____ date started _____
   If so, and if it is no longer in operation:
   person involved _____
   address _____
   date started _____ date ended _____
   reasons for failure _____
   _____

   How many inquiries have there been for the franchise from
   the area in the past six months? ___
6. What product or service will be added to franchise package:
   a. within twelve months? _____
   _____

   b. within two years? _____
   _____

   c. within two to five years? _____
   _____

7. Competition
   a. What is my competition? _____
   _____
   _____

8. Are all franchises independently owned?
   a. Of the total outlets, _____ are franchised, and _____
   are company owned.
   b. If some outlets are company owned did they start out this
   way, _____ or were they repurchased from a franchisee?
   _____ Date of most recent company acquisition. _____
9. Franchise distribution pattern:
   a. Is the franchise exclusive, _____ or nonexclusive? _____
   b. Is the franchise a distributorship, _____ or a dealership
   _____ If it is a dealership who is the distributor in my area?
   name _____
   address _____
   How long has he been a distributor? _____

10. Franchise operations:
    a. What facilities are required, and do I lease or build?

	build	lease
operated out of home ___		
office	_____	_____
building	_____	_____
manufacturing facility	_____	_____
warehouse	_____	_____
_____	_____	_____
_____	_____	_____

   b. Getting started—who is responsible for what?

	franchisor	franchisee
feasibility study	_____	_____
design	_____	_____
construction	_____	_____
furnishing	_____	_____
financing	_____	_____

Franchise company

1. The company:
   a. What is the name and address of the parent company, if different from the franchise company:
      name _____
      address _____
   b. Is the parent company public, ___ or private? ___
   c. If the company is public, where is the stock traded?
      New York Stock Exchange _____
      American Stock Exchange _____
      over-the-counter _____
      _____ _____
   d. If the company is private, the president is _____.
      This bank can be used as a reference:
      name _____
      address _____
      person to contact_____

Financial and legal:

1. Where to get advice:
   a. Lawyer
      name _____
      address _____
      telephone _____
   b. Financial
      name _____
      address _____
      telephone _____

  c. Management
   name _____
   address _____
   telephone _____
2. Total franchise cost:
  a. How much money do I have to have to get started?

item	*amount*
franchise start up (2b)	$ _____
first year operating	$ _____
first year personal	$ _____
Total	$ _____

  b. What do I have to pay the franchisor to get started?
   $ _____
   Basis of cost:

item	*amount*
franchise fee	$ _____
services	$ _____
product	$ _____
real estate	$ _____
equipment	$ _____
_____	$ _____

  c. Is any of the initial franchise cost refundable? _____
   If so, on what basis? _____
   _____

3. Financing:
  a. Is part of the initial cost to the franchisee financed? _____
   If so, how much? $ _____ This represents _____ % of
   the total initial cost.
  b. What is the interest rate? _____ % When does financing
   have to be paid back? _____
4. Forecast of income and expenses:
  a. Is a forecast of income and expenses provided? _____
   Is it:
   based on actual franchisee operations? __
   based on a franchisor outlet? __
   purely estimated? __
  b. If a forecast is provided does it:

	yes	no
relate to your market area?	_____	_____
meet your personal goals?	_____	_____
provide adequate return on investment?	_____	_____
provide for adequate promotion and personnel?	_____	_____

5. What is the best legal structure for my company?
  proprietorship _____
  partnership _____
  corporation _____

6. Are all details covered in a written franchise contract? yes
   __ no __ (get copy for lawyer and accountant review)

   a. What to look for—are these included?

	yes	no
franchise fee		
termination		
selling and renewal		
advertising and promotion		
patent and liability protection		
home office services		
commissions and royalties		
training		
financing		
territory		
exclusive vs. non-exclusive franchise		

Training

1. Initial training:
   a. Does franchisor provide formal initial training _____
      If so how long does it last? __
   b. Cost

	yes	no
included in franchise cost		
includes all materials		
includes transportation		
includes room and board		

      If not included in franchise cost, what is total cost, including
      all expenses immediately above? $____

   c. What does the training course include?

	yes	no
franchise operations		
sales		
finance		
promotion		
personnel		
management		
manufacturing and maintenance		
training		
_____		
_____		

   d. How do you train your initial staff? Is a training program
      provided? __ Does the franchisor make a staff member

from the home office available to assist? ___ What materials are included in the staff training program? _____

_____

_____

2. Continuing training:
   What is the continuing program? Is there any cost? _____
   If so how much? $ _____ Are special materials or equipment required? _____ If so, what? _____ What is the cost to the franchise? $ _____

Marketing:

1. How is the product or service sold?

	yes	no
in home—appointment	___	___
in home—on the spot	___	___
telephone	___	___
in store or place of business	___	___
at business—appointment	___	___
at business—on the spot	___	___
mail	___	___
_____	___	___

2. How do you get the sales leads?

	yes	no
franchisor	___	___
franchisee	___	___
advertising	___	___
direct mail	___	___
telephone	___	___
trade shows	___	___
_____	___	___

3. Who are the prospects for the products or services?
   Give a brief profile _____

   _____

4. What is the national advertising program of the franchisor?
   a. What is the national advertising budget?
      $ _____
   b. What are the primary advertising media?
      television ___
      radio ___
      outdoor ___
      newspaper ___
      magazine ___
      direct mail ___

5. What kind of advertising and promotional support is available for the local franchisee?

	yes	no
Is a packaged advertising program available?	_____	_____
Is there a co-op advertising program?	_____	_____
Is there a "grand opening" package?	_____	_____

6. Should you have an advertising agency? _____

Home office support

1. Principals and directors:
   a. Who are the key people in the day-to-day operation of the business?

name	title	background
_____	_____	_____
_____	_____	_____
_____	_____	_____
_____	_____	_____
_____	_____	_____

   b. Who are the directors (do not include those from a.)?

name	business association
_____	_____
_____	_____
_____	_____

2. Consultants:
   a. Who are the consultants to the company?

name	business specialty
_____	_____
_____	_____
_____	_____

3. Service departments
   a. What service departments do you have?

	yes	no
finance and accounting	_____	_____
advertising and promotion	_____	_____
sales and marketing	_____	_____

	yes	no
research and development	___	___
real estate	___	___
construction	___	___
personnel and training	___	___
manufacturing and operations	___	___
purchasing	___	___
_____	___	___
_____	___	___

4. Field support
   a. Do you have a field agent assigned to work with a set number of franchises? ___
   Who would be assigned to your franchise? ___
   How many other franchises is that agent assigned to? __
   Can you contact the agent? __

CHECKLIST C

This checklist illustrates a number of aspects that should be considered before purchasing a business. Again, there are no set answers to insure success. It is advisable to refer to Worksheet 1 in Checklist A and complete it with regard to the ongoing concern. Ignoring potential problems does not correct them. Realistically evaluating them and planning to resolve them certainly increases the chance for success.

CHECKLIST FOR BUYING A BUSINESS

What factors affect sales?
  How will these market factors behave?
    Therefore, what sales can I expect?

What makes up the cost of sales?
  How will these cost factors apply to expected sales?
    Therefore, what gross profit can I expect?

What expenses are required to run this business?
  How will expenses develop under my ownership?
    Therefore, what net profit can I predict?

What assets will the business need and possess?
  What is the condition of these assets?
    Therefore, what asset improvements will I have to make?

What credit does the business assume?

Source: Verne A. Bunn. *Buying and Selling a Small Business,* Washington, D.C.: Small Business Administration, 1969, p. 11.

What is the condition of the credit position?
　Therefore, what changes, if any, can occur in the debt structure?

How much cash do I have?
　How much cash will the business generate?
　　Therefore, what will be my available-cash position?

What immediate cash outlay must I make?
　What will be the cash needs of the business?
　　Therefore, what cash outgo will be necessary?

What will be my net cash position as things now stand?
　What additional cash resource, if any, must I have?
　　Therefore, what financing plan shall I use?

CHECKLIST D AND CHECKLIST E

Checklists D and E form the basis for deciding where you are going to establish your firm. These checklists, when used periodically, also give a current appraisal of the general trend of your area. Generally, a growth area with supportive businesses is best, and these checklists provide this information.

CHECKLIST D–CHECKLIST FOR LOCATION ANALYSIS

(Location analysis should be completed prior to site analysis.)

City or town

1. Economic considerations
　Industry
　　farming　　　　　　　　　　　　　　　_____
　　manufacturing　　　　　　　　　　　　_____
　　trading　　　　　　　　　　　　　　　_____

　Trend
　　highly satisfactory　　　　　　　　　　_____
　　growing　　　　　　　　　　　　　　　_____
　　stationary　　　　　　　　　　　　　　_____
　　declining　　　　　　　　　　　　　　_____

　Permanency
　　old and well-established　　　　　　　　_____
　　old and reviving　　　　　　　　　　　_____
　　new and promising　　　　　　　　　　_____
　　recent and uncertain　　　　　　　　　_____

Source: *Small Business Location and Layout,* Washington, D.C.: Small Business Administration, 1965.

Diversification
    many and varied lines   _____
    many of the same type   _____
    few varied lines   _____
    dependent on one industry   _____

Stability
    constant   _____
    satisfactory   _____
    average   _____
    subject to wide fluctuations   _____

Seasonality
    little or no seasonal change   _____
    mild seasonal change   _____
    periodical—every few years   _____
    highly seasonal in nature   _____

Future
    most promising   _____
    satisfactory   _____
    uncertain   _____
    poor outlook   _____

2. Population
Income distribution
    mostly wealthy   _____
    well-distributed   _____
    mostly middle income   _____
    poor   _____

Trend
    growing   _____
    large and stable   _____
    small and stable   _____
    declining   _____

Living status
    own homes   _____
    pay substantial rent   _____
    pay moderate rent   _____
    pay low rent   _____

3. Competition
Number of competing stores
    few   _____
    average   _____
    many   _____
    too many   _____

Type of management
  not progressive   _____
  average   _____
  above average   _____
  alert and progressive   _____

Presence of chains
  no chains   _____
  few chains   _____
  average number   _____
  many well-established   _____

Type of competing stores
  unattractive   _____
  average   _____
  old and well-established   _____
  are many people buying out of community?   _____

4. The town as a place to live
  Character of the city
    are homes neat and clean?   _____
    are lawns, parks, streets, neat, modern, attractive?   _____
    adequate facilities available for
      banking?   _____
      transportation?   _____
      professional services?   _____
      utilities?   _____

  Facilities and climate
    schools   _____
    churches   _____
    amusement centers   _____
    medical and dental services   _____
    climate   _____

CHECKLIST E—CHECKLIST FOR SITE ANALYSIS

(Location analysis [Checklist D] should be completed prior to site analysis.)

The actual site

1. Competition
  Number of independent stores of same kind as yours
    same block   _____
    same side of street   _____
    across street   _____

Source: *Small Business Location and Layout,* Washington, D.C.: Small Business Administration, 1965.

Number of chain stores
  same block
  same side of street   _____
  across street   _____

Kind of stores next door   _____

Number of vacancies
  same side of street
  across street   _____
  next door   _____

Dollar sales of nearest competitor   _____

2. Traffic flow
  sex of pedestrians   _____
  age of pedestrians   _____
  destination of pedestrians   _____
  number of passers-by   _____
  automobile traffic count   _____
  peak hours of traffic flow   _____

3. Transportation
  transfer points
  highway   _____
  kind (bus, streetcar, auto, railway) _____

4. Parking facilities
  large and convenient
  large enough but not convenient   _____
  convenient but too small   _____
  completely inadequate   _____

5. Side of street   _____

6. Plant
  frontage—in feet   _____
  depth—in feet   _____
  shape of building   _____
  condition
  heat—type; air conditioning   _____
  light   _____
  display space   _____
  back entrance   _____
  front entrance   _____
  display windows   _____

7. Corner location—if not, what is it? _____

8. Unfavorable characteristics
   fire hazards _____
   cemetery _____
   hospital _____
   industry _____
   relief office _____
   undertaker _____
   vacant lot with no parking possibilities _____
   garages _____
   playground _____
   smoke, dust, odors _____
   poor sidewalks and pavement _____
   unsightly neighborhood buildings _____

9. Professional men in block
   medical doctors _____
   dentists _____
   lawyers _____
   veterinarians _____
   others _____

10. History of the site _____

   _____

   _____

   _____

CHECKLIST F

This checklist is a general market analysis. It summarizes a number of factors that directly affect the success of a small business. Since this is a general listing, it is not as specific as the preceding checklists. However, it is important and offers a number of points to be periodically considered in small business.

CHECKLIST FOR MARKETING ANALYSIS

1. Does a market exist?
   A. Who are the customers?
      1. their income
         a. sources of customers' employment
         b. effective buying power
   B. How large is the market?
      1. population
         a. growth trend
         b. characteristics

    2. income
      a. average (median, range) for area and trends
      b. sales in this area of operation in past years
      c. percentage of income dollar spent in this area of endeavor
    3. potential
      a. How accurately can sales be forecasted?
      b. Are data available?
        1. sources
        2. outside assistance available
        3. What is size of trading area?
        4. What segment of population is the market?
        5. What is this firm's projected market share?
        6. Can the market expand?
  C. What is the competition?
    1. What is the nature of competition in the market area (size and characteristics of other stores in same area)?
    2. To what extent have existing competitors satisfied demand?
      a. is there a niche for the product at the present quality level?
      b. is there a niche for our product at the present price level?
    3. risk
      a. number of failures in business as percentage of starts in the area and by type
      b. stability in price of goods needed for operation
  D. Characteristics of market
    1. seasonal fluctuations
      a. What can offset seasonal fluctuations?
    2. What are the major factors that influence business in the area?
2. Find specific site in desired area
  A. Cost of land?
  B. Cost of construction?
    1. How long will construction take?
  C. Location (see Checklist D)
  D. City's present retail structure
    1. What heavily trading or traveled areas are open?
3. Factors relating to operation
  A. Channels of distribution available
  B. Sources of supplies available
  C. Transportation available
  D. Credit investigation and collection service available
  E. Parking and traffic factors
  F. Promotional activities
    1. name and identifying characteristics of business
    2. What cost of advertising is reasonable?
    3. Can we increase sales by advertising?
      a. What local media are available?

        b. assistance from suppliers
        c. regional or national affiliation or assistance
4. Factors relating to product
  A. Will this be specialty or general operation?
    1. Is this a mass appeal or limited market?
    2. What are possibilities of becoming regional?
  B. What is the service capacity?
  C. Pricing required
    1. Can we give better service or prices?
    2. What is "going price"?
    3. Can the product compare in price to competitors?
    4. What is our profit margin at competitive prices?

CHECKLIST G

This checklist demonstrates the aspects that should be considered in evaluating advertising. Those aspects particularly applicable to the small business are noted.

CHECKLIST FOR ADVERTISING (NEWSPAPER)

*Merchandise — Does the ad offer merchandise having wide appeal, special features, price appeal, and timeliness?

Medium — Is a newspaper the best medium for the ad, or would another—direct mail, radio, television — be more appropriate?

Location — Is the ad situated in the best spot, in both section and page location?

Size — Is the ad large enough to do the job expected of it? Does it omit important details, or is it overcrowded with nonessential information?

*Headline — Does the headline express the single major idea about the merchandise advertised? The headline should usually be an informative statement and not

Source: John W. Wingate and Seymore Helfant. *Small Store Planning for Growth,* Washington, D.C.: Small Business Administration, 1966, p. 69.
*The seven items starred are of chief importance to the smaller store.

simply a label. For example, "Sturdy shoes for active boys, specially priced at $6.95," is certainly better than "Boys' Shoes, $6.95."

Illustration

Does the illustration (if one is used) express the idea the headline conveys?

*Merchandise information

Does the copy give the basic facts about the goods, or does it leave out information that would be important to the reader? ("The more you tell, the more you sell.")

Layout

Does the arrangement of the parts of the ad and the use of white space make the ad easy to read? Does it stimulate the reader to look at all the contents of the ad?

Human interest

Does the ad—through illustration, headline, and copy—appeal to customers' wants and wishes?

*"You" attitude

Is the ad written and presented from the customer's point of view (with the customer's interest clearly in mind), or from the store's?

*Believability

To the objective, nonpartisan reader, does the ad ring true, or does it perhaps sound exaggerated or phony?

Type face

Does the ad use a distinctive typeface —different from those of competitors?

*Spur to action

Does the ad stimulate prompt action through devices such as use of a coupon, statement of limited quantities, or announcement of a specific time period for the promotion or impending event?

*Sponsor identification

Does the ad use a specially prepared signature cut that is always associated with the store and that identifies it at a glance? Also, does it always include these institutional details: store location, hours open, telephone number, location of advertised goods, and whether phone and mail orders are accepted?

CHECKLIST H

Checklist H offers a number of "yes—no" questions about the interior layout of a firm. Any negative answer should be taken as a potential or current problem area and corrective action should be initiated.

CHECKLIST FOR INTERIOR LAYOUT ARRANGEMENTS

Layout

	yes	no
1. Are your fixtures low enough and signs so placed that the customer can get a bird's eye view of the store and tell in what direction to go for wanted goods?		
2. Do your aisle and counter arrangements tend to stimulate a circular traffic flow through the store?		
3. Do your fixtures (and their arrangement), signs, lettering, and colors all create a coordinated and unified effect?		
4. Before any supplier's fixtures are accepted, do you make sure they conform in color and design to what you already have?		
5. Do you limit the use of hanging signs to to special sale events?		
6. Are your counters and aisle tables not overcrowded with merchandise?		
7. Are your ledges, and cashier and wrapping stations kept free of boxes, unneeded wrapping materials, personal effects, and odds and ends?		
8. Do you keep trash bins out of sight?		

Merchandise emphasis

	yes	no
1. Do your signs, referring to specific goods, tell the customer something significant about the goods, rather than simply naming the products and their prices?		
2. For your advertised goods, do you have prominent signs, including tear sheets at entrances, to inform and guide customers to their exact location in the store?		

Source: John W. Wingate and Seymour Helfant. *Small Store Planning for Growth,* Washington, D.C.: Small Business Administration, 1966, pp. 98–99.

	yes	*no*
3. Do you prominently display both advertised and nonadvertised specials at the ends of counters as well as at the point of sale?	_____	_____
4. Are both your national and private brands highlighted in your arrangement and window display?	_____	_____
5. Wherever feasible, do you give the more colorful merchandise in your stock preference in display?	_____	_____
6. In the case of apparel and home furnishings, do the items that reflect your store's fashion sense or fashion leadership get special display attention at all times?	_____	_____
7. In locating merchandise in your store, do you always consider the productivity of space—vertical as well as horizontal?	_____	_____

8. Is your self-service merchandise arranged to attract customers and assist them in selection by:

a. grouping each category under a separate sign?	_____	_____
b. arranging the merchandise in each catetory according to its most significant characteristic—need for weather protection, color, style, size, or price?	_____	_____
c. arranging in apparel categories the merchandise by price lines or zones to assist the customer in making a selection quickly?	_____	_____
d. usually devoting horizontal space to different items and styles within a category (vertical space being used for different sizes—smallest at the top; largest at the bottom)?	_____	_____
e. interspersing impulse items with demand items, and not placing them across the aisle from demand items, where many customers will not see them?	_____	_____

APPENDIX II

The Legal Aspects of Small Business

Introduction

Much has been written regarding the pros and cons of the three principal legal structures of businesses—proprietorships, partnerships, and corporations.[1]

If a small business is to operate effectively in today's climate and continue to exist when the present owners can no longer function effectively, its legal structure must be right. For this reason, many small-business owners ask: "Should a proprietorship be continued? Would a form of partnership be better? What about incorporation?" "Would a Subchapter S corporation be beneficial in my situation?"

THREE BASIC CHOICES

Broadly speaking, there are three principal legal structures for small business. Variations exist within the partnership and corporation classifications. The general description of each category is:

1. proprietorship, the easiest to begin and end, can have the most flexibility for its operations, needs no government approval, has business profits taxed as personal income, and makes the owner personally liable for debts and taxes;
2. partnership, the simplest for two or more people to start and terminate, has the same flexibility of objective as the proprietorship, has partners taxed separately, and makes all partners except limited partners liable for all debts regardless of their share of the partnership;

---

[1]A large portion of this material was condensed from Management Aid No. 80, *Choosing the legal structure for your firm;* Washington, D.C.: Small Business Administration, April, 1972.

3. corporation, the most formal structure, operates under state laws has a continuous and separate legal life, has its scope of activity and name restricted by a charter, has the business profits taxed separately from earnings of executives and stockholders, and makes only the corporation, not the owners nor managers, liable for its debts and taxes, the liability of the stockholders being generally limited to the purchase price of the corporate stock.

SIX POINTS TO CHECK PRIOR TO CHOOSING A LEGAL STRUCTURE

In analyzing a situation, it is advisable to obtain the advice and guidance of competent legal counsel. Among other things, it is worthwhile for the small-business owner to be familiar with six main points of legal structure in addition to tax considerations: costs and procedures in starting; size of risk, that is, amount of investors' liability for debts and taxes; continuity of the concern; adaptability of administration; influences of applicable laws; and attraction of additional capital.

COSTS AND PROCEDURES IN STARTING

Single proprietorships are the easiest to initiate. The costs of formation are low. Basically, all you have to do is find out whether you need a license to carry on your particular business, and whether you have to pay a state tax or licence fee.

General partnerships are also started quite simply. You can set one up by having the executives in the business sign a partnership agreement. A written document, however, is not necessarily a prerequisite, since an oral agreement can be equally effective. Moreover, a partnership may even be implied by actions that the managers of an unincorporated business have taken even though no agreement of any kind, oral or written, exists.

Limited partnerships are somewhat more difficult to initiate. To form a limited partnership you file, with the appropriate state official, a written contract drawn according to certain legal requirements. This contract permits you to limit the liability of one or more of the partners to the amount they have invested. A minimum of one general partner must be designated in addition to the limited partners. All limited partners must have actually invested in the partnership. According to the Uniform Limited Partnership Act, those investments may be either cash or tangible property, but not services. Finally, you must conform strictly to the laws of the particular state in which you organize; otherwise your business will be considered as a general partnership. When this is the case a partner's liability can exceed his or her share of the partnership.

Corporations are more complicated to form than the other forms of legal organization. A corporation may be created only by following the legal procedures of the particular state in which the corporation is being established. First, certain responsible people are needed to organize and become officials in the new corporation. Next, they must file with the designated state official a special document, articles of incorporation. An initial tax and various filing fees must be paid. Third, in order to do the business for which the corporation was formed, various official meetings must be conducted to deal with specified details of organization and operation. Fourth, stock in the corporation must be sold. Accounting records are established so that the small-business owner receives a salary on which he pays a tax. The corporation is taxed separately on profit after a salary is paid to the small-business owner.

THE SIZE OF THE RISK

The degree to which investors in your enterprise risk legal liability for the debts of your business is an important consideration. Regardless of legal structure, creditors are always entitled to be paid out of business assets before any equity capital may be withdrawn. When those assets are insufficient, the extent to which owners can be compelled to meet creditors' claims out of their own pockets varies with the type of organization.

A single proprietor is personally liable for all debts of the business to the extent of all personal property. This liability cannot be restricted in any way. Likewise, each member of a general partnership is fully responsible for all debts owed by the partnership regardless of the amount of personal investment in the business. In a limited partnership, however, the limited partners are protected; they risk only the loss of the capital they have invested. But the general partners in a limited partnership are liable jointly and severally for all debts just like any other general partner.

Corporations have an advantage here over other legal structures. Creditors can force payment on their claims only to the limit of the company's assets. Thus, while a shareholder may lose the amount of money invested in the corporation's stock, no additional funds can be required to meet business debts. This is true even though the corporate assets may be insufficient to meet creditors' claims.

CONTINUITY OF THE CONCERN

In choosing the legal structure for your business, you should also understand clearly how it influences the continuity of the business. Although single proprietorships have no time limit on them by law, they are not fundamentally perpetual. Illness of the owner may disturb the operations of the business and death legally ends the proprietorship. Partnerships are perishable in the same general sense, since they are terminated by the death or withdrawal of any one of the partners.

Corporations have the most permanent legal structure. They have a continuous life of their own. The withdrawal, insolvency, injury, illness, or death of a person officially concerned with a corporation does not terminate the firm. Moreover, the certificates of stock, which represent investments and ownership in the business, may be transferred from one person to another without hampering the concern's operation.

ADAPTABILITY OF ADMINISTRATION

In the single proprietorship, policy and operations rest in one individual. Concentration of management avoids the problems of opposing factions and divided responsibilities; however, many individuals are not competent to handle all management jobs. An owner may hire employees to assist with management, but is still responsible for all their actions. After incorporating, the owner of a small business does not necessarily lose control of the enterprise. In most small, closely held corporations, the former proprietor can retain control by the ownership of a majority of the stock in the newly formed corporation.

In general partnerships, each partner typically has an equal role in administration, with the various operating functions divided among them. The combined abilities and knowledge of several executives give the partnership an advantage over the single proprietorship.

In a partnership, decisions may be made and changes adopted simply by oral agreement among the partners. In limited partnerships, the limited partners may not engage in management functions. If they do, they may be held fully liable as general partners. They are, however, entitled to inspect the books and obtain full and complete information regarding the business.

In corporations, the stockholders do not necessarily participate either in operations or in policy formulation, but they may. In small businesses, the managers and stockholders are usually the same. In many cases the majority owner may still have to sign notes and be responsible for a number of the debts of the firm. Corporations have an advantage over partnerships. In partnerships each partner can act as general agent for the business, but in corporations, the stockholder cannot bind the firm by their acts just because they have invested capital in it.

INFLUENCE OF APPLICABLE LAWS

Single proprietorship is the oldest and most widespread legal structure of business. As a result, little doubt remains about the influences of laws regulating its legal rights and obligations. Likewise the relationships are clear between a sole owner, agents, creditors, and others who deal with the business. A private citizen working in Iowa can carry on business in Kansas without paying any greater taxes or incurring any more obligations in Kansas than a Kansas business owner.

Broadly speaking, this is also true for a partnership. Of course, a state may require the purchase of a license to carry on a particular kind of business. But the license will be equally available to business of any state as long as they conform to prescribed uniform standards. This equality of opportunity derives from the United States Constitution, which guarantees to citizens of each state "all privileges and immunities" provided to citizens of the other states. Thus, the legal structure that does not involve any artificial entity such as a corporation does provide a freedom of action in all states for single proprietorships and partnerships which corporations cannot match.

Corporations owe their legal life solely to the states in which they are organized. No other state is required to recognize them. All states do permit out-of-state corporations to function inside their boundaries. Nevertheless, out-of-state corporations must always comply with special in-state obligations such as filling certain legal papers with the proper state officials, appointment of a representative in the state to act as agent in serving process on the foreign corporation, and payment of specified fees and taxes.

Also, corporations are regulated by numerous state laws which vary considerably. Even when the language is similar, these laws can be, and have been, interpreted differently in different places. Therefore, in running a corporation effectively, competent legal counsel is virtually indispensable. The essential feature of limited liability of stockholders is preserved in every state.

ATTRACTION OF ADDITIONAL CAPITAL

Every business may require additional funds to carry on operations. It is important, therefore, in deciding upon legal structure to take into account the means for attracting new money.

In single proprietorships, the owner may raise additional money by borrowing, by purchasing on credit, and by investing additional funds. Since the owner is personally liable for all the debts of the business, banks and suppliers will look carefully at the owner's personal wealth. Consequently, the funds available will always be limted by the owner's circumstances. For this reason alone, a business requiring large amounts of capital for successful operation should probably not be organized as a single proprietorship.

Partnerships can often raise funds with greater ease, since the resources of all partners are combined in a single undertaking. Like single proprietors, partners must accept full personal liability for business debt; for this reason, a partnership may be able to borrow on better terms than can some corporations. In addition, outsiders may be willing to extend credit because of the security deriving from the individual partners' full liability.

Corporations are usually in the best position of all to attract capital. They may acquire additional funds by borrowing money by pledging corporate assets. Also, they may sell securities to the public and attract a wide range of investors. The shareholders' investment in a corporation will not subject them to any financial risk beyond the amount of their holdings. In addition, as stockowners, they have the prospect of sharing directly, through dividends and rising value of the stock, in any profits the concern makes.

A FOURTH CHOICE—SUBCHAPTER S CORPORATIONS

The Internal Revenue Code permits the formation of Subchapter S corporations, to allow various advantages to small corporations. The basic advantage of the Subchapter S corporation is that shareholders are taxed on their share of the corporate profits instead of the corporation being taxed. Substantial tax savings are possible.

A Subchapter S business corporation is defined by the Internal Revenue Service:

1. The Subchapter S corporation is required to be a domestic corporation that is not a participant in an affiliated group of corporations;
2. The corporation may not have more than fifteen shareholders. Shareholders may be individuals, estates, or trusts—if husband and wife jointly own shares, and one dies, the estate is to be treated as one shareholder;
3. The Subchapter S corporation may not have a non-resident alien for a stockholder;
4. The corporation may have only one class of stock.

If the preceding four conditions are met, the corporation may elect to become a Subchapter S corporation. Election to be such a corporation must be made either within the first month of a specific taxable year or within the prior month. In addition, all of the shareholders must agree to the election as a Subchapter S corporation.

The major purposes of Subchapter S corporations are:

1. to permit small businesses to choose a legal organization unhampered by taxation influences;

2. to assist small-business owners by taxing corporate income to shareholders rather than the corporation;
3. to permit shareholders of Subchapter S corporations to write off the corporation's losses against income from other sources;
4. to exempt shareholders from accumulated earnings, taxes and personal holding company taxes;
5. to avail shareholders of the corporation's fringe benefits.

The small-business owner would be wise to consider using the Subchapter S corporation. However, in individual cases, the advice of a qualified accountant should be sought. Generally, the Subchapter S corporation combines the advantages of both a corporation and a partnership; however, states do not recognize a Subchapter S Corporation and state taxes follow normal corporate tax procedures.

The following documents are examples of various legal documents which have been drawn to meet various situations; they will provide insight into the issues covered in such documents and how these issues have been treated in the past. These examples are *not* general-purpose forms to be used in any situation.

Legal Documents For Starting New Ventures

Item A: Articles of Organization
Item B: By-Laws
Item C: Investment Letter
Item D: Employment Agreement
Item E: Lease
Item F: Purchases and Sales Agreement (Preliminary)
Item G: Promoter's Agreement

Item A

C.D. ARO–3 (Rev. 8–69) 25M–11–69–045652

The Commonwealth of Massachusetts

JOHN F. X. DAVOREN
Secretary of the Commonwealth
STATE HOUSE
BOSTON, MASS.

ARTICLES OF ORGANIZATION

(Under G.L. Ch. 156B)

Incorporators

NAME	POST OFFICE ADDRESS

Include given name in full in case of natural persons; in case of a corporation, give state of incorporation.

Peter Cheatem

42 Crooked Lane
Boston, Massachusetts   02114

Donald Conman

"

Philip Shyster

"

The above-named incorporator(s) do hereby associate (themselves) with the intention of forming a corporation under the provisions of General Laws, Chapter 156B and hereby state(s):

1.   The name by which the corporation shall be known is:

Fly By Nite Electronics, Inc.

2.   The purposes for which the corporation is formed are as follows:

See Rider A on Page 2A

NOTE: If provisions for which the space provided under Articles 2, 4, 5 and 6 is not sufficient additions should be set out on continuation sheets to be numbered 2A, 2B, etc. Indicate under each Article where the provision is set out. Continuation sheets shall be on 8 1/2" x 11" paper and must have a left-hand margin 1 inch wide for binding. Only one side should be used.

(Item A continued)

3. The total number of shares and the par value, if any, of each class of stock which the corporation is authorized is as follows:

CLASS OF STOCK	WITHOUT PAR VALUE	WITH PAR VALUE		
	NUMBER OF SHARES	NUMBER OF SHARES	PAR VALUE	AMOUNT
Preferred				$
Common		150,000	$1.00	$150,000

4. If more than one class is authorized, a description of each of the different classes of stock with, if any, the preferences, voting powers, qualifications, special or relative rights or privileges as to each class thereof and any series now established:

NONE

*5. The restrictions, if any, imposed by the Articles of Organization upon the transfer of shares of stock of any class are as follows:

See Rider B on Page 5A

*6. Other lawful provisions, if any, for the conduct and regulation of the business and affairs of the corporation, for its voluntary dissolution, or for limiting, defining, or regulating the powers of the corporation, or of its directors or stockholders, or of any class of stockholders:

See Rider C on Page 6A

(Item A continued)

7. By-laws of the corporation have been duly adopted and the initial directors, president, treasurer and clerk, whose names are set out below, have been duly elected.

8. The effective date of organization of the corporation shall be the date of filing with the Secretary of the Commonwealth or if later date is desired, specify date, (not more than 30 days after date of filing.)

9. The following information shall not for any purpose be treated as a permanent part of the Articles of Organization of the corporation.

   a. The post office address of the initial principal office of the corporation in Massachusetts is:

   42 Crooked Lane, Boston, Massachusetts 02114

   b. The name, residence, and post office address of each of the initial directors and following officers of the corporation are as follows:

	NAME	RESIDENCE	POST OFFICE ADDRESS
President:	Peter Cheatem	Concord, Mass.	42 Crooked Lane Boston, Mass. 02114
Treasurer:	Donald Conman	Lexington, Mass.	"
Clerk:	Philip Shyster	Charlestown, Mass.	"

Directors:
   Each of the above named officers is also a Director.

   c. The date initially adopted on which the corporation's fiscal year ends is: June 30

   d. The date initially fixed in the by-laws for the annual meeting of stockholders of the corporation is:
   Third Tuesday in September

   e. The name and business address of the resident agent, if any, of the corporation is:
   NONE

IN WITNESS WHEREOF and under the penalties of perjury the above-named INCORPORATOR(S) sign(s) these Articles of Organization this 31st day of February 19 7/ .

The signature of each incorporator which is not a natural person must be by an individual who shall show the capacity in which he acts and by signing shall represent under the penalties of perjury that he is duly authorized on its behalf to sign these Articles of Organization.

(Item A continued)

THE COMMONWEALTH OF MASSACHUSETTS

ARTICLES OF ORGANIZATION
GENERAL LAWS, CHAPTER 156B, SECTION 12

I hereby certify that, upon an examination of the within-written articles of organization, duly submitted to me, it appears that the provisions of the General Laws relative to the organization of corporations have been complied with, and I hereby approve said articles; and the filing fee in the amount of $ having been paid, said articles are deemed to have been filed with me this   day of
                                            19

Effective date

Secretary of the Commonwealth

TO BE FILLED IN BY CORPORATION
PHOTO COPY OF ARTICLES OF ORGANIZATION TO BE SENT

TO:

....

....

....

FILING FEE: 1/20 of 1% of the total amount of the authorized capital stock with par value, and one cent a share for all authorized shares without par value, but not less than $75. General Laws, Chapter 156B. Shares of stock with a par value of less than one dollar shall be deemed to have par value of one dollar per share.

Copy Mailed

(Item A continued)

RIDER A

1. To manufacture and sell electronic devices designed to enable entrepreneurs to fly by night.

2. To carry on any manufacturing, mercantile, selling, management, service or other business, operation or activity which may be lawfully carried on by a corporation organized under the Business Corporation Law of The Commonwealth of Massachusetts, whether or not related to those referred to in the foregoing paragraph.

3. To carry on any business, operation or activity through a wholly or partly owned subsidiary.

4. To carry on any business, operation or activity referred to in the foregoing paragraphs to the same extent as might an individual, whether as principal, agent, contractor or otherwise, and either alone or in conjunction or a joint venture or other arrangement with any corporation, association, trust, firm or individual.

5. To have as additional purposes all powers granted to corporations by the laws of the Commonwealth of Massachusetts, provided that no such purpose shall include any activity inconsistent with the Business Corporation Law or the general laws of said Commonwealth.

6. To be a partner in any business enterprise which the corporation would have power to conduct by itself.

(Item A continued)

RIDER B

Any stockholder, including the heirs, assigns, executors or administrators of a deceased stockholder, desiring to sell or transfer such stock owned by him or them, shall first offer it to the corporation through the Board of Directors, in the manner following:

He shall notify the directors of his desire to sell or transfer by notice in writing, which notice shall contain the price at which he is willing to sell or transfer and the name of one arbitrator. The directors shall within thirty days thereafter, either accept the offer, or by notice to him in writing name a second arbitrator, and these two shall name a third. It shall then be the duty of the arbitrators to ascertain the value of the stock, and if any arbitrator shall neglect or refuse to appear at any meeting appointed by the arbitrators, a majority may act in the absence of such arbitrator.

After the acceptance of the offer, or the report of the arbitrators as to the value of the stock, the directors shall have thirty days within which to purchase the same at such valuation, but if at the expiration of thirty days, the corporation shall not have exercised the right so to purchase, the owner of the stock shall be at liberty to dispose of the same in any manner he may see fit.

No shares of stock shall be sold or transferred on the books of the corporation until these provisions have been complied with, but the Board of Directors may in any particular instance waive the requirement.

(Item A continued)

RIDER C

(a) The directors may make, amend or repeal the by-laws in
whole or in part, except with respect to any provision thereof
which by law or the by-laws requires action by the stockholders.

(b) Meetings of the stockholders may be held anywhere in the
United States

(c) No stockholder shall have any right to examine any
property or any books, accounts or other writings of the corporation if there is reasonable ground for belief that such examination will for any reason be adverse to the interests of the corporation, and a vote of the directors refusing permission to make
such examination and setting forth that in the opinion of the directors such examination would be adverse to the interests of the
corporation shall be prima facie evidence that such examination
would be adverse to the interests of the corporation. Every such
examination shall be subject to such reasonable regualtions as
the directors may establish in regard thereto.

(d) The directors may specify the manner in which the accounts of the corporation shall be kept and may determine what
constitutes net earnings, profits and surplus, what amounts, if
any, shall be reserved for any corporate purpose, and what amounts,
if any, shall be declared as dividends. Unless the board of directors otherwise specifies, the excess of the consideration for
any share of its capital stock with par value issued by it over
such par value shall be paid-in surplus. The board of directors
may allocate to capital stock less than all of the consideration
for any share of its capital stock without par value issued by it,
in which case the balance of such consideration shall be paid-in
surplus. All surplus shall be available for any corporate purpose, including the payment of dividends.

(e) The purchase or other acquisition or retention by the
corporation of shares of its own capital shall not be deemed a
reduction of its capital stock. Upon any reduction of capital or
capital stock, no stockholder shall have any right to demand any
distribution from the corporation, except as and to the extent
that the stockholders shall so have provided at the time of
authorizing such reduction.

(Item A continued)

(f)   Each director and officer of the corporation shall, in the performance of his duties, be fully protected in relying in good faith upon the books of account of the corporation, reprots made to the corporation by any of its officers or employees or by counsel, accountants, appraisers or other experts or consultants selected with reasonable care by the directors, or upon other records of the corporation.

(g)   The directors shall have the power to fix from time to time their compensation. No person shall be disqualified from holding any office by reason of any interest. In the absence of fraud, any director, officer or stockholder of this corporation individually, or any individual having any interest in any concern which is a stockholder of this corporation, or any concern in which any such directors, officers, stockholders or individuals have any interest, may be a party to, or may be pecuniarily or otherwise interested in, any contract, transaction or other act of this corporation, and

   (1)   such contract, transactions or act shall not be in any way invalidated or otherwise affected by that fact;

   (2)   no such director, officer, stockholder or individual shall be liable to account to this corporation for any profit or benefit realized through any such contract, transaction or act; and

   (3)   any such director of this corporation may be counted in determining the existence of a quorum at any meeting of the directors or of any committee thereof which shall authorize any such contract, transaction or act, and may vote to authorize the same;

provided, however, that any contract, transaction or act in which any director or officer of this corporation is so interested individually or as a director, officer, trustee or member of any concern which is not a subsidiary or affiliate of this corporation, or in which any directors or officers are so interested as holders, collectively, of a majority of shares of capital stock or other beneficial interest at the time outstanding in any concern which is not a subsidiary or affiliate of this corporation, shall be duly authorized or ratified by a majority of the directors who are not so interested and to whom the nature of such interest has been disclosed;

(Item A continued)

the term "interest" including personal interest and
interest as a director, officer, stockholder, shareholder, trustee, member or beneficiary of any concern;

the term "concern" meaning any corporation, association
trust, partnership, firm, person or other entity other
than this corporation; and

the phrase "subsidiary or affiliate" meaning a concern
in which a majority of the directors, trustees, partners
or controlling persons are elected or appointed by the
directors of this corporation, or are constituted of
the directors or officers of this corporation.

To the extent permitted by law, the authorizing or ratifying vote
of a majority in interest of each class of the capital stock of
this corporation outstanding and entitled to vote for directors
at an annual meeting or a special meeting duly called for the
purpose (whether such vote is passed before or after judgment
rendered in a suit with respect to such contract, transaction or
act) shall validate any contract, transaction or act of this
corporation, or of the board of directors or any committee
thereof, with regard to all stockholders of this corporation,
whether or not of record at the time of such vote, and with regard to all creditors and other claimants under this corporation;

provided, however, that with respect to the authorization or ratification of contracts, transactions or acts
in which any of the directors, officers or stockholders
of this corporation have an interest, the nature of
such contracts, transactions or acts and the interest
of any director, officer or stockholder therein shall
be summarized in the notice of any such annual or
special meeting, or in a statement or letter accompanying such notice, and shall be fully disclosed at any
such meeting;

(Item A continued)

provided, also, that stockholders so interested may vote at any such meeting; and

provided, further, that any failure of the stockholders to authorize or ratify such contract, transaction or act shall not be deemed in any way to invalidate the same or to deprive this corporation, its directors, officers or employees of its or their right to proceed with such contract, transaction or act.

No contract, transaction or act shall be avoided by reason of any provision of this paragraph (g) which would be valid but for those provisions.

Item B

BY-LAWS
of
FLY BY NITE ELECTRONICS, INC.

Section 1.   ARTICLES OF ORGANIZATION

The name and purposes of the corporation shall be as set forth in the articles of organization. These by-laws, the powers of the corporation and of its directors and stockholders, or of any class of stockholders, if there shall be more than one class of stock, and all matters concerning the conduct and regulation of the business and affairs of the corporation shall be subject to such provisions in regard thereto, if any, as are set forth in the articles of organization as, from time to time, in effect.

Section 2.   STOCKHOLDERS

2.1.   *Annual Meeting.*   The annual meeting of the stockholders shall be held at 2 o'clock in the afternoon on the third Tuesday in September in each year, unless a different hour is fixed by the president or the directors. If that day be a legal holiday at the place where the meeting is to be held, the meeting shall be held on the next succeeding day not a legal holiday at such place. Purposes for which an annual meeting is to be held, additional to those prescribed by law, by the articles of organization or by these by-laws, may be specified by the president or by the directors.

2.2.   *Special Meeting in Place of Annual Meeting.*   If no annual meeting has been held in accordance with the foregoing provisions, a special meeting of the stockholders may be held in place thereof, and any action taken at such special meeting shall have the same force and effect as if taken at the annual meeting, and in such case all references in these by-laws to the annual meeting of the stockholders shall be deemed to refer to such special meeting. Any such special meeting shall be called as provided in Section 2.3.

2.3. *Special Meetings.*   A special meeting of the stockholders may be called at any time by the president or by the directors. Each call of a meeting shall state the place, date, hour, and purposes of the meeting.

2.4.   *Place of Meetings.*   All meetings of the stockholders shall be held at the principal office of the corporation in

(Item B continued)

Massachusetts or, to the extent permitted by the articles of organization, at such other place within the United States as shall be fixed by the president or the directors. Any adjourned session of any meeting of the stockholders shall be held at the same city or town as the initial session, or within Massachusetts, in either case at the place designated in the vote of adjournment.

2.5. *Notice of Meetings.* A written notice of each meeting of stockholders, stating the place, date and hour and the purposes of the meeting, shall be given at least seven days before the meeting to each stockholder entitled to vote thereat and to each stockholder who, by law, by the articles of organization or by these by-laws, is entitled to notice, by leaving such notice with him or at his residence or usual place of business, or by mailing it, postage prepaid, addressed to such stockholder at his address as it appears in the records of the corporation. Such notice shall be given by the clerk, or an assistant clerk, or by an officer designated by the directors. Whenever notice of a meeting is required to be given to a stockholder under any provision of the Business Corporation Law of the Commonwealth of Massachusetts or of the articles of organization or these by-laws, a written waiver thereof, executed before or after the meeting by such stockholder or his attorney thereunto authorized and filed with the records of the meeting, shall be deemed equivalent to such notice.

2.6. *Quorum of Stockholders.* At any meeting of the stockholders, a quorum shall consist of a majority in interest of all stock issued and outstanding and entitled to vote at the meeting; except that if two or more classes or series of stock are entitled to vote as separate classes or series, then in the case of each such class or series a quorum shall consist of a majority in interest of all stock of that class or series issued and outstanding; and except when a larger quorum is required by law, by the articles of organization or by these by-laws. Stock owned directly or indirectly by the corporation, if any, shall not be deemed outstanding for this purpose. Any meeting may be adjourned from time to time by a majority of the votes properly cast upon the question, whether or not a quorum is present, and the meeting may be held as adjourned without further notice.

2.7. *Action by Vote.* When a quorum is present at any meeting, a plurality of the votes properly cast for election to any office shall elect to such office, and a majority of the votes properly cast upon any question other than an election to an office shall decide the question, except when a larger vote is required by law, by the articles of organization, or by these

(Item B continued)

by-laws. No ballot shall be required for any election unless requested by a stockholder present or represented at the meeting and entitled to vote in the election.

2.8. *Voting.* Stockholders entitled to vote shall have one vote for each share of stock entitled to vote held by them of record according to the records of the corporation, unless otherwise provided by the articles of organization. The corporation shall not, directly or indirectly, vote any share of its own stock.

2.9. *Action by Writing.* Any action required or permitted to be taken at any meeting of the stockholders may be taken without a meeting if all stockholders entitled to vote on the matter consent to the action in writing and the written consents are filed with the records of the meetings of stockholders. Such consents shall be treated for all purposes as a vote at a meeting.

2.10. *Proxies.* Stockholders entitled to vote may vote either in person or by proxy in writing dated not more than six months before the meeting named therein, which proxies shall be filed with the clerk or other person responsible to record the proceedings of the meeting before being voted. Unless otherwise specifically limited by their terms, such proxies shall entitle the holders thereof to vote at any adjournment of such meeting but shall not be valid after the final adjournment of such meeting.

Section 3.   BOARD OF DIRECTORS

3.1. *Number.* A board of not more than nine nor less than three directors shall be elected at the annual meeting of the stockholders, by such stockholders as have the right to vote at such election. The number of directors may be increased at any time or from time to time either by the stockholders or by the directors by vote of a majority of the directors then in office. The number of directors may be decreased to any number not less than three at any time or from time to time either by the stockholders or by the directors by a vote of a majority of the directors then in office, but only to eliminate vacancies existing by reason of the death, resignation or removal of one or more directors. No director need be a stockholder.

3.2. *Tenure.* Except as otherwise provided by law, by the articles of organization, or by these by-laws, the directors shall hold office until the next annual meeting of the stockholders and until their successors are elected and qualified, or until a director sooner dies, resigns, is removed, or becomes disqualified.

(Item B continued)

3.3. *Powers.* Except as reserved to the stockholders by law, by the articles of organization, or by these by-laws, the business of the corporation shall be managed by the directors who shall have and may exercise all the powers of the corporation. In particular, and without limiting the generality of the foregoing, the directors may at any time issue all or from time to time any part of the unissued capital stock of the corporation from time to time authorized under the articles of organization and may determine, subject to any requirements of law, the consideration for which stock is to be issued and the manner of allocating such consideration between capital and surplus.

3.4. *Committees.* The directors may, by vote of a majority of the directors then in office, elect from their number an executive committee and other committees and may by vote delegate to any such committee or committees some or all of the powers of the directors except those which by law, by the articles of organization or by these by-laws they are prohibited from delegating. Except as the directors may otherwise determine, any such committee may make rules for the conduct of its business, but unless otherwise provided by the directors or such rules, its business shall be conducted as nearly as may be in the same manner as is provided by these by-laws for the conduct of business by the directors.

3.5. *Regular Meetings.* Regular meetings of the directors may be held without call or notice at such places and at such times as the directors may from time to time determine, provided that notice of the first regular meeting following any such determination shall be given to absent directors. A regular meeting of the directors may be held without call or notice immediately after and at the same place as the annual meeting of the stockholders.

3.6. *Special Meetings.* Special meetings of the directors may be held at any time and at any place designated in the call of the meeting, when called by the president or the treasurer or by two or more directors, reasonable notice thereof being given to each director by the secretary or an assistant secretary, or, if there be none, by the clerk or an assistant clerk, or by the officer or one of the directors calling the meeting.

3.7. *Notice.* It shall be sufficient notice to a director to send notice by mail at least forty-eight hours or by telegram at least twenty-four hours before the meeting addressed to him at his usual or last known business or residence address or to give notice to him in person or by telephone at least twenty-four hours before the meeting. Notice of a meeting need not be given

(Item B continued)

to any director if a written waiver of notice, executed by him before or after the meeting, is filed with the records of the meeting, or to any director who attends the meeting without protesting prior thereto or at its commencement the lack of notice to him. Neither notice of a meeting nor a waiver of a notice need specify the purposes of the meeting.

3.8. *Quorum.*   At any meeting of the directors a majority of the directors then in office shall constitute a quorum. Any meeting may be adjourned from time to time by a majority of the votes cast upon the question, whether or not a quorum is present, and the meeting may be held as adjourned without further notice.

3.9. *Action by Vote.*   When a quorum is present at any meeting, a majority of the directors present may take any action, except when a larger vote is required by law, by the articles of organization or by these by-laws.

3.10. *Action by Writing.*   Unless the articles of organization otherwise provide, any action required or permitted to be taken at any meeting of the directors may be taken without a meeting if all the directors consent to the action in writing and the written consents are filed with the records of the meetings of the directors. Such consents shall be treated for all purposes as a vote at a meeting.

Section 4.   OFFICERS AND AGENTS

4.1. *Enumeration: Qualification.*   The officers of the corporation shall be a president, a treasurer, a clerk, and such other officers, if any, as the incorporators at their initial meeting, or the directors from time to time, may in their discretion elect or appoint. The corporation may also have such agents, if any, as the incorporators at their initial meeting, or the directors from time to time, may in their discretion appoint. Any officer may be, but none need be, a director or stockholder. The clerk shall be a resident of Massachusetts, unless the corporation has a resident agent appointed for the purpose of service of process. Any two or more offices may be held by the same person. Any officer may be required by the directors to give bond for the faithful performance of his duties to the corporation in such amount, and with such sureties, as the directors may determine.

4.2. *Powers.*   Subject to law, to the articles of organization, and to the other provisions of these by-laws, each officer shall have, in addition to the duties and powers herein set forth, such duties and powers as are commonly incident to his

(Item B continued)

office, and such duties and powers as the directors may from time to time designate.

4.3. *Election.* The president, the treasurer, and the clerk shall be elected annually by the directors at their first meeting following the annual meeting of the stockholders. Other officers, if any, may be elected or appointed by the board of directors at said meeting or at any other time.

4.4. *Tenure.* Except as otherwise provided by law or by the articles of organization or by these by-laws, the president, the treasurer and the clerk shall hold office until the first meeting of the directors following the next annual meeting of the stockholders and until their respective successors are chosen and qualified, and each other officer shall hold office until the first meeting of the directors following the next annual meeting of the stockholders unless a shorter period shall have been specified by the terms of his election or appointment, or in each case until he sooner dies, resigns, is removed or becomes disqualified. Each agent shall retain his authority at the pleasure of the directors.

4.5. *President and Vice Presidents.* The president shall be the chief executive officer of the corporation and, subject to the control of the directors, shall have general charge and supervision of the business of the corporation. The president shall preside at all meetings of the stockholders and of the directors at which he is present, except as otherwise voted by the directors.

Any vice presidents shall have such duties and powers as shall be designated from time to time by the directors.

4.6. *Treasurer and Assistant Treasurers.* The treasurer shall be the chief financial and accounting officer of the corporation and shall be in charge of its funds and valuable papers, books of account and accounting records, and shall have such other duties and powers as may be designated from time to time by the directors or by the president.

Any assistant treasurers shall have such duties and powers as shall be designated from time to time by the directors.

4.7. *Clerk and Assistant Clerks.* The clerk shall record all proceedings of the stockholders in a book or series of books to be kept therefor, which book or books shall be kept at the principal office of the corporation or at the office of its transfer agent or of its clerk and shall be open at all reasonable times to the inspection of any stockholder. In the absence of the clerk from any meeting of stockholders, an assistant clerk, or if there be none or he is absent, a temporary clerk chosen at the meeting, shall record the proceedings thereof in the aforesaid book.

(Item B continued)

Unless a transfer agent has been appointed, the clerk shall keep, or cause to be kept, the stock and transfer records of the corporation, which shall contain the names and record addresses of all stockholders and the amount of stock held by each. If no secretary is elected, the clerk shall keep a true record of the proceedings of all meetings of the directors and in his absence from any such meeting an assistant clerk, or if there be none or he is absent, a temporary clerk chosen at the meeting, shall record the proceedings thereof.

Any assistant clerk shall have such duties and powers as shall be designated from time to time by the directors.

4.8. *Secretary and Assistant Secretaries.* If a secretary is elected, he shall keep a true record of the proceedings of all meetings of the directors and in his absence from any such meeting an assistant secretary, or if there be none or he is absent, a temporary secretary chosen at the meeting, shall record the proceedings thereof.

Any assistant secretaries shall have such duties and powers as shall be designated from time to time by the directors.

Section 5. RESIGNATIONS AND REMOVALS

Any director or officer may resign at any time by delivering his resignation in writing to the president, the treasurer or the clerk or to a meeting of the directors. Such resignation shall be effective upon receipt unless specified to be effective at some other time. A director (including persons elected by directors to fill vacancies in the board) may be removed from office (a) with or without cause, by the vote of the holders of a majority of the shares issued and outstanding and entitled to vote in the election of directors, provided that the directors of a class elected by a particular class of stockholders may be removed only by the vote of the holders of a majority of the shares of such class; or (b) for cause, by vote of a majority of the directors then in office. The directors may remove any officer elected by them with or without cause by the vote of a majority of the directors then in office. A director or officer may be removed for cause only after reasonable notice and opportunity to be heard before the body proposing to remove him. No director or officer resigning, and (except where a right to receive compensation shall be expressly provided in a duly authorized written agreement with the corporation) no director or officer removed, shall have any right to any compensation as such director or officer for any period following his resignation or removal, or any right to damages on account of such removal, whether his compensation be by the month or by the year or otherwise; unless in the

(Item B continued)

case of a resignation, the directors, or in the case of a removal, the body acting on the removal, shall, in their or its discretion, provide for compensation.

Section 6. VACANCIES

Any vacancy in the board of directors, including a vacancy resulting from the enlargement of the board, may be filled by the stockholders or, in the absence of stockholder action, by the directors by vote of a majority of the directors then in office. If the office of the president or the treasurer or the clerk becomes vacant, the directors may elect a successor by vote of a majority of the directors then in office. If the office of any other officer becomes vacant, the directors may elect or appoint a successor by vote of a majority of the directors present. Each such successor shall hold office for the unexpired term, and in the case of the president, the treasurer and the clerk, until his successor is chosen and qualified, or in each case until he sooner dies, resigns, is removed or becomes disqualified. The directors shall have and may exercise all their powers notwithstanding the existence of one or more vacancies in their number.

Section 7. CAPITAL STOCK

7.1. *Number and Par Value.*   The total number of shares and the par value, if any, of each class of stock which the corporation is authorized to issue shall be as stated in the articles of organization.

7.2. *Fractional Shares.*   The corporation shall not issue fractional shares of stock but may issue scrip, in registered or bearer form, which shall entitle the holder to receive a certificate for a full share upon surrender of such scrip aggregating a full share, the terms and conditions and manner of issue of such scrip to be fixed by the directors.

7.3. *Stock Certificates.*   Each stockholder shall be entitled to a certificate stating the number and the class and the designation of the series, if any, of the shares held by him, in such form as shall, in conformity to law, be prescribed from time to time by the directors. Such certificate shall be signed by the president or a vice president and by the treasurer or an assistant treasurer. Such signatures may be facsimiles if the certificate is signed by a transfer agent, or by a registrar, other than a director, officer or employee of the corporation. In case any officer who has signed or whose facsimile signature has been placed on such certificate shall have ceased to be such officer before such certificate is issued, it may be issued by the

(Item B continued)

corporation with the same effect as if he were such officer at the time of its issue.

7.4. *Loss of Certificates.* In the case of the alleged loss or destruction or the mutilation of a certificate of stock, a duplicate certificate may be issued in place thereof, upon such terms as the directors may prescribe.

Section 8.   TRANSFER OF SHARES OF STOCK

8.1. *Transfer on Books.*   Subject to the restrictions, if any, stated or noted on the stock certificates, shares of stock may be transferred on the books of the corporation by the surrender to the corporation or its transfer agent of the certificate therefor properly endorsed or accompanied by a written assignment and power of attorney properly executed, with necessary transfer stamps affixed, and with such proof of the authenticity of signature as the directors or the transfer agent of the corporation may reasonably require. Except as may be otherwise required by law, by the articles of organization or by these by-laws, the corporation shall be entitled to treat the record holder of stock as shown on its books as the owner of such stock for all purposes, including the payment of dividends and the right to receive notice and to vote with respect thereto, regardless of any transfer, pledge or other disposition of such stock until the shares have been transferred on the books of the corporation in accordance with the requirements of these by-laws.

It shall be the duty of each stockholder to notify the corporation of his post office address.

8.2. *Record Date and Closing Transfer Books.*   The directors may fix in advance a time, which shall not be more than sixty days before the date of any meeting of stockholders or the date for the payment of any dividend or making of any distribution to stockholders or the last day on which the consent or dissent of stockholders may be effectively expressed for any purpose, as the record date for determining the stockholders having the right to notice of and to vote at such meeting and any adjournment thereof or the right to receive such dividend or distribution or the right to give such consent or dissent, and in such case only stockholders of record on such record date shall have such right, notwithstanding any transfer of stock on the books of the corporation after the record date; or without fixing such record date the directors may for any of such purposes close the transfer books for all or any part of such period.

(Item B continued)

Section 9. INDEMNIFICATION OF DIRECTORS AND OFFICERS

The corporation shall, to the extent legally permissible, indemnify each of its directors and officers (including persons who serve at its request as directors, officers, or trustees of another organization in which it has any interest, as a shareholder, creditor, or otherwise) against all liabilities and expenses, including amounts paid in satisfaction of judgments, in compromise or as fines and penalties, and counsel fees, reasonably incurred by him in connection with the defense or disposition of any action, suit, or other proceeding, whether civil or criminal, in which he may be involved or with which he may be threatened, while in office or thereafter, by reason of his being or having been such a director or officer, except with respect to any matter as to which he shall have been adjudicated in any proceeding not to have acted in good faith in the reasonable belief that his action was in the best interests of the corporation; provided, however, that as to any matter disposed of by a compromise payment by such director or officer, pursuant to a consent decree or otherwise, no indemnification either for said payment or for any other expenses shall be provided unless such compromise shall be approved as in the best interests of the corporation, after notice that it involves such indemnification: (a) by a disinterested majority of the directors then in office; or (b) by a majority of the disinterested directors then in office, provided that there has been obtained an opinion in writing of independent legal counsel to the effect that such director or officer appears to have acted in good faith in the reasonable belief that his action was in the best interests of the corporation; or (c) by the holders of a majority of the outstanding stock at the time entitled to vote for directors, voting as a single class, exclusive of any stock owned by any interested director of officer. The right of indemnification hereby provided shall not be exclusive of or affect any other rights to which any director or officer may be entitled. As used in this Section, the terms "director" and "officer" include their respective heirs, executors and administrators, and an "interested" director or officer is one against whom in such capacity the proceedings in question or another proceeding on the same or similar grounds is then pending. Nothing contained in this Section shall affect any rights to indemnification to which corporate personnel other than directors and officers may be entitled by contract or otherwise under law.

Section 10. CORPORATE SEAL

The seal of the corporation shall, subject to alteration by the directors, consist of a flat-faced circular die with the word

(Item B continued)

"Massachusetts," together with the name of the corporation and the year of its organization, cut or engraved thereon.

Section 11. EXECUTION OF PAPERS

Except as the directors may generally or in particular cases authorize the execution thereof in some other manner, all deeds, leases, transfers, contracts, bonds, notes, checks, drafts and other obligations made, accepted or endorsed by the corporation shall be signed by the president or by one of the vice presidents or by the treasurer.

Section 12. FISCAL YEAR

Except as from time to time otherwise provided by the board of directors, the fiscal year of the corporation shall end on the last day of June of each year.

Section 13. AMENDMENTS

These by-laws may be altered, amended or repealed at any annual or special meeting of the stockholders called for the purpose, of which the notice shall specify the subject matter of the proposed alteration, amendment or repeal or the sections to be affected thereby, by vote of the stockholders, or if there shall be two or more classes or series of stock entitled to vote on the question, by vote of each such class or series. These by-laws may also be altered, amended or repealed by vote of the majority of the directors then in office, except that the directors shall not take any action which provides for indemnification of directors or affects the powers of directors or officers to contract with the corporation, nor any action to amend this Section 13, and except that the directors shall not take any action unless permitted by law.

Any by-law so altered, amended or repealed by the directors may be further altered or amended or reinstated by the stockholders in the above manner.

Item C—investment letter

Fly By Nite Electronics
42 Crooked Lane
Boston, Massachusetts   02114

Dear Sirs:

The undersigned hereby represents and agrees that the shares of the Common Stock, par value of $0.10 per share, of Fly By Nite Electronics, Inc., a Massachusetts corporation ("Fly By"), being acquired by the undersigned, are being acquired by the undersigned for investment only and not with a view to, or for sale in connection with, a distribution thereof, and not with a view to their resale. The undersigned hereby further represents and agrees that such shares are being acquired by the undersigned for the undersigned's own account, and not with a view to their division among others, and that no other person has any direct or indirect beneficial interest in such shares.

The undersigned hereby agrees that such shares will not be sold or otherwise transferred (a) unless there is in effect, with respect to such shares, a Registration Statement under the Securities Act of 1933, as amended, or (b) unless an appropriate no-action letter issued by the Securities and Exchange Commission shall have been obtained, or (c) unless a written opinion of counsel for Fly By shall have been obtained stating that such a Registration Statement is not required.

The undersigned acknowledges that Fly By's Transfer Agent, if any, shall be advised of this agreement and instructed by Fly By to restrict transfer of such shares in accordance with the terms hereof.

The undersigned further agrees that the stock certificate or certificates to be issued for such shares shall bear the following legend:

> THE SHARES REPRESENTED BY THIS CERTIFICATE HAVE BEEN ACQUIRED FOR INVESTMENT AND MAY NOT BE SOLD OR OTHERWISE TRANSFERRED UNLESS A REGISTRATION STATEMENT UNDER THE SECURITIES ACT OF 1933, AS AMENDED, IS IN EFFECT WITH REGARD THERETO, OR AN APPROPRIATE NO-ACTION LETTER ISSUED BY THE SECURITIES AND EXCHANGE COMMISSION SHALL HAVE BEEN OBTAINED, OR A WRITTEN OPINION OF COMPANY COUN-

(Item C continued)

SEL SHALL HAVE BEEN OBTAINED STAT-
ING THAT SUCH A REGISTRATION STATE-
MENT IS NOT REQUIRED.

Very truly yours,

Dated: _____

Item D

EMPLOYMENT AGREEMENT

THIS AGREEMENT made by and between _____ (hereinafter called the Employee), residing at _____ _____, and _____ Corporation (hereinafter called the company), a corporation organized under the laws of Delaware with an office and place of business at _____ .
_____ .

WITNESSETH

WHEREAS, the Employee has accepted employment by the Company at a stated compensation which is hereby made a part of the consideration of this Agreement; and

WHEREAS, the Company is engaged in the business of design, manufacture, selling, servicing, and otherwise general research, development, and promotion of instruments, equipment, mechanisms, electronic and other components and machinery for computers, data processing equipment and systems, and allied or related products; and

WHEREAS, by reason of such employment the Employee is put in contact with developments and ideas and has access to developments, inventions, and ideas relating to the business of the Company; and

WHEREAS, the Employee by reason of such employment has the advantage of working with and contacting other employees of the Company engaged upon work relating to the business of the Company;

NOW, THEREFORE, in consideration of the premises herein-above recited, it is agreed as follows:

1. The Employee hereby agrees promptly to disclose and

(Item D continued)

assign to the Company the Employee's entire right, title, and interest in and to any and all inventions and discoveries solely or jointly conceived, and/or reduced to practice by the Employee during the term of this Agreement relating, directly or indirectly, to the current or projected business of the Company.

2. The Employee agrees that all of the inventions and discoveries specified in this Agreement are entirely the property of the Company.

3. The term of this Agreement shall be for the entire period of the Employee's employment and for one year subsequent thereto. The obligation of the Employee to render assistance in obtaining patents on inventions and discoveries made by him during the term of this Agreement shall continue after the termination of such term.

   Any assistance given by the Employee to the Company at its request, after termination of his employment by the Company, is to be paid for by the Company either at the rate of pay received by the Employee at the termination of employment or at the rate of pay earned by Employee when such assistance is rendered, whichever rate is greater.

4. The Employee agrees to execute without further consideration all documents and to perform all acts, at the expense of the Company, as may, in the opinion of the Company, be required to effectuate the provisions and intent of this Agreement, including the execution of all papers required to obtain and assign to the Company United States and Foreign Letters Patents, divisions, continuations, renewals and reissues thereof.

5. The Employee will also, at the request and expense of the Company, assist it by testifying in patent interferences and patent litigations and other proceedings in which the Company is or may be concerned.

6. The Employee agrees to receive confidential and proprietary information of the Company in confidence, and not to disclose to others, assist others in the application of, or use for the Employee's own gain, such information or any part thereof, unless and until it has become public knowledge or has come into the possession of such other or others by legal and equitable means.

7. To assist in carrying out the intent of Paragraph 6 above, the Employee, during the term of his employment, agrees to refrain from engaging on his own behalf or on behalf of any third party in the design, manufacture, use, servicing

(Item D continued)

or sale of instruments, equipment, mechanisms, electronic and other components and machinery for computers, data processing equipment and systems and allied or related products, or any research or other general development work in this field of activity.

8. In the event that applications for patents for inventions made by the Employee individually or jointly during the term of this Agreement shall not have been filed during said term or in the event that assignments with reference to the aforesaid inventions shall not have been executed by the Employee during said term, then the Employee agrees to execute such papers whenever so requested by the Company.

9. The Employee expressly authorizes and directs his executors, administrators or legal representatives whenever requested to do so by the Company, in the event of his death or incapacity to act for any reason whatsoever, to sign any and all applications for Letters Patent and any and all assignments thereof which the Company shall deem necessary to vest in it the full and complete title to said inventions.

10. The rights accruing to the Company under this Agreement shall pass to its successors or assigns.

11. The Employee agrees that no supplemental compensation shall be due the Employee from the Company for inventions within the scope of this Agreement and that all the Employee's inventions shall be presumed to be the property of the Company subject to the right of rebuttal of this presumption.

   IN WITNESS WHEREOF, the Employee has hereunto affixed his hand and seal and the Company has caused this Agreement to be signed by its ___ herebefore duly authorized, and its seal to be hereto affixed this ___ day of _____ 19 __.

Witness   /s/_____ (Seal)
                                            Employee
/s/ _____   _____CORPORATION
/s/ _____   By /s/ _____ (Seal)
                                            Secretary

Item E

LEASE

LEASE made this 1st day of April, 1971, by and between LAND ASSOCIATES, a partnership (the "Lessors") and FLY BY NITE ELECTRONICS, INC., a Massachusetts corporation (the "Lessee").

I. *PREMISES, TERM AND RENT*

(a) *The Premises.* The Lessors, in consideration of the rents, covenants and agreements to be paid, kept and performed by the Lessee, hereby lease to the Lessee and the Lessee hereby leases from the Lessors the land located at 42 Crooked Lane, Boston, Middlesex County, Massachusetts, which is more fully described in Schedule A attached hereto, together with all buildings thereon (the "Premises").

(b) *The Term.* TO HAVE AND TO HOLD the Premises for a term of six years commencing on the 1st day of April, 1971, and ending on the 31st day of March, 1977, and thereafter from year to year unless terminated by either party at the end of the original term or any anniversary thereof by giving at least three months' written notice to the other party, or as otherwise provided herein.

(c) *Rent.* YIELDING AND PAYING THEREFOR the Annual Rental or $24,000 in equal monthly installments of $2,000 each, in advance, on the first business day of each month during the term, the first payment to be made on the 1st day of April, 1971.

(d) *Additional Rent.* In addition to the rent set forth to be paid by the Lessee to the Lessors, and as part of the total rent to be paid under this Lease by the Lessee, the Lessee covenants and agrees to pay to the Lessor, with respect to each year of the term of this Lease beginning after April 1, 1971, the amount, if any, by which the total real estate taxes (or other like or substitute taxes) assessed for such year against or with respect to the Premises, exceed those so assessed for the year 1970. Payment shall be made by the Lessee to the Lessors not later than ten days before the last day on which such taxes may be paid without interest or penalty, provided that prior to such day the Lessors have presented to the Lessee a statement containing the relevant figures and a computation of the amount due hereunder, and except that payment for an appropriate portion of such taxes for any portion of a tax period included within the term of this Lease shall, upon termination of this Lease for any reason or at the expiration of the term, be payable upon such termination or at the end of said term, and, if the amount is not

(Item E continued)

then determinable, shall be made on the basis of the last prior tax with readjustment as soon as the correct amount is determinable. Any sums paid to the Lessor pursuant to this paragraph shall be held as a trust fund to be applied to payment of the taxes on or before the last day on which such taxes may be paid without interest or penalty.

II. *LESSOR'S COVENANTS*

For the consideration aforesaid, the Lessors covenant and agree with the Lessee as follows:

(a) *Quiet Enjoyment.* The Lessors represent and warrant that they have good right and title to lease the Premises to the Lessee and will defend the Lessee in the peaceful and quiet enjoyment thereof against the claims of all persons whomsoever.

III. *LESSEE'S COVENANTS*

The Lessee agree during said term and any extension thereof, and so long as Lessee's occupancy continues:

(a) Payments. To pay when due (i) said rent, (ii) all license and permit fees and all similar charges affecting the Premises and the occupancy and use thereof by the Lessee. The Lessors agree to join with the Lessee in making application for licenses and permits and utility installations as requested by the Lessee.

(b) *Utilities, Repairs, and Maintenance.* The Lessee will bear the cost of all utilities supplied to the Premises and shall maintain and repair the Premises in accordance with customary standards for first class office buildings as established from time to time by the National Association of Building Owners and Managers, and shall keep the Premises in as good order as when they were entered upon, reasonable wear and tear, and fire, and other casualty excepted, and shall pay all other charges arising from the Premises so that the rent paid by the Lessee shall, with the exception of local real estate taxes, be absolutely net to the Lessors.

(c) *Exoneration and Indemnity.* Not to hold the Lessors responsible for any loss or damage to person or property on the Premises unless occasioned by wrongful act or negligence of the Lessors; and to save the Lessors harmless and indemnified from any liability, injury, loss, accident, or damage to any person or property, and from any claims, actions, proceedings and costs in connection therewith, including reasonable counsel fees, arising from wrongful act or negligence of Lessee and not due to wrongful act or negligence of Lessors.

(d) *Waste.* Not to suffer or permit any waste or destruction of the Premises or do any act or thing on the Premises that

(Item E continued)

shall be contrary to any applicable requirement of law, ordinance, or any order or regulation of public authority.

(e) *Mechanics' Liens.* Not to permit any mechanics', laborers', materialmen's liens or other charges or encumbrances for any labor or material furnished to the Lessee or claimed to have been furnished to the Lessee, its agents or contracts in connection with work of any character performed or claimed to have been performed on the Premises, to become delinquent, or otherwise to affect adversely the Lessor's interest in the Premises, except that the Lessee shall have the right in good faith to contest the validity or amount of any such lien upon the Lessors' interest in the Premises upon providing reasonable security to the Lessors to prevent any sale, foreclosure or forfeiture of the Lessors' interest in the Premises by reason of the non-payment of such lien.

(f) *Inspection.* To permit to Lessors to examine the Premises at reasonable times and to enter upon the Premises at reasonable times and in case of emergency.

(g) *Heat.* To keep the building adequately heated.

IV. *ALTERATIONS AND IMPROVEMENTS BY THE LESSEE*

The Lessee shall have the right, at its own expense, to make any alteration or improvement to the building which it deems necessary or appropriate for the carrying on of its business and all activities necessary or incidental thereto, provided, however, that before making any major structural change or any alteration to the exterior of the building the Lessee shall first obtain the written consent of the Lessors. All such alterations and improvements shall be done in compliance with all applicable laws, ordinances, rules, and regulations of governmental authority. Title to all such alterations and improvements shall remain in the Lessee for the term of this Lease and any extensions thereof.

V. *EMINENT DOMAIN*

In case of taking by eminent domain of the Building or such portions thereof as reduce the floor area of the Premises by more than one-fourth (1/4), the Lessee may, by notice to the Lessor within thirty (30) days thereafter, terminate this lease as of the date when the Lessee is required to vacate the portions taken. The Lessors reserve and except all rights to damages to said premises and building and the leasehold thereby created accruing in case of taking or act of public or other authority, and the Lessee hereby grants to the Lessors all the Lessee's rights to such damages and agrees to deliver such further instruments of assignment thereof as the Lessor may from time to time reasonably request. The Lessors shall, however, pay to

(Item E continued)

the Lessee from such damages when received the amounts, if any, by which the same were increased by reason of inclusion therein of any award for fixtures and equipment which Lessee is entitled to remove, and for cost to the Lessee of such repairs and of moving from the premises taken. In the event that Lessee does not terminate the lease after a partial taking a just proportion of the rent shall be abated until what remains of the Premises shall have been restored by the Lessors to proper condition for use and occupation and thereafter a just proportion of the rent according to the nature and extent of the taking shall be permanently abated.

VI. *DAMAGE*

It is agreed that, if the Premises, or any part thereof, shall, during the term, be destroyed or damaged by fire or other casualty so that the Premises shall be thereby rendered unfit for occupancy, unless such damage shall have been caused by the neglect, default or misuse of the Premises by the Lessee or his employees, the rent hereinbefore reserved, or a just and proportionate part thereof according to the nature and extent of the damage sustained, shall be abated until the Premises shall have been put in proper total condition by the Lessors; *provided, however,* that if 25% or more of the floor area of the building is rendered untenantable by such damage, either party may, by notice to the other party given within thirty (30) days after the occurrence of such destruction or damage, terminate this Lease.

VII. *INSURANCE*

Each insurance policy carried by either party with respect to the Premises or occurrences thereon, which insures the interest of one party only, shall, if the other requests and it can be so written, and does not result in additional premiums or the party making such request agrees to pay any additional premiums resulting, include provisions denying to the insurer acquisition by subrogation of rights of recovery against the other to the extent such rights have been waived by the insured prior to occurence of loss or injury. Each party, notwithstanding any provision of this Lease otherwise permitting such recover, hereby waives any rights of recovery against the other for loss or injury against which such part is protected by insurance, to the extent of the coverage provided by such insurance.

VIII. *DEFAULT*

This lease is made upon the express condition that if default shall be made in the payment of said rent or any part thereof, or in the payment of any other sums due hereunder, at the times and places fixed for the payment thereof, and said

(Item E continued)

default shall continue for ten (10) days, or if default shall be made in the performance of any other of the covenants herein contained on the part of the Lessee to be kept and performed, the Lessors may give to the Lessee notice of such default and the nature thereof, and if the Lessor does not receive payment within ten (10) days after the giving of the notice or if said default in the performance of any other such covenant of this Lease is not corrected or removed within sixty (60) days after the giving of the notice, or if the Lessee shall make an assignment for the benefit of creditors, or file a voluntary petition in bankruptcy or insolvency, or shall be adjudged a bankrupt, or if a permanent receiver of the property of the Lessee shall be appointed, or the Lessee shall be declared bankrupt or insolvent according to law, or if the estate hereby created shall be taken by process of law, or if the Premises shall be deserted or vacated, then and in any of the said cases, notwithstanding any license or waiver of any former breach of covenant or consent in a former instance, the Lessors shall be at liberty thereupon or at any time thereafter while such default, assignment, insolvency, legal proceedings, desertion, vacancy or neglect shall continue, or be in effect, and without demand or notice, to discontinue furnishing any services to the Premises or to the Lessee, without liability to any person for such discontinuance, or to enter upon and into the Premises or any part thereof in the name of the whole, or otherwise to recover possession of the Premises discharged of this Lease, without prejudice, however, to the Lessor's claims for rent or other claims for breach of convenant hereunder, it being expressly understood and agreed that this Lease shall not continue to inure to the benefit of any assignee, receiver or trustee in bankruptcy, except at the option of the Lessors. The Lessee covenants that, in case of the termination of this Lease in any manner specified above, the Lessee will indemnify and save harmless the Lessor against all loss of rent or other damage which it may suffer by reason of such termination, including damages for anticipatory breach.

IX. WAIVER

The Lessors and Lessee covenant with each other that the failure of either to insist in any one or more instances upon the strict and literal performance of any of the covenants. terms or conditions of this Lease, or to exercise any option herein contained, shall not be construed as a waiver or a relinquishment for the future, of such covenant, term, condition or option, but the same shall continue and remain in full force and effect. The receipt by the Lessors of rent, with or without knowledge of the breach of any covenant, term or condition hereof, shall not be deemed to be a waiver of such breach,

(Item E continued)

and no waiver by the Lessors or Lessee of any covenant, term, condition or provision of this Lease, or of the breach thereof, shall be deemed to have been made by the Lessors or Lessee, unless expressly acknowledged in writing by said Lessors or Lessee.

X. *NOTICE*

Any notice to be given to the Lessors shall be in writing and sent to the Lessors by registered or certified mail addressed to 2000 Massachusetts Avenue Associates, 2000 Massachusetts Avenue, Cambridge, Massachusetts, and any notice to be given the Lessee shall be in writing and shall be sent to the Lessee by registered or certified mail addressed to the Lessee at the Premises, or in either case, to such other address as either party may from time to time notify the other party in writing as the address to which notices shall be sent. Any notice given by registered or certified mail shall be deemed to have been given when deposited in the mail.

XI. *PLACE OF PAYMENT*

The rent and other charges reserved in this Lease are to be paid by the Lessee to 2000 Massachusetts Avenue Associates, 2000 Massachusetts Avenue, Cambridge, Massachusetts, or in such other manner as the Lessor shall from time to time designate in writing to the Lessee.

XII. *SUCCESSORS AND ASSIGNS*

All terms, conditions and covenants to be observed and performed by the parties hereto shall be applicable to and binding upon their respective heirs, administrators, executors, successors and assigns, except where otherwise provided.

IN WITNESS WHEREOF, the parties hereto have executed and delivered this Lease as an instrument under seal the day and year first above written.

FLY BY NITE ELECTRONICS, INC.

[SEAL]

By_____
Donald Conman, Treasurer

ATTEST:

_____
Philip Shyster, Clerk

LAND ASSOCIATES

By_____

_____
Peter Cheatem, Partner

_____
Donald Conman, Partner

_____
Philip Shyster, Partner

Item F

PURCHASE & SALES AGREEMENT (PRELIMINARY) VENTURE DEVELOPMENT CORPORATION BOSTON, MASS.

International Corporation
Washington, D.C.   January 1, 1961

Attention: _____, President

Gentlemen:

This is to confirm to you our general proposal, as follows, to purchase substantially all the Property and Equipment of your company and to assume the principal existing or pending government prime or sub-contracts, and to purchase the related inventories or accounts receivable and other assets (including patents, trade secrets, drawings, etc.):

1. The specific description of said assets, contracts, and terms and conditions of our purchase and assumption thereof, will be set forth in a written Purchase and Sale Agreement between us which will include appropriate representations and warranties as to your unencumbered title and full corporate and other authority to effect such sale and assignments, conditions of closing, details of determination of price and payment, undertakings of further

(Item F continued)

assurance, and such other matters as are commonly included in an agreement of this kind, in form mutually agreeable to us and our respective legal counsel.

2. The tangible property and equipment of your company would be purchased at their depreciated book value, the inventories at their cost or fair market value (not in excess of the amounts recoverable therefor under contracts), and the accounts receivable (billed or unbilled) at their book value, it being understood that the value of such accounts will be guaranteed by you, all as will be determined as of the closing date after audit by, and in the absolute discretion of, Messrs. _____ or some other independent public accountants satisfactory to us. The fees and expenses of such accountants in this matter would be borne equally between us.

3. The closing of the transaction would be scheduled for as early a date (not later than 60 days from the date hereof) as would be reasonably possible after completion of arrangements for effective transfer of the contracts (including acceptance of the assignment thereof by the contractors, i.e., _____ etc.).

   A. During the period from the date of your acceptance of this preliminary proposal to the closing date, you will carry on the work of the company and the performance of said contracts in the usual course of business only, and make no material changes in said contracts or business without our concurrence.

4. We would expect at the closing to take over the pertinent operations of your company without unnecessary disruptions and to employ such of your personnel now engaged in such work as we believed necessary or desirable and to the extent they were willing to remain, but we would assume no obligations then existing on account of collective bargaining agreements, back wages, termination pay or existing employment contracts or benefits of your employees.

   A. We would expect to obtain from you or your landlord a satisfactory sublease or lease, effective on the closing date, relating to the premises at _____.

   B. You will undertake to effect complete physical removal within 120 days from the closing date of any property retained by you on these premises.

5. The purchase price would be paid to you as follows:

   A. At the closing, ___ in cash (including therein application of the sum of ___ being deposited

(Item F continued)

with you upon your acceptance of this preliminary proposal as "earnest money");

B. The balance, when determined by the independent public accountants, by our installment promissory note to your order, bearing no interest and being re-payable in annual installments each equal to at least 20% of the principal of the note. This note would be secured by a mortgage and pledge in the usual form of a security agreement under the Uniform Commercial Code covering the assets acquired by us. Such secur-ity agreement will not require the application of the proceeds of the collateral except in the event of de-fault and will permit substitution of collateral. The note will be subordinated to bank borrowings.

6. It is understood that in lieu of our being the purchaser, another corporation organized by us to carry on this business could be substituted.

If this preliminary proposal is acceptable to you, will you kindly indicate your acceptance by executing and returning to us one of the copies of this letter; whereupon, we will deposit with you as "earnest money" to insure our good faith in acting to consummate this purchase transaction with you, the sum of _____. It is understood further that upon your acceptance of this proposal and said deposit, (1) you will, of course, refrain from negotiating with others for any sale or dis-position of such assets or contract rights outside of the ordinary course of business unless or until said 60 day closing period has expired or we have mutually agreed to abandon this proposed transaction (in which event you shall promptly return said de-posit to us), and (2) we will both proceed immediately to make arrangements for preparation of the definitive Purchase and Sale Agreement by our respective legal counsel and to arrange for the audit and determinations of the purchase price by the accountants.

Very truly yours,
VENTURE DEVELOPMENT CORPORATION

By _____
President

Accepted _____, 1961

INTERNATIONAL CORPORATION

By _____
President

Item G—promoter's agreement

Law Offices
John Harvard Law
430 State Street
Boston 63, Massachusetts

January 15, 1960

Mr. Hubert P. Inventor
20 Hancock Avenue
Lexington, Massachusetts

                     Re: Invention filed under Serial No._____
                    in the U.S. Patent Office on_____
                    for "Data Processing Apparatus"

Dear Sir:

In accordance with our understanding with respect to the above invention, I agree to aid you in any negotiations and promotion of the said invention, or any improvements thereof, for the term of the pendency of said application and any patent or patents that may issue thereon.

I further agree that you will not be billed or charged by me for any legal work in connection with the license or sale of said invention, or any improvement thereof, and any such agreement, or agreements, must first be acceptable, approved and signed by you before it shall become effective.

In consideration of the above, you hereby grant to me twenty-five (25%) per cent of any royalties, or other payments, or stock, or other considerations received by you from the said invention, upon receipt of same.

If the above is in accordance with our understanding, please sign below the word "Accepted."

Very truly yours,

J. H. Law

Accepted, Boston, Massachusetts
January_____, 1960

_____
Hubert P. Inventor

STUDY QUESTIONS

1. Given the advantages of a Subchapter S corporation, why would a small-business owner elect to organize either as a propprietorship or as a general partnership?

2. Speak to an accounting professor. What advantages accrue to a Subchapter S corporation under Section 1244 of the Internal Revenue Code?

3. What advantages do limited partnerships have over a Subchapter S corporation?

4. Speak to an attorney. What is the cost to set up a corporation in your state? What specific requirements does the state in which you live impose on corporations?

5. How is the legal form of organization related to the estate planning of the owners of a small business?

CASE 1

STUDENT ENTERPRISES

In February, 1971, Barry Stratton and Rodney Watson were considering an opportunity to bid on a contract for the final assembly and packaging of "Snappet," a small recreational toy. Both men were Master of Business Administration students at a large university and had taken a course in starting and managing new companies. One of their professors had mentioned to them that Killebrew, Incorporated, was having difficulty manufacturing enough Snappets to fill its orders and was looking for someone to final-assemble and package additional quantities of the toy, which was being retailed throughout the United States for about one dollar.

The Snappet was a small athletic toy which could be used either by one person or by two or more people playing together. It was made out of two one-half inch dowels fifteen inches long, connected by a one-fourth inch mesh nylon net approximately eight inches wide by twelve inches long. Two lengths of elastic cord six to eight inches long, strung through the top and bottom of the netting, formed a pocket in which a small rubber ball could be caught and thrown. A quick outward jerk on the dowels caused the ball to be "snapped" into the air.

Killebrew, Incorporated, was in the business of marketing athletic equipment and toys, most of which it purchased already made or had manufactured on contract. Killebrew was producing Snappets in its own warehouse facility. When orders began to come in faster than Snappets could be made, it became clear to Killebrew's management that owing to the seasonal nature of toys (Snappet was intended for the spring season), a considerable number of orders might be canceled if not filled promptly. Killebrew then contracted with a school for the handicapped,

Adapted from "Student Enterprises (A), (B), and (C)." Copyright 1974 by Brigham Young University. This case was written by Professor Melvin J. Stanford as a basis for class discussion, and is distributed by the Intercollegiate Case Clearing House, Soldiers Field, Boston, Mass. 02163.

which was associated with the Easter Seal organization, to have its handicapped students do some of the final assembly and packaging of Snappets. Killebrew stapled the nylon netting to the dowels and cut the netting. The handicapped students at the school would thread the elastics, staple them to the dowels, and test and package the toy. Killebrew paid five cents per unit to the school for this work.

Production by the school, however, varied a great deal from day to day because students of different capabilities would work intermittently. Moreover, a typical rate of individual output was hard to determine because of these variations and the different degrees of handicap among students doing the work. The school viewed the project as useful therapy for the students.

Killebrew's general manager estimated that within the next two months, 150,000 Snappets would be needed in addition to what both the school and Killebrew could finish. The company would provide the nets stapled to the dowels, the balls, packages, elastics, labels, and instruction sheets. The contractor would have to provide facilities, equipment, and operating supplies, such as staples and tape. Moreover, a prospective contractor would have to demonstrate to Killebrew a capability to complete the contract work on time and with good quality control. Excessive loss of or damage to parts furnished would be charged to the contractor.

Barry Stratton had a bachelor's degree, with honors, in chemistry. He was 26 years of age and married. A Distinguished Military Graduate of the Army R.O.T.C. program, he had served as Cadet Colonel and Brigade Commander of the Army R.O.T.C. unit at his college. Barry was fluent in the German language and had lived in Germany. He was interested in computers, and financial and systems analysis. His prior work experience included graduate assistantships in college, selling real estate and life insurance, and summer work with a trucking company and an engineering firm. He and Rod both ranked in the top third of their MBA class.

Rodney Watson was interested in line management and in finance. During the previous summer he had worked in the Corporate Economic Planning and Development Department of Dow Chemical Company. He also had an undergraduate degree in chemistry and was a member of Phi Beta Kappa. In college, he had been president of his social fraternity. He had lived in Germany and was fluent in that language. Rod had an R.O.T.C. commission and held a graduate assistantship. He was 25 years of age and married.

Barry and Rod were recommended to Killebrew, Incorporated, by the professor who had told them about the opportunity. They visited the Killebrew warehouse and observed the Snappet manufacturing operation, which was then producing both finished Snappets and the partially completed units, consisting of nets stapled to dowels. There was no finishing and packaging operation that could be observed from the earlier assembly steps. However, they did get an idea of what tasks were involved.

The school for the handicapped was then visited by the two MBA students. Although their observations were complicated by the wide variations in capability and output, they estimated, after visiting the school and Killebrew, that college students working in small groups ought to be able to take the two dowels with net already fastened, thread the elastic and staple it to the dowels, label, test, and package the finished Snappet at an expected rate of about thirty-three to thirty-seven units per person per hour. They thought an optimistic rate might be forty per hour. Their estimate for average, full-time production workers was about thirty per hour.

Working space could be rented in a wing of a local manufacturing facility for $275 per month, including utilities. Barry and Rod estimated that it would be necessary to spend about $400 for air-driven stapler guns, $25 for air hose, and $10 to $25 for miscellaneous items, such as tape holders. It also appeared that an air compressor would need to be rented at a cost of about $185 per month and that rental of chairs would cost about $75 per month. Also, some plain wooden tables would need to be built, along with some simple assembly fixtures (such as a slot to hold dowels in place while the elastic was being stapled onto them). Transportation costs were not known, but at the desired rate of production, it appeared that about eighty miles one day per week for a truck and driver would be needed. Killebrew handled transportation in its contract with the school for the handicapped, but the possible university student operation would be further away.

Labor could be readily obtained. The university employment office indicated that there were plenty of students looking for part-time work and that the employment office would be pleased to help recruit students for an enterprise that would provide employment. Full-time university students were limited to twenty hours per week of part-time work in jobs referred by the university employment office. The minimum pay rate for campus jobs was $1.60 per hour, although that rate was not binding for off-campus work.

Barry and Rod began to analyze the potential profits and risks in the situation. They believed it was possible that college students, if properly trained and motivated for a task, could outperform the average production worker. The question in their minds was how that training and motivation might be given in a way to pay both wages and overhead and leave a profit to compensate for risk. Barry had $300 in the bank as an emergency fund, but his school and living expenses took about all else he had coming in. Rodney had used nearly all his funds to pay school costs.

There wasn't much time to consider the opportunity. Killebrew, Incorporated, wanted production started right away and expected a bid on the job from either or both of the students. Otherwise, Killebrew would quickly seek alternative means of getting the additional assembly capacity it needed.

On February 9, 1971, Barry Stratton entered into a contract with Killebrew, Incorporated, to final-assemble and package 150,000 Snappets by the end of March at a price of eight cents per unit. Barry decided to bid on the Killebrew contract by himself when Rod felt that he did not want to take the risk.

Under the name "Student Enterprises," Barry rented space in a local manufacturing plant for $275 per month, including utilities and compressed air. He purchased six staple guns at a cost of $50 each, which took all of his meager savings. Using his bank credit card to nearly the full $500 limit, he purchased wood for tables and fixtures, air hoses, and minor items. He first hired six male students through the university employment office. With these students, he built the tables and assembly jigs and worked out an assembly layout (see Case exhibit 1–1) and a list of team tasks (see Case exhibit 1–2). He then appointed each of those fellows as team leaders and hired twenty-four female students to form six teams, each consisting of four women and one man. The team leader was responsible for getting the women on his team a ride to work and home again and for supervising their work on the job.

Team leaders and members agreed to work as independent subcontractors (see Case exhibit 1–3). Barry Stratton believed

Case exhibit 1–1   Assembly Line

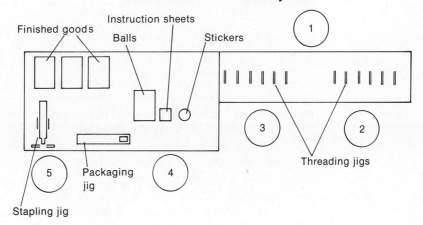

Case exhibit 1–2

STUDENT ENTERPRISES

Team Tasks

Stations 1, 2
Using needles fashioned from heavy clothes-hanger wire, team members one and two thread the elastic provided through the outside rows of the nylon mesh, threading the elastic through every other hole in the net and continuing through five Snappets.

Station 3
Using the air driven stapler, the team leader fastens the threaded elastic to the dowels by driving a staple on the inside of, parallel to, and one-eighth inch away from the last staple holding the mesh to the dowel.

Station 4
Team member four tests the Snappet by giving it two quick jerks to fully extend the elastic on each edge of the net. If the elastic pulls out, it must be rethreaded. Team member four then places a "Snappet" sticker on the upper part of the dowel, places a ball and instruction sheet in the Snappet itself and then guides Snappet into the package jig and the poly-bag held by the team member at Station five.

Station 5
Team member five holds poly-bag while team member at Station 4 guides the Snappet through the packaging jig and into the poly-bag, then uses the stapling jig to fasten the headed card to the top of the poly-bag, four staples per header. After enough Snappets of each color have been made to complete a box, they are then placed in a carton, the team member checking to assure proper numbers and colors in each container.

that this arrangement would facilitate good quality control and, of particular importance, provide the workers an incentive to increase production.

Teams were paid four cents each for the first 500 Snappets made on each four-hour shift and six cents for all above 500. Team members each received an equal share of team earnings based on team production. Barry also hired a production supervisor at $2.50 per hour and a transportation worker. He told the team leaders and the supervisor (a fellow MBA student) that some kind of profit sharing plan would include them, but that he hadn't worked out the plan as yet.

By mid-February, Student Enterprises was producing fin-

Case exhibit 1-3

STUDENT ENTERPRISES

ASSEMBLY AGREEMENT

It is understood that I am not an employee of Student Enterprises, but that I am acting in my own behalf and that I am purchasing uncompleted Snappets and all materials to complete, package and box the Snappets at $ .20 each. It is further understood that Student Enterprises agrees to purchase the completed and boxed Snappets at a price of no less than $ .24 each and no greater than $ .26 each, provided the Snappets are completed as to the specifications.

Signed, Buyer   _Address_

Signed, Student Enterprises   _Date_

---

ished Snappets. Team production started in the range of 450 to 500 units per shift and soon began to climb above 500. Shortly thereafter, Killebrew asked Student Enterprises if it could double production.

In response to this request, Barry Stratton, proprietor of

Case exhibit 1-4 Organization chart

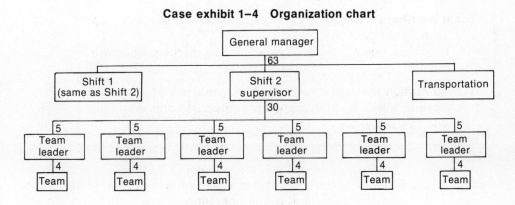

Note: numbers indicate the number of people for whom the next person up on the chart is responsible.

Case exhibit 1-5

STUDENT ENTERPRISES

Job Descriptions

General manager: responsible for effective functioning of the total operation. Duties include, but are not limited to:
1. personnel—employment and disemployment
2. finance—payroll for all personnel, expenditures for supplies, rent, startup costs
3. inventory—keep general records of materials received and products shipped, and assure adequate materials for production
4. quality control

Shift supervisor: responsible for effective functioning of shift operation. Duties:
1. keep records of hours, production of teams, absences
2. supply teams with some items needed for operation from inventory (balls, boxes)
3. take care of problems as they arise on the shift
4. quality control

Team leader: responsible for effective functioning of team operations. Duties:
1. transportation of workers to plant
2. keep record of hours and production of own team
3. serve as line of communication from shift-supervisor and general manager to team members
4. work as stapler on team
5. quality control of product
6. coordinate with general manager on rehiring and discharging team personnel

Team members: responsible for dependable quality work on team production line. Duty:
1. serve on team in one of five positions on the production line.

Transportation manager: responsible for making one trip per week to Killebrew with completed Snappets and returning with raw materials.

Student Enterprises, decided that he would have to add a second four-hour shift to the operation.

As a basis for the company operating with two shifts, Barry drew up an organization chart (see Case exhibit 1-4) and a description of duties (see Case exhibit 1–5). He decided to hire another supervisor for the second shift.

Killebrew wanted the production to ship quickly and began to help out with transportation for the increased quantity and with no change in the contract price.

As an incentive for efficient supervision, Barry worked out a profit sharing plan, in addition to the piece rate system, which would include team leaders and supervisors (see Case exhibit 1–6). By this means he hoped that they would strive for profit-able operation and high output without his having to manage

Case exhibit 1–6
STUDENT ENTERPRISES

Snappet operation — profit sharing plan for student enterprises

A bonus will be distributed to qualified team leaders and super-visors. The bonus will be determined:

1. a bonus will be given to those who are working at the completion of the project, or May 7, whichever occurs first;
2. the amount of bonus will be calculated on a contribution to profits basis, the basis being the total amount earned by the team and/or shift of which the team leader is a member;
3. the maximum bonus to be distributed to any individual will not be more than 2 per cent of the profits of the shift.
4. profits will be determined as follows:

Gross revenues		$XXXX
Less expenses:		
direct labor	$XXX	
indirect labor	XXX	
rent of facilities	XXX	
supplies	XXX	
transportation	XXX	
administrative expenses	XXX	
miscellaneous (start-up)	XXX	
Total expenses		XXXX
Gross profit		XXXX
less: estimated taxes		XXXX
Net profits		$XXXX
(upon which bonus is based)		

the business so closely that it interfered with his final semester of graduate school.

SUGGESTED QUESTIONS FOR DISCUSSION

1. Evaluate Barry Stratton's qualifications for starting his new business.

2. Do you consider this an "on-going" venture?

3. Is the present set-up going to motivate college students?

4. What other types of venture are open to the entrepreneur-student?

5. What type of profit should the new firm produce?

EDGAR SPEER

In July, 1974, Edgar Speer was faced with the decision whether or not to acquire a Paperback Booksmith (PB)[1] store in Bradford, Pennsylvania. For six months, Edgar had been searching for an opportunity to buy or start a bookstore of his own. He had hoped to locate something in the Boston area, (where he could continue to live rent-free in his duplex), but Paperback Booksmith's latest offer had caused him to reconsider. Mr. Supovitz, PB's vice president, had agreed to purchase the store back (including the license fee) after one year, at the same price Edgar had paid for the store (less 10 per cent depreciation fee on the fixtures).

While taking on the Bradford store would make it necessary to sell his duplex and move his wife and two children to Pennsylvania, the buy-back offer would considerably reduce his risk of starting a business of his own. Furthermore, if he bought the Bradford store, there was the possibility that he would be given an inside track on any new store opportunities that might develop in the Boston area. Such preferential treatment had been given other PB store owners.

For several months, Edgar had worked part-time for the New England Book Store, a full-line retail book store in Boston. This work sparked his interest in owning a bookstore of his own. "It was a moment of truth," he said, "as if I had been looking for the right thing for myself my whole life, and then there it was—I had found my home! I consider myself a humanist, an intellectual, and somewhat of a scholar, and the thought of being around books in a business of my own would give me a deep feeling of being exactly where I ought to be in life."

---

[1]Paperback Booksmith is a division of Learning Resources, Inc., a Boston-based book wholesaler. PB distributes through 12 company-owned retail stores and 37 licensed outlets along the eastern seaboard.

Prior to discovering the bookstore business, Edgar had taught American History in high school for six years. By necessity, he had earned his own way through college and graduate school. His college education was interrupted for three years while he saved money by working as a dispatcher for a steamship line. His only other business experience — real estate — had been remarkably successful. Starting with a $3000 inheritance from a distant relative, in 1968 he purchased a small investment property on Beacon Hill in Boston, and doubled his money in 24 months. He purchased several more properties during the next four years, and by 1974 had a net worth of over $50,000. He had $4000 in cash, $11,000 in a limited real estate partnership (which he felt he could turn to cash at any time), and he was sure he could get another $10,000 on his real estate equity to invest in a business of his own.

During the last six months, Edgar had visited dozens of bookstores in the Boston area. He asked each manager or owner every question politeness would allow, and made several conclusions from his interviews. First of all, most owners were happy to be in the bookstore business. Only one owner was interested in selling, but he wanted $85,000, more than double what he had paid for the store nine months earlier. The PB licensees indicated that they were all doing as well as, or better than, the PB Company had originally projected. One owner reported that he was doing triple the break-even volume of $250,000.

In addition, he spoke to every book sales representative who visited the New England Book Store. He learned that publishers gave a 40 to 50 per cent discount off list to a bookstore owner, and would allow a 100 per cent return allowance if the front covers were torn off the paperback books and returned within one year. He also learned that the publishers' sales representatives could be helpful in selecting the titles that were moving well in other stores.

The book sales representatives and the store owners were unanimous in advising that the most important ingredient to success was location. Books are largely an impulse item, and a successful paperback bookstore had to be located where there was a high foot-traffic count. Bookstores located in busy shopping malls seemed to do better than any other location. Unfortunately for Edgar, he learned that space in new shopping centers was tied up by well-known retailers like PB years before construction was started. Since shopping center owners wanted to rent to "name" retailers with strong balance sheets, Edgar felt that he had no chance of ever securing space in a substantial shopping center, unless he purchased a store from someone like PB.

As an alternate, Edgar considered opening his own bookstore in a 3500 square foot vacant store in Central Square, Cambridge, about two miles from both Harvard University and M.I.T. There were several other vacant stores in the vicinity but Edgar noted that there was a lot of foot traffic in the area, especially college students. While there was no other bookstore in Central Square, Edgar had learned that another bookstore in the same location had been opened two years ago, and closed after three months in business. The rent for this store would be $600 per month on a two-year lease. Since the store had already served as a bookstore, many fixtures were still usable. Edgar guessed that it would take about $10,000 to prepare the store for opening, including necessary renovations, furniture, and fixtures. He expected that his first-year expenses would be similar to those PB had projected for the Bradford store. He had visited the Small Business Administration, and was told he might be able to get an SBA-guaranteed loan of $15,000 to $20,000 to start a bookstore. This would give him a total of $40,000 to $45,000 to invest.

On the other hand, Edgar felt overwhelmed by the thought of starting a bookstore from scratch without the kind of training he would receive from a program like PB's four-week training course. His only real business experience at the retail store level had come while working at the New England Book Store. Many nights, he had stayed after hours with the owner and discussed such problems as training personnel, laying out stock, and taking inventory. But still he felt ill-prepared. "It's not that I am incompetent," he said, "but I just lack business training. For example, I know nothing about bookkeeping, filling out business tax forms, finding a profitable location, or placing advertising."

A further advantage of the PB program was its buying system, which provided a store with automatic and immediate distribution of new book titles, thereby virtually eliminating the need for an experienced book buyer on the store's payroll. PB also offered a unique inventory control system to assist in maximizing turnover of inventory.

Buying a PB license was not as easy as he had anticipated. The first opening in the Boston area was a new shopping center in Swampscott scheduled to open in March, 1975. He wasn't sure he could stand to wait that long, so he considered the six locations which were presently available—Seminole and St. Petersburg, Florida; Wayne, New Jersey; Washington, D.C.; Baltimore, Maryland; and Bradford, Pennsylvania. He ruled out the Florida locations because of their distance. Washington would have been his first choice, but PB had not made up its prospectus yet, so he could not consider it right now. Bradford, Pennsylvania, seemed to be in the middle of nowhere, and Edgar wondered whether a 35,000 population could support a paperback bookstore that needed over $200,000 in annual sales to break even.

Edgar drove to Wayne and Baltimore to inspect those locations. Both were in shopping centers scheduled for opening within a couple of months. He preferred the Baltimore location because the Wayne shopping center was a small group of stores adjacent to a larger mall, and he feared that most of the foot traffic would not pass by his store.

For experience as much as anything, he visited commercial banks in both Baltimore and Wayne, taking along the PB prospectus (see Case exhibit 2–1), and a letter from PB (Case exhibit 2–2), as well as his personal balance sheet. He asked for a bank loan of $22,500.

Two weeks later, he had heard nothing from either bank. He called Mr. Supovitz at PB and asked him if it generally took banks that long to make a decision. In the course of his conversation, he learned that the Baltimore license had already been purchased, and that PB, itself, had opened the Wayne location. Mr. Supovitz reported that the Wayne store's first week only grossed $2000, well below the break-even volume of $3500. "It will do poorly," he said; "therefore I wouldn't even sell it to you at its present sales level."

Mr. Supovitz's attitude confirmed Edgar's faith in the integrity of the PB organization, a faith up to now founded upon his conversations with many loyal PB licensees. (The Baltimore bank had also made inquiries, and found PB to have a reputation for honorable dealings.) Now more than ever, he wanted to tie up a license before any more opportunities slipped away.

Edgar decided to put a deposit down on the Swampscott store immediately. While it would mean a wait of eight months, perhaps he could use the time to complete his Master's thesis. (While he really wouldn't need a Master's degree in the bookstore business, it was one of those unfinished jobs that bothered him from time to time.) He took the 80-page PB license agreement to his lawyer for review, and drove at once to offer Mr. Supovitz a $5000 deposit on the Swampscott store.

Much to his disappointment, he learned that the Swampscott store had already been promised to someone else. Mr. Supovitz was sympathetic to his plight, however, and made him the unusual offer for the Bradford location. Not only would he guarantee to buy the store back in one year (including the license fee) but he would reduce the cash required to $15,000 so Edgar would not have to borrow additional money from outside banking sources to get started.

Edgar returned home to consider this new turn of events. His wife greeted him with a copy of the morning paper. An article in the business section indicated that his limited real estate partnership investment was most likely worthless. The partner-

Text continued on page 238.

"Dedicated to the fine art of browsing"

TO: Prospective Owner

FROM: Paul A. Supovitz, Vice President

RE: Paperback Booksmith Store
            Bradford Mall
            Bradford, Pennsylvania

The following enclosures are our prospectus on the licensing of our forthcoming store in Bradford, Pennsylvania. The enclosures include:

    terms and conditions of the sale, and total cost of the store;

    outline and breakdown of costs;

    lease and location information;

    first year break-even analysis;

    pre-opening schedule and timetable.

Our store is scheduled to open in May, 1974.

Case exhibit 2–1B

Bradford Mall
Bradford, Pennsylvania

The terms for the sale of this store will be as follows:

1. The buyer would purchase the license to operate a Paperback Booksmith store in this location for $10,000. This fee covers the site search and evaluation, lease and license negotiations, training and store-opening costs, and the use of the Paperback Booksmith name, marks, and systems.

2. The total opening cost of this store is projected to be as follows:

License fee	$10,000
Furniture, fixtures, and improvements	33,000
Sub-total	$43,000
Inventory	$35,000
Total opening cost	$78,000

3. The proposed financing schedule for this store is as follows:

Cash investment	$23,000
Bank financing	20,000
Inventory financing	35,000
	$78,000

The prospective owner should have a minimum cash

(Case exhibit 2–1B continued)

investment (unencumbered) of $23,000 plus $2,000 in working capital, or a total of $25,000. Local bank financing should be available to cover the balance of the improvement costs. The open inventory can be financed by Paperback Booksmith if desired, and will be repaid after the bank loan is retired. During the period that the opening inventory indebtedness is due Paperback Booksmith, payment for current merchandise purchased from Booksmith Distributing Company shall be on a weekly basis.

4. The license fee plus a $10,000 deposit on construction costs is due at signing. Balance of improvement costs to be paid when the store opens.

5. There is a goodwill charge based upon third-year sales. This is a One-Time Charge of 10 per cent of sales in excess of $200,000 for the third year. This covers the value and goodwill of the bookstore itself, its location, and the value of Paperback Booksmith's signature on the lease. This is the only intangible charge associated with the cost of the store.

6. The construction or improvement costs and the furniture and fixture costs are completely turnover if you elect to use us as your general contractor. Approximately one-half of this amount is removable fixtures.

7. As is the industry-wide practice, the inventory is 99 per cent returnable for full credit at any time. Book inventory is sold at a 35 per cent gross margin. We prepay all incoming trucking costs; owner pays freight-out on returns.

Case exhibit 2–1C

Bradford Mall
Bradford, Pennsylvania

BREAKDOWN OF COSTS

Furniture, Fixtures, and Improvements $33,000

This is totally a turnover cost, and our best estimate based on costs of the numerous mall stores which we have opened over the past years. There is a 20 per cent adjustment allowed in construction costs. All invoices are open for inspection and the cost is net after any landlord contribution towards construction. It includes:

HVAC	Painting
Plumbing	Store front
Sprinkler	Floor
Wall	Ceiling
Store design	Signs
Fixtures	Cash register
Electrical installation	Miscellaneous

Inventory at Wholesale $35,000

Working Capital $ 2,000

In addition to the above, it is recommended that the owner have available sufficient working capital to cover initial expenses:

First month rent	$ 618
Pre-opening labor costs	500
Cash register change	100
Petty cash	300
Back room needs	300
Miscellaneous	182
	$2,000

Case exhibit 2–1D

Bradford Mall
Bradford, Pennsylvania

<u>Bradford Mall</u>

<u>LEASE AND LOCATION INFORMATION</u>

Location:	U.S. Route 219 and Bolivar Drive, Bradford, Pennsylvania 16701
Mall description:	200,000 sq. ft. of gross leasable space; 20 stores. Major tenants are J. C. Penney's, Woolworth's, and Loblaw's Supermarket.
Size of store:	17′ × 120′, or 2016 square feet
Store due to open:	May 1974
Length of lease:	10 years plus a 5-year option
Annual base rent:	1st year—$6,048 ($3.00 per sq. ft.) 2nd year—$6,552 ($3.25 per sq. ft.) 3rd through 10th year—$7,245 ($3.60 per sq. ft.)
Percentage rent payment:	5 per cent of all sales over $120,960 (commencing with the third year)
Common area charges:	$1,370 annually (68¢ per sq. ft. estimated)
Use of premises:	Books; and as incidentals, records, tapes, magazines, newspapers, posters, adult games, puzzles, art objects, and educational toys

Case exhibit 2–1E

Bradford Mall
Bradford, Pennsylvania

PROJECTED FIRST YEAR BREAK-EVEN ANALYSIS

Sales for a new store are extremely difficult to forecast. As a means of providing you with some basis for projecting the possible sales volume for this store, we can refer to the experience of our existing stores. Most sales projections for retail operations are made on a per-square-foot basis. For the calendar year 1973, the average sales per-square-foot for PB stores open the full year was $141. Those stores that were open for their first full year averaged $114 in sales per-square-foot.

Operating expenses and overhead are fairly accurately predictable, based upon our past experience and the known fixed costs. We are therefore able to project the sales volume required to sustain this store on a cash break-even basis.

The figures quoted are comparable to actual expenses of existing mall stores and the projections are on a cash flow basis (i.e., do not include non-cash items such as depreciation and amortization). They do contain all normal controllable cash outflow, including debt repayment, interest expense, and owner's draw.

(Case exhibit 2–1E continued)

Sales		$204,500
Cost of goods sold @ 66%		135,000
Gross profit @ 34%		$ 69,500
Operating expenses		
Rent	$ 6,048	
Mall charges	1,370	
Salaries	13,000	
Owner's draw	15,000	
Payroll taxes	3,000	
Utilities	1,500	
Insurance	1,000	
Telephone	1,000	
Supplies	1,500	
Freight	500	
Shortages @ 1%	2,050	
Repairs and maintenance	500	
Miscellaneous	500	
Total operating expenses	$46,968	
Administrative expenses		
Royalties @ 4.25% (payable to PB)	$ 8,700	
Advertising @ 1%	2,050	
Accounting and legal	2,500	
Bank payment—principal and interest	5,400	
Interest on inventory loan	3,850	
Total administrative expenses	$22,500	
Total cash outlay		$ 69,468

Case exhibit 2–1F

Bradford Mall
Bradford, Pennsylvania

PRE-OPENING TIMETABLE

If you are accepted by Paperback Booksmith as the owner of this store, the following timetable is scheduled.

1. Proposed owner secures financing (subject to Paperback Booksmith approval) and reviews contract.

2. Formal signing of contract.

3. Training Program—4 weeks.

    Paperback Booksmith will provide rooming accommodations for new store owners during their training in Boston. Transportation and meals are at the expense of the owner.

First week	—general meeting with Paperback Booksmith staff.
	introduction and formal training in Paperback Booksmith systems, merchandising, retailing, and procedures, etc.
Second week	—develop and order opening inventory.
Third and fourth weeks	—continue with formal training; work experience in stores and warehouse.

4. The week prior to the store opening will be spent hiring and training your employees, installing fixtures, stocking the store, and attending to opening details. Booksmith will provide supervisory assistance during this pre-opening week, but it will be the owner's responsibility to provide sufficient labor to install the fixtures and stock the store.

"Dedicated to the fine art of browsing"

June 19, 1974

Mr. Edgar Speer
12 Lawrence Road
Brookline, Massachusetts   02146

Dear Mr. Speer:

In arranging for the finances of a Paperback Booksmith, I am sure that you will be discussing a business loan from a local bank. As I have related to you, it would be pertinent to inform any bank you are dealing with that Paperback Booksmith would be willing to repurchase the removable fixtures (i.e., bookcases, tables, front cash and wrap desk, and cash register) at their depreciated value using a 10-year straight line depreciation schedule, less any transportation costs to relocate these fixtures. This agreement would naturally be predicated upon these items being in an acceptable physical condition.

It would also be worthy of mention to any of these banks that the net worth of Learning Resources, Inc., as of December 30, 1973 was $1,207,718 and that we would be pleased to supply any bank with a copy of our financial statement at the appropriate time.

Sincerely yours,

Paul A. Supovitz
Vice President

PAS:mr
enclosure

ship had been forced into bankruptcy when the first mortgagee instituted foreclosure on all the partnership's real estate. "Even if the shares have a value," the article concluded, "it will be months (and perhaps years) before investors can convert them to cash."

SUGGESTED QUESTIONS FOR DISCUSSION

1. Evaluate Mr. Speer's background, regarding his probability of successfully managing a bookstore.

2. Evaluate Mr. Speer's financial condition at the end of the case.

3. What advice would you offer Mr. Speer at this time?

THE CASE OF THE MISSING TIME

It was 7:30 Tuesday morning when Chet Craig, general manager of the Norris Company's Central Plant, swung his car out of the driveway of his suburban home and headed toward the plant in Midvale, six miles away. The trip to the plant took about twenty minutes and gave Chet an opportunity to think about plant problems without interruption.

The Norris Company operated three printing plants and did a nationwide business in quality color work. It had about 350 employees, nearly half of whom were employed at the Central Plant. The company's headquarters offices were also located in the Central Plant building.

Chet had started with the Norris Company as an expeditor in its Eastern Plant ten years ago, after his graduation from Ohio State. After three years he was promoted to production supervisor, and two years later he was made assistant to the manager of the Eastern Plant. A year and a half ago he was transferred to the Central Plant as assistant to the plant manager, and one month later, when the manager retired, Chet was promoted to general plant manager. (See Case exhibit 3–1.)

Chet was in good spirits this morning. Various thoughts occurred to him as he said to himself, "This is going to be the day to really get things done." He thought of the day's work—first one project, then another—trying to establish priorities. He decided that the open-end unit scheduling was probably the most important—certainly the most urgent. He recalled that on Friday the vice president had casually asked him if he had given the project any further thought. Chet realized that he had not been giving it any attention lately. He had been meaning to get to work on his idea for over three months, but something else always seemed to crop up.

This case was prepared by G. L. Bergen; copyright 1971, Northwestern University. Reproduced by permission.

Case exhibit 3–1 Organization Chart of the Norris Company

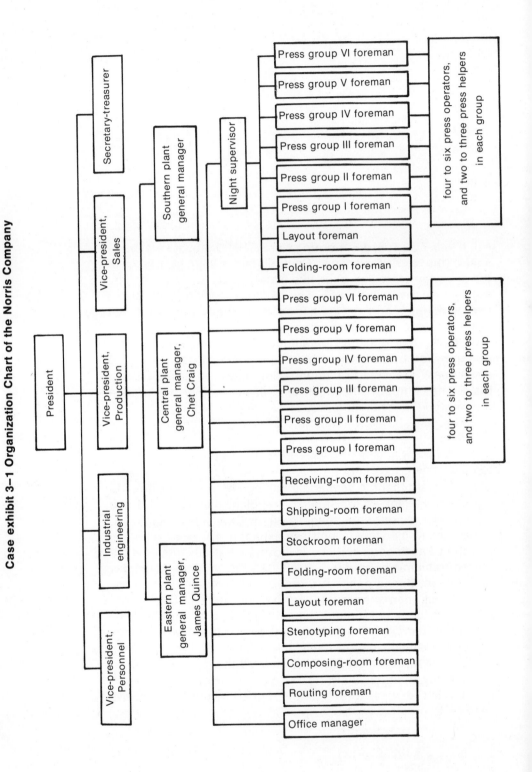

"I haven't had time to really work it out," he said to himself. "I'd better get going and finish it off one of these days." He then began to break down the objectives, procedures, and installation steps in the project. It gave him a feeling of satisfaction as he calculated the anticipated cost savings. "It's high time," he told himself. "This idea should have been completed a long time ago."

Chet had first conceived the open-end unit scheduling idea almost two years ago, just prior to leaving the Eastern Plant. He had talked it over with the general manager of the Eastern Plant, and both agreed that it was a good idea and worth developing. The idea was temporarily shelved when Chet was transferred to the Central Plant a month later.

His thoughts returned to other plant projects he was determined to get under way. He started to think through a procedure for simplifying the transport of dies to and from the Eastern Plant. He thought of the notes on his desk: the inventory analysis he needed to identify and eliminate some of the slow-moving stock items; the packing controls that needed revision; and a new special order form that needed designing. He also decided that this was the day to settle on a job printer to do the outside printing of simple office forms. There were a few other projects he could not recall offhand, but he felt sure that he could tend to them sometime during the day. Again he said to himself: "This is the day to really get rolling."

When he entered the plant, Chet was met by Al Noren, the stockroom foreman, who appeared troubled. "A great morning, Al," said Chet, cheerfully.

"Well, I don't know, Chet; my new man isn't in this morning," said Noren morosely.

"Have you heard from him?" asked Chet.

"No, I haven't."

"These stock handlers take it for granted that if they're not here, they don't have to call in and report. Better ask Personnel to call him."

Al hesitated a moment. "Okay, Chet," he said, "but can you find me a replacement? I have two cars to unload today."

Making a note of the incident, Chet headed for his office. He greeted some workers discussing the day's work with Marilyn, the office manager. As the meeting broke up, Marilyn took some samples from a clasper and showed them to Chet, asking if they should be shipped that way or if it would be necessary to inspect them. Before he could answer, Marilyn went on to ask if he could suggest another clerical operator for the sealing machine to replace the regular operator, who was home ill. She also told him that Gene, the industrial engineer, had called and was waiting to hear from him.

Chet told Marilyn to ship the samples, and he made a note of the need for a sealer operator, and then called Gene. He agreed to stop by Gene's office before lunch, and started on his routine morning tour of the plant. He asked each foreman the volumes and types of orders running, the number of people present, how the schedules were coming along, and the orders to be run next; he helped the folding-room foreman find temporary storage space for a carload shipment; he discussed quality control with a press operator who had been running poor work; he arranged to transfer four people temporarily to different departments, including two for Al in the stock room; and he talked to the shipping foreman about pickups and special orders to be delivered that day. As he continued through the plant, he saw to it that reserve stock was moved out of the forward stock area; talked to another press operator about his requested change of vacation schedule; had a "heart-to-heart" talk with a press helper who seemed to need frequent assurance; and gave okays for two type and one color procedures for different press operators.

Returning to his office, Chet reviewed the production reports on large orders against his initial projections and found that the plant was running slightly behind schedule. He called in the folding-room foreman, and together they went over the lineup of machines and made several changes.

During this discussion the composing-room foreman stepped in to cover several type changes and the routing foreman telephoned for approval of a revised printing schedule. The stockroom foreman called twice—first to inform him that two standard, fast-moving stock items were dangerously low, and later to advise him that the paper stock for the urgent Dillon job had finally arrived. Chet telephoned this information to the people concerned.

He then began to put delivery dates on important inquiries received from customers and sales people. (The routine inquiries were handled by Marilyn.) While he was doing this he was interrupted twice, once by a sales correspondent calling from the West Coast to ask for a better delivery date than originally scheduled, and once by the vice president of personnel, asking Chet to set a time when he could hold an induction interview with a new employee.

After dating the customer and sales inquiries, Chet headed for his morning conference in the executive office. At this meeting he answered the vice president for sales' questions in connection with "hot" orders, complaints, the status of large-volume orders, and potential new orders. Then he met with the vice president and general production manager to answer "the old man's" questions on several production and personnel problems. Before leaving the executive offices, he stopped at the office of the purchasing agent to inquire about the delivery of some cartons, paper, and boxes, and to place an order for some new paper.

On the way back to his own office Chet conferred with Gene about two current engineering projects. When he reached his desk, he lit a cigarette and looked at his watch. It was ten minutes before lunch—just time enough to make a few notes of the details he needed to check in order to answer knotty questions raised by the vice president for sales that morning.

After lunch Chet started again. He began by checking the previous day's production reports, did some rescheduling to get out urgent orders, placed delivery dates on new orders and inquiries received that morning, and consulted with a foreman about a personal problem. He spent about twenty minutes at the TWX* going over mutual problems with the Eastern plant.

By midafternoon Chet had made another tour of the plant, after which he met with the vice president of personnel to review a touchy personal problem raised by one of the clerical employees, the vacation schedules submitted by his foremen, and the pending job evaluation program. Following this conference, Chet hurried back to his office to complete the special statistical report for Universal Waxing Corporation, one of Norris's biggest customers. When he finished the report he discovered that it was ten after six and he was the only one left in the office. Chet was tired. He put on his coat and headed for the parking lot. On the way out he was stopped by the night supervisor and the night layout foreman for approval of type and layout changes.

As he drove home Chet reviewed the day he had just completed. "Busy?" he asked himself. "Too much so—but did I accomplish anything?" The answer seemed to be "Yes, and no." There was the usual routine, the same as any other day. The plant kept going and it was a good production day. "Any creative or special project work done?" Chet winced. "I guess not."

With a feeling of guilt Chet asked himself: "Am I an executive? I'm paid like one, and I have a responsible assignment and the authority to carry it out. My superiors at headquarters think I'm a good manager. Yet one of the greatest returns a company gets from an executive is his innovative thinking and accomplishments. What have I done about that? Today was just like other days, and I didn't do any creative work. The projects that I was so eager to work on this morning are no further ahead than they were yesterday. What's more, I can't say that tomorrow night or the next night they'll be any closer to completion. This is a real problem, and there must be some answer to it.

"Night work? Yes, sometimes. This is understood. But I've been doing too much night work lately. My wife and family deserve some of my time. After all, they are the people for whom

---

*Leased private telegram communication system using a teletypewriter.

I'm really working. If I spend much more time away from them, I'm not meeting my own personal objectives. I spend a lot of time on church work. Should I eliminate that? I feel I owe that as an obligation. Besides, I feel I'm making a worthwhile contribution in this work. Maybe I can squeeze a little time from my fraternal activities. But where does recreation fit in?''

Chet groped for the solution. ''Maybe I'm just rationalizing because I schedule my own work poorly. But I don't think so. I've studied my work habits, and I think I plan intelligently and delegate authority. Do I need an assistant? Possibly, but that's a long-time project and I don't believe I could justify the additional overhead expense. Anyway, I doubt whether it would solve the problem.''

By this time Chet had turned off the highway into the side street leading to his home. ''I guess I really don't know the answer,'' he said to himself as he pulled into his driveway. ''This morning everything seemed so simple, but now ——''

SUGGESTED QUESTIONS FOR DISCUSSION

1. What can Chet Craig do to improve his time utilization?

2. What does this case demonstrate about the need for planning?

3. Is Chet Craig's organizational position similar to most small-business owners'? What does this suggest?

EXPRESSWAY LUMBER COMPANY

Jack Parker, president of Expressway Lumber Company, was reviewing sales figures for the past month one morning early in May. He was pleased, and thought to himself that if sales kept increasing at the current rate, 1974 would be a very profitable year. He knew, however, the tremendous success experienced in April was primarily the result of two large contracts with Farwell Construction and Southtown Builders, which had been secured by the estimating department. Even though the national economy was suffering from rapid inflation and threatened by recession, it appeared to Jack Parker that 1974 might be the most lucrative year ever experienced in the company's 24 year history.

Following World War II, having served three years, Jack Parker began building homes with his brother and an army buddy. By 1949 the reputation and success of Parker Home Builders was well known, but Jack disliked the fact that his brother always received recognition for the company's accomplishments, and he was easily persuaded by several prominent business people to sell his share in the partnership and manage a soon-to-be formed building supply company. The operation first opened its doors in January, 1950, with Jack at the controls and grew gradually, reaching sales of $1,600,000 in 1973. Throughout this growth period Jack gained the respect of the community and business associates by working hard and always dealing honestly with customers. During the first year of business, Expressway Lumber specialized in wood products for construction, but soon added a wide variety of building materials, hardware, and hand tools.

This case was prepared by Christopher E. Fuhrmann, graduate student at the University of Notre Dame, under the supervision of Assistant Professor Francis A. Yeandel. Distributed by the Intercollegiate Case Clearing House, Soldiers Field, Boston, Mass. 02163.

Jack had seen a number of employees stay with the company for only a short time (especially yard laborers and truck drivers), but his reliable bookkeeper and secretary, Ellen McGraw, had served the organization for nearly 21 years. Besides himself, Ellen was the only person completely familiar with the company's books. Three years ago Jack's son, Mike, was added to the sales department, after graduating from the area's community college. Mike joined Charlie Jackson and Ken Williams, both experienced sales personnel. Last year, two more of Jack's children were put on the company payroll: Jim, a recent high school graduate, served as a yard laborer in charge of building and equipment maintenance, and Mary filled the need for part-time secretary. As the company expanded and additional personnel were hired, all new employees learned the trade through experience rather than a formal training program: inexperienced truck drivers, salesmen, and yard laborers were taught operating procedures by their senior co-workers through informal, on-the-job training.

Every morning, Jack would jot down items he intended to handle sometime during the day. This particular morning's list was brief, but included the following items:

1. Order lumber to replenish depleted stocks — 2×4s, 2×6s, and 4×4s especially low!
2. Send advertisement to newspaper.
3. Prepare employee vacation schedule.
4. Discuss driver tardiness and sloppy condition of yard with John.
5. Golf at 4:00 with Ed.

Jack also decided it was necessary to squeeze in some time analyzing a few problems which required prompt action. For over a year, it seemed that no one in the sales department (physically, the customer service area in the store) or out in the yard (the shipping and receiving building plus material storage areas) accepted fully the responsibilities of the job. To make sure things ran more smoothly, Jack often handled the assortment of unfinished tasks left by others. This resulted in excessive work for Jack and, consequently, he was frequently unable to attend to his more important duties as president of the company. It seemed certain to Jack that some day his son, Mike, would take charge of sales, but until then, a system was needed to coordinate store and yard activities more efficiently. In addition to the poor attitude displayed by employees toward their work, direct communication between the store and the yard had become progressively worse; however, Jack made sure that the flow of critical information was not restrained. Except for the estimating department, Jack, and his secretary, Ellen McGraw, it appeared that most Expressway Lumber Company employees exerted minimal effort in doing their job. This distressed Jack because he believed in "a fair day's pay for a fair day's work."

Around 10:30 A.M. Jack Parker received a phone call from Al Farwell, out at the Springville nursing home construction site:

Jack, this is Al, out at Springville. Our men can't work because that load of 2×4s and roofing you promised us first thing this morning hasn't arrived yet. If my men aren't working I lose money and if I send them home I'll have the union on my back until this job's over. We schedule work according to delivery, and when materials don't come we're stuck. This job's already behind schedule and I can't afford any more delays. To put it bluntly, I can't afford to pay for your mistakes!

It was usually Jack's style to handle these problems personally, so he assured Al that the materials would be at the site this afternoon and then politely closed the conversation.

Irritated, Jack proceeded to call around the yard on the speaker system (see Case exhibit 4–1), attempting to locate John Eckman, the yard foreman. John, a "veteran" lumberman, knew the lumber business, but lacked enthusiasm for his work, anticipating his official retirement at the end of the year. Failing to reach him over the intercom, Jack headed out into the yard

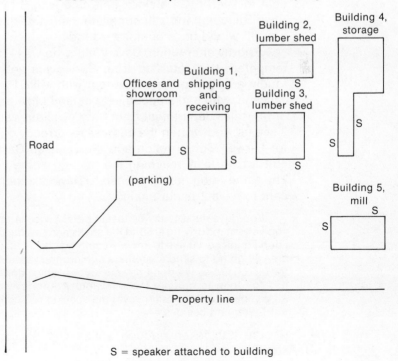

Case exhibit 4–1 Expressway lumber company

S = speaker attached to building

searching for John, or someone who might tell him where John was. After walking back to Building 4, he found John sorting spilled pallets and emotionally related Al Farwell's conversation to him. John thought he had sent the order out about three hours ago with Dave Wald and since Springville was only eighteen miles away he figured Dave would be back soon. Because most of the drivers had a poor reputation for punctuality, Jack made it clear that John should speak with Dave when he returned about his excessively long delivery time.

Jack hurried back to his office and on his way passed through the sales showroom only to find six or seven customers waiting at the counter for service. He wiped the perspiration off his forehead with the back of his hand, stepped behind the counter, and took orders for the impatient patrons. When store traffic cleared, Jack asked Ken Williams why he had been on the phone so long and why Mike and Charlie were not in the store handling the backlog of customers. Ken responded:

> My wife couldn't get the car started and so I had to explain what to do ... ah, I think the carburetor was probably flooded. Oh — Mike left for lunch already, he usually leaves early on Wednesday, and Charlie ... let me see ... Charlie might be back in the stock room, but I'm not sure.

These "rescue" situations were nothing new, but Jack realized that he could no longer run his organization as he had in the past and expect it to be profitable. Jack hastily left the sales counter and walked back to his office wondering if he would be able to keep his 4 o'clock golf date with Ed Donovon (Southtown Builders) and still complete the list of things he promised himself would be accomplished today.

Shortly after lunch, Dave Wald, who was known to be short-tempered, had returned from Springville and could be heard loudly arguing in the showroom with Mike Parker and Charlie Jackson, who had stepped in to defend Mike and the reputation of the sales department from Dave's vicious verbal blasts. Mike, it seems, had written the address incorrectly on the delivery slip for Farwell Construction and thus caused Dave about an hour and a half delay reaching the nursing home construction site. The same thing had happened to Dave last month and he didn't care to have it occur again:

> You guys must really be lost in here! Twice in the last three weeks you've sent me driving around the sticks and I've had it! Can't you read? I don't think so. I'd like to know something else — how many more times are you going to send customers out into the yard with a purchase slip for merchandise we don't have in stock — why, I don't know what good it is for John to prepare those inventory reports — no one reads them. All you have to do is call us over the speaker to find out what we've got out there, and besides —

Charlie had taken enough abuse and decided to set things straight:

We don't ever claim to be perfect, because we do slip up now and then, but listen, at least once a day we yell for a driver or yard man over the speaker trying to get some information and nobody answers... and each customer we don't satisfy walks right out the door and heads over to Garden City Lumber. You know, a few times I've walked back in the yard and seen four or five of you just sitting around in the mill doing nothing. John knows what's goin' on, so don't think you're getting away with anything—and don't think *we* are the cause of problems around here.

The commotion was noticeable and disruptive. Annoyed, Jack left his office to settle the quarrel before either one could respond with further insults. After spending a few minutes to temporarily resolve the discord, Jack asked Dave to come in his office for a second. Several brief questions indicated that John had never spoken to Dave concerning his inordinately long delivery runs; Jack then went out to the shipping building and asembled a delivery schedule to occupy Dave the remainder of the day.

Jack was again at his desk reviewing purchase orders and calling various wholesalers for quotes when Fran Long stopped by to show him the final estimates on some important projects. It took about half an hour to review some of the critical cost figures, but the bids looked both profitable and competitive, and Jack okayed Fran's work. Shortly thereafter, Ellen stepped inside Jack's office doorway and indicated that help was needed at the counter to handle an order for Bird Company's new polyvinyl siding which was recently added to Expressway's line of stocked items. Since it was a relatively new product on the market none of the sales personnel were familiar with its specifications or price, except Jack who had attended a home show in March, conferred with sales representatives, and studied accompanying literature.

Art Jenkins, the village fire chief, was interested in purchasing enough siding to cover the new addition to the fire station and had come prepared with a sketch and the building's dimensions. Jack explained in detail many of the outstanding features of this product which included easy installation and maintenance and the fact that it was rust-proof and dent-proof and had insulating qualities. An estimate was put together and the fire chief decided to purchase the siding immediately, so that the fire house addition could be completed soon. Jack ended the transaction by handing Art the purchase slip and instructing him to drive his pick-up over to Building 1 where Roy Becker or one of the other yard men would load his truck.

Walking out of the store, Art met Jim Parker and handed him the purchase slip; together they drove back to Building 4 and Jim began loading Art's truck. Although it was against company policy to issue any materials without proper authorization, Jim passively watched Art Jenkins throw a couple of 5-gallon cans of driveway sealer into the cab as he finished sliding the last length of siding over the tailgate and into position. Before Jim spoke up, Jenkins started away, but mentioned he'd pay for the stuff up at the store. Art's word was good, of course, but customer theft was thought to occur almost regularly.

Busy days frequently coincided with warm, sunny weather and this welcome spring day kept store traffic heavy throughout the afternoon. Customers were continually demanding advice or simply a few minutes of "neighborly" conversation with Jack, pushing him farther behind schedule and placing him under extreme pressure to finalize purchasing plans for the summer months. Also, a decision had to be made concerning an equitable employee vacation schedule, since Jack had promised this information would be available on pay day, which was tomorrow.

Every Wednesday after school, Mary Parker stopped by the office to assist Ellen with the weekly payroll, typing, and other secretarial duties. The checks were already prepared when Mary arrived, so she simply arranged them in a neat stack and took them to her father's office for his signature. Before leaving, Mary reminded her dad about his meeting with Ed Donovon at 4 P.M. Jack glanced at his watch—the afternoon had slipped by quickly, it was already ten minutes to four. He had to decide now whether to call Ed and cancel out on the golf date, or stay at the office and tackle what seemed to be a growing list of management problems. Jack intensely disliked making this call because he knew that future sales depended upon his ability to maintain outside contacts. During the next several moments Jack speculated whether he should make that call.

SUGGESTED QUESTIONS FOR DISCUSSION

1. How would you evaluate Jack's style of management?

2. How can the management situation at Expressway be improved?

3. How important does this case show experience and training to be?

4. What advice can you offer Jack regarding time management?

5. Why is time management often a problem in the small business?

STAR TOOL AND MACHINE COMPANY, INCORPORATED

HISTORY OF THE FIRM

Star Tool Company is a small machine shop engaged in the design and fabrication of equipment and tools. The company was founded as a corporation in 1970 by Armando Antonio and Louis Gonzales in Mobile, Alabama. Both men are Cuban refugees who came to the United States in 1960, after the Communist government of Fidel Castro seized their respective businesses.

Armando Antonio, the president of Star, was born in Havana, Cuba, and has the equivalent of a high school education, including three years of commerce training. He was 25 per cent owner in a brick plant in Havana, which was formed by his father in 1913 and had yearly sales of approximately $600,000. In 1952, Antonio and a brother, along with two partners, founded a second brick plant, which had a sales volume reaching about $350,000 per year. After Castro seized the companies, Antonio emigrated to Alabama, where he was employed first by Alabama Ceramics and later by Cointat Brick Works, which paid him an annual salary of $9,000. Mr. Antonio is now 59 years old and has 26 years of experience in machine shop work.

Mr. Gonzales, the manager of Star Tool, was born in Murskasobota, Yugoslavia, and has sixteen years of formal education, including four years of toolmaking. He began his apprenticeship in 1937 at age 13, under his brother-in-law in Camagüey, Cuba, at Jorge Lucas Machine Shop. Gonzales completed his high school education at night. In 1948, he was made a partner. In 1954, he became manager of the business with 33 per cent ownership. He held this position until 1960, when the government took over the shop, at which time Gonzales came to the United States. In this country, he worked in different areas of machine and tool manufacture and repair, including a position as process engineer at Smith Corona Corporation in Orange-burg, South Carolina, where he earned a salary of $10,000 per year. He also worked as a part-time machinist to supplement his salary. Mr. Gonzales is now 53 years old and has 26 years' experience as a machinist and two years as a process engineer.

At Smith Corona, Mr. Gonzales worked with Mr. Antonio's son and, through him, the two families met and became close friends. Mr. Antonio originated the idea of setting up a machine shop and Gonzales, though reluctant at first, agreed. The two men then began making plans for the business to employ Mr. Gonzales as manager, and one other employee, later to be joined by Antonio after the business was soundly established. The business was to engage in design, fabrication, and repair of small machines and tools. Mr. Antonio and Mr. Gonzales each obtained letters of reference from their U.S. employers that indicated their work was outstanding. They then called on prospective customers and obtained letters stating that a great need existed for the type of business they proposed to establish.

A bank loan for starting the business was refused, and the men were referred to the Small Business Administration. The bank had no adverse information on either man, and each had maintained satisfactory checking accounts. Mr. Antonio's net worth at the time was $6876, and Mr. Gonzales' was somewhat higher, at $9956. The bank considered a guaranty loan, but declined because of the request for a ten year maturity.

A loan inquiry was made of the SBA in September, 1969, and a 100 per cent SBA ten year loan of $25,000 at 5.5 per cent interest was granted on June 4, 1970. The loan was granted under EOL–11, because the applicants were of foreign nationality, with limited resources, to whom finances would not be readily available from other lending institutions. The business did not qualify for a loan under the 7(a) loan program because of its disproportionate debt-to-worth ratio and limited collateral. The SBA management evaluation indicated good management capabilities and a Dun and Bradstreet report revealed good credit and that both men were considered good credit risks.

The loan was to enable the applicants to start a tool and machine making and repair business. The proceeds from the loan were to be divided: $18,000 to purchase equipment, $1000 to purchase supplies inventory, and $6000 for working capital. The SBA considered these funds, along with the cash, tools, and equipment injected by Antonio and Gonzales, sufficient to allow business to be established on a small scale. Collateral for the loan consisted of all their business equipment, valued at $19,450, and a business inventory of $1000. As a loan condition, hazard insurance on equipment and inventory in the amount of $20,000, was required, along with copies of invoices for initial purchase of equipment. Monthly loan payments of $277 began on November 6, 1970.

Star Tool opened for business at 414½ Center Street. The greatest initial problem was obtaining good labor. The business progressed well, and by November, 1971, Mr. Antonio was working full-time in the business, while also working as a part-time consultant with Cointat Brick Works. An agreement was made in which Mr. Gonzales' salary would be the same as Mr. Antonio's combined salaries from Cointat Brick and Star Tool; this agreement has remained in effect to the present time. Mr. Antonio received $450 per month as consultant, which required one hour of his time each day; he was now drawing $650 per month from Star. The business was progressing better than expected, and each partner drew a bonus of $1450 at the end of 1970. All loan payments have been made on time.

By 1975, the shop on Center Street was too small for the business; therefore, the present site, consisting of one and a half acres of land on an interstate highway, was acquired from Cointat Brick. Star obtained the land for $7500, which was very inexpensive in relation to similar nearby tracts at the time. Cointat Brick was anxious to have the shop conveniently located to a plant they proposed to build on the adjacent site. In addition, Cointat made a loan of $43,000 to Star for construction of a new shop. The payment on the loan is $1400 per quarter, so Star's payments for the building are less expensive than rent would have been on a similar building. The shop was moved into the new building in mid-1975.

The management at Cointat had for some time tried to coax Mr. Antonio into coming back to work full-time, and in May, 1976, he returned as a plant manager for Cointat.

PRESENT MANAGEMENT

Both Mr. Antonio and Mr. Gonzales are experienced managers. Mr. Gonzales, as manager, makes all the day-to-day decisions for the business; Mr. Antonio is only involved in major decisions. Realistic goals were set for the business; in fact, they have nearly been attained. Mr. Gonzales states that he would like to have ten to twelve good men, and sales around $300,000 per year. He does not wish to go beyond these goals because he does not want the business to "get out of hand, which will cause too many headaches."

Mr. Gonzales believes one of his major problems is obtaining qualified personnel. He has advertised for employees, but the experienced people he would like to have seldom apply for jobs; he has recruited at the local technical schools, but states that people from schools must still be trained. There is a high turnover rate for employees; in fact, Mr. Gonzales recently lost his foreman. It is estimated that the firm has employed fifty different people since its inception. The number of employees needed fluctuates with contracts successfully bid for, and at times Mr. Gonzales "hires anyone who walks in."

Wages range from $2.25 per hour for cleanup men to $4.75 per hour for experienced machinists. In addition, a Christmas bonus of approximately $150 is given, depending on how well the business is doing. The firm has a group hospitalization plan for which it pays the total cost for the employee and half the cost for any dependents. Raises are generally given across-the-board and depend on the firm's financial success for the period. Increases are given one or two times a year, in accordance with the labor market.

Since losing his foreman, Mr. Gonzales schedules all work in the shop, generally oversees shop activity, and occasionally does machining work, in addition to estimating all work, calling on customers, and acting as business manager. He works from ten to fourteen hours per day, and expects his machinists to do the same if need be. In the past, this has caused some problems. Mr. Gonzales is a strong-willed person who expects hard work and high quality work from his employees. He takes pride in his own ability to perform difficult machining tasks and tries to satisfy his customers in every way. Mr. Gonzales does not mind getting his hands dirty and does not care about the frills that others in his position might desire; he has an office space in the new shop, but he has not bothered to furnish it yet, saying "I can be comfortable and act like a big-shot later; right now I have too much work to do. I have no delusions of grandeur."

Mr. Gonzales attributes his success to hard work, good service, quality work, and honesty, but another reason for his success is that he recognizes some basic principles of business. When speaking of small business in general, he stated, "In my opinion, most small businesses fail due to lack of working capital."

Since moving to the new location near the intersection of the interstate highway and a U.S. highway, the shop has a good layout with considerably more space than in the old location. The shop is well-lighted and well-ventilated, and has a generally clean and comfortable working environment. The shop has met all Occupational Safety and Health Administration requirements to date without difficulty. Since Star is a small job shop, machine arrangement is not as critical as in a manufacturing shop, so machines are grouped according to function. However, drill presses have been conveniently located throughout the shop owing to the many drilling jobs that come up throughout the machining operation. The welding bench and equipment are

Case exhibit 5–1

PLANT LAYOUT
STAR TOOL

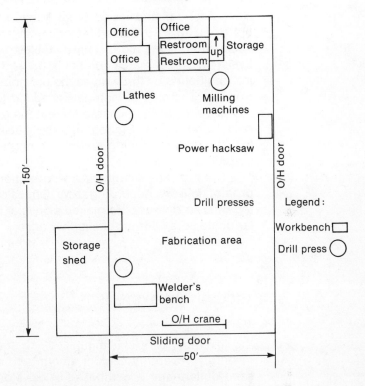

located in the rear of the building where space is ample for fabrication. The power hacksaw is located in front of one of the large overhead doors, which is convenient for cutting off long pieces of stock without blocking passage through the shop. A sketch of the layout is shown in Case exhibit 5–1. Storage space is adequate since only a small inventory of bar stock and standard items is maintained.

MARKETING

Mr. Gonzales makes all the contacts with customers and potential customers; there is no other form of advertising, such as a Yellow Page listing and bold printing in the White Pages of the telephone book, both of which his competitors have. Star's chief competitors in the area include Mobile Machine Tool

Service, Gibbes Machinery Company, John A. Willenborg Tool Making Company, Fryer Engineering and Manufacturing Company (fabrication), and Mobile Supply Company (fabrication).

Star's major customers include Tamper, Alabama Eastman, Westinghouse, Allis-Chalmers, Alabama Ceramics, Cointat Brick, Richley Brick, Merry Brothers Brick (Mississippi), Indian Brick (Florida), and Trojan Steel. Most jobs are on a competitive bid basis. Mr. Gonzales bids solely on the basis of his experience, without the aid of charts, tables, or diagrams. His bid is based on the estimated number of hours it will take him to do the job, multiplied by three times the per hour wage he must pay his workers. The cost of materials is added to this. Occasionally, a 10 per cent handling charge for materials is added, if he doesn't really need the job. Star obtains about 80 per cent of the jobs bid for. The goal of bidding policy is to make an annual profit of 10 per cent after salaries.

The firm has established a reputation for quality work and prompt delivery. According to Mr. Gonzales, he has rarely missed a promised delivery. He makes a special effort to help his regular customers with problems that arise.

ACCOUNTING SYSTEMS

Inventory control is minimal since Star maintains little or no inventory. Inventory seldom amounts to more than a few thousand dollars and is composed of bar stock and a few standard items. The purpose of this inventory is primarily to allow the possibility of starting a job the same day that an order is received. Almost all of the material used is secured on an "as needed" basis for a specific job.

Whether to make or buy an item is more a question of time and needed equipment than of calculated economics. Availability of manpower and machinery will dictate whether an item will be secured outside the company or produced internally.

Financial records and the actual payments of vendor invoices are handled by the Davison Tax Service. This firm also handles computation of taxes, preparation of financial statements, and maintenance of accounts receivable. The source data necessary for these activities are gathered at the shop, consolidated, and sent on to Davison Tax Service by the shop secretary, after Mr. Gonzales' review, if necessary. Preparation of the weekly payroll and maintenance of supplemental information on shop hours are handled by the secretary. Detailed job cost sheets are maintained for each job, indicating materials used (vendor, cost), hours charged to that job (from payroll time cards), and a comparison of actual costs of completed jobs against the estimated costs that were the basis for securing the job.

The cost structure and general expense level of this firm are highly variable, which is typical of the industry. Because of the individual nature of the jobs, and both the bid and sale prices being individually structured, the prime cost is labor, and computation of the total bid is based on a multiple of three times labor costs to cover overhead and allow for profit. The use of a standard multiplier is further complicated by difficulties in estimating the total hours required. Generally, Mr. Gonzales appears to be underestimating the required hours and overestimating the necessary multiplier to cover overhead and profit.

Materials are generally purchased on credit, from several suppliers. Star's purchases from any one supplier are comparatively small. Mr. Gonzales believes this to be an advantage since he can always obtain the necessary materials, even when in short supply, from one or more of the vendors.

In some instances, Mr. Gonzales and Mr. Antonio have found it necessary to personally guarantee major loans to the business. An open line of credit is maintained with the Gulf Bank and Trust Company for $15,000, which is available to handle current operating needs. Most of the credit line is currently not being used.

FINANCIAL DATA

A pro forma balance sheet was prepared, shown in Case exhibit 5–2. The earnings projection indicated decreasing losses over the first three months of operation and increasing profits beginning in the fourth month. After the sixth month, sales and profits were projected to level off for the remainder of the year and until sufficient profits were retained in the business for additional employees and equipment. The first twelve months of operation were expected to result in profits of about $5500 after depreciation and partners' salaries. Total salaries were expected to be about $40,000 during the first year.

In the second year of operation, sales of $50,000 were projected, with a profit of $11,652. The partners felt that the second year would be substantially better than projected, because they hoped to expand the business before that time. A summary of the financial data is shown in Case exhibits 5–3 and 5–4.

Case exhibit 5-2

STAR TOOL AND MACHINE CO., INCORPORATED

Pro forma balance sheet prior to starting operations

Cash	$11,000	
Parts and supplies	1,000	
Fixed assets	19,450	
Total assets		$31,450
SBA loan	$25,000	
Owner's equity	6,450	
		$31,450

Case exhibit 5-3

STAR TOOL AND MACHINE COMPANY, INCORPORATED

Balance Sheet

	1972	1973	1974	1975	1976
Assets					
Cash	2,875.25	15,714.93	13,977.51	9,744.51	21,503.58
Accounts Receivable	4,561.20	10,202.13	12,502.10	20,847.78	13,136.32
Inventory	750.00	1,350.00	1,220.00	2,550.00	1,600.00
Work in process	1,983.46	1,593.36	7,000.00	43,300.00	2,350.00
Machinery and equip.	27,605.68	28,333.02	34,147.82	50,675.47	52,172.16
Truck	1,400.00	1,400.00	1,400.00	1,400.00	1,400.00
Total	29,005.68	29,733.02	35,547.82	52,075.47	53,572.16
Less acc. depr.	4,899.26	8,143.99	11,818.34	15,799.58	20,348.12
	24,106.42	21,589.03	23,729.48	36,275.89	33,224.04
Building and land				55,102.26	55,102.26
Less acc. depr.				238.88	1,672.21
				54,863.38	53,430.05
Lease hold improve	685.30	456.90	228.50		
Organization cost	255.00	255.00	255.00	255.00	255.00
Utility deposit	190.00	190.00	190.00	190.00	187.00
Prepaid income tax	20.00	20.00	160.00	800.35	
Loans to employee				147.28	
Total assets	35,426.63	51,371.35	59,262.59	168,974.19	125,685.99
Liabilities					
Accounts payable	1,825.26	7,306.81	3,289.49	49,033.48	6,355.43
Notes pay. – SBA	21,664.55	19,492.02	17,172.66	14,708.20	12,163.09
Notes pay. – other	3,518.40	8,638.80	1,759.20	8,813.51	5,240.94
Notes pay. – building				42,800.00	32,375.00
Payroll taxes accrued	684.70	830.24	1,175.14	2,054.97	12,106.85
Accrued salaries	981.40	6,417.04	14,625.74	19,290.40	15,763.45
Income tax payable	106.46	544.42	785.90	709.15	657.32
Total liabilities	28,780.77	43,229.33	38,808.13	137,409.71	84,662.08
Net Worth					
Common stock	6,400.00	6,400.00	6,400.00	6,400.00	6,400.00
Retained earnings	245.86	1,742.02	14,054.46	25,164.48	34,623.91
Total net worth	6,645.86	8,142.02	20,454.46	31,564.48	41,023.91
Total liab. and N.W.	35,426.63	51,371.35	59,262.59	168,974.19	125,685.99

Case exhibit 5-4

STAR TOOL AND MACHINE COMPANY, INCORPORATED

Income statement

	1972	1973	1974	1975	1976
SALES	90,102.95	91,047.01	172,979.15	234,497.44	297,330.27
Cost of Goods Sold					
Mat'l inv. 8/1	502.07	750.00	1,350.00	1,200.00	2,550.00
Work in process 8/1		1,973.46	1,593.36	7,000.00	43,300.00
Mat'l purchased	30,002.15	23,106.29	71,918.05	129,806.98	72,809.27
Labor	37,580.71	38,849.55	45,212.32	66,919.32	86,001.61
Freight	198.25	80.86	1,025.87	649.61	228.27
Outside service	3,604.49	943.71	4,866.47	3,949.33	1,146.01
Indirect cost	3,365.33	4,959.91			
Shop expense			5,659.03	9,735.27	12,606.78
Total	75,253.00	70,663.78	131,625.10	219,260.51	218,641.94
Mat'l inv. 7/31	750.00	1,350.00	1,200.00	2,505.00	2,350.00
Work in process 7/31		1,593.36	7,000.00	43,300.00	1,600.00
Total	750.00	2,943.36	8,200.00	45,805.00	3,950.00
Cost of goods sold	74,503.00	67,720.42	123,425.10	173,455.51	214,691.94
Gross profit	15,599.95	23,326.59	49,554.05	61,041.93	82,638.33

Other Expenses

Salaries	1,686.32	6,844.32	16,946.62	26,127.13	30,305.78
Rent	1,920.00	1,920.00	2,340.00	2,535.00	2,145.00
Utilities	834.77	910.73	953.44	1,207.84	2,332.98
Telephone	445.73	459.02	950.21	1,039.65	498.69
Tax and License	2,423.08	2,730.25	3,583.58	5,258.18	8,175.73
Auto, truck, travel	1,279.50	459.61	1,110.36	1,205.85	1,693.68
Professional fees	295.00	629.50	1,365.25	980.00	1,227.75
Contributions		60.00	50.00	62.10	75.00
Office expense	740.41	807.16	640.14	128.23	707.87
Depreciation	2,993.44	3,244.73	3,674.35	4,361.54	5,981.87
Interest expense	1,263.68	1,275.07	1,353.74	1,080.41	3,158.65
Insurance	1,360.54	1,512.20	2,670.80	3,330.98	4,915.80
Advertising		102.40	588.92	780.59	132.61
Amortization	228.34	228.40	228.40	228.50	
Sales expense		102.62		112.06	134.75
Storage				130.00	
Dues and subscription				159.75	855.15
Uniforms				215.97	169.20
Miscellaneous				278.98	
Total	15,470.81	21,286.01	36,455.81	49,222.76	62,510.51
Income before tax	129.14	2,040.58	13,098.24	11,819.17	20,127.82
Federal income tax	6.46	421.99	785.80		
Alabama income tax	122.68	122.43	12,312.44	709.15	1,207.67
Net income		1,496.16		11,110.02	18,920.15

SUGGESTED QUESTIONS FOR DISCUSSION

1. Evaluate the qualifications of Antonio and Gonzales as potential small-business owners.

2. Comment on their market survey.

3. A major problem in this case is total dependence on one or two individuals. What suggestions can you make to change this?

4. What suggestions can you make to alleviate Antonio's personnel problems?

THE WHEEL, INCORPORATED

DESCRIPTION OF THE FIRM

The Wheel, Incorporated is a retail bicycle firm located in Covington, Kentucky. The firm is part of an organizational system that owns two bicycle shops and one combination stereo and high-fidelity store. One of the owners is involved in all three establishments. The Wheel, Incorporated has been in operation since November, 1973 and is a branch of The Wheel bicycle shop located near the campus of the University of Cincinnati, across the Ohio River. The Wheel, Incorporated offers a complete service and repair facility and, in addition, handles a multitude of parts and accessories—anything the complete bicyclist would require.

The owner of The Wheel, Joseph Waldman, age 23, and one of his former full-time employees, William Estafen, age 26, each contributed $3000 as an initial investment to start The Wheel, Incorporated in the second location. Immediately prior to this endeavor, Estafen worked part-time for the Post Office and was involved in a small operation which sold soap.

The decision to add another shop was a function of four factors: the success of the Campus shop, an opportunity to expand to a new market in a location where no competition existed, Bill Estafen's desire to enter the bicycle business, and the fact that the Covington shop was already under lease by Waldman, housing a high fidelity and stereo shop in which Waldman and another friend are in partnership, and available to house such a bicycle outlet.

Initially, the Covington shop was designed to appeal to a different type of bicyclist than patronized the Campus shop. It was not to be merely an extension of the Campus shop services, but an effort to compete in an additional market segment. The original Wheel Campus Shop catered directly, and almost solely, to college students, providing them with inexpensive and efficient transportation. To meet this need, touring, racing, and recreational bicycles are for sale at both shops. The expansion to Covington was an attempt to reach the potentially large children's bicycle market, and the increasing market of young adults, not in college, who use the bicycle as a means of free-time fun and exercise. These objectives were to be fulfilled while maintaining the image of a small, friendly business, a factor believed by Waldman to play a major role in the success of the Campus shop.

LOCATION

The area surrounding the Covington shop comprises other small businesses, vacant buildings, and a residential section. The residential area is a relatively low income, white neighborhood, with old two-story structures. The individuals living in this area are middle-aged. The immediate business sector is made up of many old buildings that once made up the business district around the intersections of several main local streets, a state highway, and a U.S. highway.

The location has positive aspects in that it lies on one of the main routes to more affluent Covington residential areas. It is within three blocks of the Bluegrass Square Shopping Center, which is a new shopping center completed in July, 1974, and in contrast to the other business structures close by, the building that houses The Wheel, Incorporated and the stereo concern is modern in design and well-kept. The building itself is leased on a three-year term for $200 per month, split equally between the bicycle shop and the stereo shop.

Although the location has no direct competition, bikes are carried by a department store in the Bluegrass Square Shopping Center. Other than that, the closest competition dealing only in bicycles is the Northern Kentucky Bicycle Shop located in Triangle City, a business district twelve blocks away.

MANAGEMENT

Estafen, an avid cyclist, entered the business as an employee of Waldman at the campus location. Because of the success of the campus shop, the two decided to join in partnership and expand, to tap a new and larger market. Estafen contributed his personal resources for the expansion and took over the operation of the expansion shop in Covington as owner-operator. Waldman is still attending the University of Cincinnati on a part-time basis. Estafen graduated from Ball State University as an English major.

Waldman is stern and outspoken when it comes to his business policy. He presents an air of determination and knowledge when speaking about his business, and is autocratic. Estafen is easy-going. He understands what is required to run the business, but unlike Waldman's business orientation, his interests lie with bicycles themselves more than with the bike business.

Although the Covington shop is the direct responsibility of Bill Estafen, Joe Waldman handles all financial matters and personnel hiring, and the bulk of purchasing and ordering for the Covington shop. Estafen's duties consist mostly of the day-to-day management and operation of the shop: selling, supervising, and stock work.

The shop itself is operated by Estafen on a full-time basis, with two college students as part-time employees. The part-time help works almost exclusively in the repair shop and rarely participates in the selling effort. Most employees are hired by Mr. Waldman at the Campus shop and then transferred to the Covington shop. Generally, the people hired are those who frequent the shop near campus. If a position becomes available, Waldman considers applicants on his perception of "how well they can be relied upon to do a good job." Part-time help is paid the minimum wage.

SERVICES OFFERED

The Wheel, Incorporated is open from 10 A.M. to 6 P.M., Monday through Saturday, and provides a variety of goods and services for the cycling enthusiast. Heading the list, of course, is a variety of completely assembled 3-speed, 10-speed, and children's bicycles. The adult models consist of both touring and racing bikes, and are listed in Case exhibit 6–1.

The children's bicycles are made by Murray. They sell for $54.80 and come in only one model. This model has both a boy's and a girl's style. Four of the original inventory of six Murray bicycles were still in stock, as of September 30, 1974.

In addition to the bikes, The Wheel, Incorporated also offers a complete supply of parts and accessories. The accessory list runs from backpacks, locks, and chains, to bicycling magazines, newspapers, and T-shirts. A complete inventory of replacement parts is also offered, as are the tools required for the do-it-yourselfer to accomplish repairs. The parts inventory is utilized as a source of supply for the shop's repair service, located in the basement. The shop offers repair services on any make or model of bicycle. The repair service is utilized primarily in the assembly of the firm's inventory, and the shop prides itself on the care and professionalism that it exhibits in putting a bicycle together: a 90-day warranty is offered on all parts and work for any bicycle

Case exhibit 6-1

THE WHEEL, INCORPORATED

List of adult bicycles carried

Make		Wholesale Cost	Price	Profit
Sutton	3-speed	$ 56.60	$ 89.50	$ 32.90
Torrot	10-speed Men's Frame	79.38	115.00	35.62
Torrot	10-speed Mixte Frame	91.95	125.00	33.05
Royce-Union	10-speed	80.00	123.95	43.95
St. Etienne	10-speed	90.00	130.00	40.00
Liberia	10-speed DemiCourse	94.50	144.50	50.00
	10-speed SemiPro	145.00	225.00	80.00
Zeus	10-speed Competition	160.00	250.00	90.00
	10-speed Professional	245.00	350.00	105.00
	10-speed Suprema	335.00	450.00	115.00

sold. The service department accounts for about four per cent of the total sales of the firm (see Case exhibit 6-3).

Two additional services offered by the firm include the sale of used bikes, and the ability to provide expertise in the field of cycling. The corporation has also instigated "Saturday Cycling Tours" for those interested. The Wheel, Incorporated personnel can provide any information that either a cycling novice or confirmed enthusiast may seek.

PURCHASING AND INVENTORY CONTROL

No formula exists for ordering or maintaining inventory levels. Generally, all items to be stocked are the same at both locations. Therefore, Estafen will just inform Waldman of low stock levels or out-of-stock items. Replacements can be ordered in conjunction with the Campus shop, or they can be sent on loan, as accounts payable, from the Campus shop. In some cases, Estafen may submit an independent order to the distributor for items that are unique to the Covington shop. The basic inventory formula was expressed as "just try to keep as many in stock as possible." Orders are placed to take advantage of both volume discounts and credit terms offered by the distributors.

PRICING AND MARKETING STRATEGIES

The retail prices of bicycles are determined by a 50 per cent mark-up over wholesale cost, with some variations. However, the general formula for pricing the parts and accessories is to mark them up at 100 per cent over cost, and then adjust them either up or down to keep them in line with the competition. Personnel from the shops periodically visit competitive establishments to get a view of their operations, and to note any competitive advantages or disadvantages.

The marketing effort can probably best be described as low-key. Personal selling is done almost exclusively by Estafen, and it is usually a spin-off of a discussion concerning bicycles and cycling in general. The initial communication between buyer and seller tends to be information-seeking about a given product or its usage. Waldman states that he prefers to push a specific brand. He feels the Liberia brand of bicycle is superior to the others. Consequently, it receives most of the selling effort.

Because it is financially advantageous to advertise both bicycle shops in the same commercial messages, all the advertising for The Wheel, Incorporated is the same as that employed by the Campus shop. Monthly advertising expenditures are distributed among the two campus newspapers and spot radio commercials. The radio spots appear throughout the day on various AM and FM radio stations. The emphasis of the advertisements is placed on informative presentations, giving names, addresses, phone numbers, and services offered. Special ads usually highlight the qualities of the Liberia brand bicycles.

In-store displays consist of distributors' or manufacturers' pamphlets, the company's newspaper ads on the bulletin board, and hand-painted signs depicting brand names and prices. Sales promotions (discounted prices) are offered occasionally, but only on slow turnover parts and accessories, not on bicycles. Another form of advertising is the one-eighth page ad that appears in the Yellow Pages of the phone directory. Twenty-four dollars per month are currently spent on this ad. Its importance is emphasized by the fact that a vast quantity of prospective customers locate the shop by this means, according to Estafen.

Although The Wheel, Incorporated does not offer a credit plan, the owners allow buyers to put some money down (no specified amount), and pay whatever they can, whenever they can. Although Estafen makes it known that he prefers to have half of the stated price as a down payment, and the balance paid before the end of the month, there is no enforcement of this and the plan is quite lenient. The shop holds the bike until the full amount has been paid. Two major credit cards, Mastercharge and BankAmericard, are honored. However, only three bicycle purchases in the first year of operation were credit card purchases.

COMPETITION

Those shops competing for the sale of bicycles can be divided into two categories: small, exclusive bicycle outlets, and major-chain discount stores. There are about ten shops in the Cincinnati metropolitan area that could be classified as the former. They all deal in a specialized brand of bicycle, either foreign or domestic (Raleigh or Schwinn), emphasizing quality and service as major selling points. The latter category is made up of stores such as K-Mart, Sears, and Woolco, which offer a private label brand, emphasizing discount prices and savings. These brands run in price from $20.00 to $44.00 less than The Wheel's least expensive bike. With private brands, the bicycle purchased will have to be assembled by the buyer, and no other services are offered. In contrast, the small shops assemble their bikes so that they are ready to ride at the time of purchase.

THE CONSUMER MARKET

The two categories of bicycle retailers are directly related to two types of cycle purchasers. Some prospective buyers are interested in obtaining a three-speed or ten-speed bicycle at the lowest possible price. This kind of customer's first question is usually aimed at finding out which is The Wheel's least expensive model. These people are first-time buyers, and rarely make their purchase at The Wheel Incorporated, once they have seen the price list. Estafen assumes that they buy at one of the discount outlets, since many of them mention the chain stores' competitive prices.

The second type of bicycle buyer knows bicycles. These are people much like Estafen himself, and they would rarely purchase a bike from a discount establishment. Bill explains that "there are significant differences among brands along quality lines, and knowledgeable cyclists can easily spot them." These people are previous bicycle owners, and generally use the bikes for reasons other than recreation riding and exercise. Their interest in bikes usually lies in their value as transportation. Small, exclusive bike shops are also frequented by racing enthusiasts who place great emphasis on quality products, and service after the sale.

Both types of buyers appear to frequent The Wheel, Incorporated, but the second type of buyer is the one most likely to purchase a bicycle. Most of these individuals are in the 18 to 30 year age group, and are college students. Approximately one-third of the bicycle sales of The Wheel, Incorporated have been to females. Many of the women buy the same ten-speed style that the men buy, making it unnecessary to differentiate required styles at order time. Two children's bicycles have sold in the first eleven months of operations.

INVENTORY

An inventory of all property was taken by Mr. Waldman. Normally, the inventory is taken only once each year, a requirement for filing tax returns. The whole procedure is accomplished in less than one hour, and is done entirely by visual observation.

The bicycles on hand are counted and multiplied by their respective wholesale costs to give an accurate measure. A list of the inventory on hand on September 30, 1974, appears in Case exhibit 6–2.

FINANCIAL DATA

The filing system for the shop is maintained both by Estafen as a daily log of his transactions, and by Waldman as a monthly update of the operation. The files consist of two records. One is a daily register of all sales receipts that have been processed to date. It consists of a binder that holds a copy of every sales transaction that has taken place since the inception of the shop. The second file is a log book that sums up the amount of sales on a daily basis for each month. The final entry is a sum total of the daily receipts and gives a monthly total divided into retail sales and service sales. Case exhibit 6–3 illustrates this type of information. No similar logs are maintained for expense ac-

Text continued on page 273

Case exhibit 6–2

THE WHEEL, INCORPORATED

Inventory of Brands on Hand, September 30, 1974

Make	Number on hand	% of total
Royce-Union	21	34%
Liberia	11	18%
Torrot	3	5%
Sutton	18	30%
St. Etienne	8	13%
Zeus*	0	0%

*One personally owned bike is on display, but not for sale.

Case exhibit 6–3

THE WHEEL, INCORPORATED

Monthly Sales Receipts

Month	Retail Sales	Service Sales	Less Refund	Total
November, 1973	$ 405.03	$ 5.00	—	$ 410.03
December, 1973	2760.69	34.00	—	2794.69
January, 1974	1751.71	84.00	$18.72	1816.99
February, 1974	3088.29	58.00	14.32	3131.97
March, 1974	4014.68	146.50	—	4161.18
April, 1974	2743.18	141.25	69.39	2815.04
May, 1974	2213.12	152.00	23.46	2341.66
June, 1974	2160.60	145.75	5.20	2301.15
July, 1974	3681.52	132.68	8.43	3805.77
August, 1974	2796.16	192.67	—	2988.83
Total		$1091.85		$26,567.31
% of Total		4.1%		100%

Case exhibit 6–4

THE WHEEL, INCORPORATED

Balance Sheet (as of September 30, 1974)

Assets		Liabilities	
Cash	2145.00	Accts. payable	$ 2275.00
Inventories:		Notes payable	1750.00
bicycles	4924.00	Accrued expenses	174.00
parts/access.	1768.00	Accrued sales tax	101.00
Tools and fixtures	780.00	Total Liabilities	4300.00
Depreciation	156.00		
Prepaid insurance	105.00	**Owner's Equity**	
Other assets	240.00		
		Equity	6000.00
		Retained earnings	(182.00)
Total assets	$10,118.00	Total equity and liabilities	$10,118.00

Case exhibit 6–5

THE WHEEL, INCORPORATED

Income Statement
(for a typical month)

Sales—bicycles, parts, and accessories $2796.16
   Service.. 192.67
                              Total sales $2988.83
Cost of goods sold 1749.40
                              Gross margin...$1239.43

Expenses
   Rent...$100.00
   Advertising
      Yellow Pages 24.00
      other 75.00
   Salaries*...........$191.81
             193.38   385.19

   Utilities....................................... 62.00
   Alarm system 25.00
   Administration 42.00
                            Total expenses... 713.19

                            Net margin ....$ 526.24
Taxes at 25% 131.56
                            Profit after tax 394.68

*Does not include a salary figure for Estafen.

Case exhibit 6–6

The firm maintains a log of all sales receipts that have been processed since the first day of business. For those transactions that involved the sale of a bicycle, these items were recorded: the name and address of the purchaser, the date, the brand of bicycle sold, and the method of payment at the time of purchase. From these receipts, a list of tables was prepared. No names and addresses, nor lists of specific items sold were recorded for sales involving parts and accessories. The data presented below only typify the information on purchases of bicycles.

Table A   UNIT BICYCLE SALES PER MONTH (INCLUDES USED BIKES)

Month	Number of bikes sold
November, 1973	2
December, 1973	30
January, 1974	12
February, 1974	22
March, 1974	25
April, 1974	16
May, 1974	14
June, 1974	17
July, 1974	19
August, 1974	16
September, 1974	15
Total	188

Table B   UNIT SALES BY BRAND*

Brand	# of Units Sold	% of Total
Royce-Union	65	38%
Liberia	77	45%
Sutton	7	4.1%
Zeus	3	1.75%
St. Etienne	3	1.75%
Torrot	1	.6%
Used	15	8.8%
	171	

Table C   BICYCLE SALES BY SEX OF PURCHASER

Sex	# Purchasing	% of Total
Male	126	69.23%
Female	56	30.77%
	182	

*Does not include some special orders or one-of-a-kind items that were in stock.

(Case exhibit 6–6 continued)

Table D BICYCLE SALES BY PURCHASER'S RESIDENCE

Place of Residence	# of Purchases	% of the Total
Cincinnati	87	48.33%
Covington	48	26.67%
Covington suburbs	17	9.44%
Outside the greater Cincinnati area	28	15.56%
	180	

Table E SALES BY METHOD OF PAYMENT

Amount of Down Payment	# of Purchasers Using	% of Total
Paid in full at time of purchase	137	82.54%
$150	1	
130	2	
100	1	
80	2	
70	3	
60	2	17.46%
50	7	
45	1	
40	1	
25	4	
20	2	
5	3*	

*Two of these people decided not to purchase, and were refunded their money; all others completed the sales.

counts, although the checkbooks designate to whom and for what purpose any expenditure is made. All bills and invoices are filed in manila folders and maintained in a filing cabinet. No monthly totals or breakdowns of expenses are incorporated into a single document as are the sales figures.

SUGGESTED QUESTIONS FOR DISCUSSION

1. Evaluate the two men in this case on their qualifications to be in business.

2. Should the firm maintain the Covington location? Why or why not? How was the location selected?

3. How would you evaluate the advertising relative to the objectives of the Covington location?

4. Do the present level and projected levels of sales justify both individuals being involved full-time in the operation?

FU CHOW HOUSE

The Fu Chow House is a small Chinese restaurant, situated among 25 other retail establishments within the Boulevard Plaza in Springfield, Massachusetts. The area is under reconstruction and experiencing rapid population and income growth.

The Fu Chow House was organized as a single proprietorship under the name of Mae Chang. Mrs. Chang is assisted by her husband, Jim Chang, in the operation of the restaurant.

The business specializes in Chinese cuisine. Forty per cent of the sales are from take-out orders, and the remainder are from dinners served in the restaurant. Sales for the first twelve months of operation were $104,504 and the gross margin was 65 per cent of net sales.

BACKGROUND

In 1970, Jim and his wife Mae Chang became United States citizens. Originally citizens of China, they lived in Gyang-tse for 22 years before migrating to the United States.

Mae Chang, 35 years old, a hair dresser by profession, continued as such after entering the United States. Jim Chang, 37 years old, a lab technician, also found employment in his field.

In 1972, both Jim and Mae were laid off from their jobs, and remained unemployed. After experiencing the frustration and insecurity of unemployment, they sought to stabilize their finances by operating their own business.

Since their cultural background was Chinese, it was natural

This case was prepared by Dean Joseph A. Parker; Mr. Howard Fidler, Chairman, Department of Hotel, Restaurant, Institutional Management, Tourism, and Travel; and Ms. Susan Moody, Research Assistant, University of New Haven, as a basis for class discussion rather than to illustrate either effective or ineffective handling of an administrative situation. Presented at a Case Workshop and distributed by the Intercollegiate Case Clearing House, Soldiers Field, Boston, Mass. 02163. All rights reserved to the contributors. Printed in the U.S.A.

Case exhibit 7-1

FU CHOW HOUSE

Capital Requirement

Total cash available	$ 7,500.00
Loan proceeds	43,000.00
Total available	$50,500.00
Capital expenditures:	
Organizational expenses (legal & acct.)	1,500.00
Furniture and fixtures	33,000.00
Miscellaneous supplies	5,050.00
Prepaid items:	
Rent	1,500.00
Insurance and taxes	2,000.00
Utility deposits	300.00
Licenses and liquor	2,200.00
Inventory	1,800.00
Total expenditures	$47,350.00
Ending cash balance	3,150.00

for them to open a Chinese restaurant. However, neither had any experience or training in this field. But being of a single mind, they decided that the first priority was to find a suitable location. Their search was conducted by car, driving all over town and through nearby communities. No realtors were contacted. They decided that the Boulevard Plaza, though still being constructed, seemed to be the ideal location. Since the nearest Chinese restaurant was over five miles away, they assumed that there would be little competition. Moreover, the new Plaza was expected to open within five months.

The Changs chose an open space at the end of the Plaza between two banks, with the dimensions 120' by 20', or 2400 square feet. The lease was signed with the agreement that the restaurant must be established by March 1, 1973, only five months away.

The total capital requirement to establish the Fu Chow House was estimated at $47,350 (see Case exhibit 7-1). With $7500 in cash to invest, Mrs. Chang approached the Small Business Administration for a loan of $43,000. At that time, the SBA had established that 3 per cent of their total funds were to be allocated to minorities. Mrs. Chang was fortunate in seeking a loan at a very opportune time. She received a loan for $43,000, with the security being her home (approximate value of $38,000), for which she had paid cash.

The Changs had to rush to choose an equipment purveyor

Case exhibit 7–2

FU CHOW HOUSE

Equipment Bids

Company	Bid
Bottoms Equipment Supply Company	$28,744.48
White Store Fixture	49,941.18
HA Restaurant Supplies	28,355.00
Modern Food Equipment Company	33,000.00

by January 12, to permit the landlord to plan how to pour the cement floor. Four equipment companies were contacted. The bids are summarized in Case exhibit 7–2.

White Store Fixtures was an excellent company for those with adequate funding. Their layout proposals for the Changs were magnificent. Bottoms Equipment Supply Company had a low price but did not seem qualified to do the job. The equipment and the layout proposal of the Modern Food Company was viable, but the bid was too high. HA Restaurant Supplies gave the lowest bid, but the equipment was of poor quality. Using the criteria of price alone, that is, the lowest bid, the Changs decided on HA Restaurant Suppliers.

The Changs next contacted three companies who would handle the heating, air conditioning, plumbing, wiring, and carpentry of the new restaurant. The Levino Company agreed to install one Fedders roof-top model combination air conditioner and heating unit, with a cooling capacity of 72,000 BTUH and a heating capacity of 150,000 BTUs. The duct work would be insulated and weatherproofed. The kitchen would also have a Fedders heating/cooling combination unit installed with a cooling capacity of 157,000 BTUH and a heating capacity of 140,000 BTUs. The total installation cost of both units was $7500. This included all labor, freight, rigging, and miscellaneous material needed. This bid did not include any plumbing or electrical work.

The Reynolds Company agreed to install a 7.5-ton Fedders air conditioner and heating system as well as the exhaust fans in the bathrooms. All plumbing pertaining to the kitchen and the two bathrooms would be installed. The electrical work included lighting, and wiring for the air conditioners. Included in the Reynolds bid was the carpentry work, such as paneling, partitions, and paint. The total bid received from Reynolds was $18,200.

Mr. and Mrs. Chang conferred with the Walterman Company about a 10-ton air conditioner. Walterman's proposal appeared more suitable to Mrs. Chang's needs. They were quoted a price of $2200 for all the plumbing and $6040 for the air conditioning and heating. However, the bid did not include the needed roof sealing which would cost another $200.

The Walterman Company was chosen by the Changs to install the plumbing, heating, and air conditioner, even though the Levino Company was highly recommended by the SBA. Mr. Robert Benevento, a union man unemployed because of a layoff, agreed to do the carpentry if Mr. Chang would buy the paneling. He was paid $8.00 per hour, completion of the job taking 3 days. Al's Electric Company was awarded the contract for all the electrical work. The total electrical cost bid was $3417 including materials, labor, and fixtures (lighting and exhaust fans). The Changs did not wish to use his fixtures and exhaust fan, so the bid was lowered to $2600.

A highly reputable New York City interior decorator was contracted to coordinate the selection of lighting fixtures, carpets, partitions, layout, types of tables, colors, and so on. The Changs wanted to use a panda bear as their trademark because of its significance following then-President Nixon's return from China, when he carried a panda bear, given to him as a gift from the Chinese people. Since his return, profits had improved in many New York City Chinese restaurants and the Changs hoped that everyone would remember the bear. The decorator submitted sketches of her ideas and a picture of the trademark, drawn by her. The Changs then decided they could not afford the interior decorator. They made a settlement with the decorator and terminated the contract. The lighting was selected from a Sears catalog (American design). The paint for the walls in the dining room was beige, only because Sears had it on "special."

The food industry was totally new to the Changs. Therefore, they hired a Chinese chef, Mr. Wong, who could not speak or comprehend any English. They agreed to provide him with a basic subsistence allowance, plus full maintenance and care for his family, including food and clothing. A Chinese woman was hired and paid by the hour. She was to assist the chef in the preparation of food. All employee training was conducted by the Changs, who had no such experience.

In preparing the menu, the Changs decided they wanted to compete with the busiest Chinese restaurants in the city. Hence, the menu consisted of 118 items plus combination dishes, very similar to their competitors. Liquor would also be served. However, the prices were established at rates slightly higher than their competitors.

Case exhibit 7–3

FU CHOW HOUSE—

Income statement for the year ended December 31, 1973

Net sales		$104,504.00
Cost of goods sold		36,307.00
Gross profit on sales		68,197.00
Operating expenses:		
Selling expenses:		
Building occupancy expense	6,000.00	
Salaries	31,800.00	
Telephone	480.00	
Heat, light, water	3,600.00	
Postage	100.00	
Advertising	1,100.00	
Travel	300.00	
Vehicle expense	600.00	
Payroll taxes	3,000.00	
Supplies	2,000.00	
Insurance	2,000.00	
Total selling expenses		50,980.00
General and administrative expenses:		
Administrative salaries	7,500.00	
Property taxes	1,000.00	
Other	1,100.00	
Total general and administrative expenses	9,600.00	
Total operating expenses		60,580.00
Other expenses:		
Interest and mortgage		6,657.00
Income before taxes		960.00

CONSUMER MARKET

The Boulevard Plaza was under redevelopment when the Fu Chow House opened. To the rear of the Plaza was a 45-unit apartment building, with the average rental being $190 to $210 per month. To the right of the Plaza was a 15-story high-rise apartment house for elderly citizens. Directly across the street was a 25-unit condominium development. The average purchase price was between $25,000 and $32,000. According to The Springfield Redevelopment Agency, two additional 15-story high-rise apartment buildings as well as two additional 25-unit condominiums would be constructed within the next three years.

MARKET FEASIBILITY

Two months before the restaurant was to commence operation, an SBA team began the first phase of the market study to determine the profitability of the Fu Chow House.

They chose to conduct a person-to-person convenience sample at the proposed site. Two passersby were stopped and asked various questions concerning the Fu Chow House. The first woman told them to go away or she would call the police. The second woman just turned around and walked away. By majority vote, the SBA team decided to suspend the sample.

ADVERTISING

While limited to a budget, the Changs wanted the best advertising available. Newspaper ads were mandatory. *The Springfield Times* offered the widest coverage and the highest price for their ad space. A 2" × 2" ad would cost $20.50 per week, or $82 per month. The ad was placed in the entertainment section of the newspaper and would run once a week on Friday for an entire year.

Besides the newspaper ad, the only other advertising was a neon sign placed outside the restaurant. The sign was clear red, with 6-inch letters and spelling the name "Fu Chow House." The visibility of the sign was 110 feet.

SUGGESTED QUESTIONS FOR DISCUSSION

1. Evaluate the marketing survey.

2. How would you evaluate Jim and Mae Chang's qualifications for this business?

3. Evaluate the site and location analysis of the Fu Chow House.

THE RICHARD TRACY DETECTIVE AGENCY

INTRODUCTION

The Richard Tracy Detective Agency is owned and operated by Philip Spade. The agency provides security and investigative services to private individuals, and to a number of organizations engaged in commercial activities.

The agency is located in Jacksonville, Florida, with an answering service in Orlando. There is currently one security contract maintained in St. Augustine. Investigative work is conducted in any locality dictated by a particular case. The agency currently maintains an office at 37 Cannon Lane, in Jacksonville. A receptionist is on duty daily, Monday through Saturday. A telephone answering service records messages which come in during the hours when the office is not staffed.

HISTORY OF THE FIRM

Operations began in the fall of 1970 and office space was leased at the FNC Bank Building in Jacksonville. Operations were quickly expanded to include Orlando, Gainesville, Daytona Beach, and St. Augustine. A branch office was established in Daytona Beach to handle the contacts in that area. The following spring, the main office was shifted to its present address. This rapid growth created severe problems of organization, supervision, and financing for the young company, and Mr. Spade concluded that he would need a loan to solve some of these problems.

By early 1972, Mr. Spade had reached the conclusion that the operation of his agency was hampered by a lack of radio equipment necessary for surveillance and patrol, and a shortage of working capital. He sought a loan from National Bank, in the amount of $10,000, but his application was denied. In April of 1972 he turned to the Small Business Administration for aid.

Mr. C. E. Jenners was assigned by the SBA to investigate the eligibility and financial condition of Mr. Spade and the Richard Tracy Detective Agency. In his report:

1. he noted that while the agency's net profit in 1971 had been very small, income statements for the first two months of 1972 showed an encouraging upswing in earnings;
2. he felt that Mr. Spade's proffered collateral was weak, but adequate with the $5000 personal guarantee of Spade's parents, Edward and Clara S. Spade;
3. he was impressed by Mr. Spade's intelligence and energy.

Having received a favorable review of Mr. Spade's management ability from Mr. Sam Gulick, SBA management ability officer for Jacksonville, Mr. Jenners recommended approval of a $10,000 non-participation loan. It was understood that $6000 would be used to purchase the necessary radio equipment, and $4000 would be used to furnish working capital. Maturity was set for six years. The loan was authorized on April 12, 1972 and disbursed on May 2, 1972.

Mr. Spade soon began to have difficulty meeting the obligations of the loan. He fell behind in his monthly payments, and by November 2, 1972 was two months in arrears. Mr. Paul R. Simonds of the SBA made a field visit to the agency on that date. He was unable to interview Mr. Spade at that time, but he did make telephone contact on November 7, 1972. Mr. Spade reported that business was good and that payments had been late because of a temporary strain on working capital. Mr. Spade continued to have difficulty meeting his SBA loan obligations in 1973. His payments were consistently two months late, and SBA personnel had little success in obtaining satisfactory explanations.

Mr. George Harris was engaged by the SBA through the Active Corps of Executives (ACE) program and filed a Management Counseling Report on September 26, 1973. He advised that the agency's future was handicapped by inadequate capital investment, excessive debt, and minimal financial records. He recommended semi-monthly billing to ease working capital requirements, and suggested that a part-time bookkeeper be hired. His overall prognosis was pessimistic. A Service Corps of Retired Executives (SCORE) report filed in the same month by Mr. Jack Soque noted that Mr. Spade was having trouble with sales promotion, market research, and records and collections.

The Richard Tracy Detective Agency was also having problems meeting its federal tax liabilities. Mr. Simonds of the SBA learned that the IRS intended to lock the doors of the agency at 12 noon on October 24, 1973. The IRS wanted payment of $3000 on an outstanding liability of $14,000. Operations were suspended, but Mr. Spade satisfied the IRS of his intent to discharge the obligation and was permitted to reopen his office on October 29, 1973.

Contact between the SBA and Mr. Spade throughout the remainder of 1973 was infrequent. It proved to be very difficult to meet with Mr. Spade at his office, or even to contact him by telephone. The demands of supervision and investigations kept Mr. Spade on the road much of the time.

Mr. Spade's payments on his SBA loan continued to be late in the early months of 1974. On March 13, 1974 the SBA received two checks in payment of the January and February installments. These checks were returned by the bank because of insufficient funds.

On April 17, 1974, Mr. Spade visited the office of L. C. Coner, an SBA loan assistant. He reported that he was selling his Daytona Beach and St. Augustine operations for $10,000 in cash and a $9000 note. He explained that he would use the money to pay his back taxes and would make two loan payments to the SBA. On April 19, 1974 Spade delivered three installment payments to the SBA office. On June 10, 1974 he made two more payments, bringing his account up-to-date through May, 1974. (See Case exhibit 8-1.)

THE SECURITY INDUSTRY

The Richard Tracy Detective Agency is in an industry that is expected to make major advances in the coming years. As the crime rate rises, the need for security services increases, and those firms already established in the market will have an advantage in obtaining the new accounts. However, the present economic slump has badly injured most firms in the security business.

FINANCIAL RECORDS

During its short history, the agency has experimented with a variety of bookkeeping systems and bookkeepers; however, it has not settled on any single system. At present the agency is testing a Safeguard plan which is complex and expensive — in excess of $400 for the full range of books.

The agency has not utilized the benefits of the Safeguard system. At present it is keeping no current bank balance in either the receipts or the disbursement journal. This has caused it to pay as much as $100 in one month for checks not covered. The

Case exhibit 8–1

RICHARD TRACY DETECTIVE AGENCY

Payment record on SBA loan as of August 31, 1974 (Payment of $169)

Due date	Date paid
8/2/72	on time
9/2/72	on time
10/2/72	11/10/72
11/2/72	11/10/72
12/2/72	1/8/73
1/2/73	1/8/73
2/2/73	3/5/73
3/2/73	3/5/73
4/2/73	on time
5/2/73	on time
6/2/73	7/2/73
7/2/73	10/9/73
8/2/73	10/9/73
9/2/73	11/29/73
10/2/73	11/29/73
11/2/73	2/8/74
12/2/73	2/8/74
1/2/74	4/22/74
2/2/74	4/22/74
3/2/74	4/22/74
4/2/74	6/10/74
5/2/74	6/10/74
6/2/74	7/29/74
7/2/74	7/29/74
8/2/74	– –

income and expense accounts in the journals have not been totaled for nearly eight months.

The accounting data that is compiled is not used to generate decision information. Balance sheets and income statements for the years 1972 and 1973 were unavailable until 1974. Cash budgeting has never been attempted, nor has a careful scrutiny of expenses ever been undertaken.

CREDIT AND COLLECTIONS

The shortage of working capital available to the agency makes careful budgeting mandatory. It was suggested by SCORE that Mr. Spade improve the coordination of his collections and disbursements, since at present many of his payables and receivables come due on the same date.

The agency has been plagued by a high incidence of bad debts, since industry has been hurt during the recent slump, particularly the firms that the agency relies upon heavily. The failure of many of these firms destroyed much of the agency's profit margin. Mr. Spade had no alternative but to assign these delinquent accounts to a collection agency.

Collection problems have also arisen in investigative work, which is conducted, at least in theory, on a payment-in-advance basis. The client is required to make some initial payment, and assumes the obligation of the expenses incurred by the investigator. However, the "retainer" clause of the standard agreement is very weak, and clients frequently succeed in canceling their commitment and recovering all or part of the retainer.

ORGANIZATIONAL STRUCTURE

The Richard Tracy Detective Agency is a single proprietorship, owned and managed by Mr. Philip Spade. Mr. Spade has considered incorporation as a means of attracting investors but has not actively investigated this possibility. Mr. Spade is an intelligent and energetic proprietor whose ambitions seem to have been thwarted by his unfamiliarity with the essentials of business management. He is thoroughly competent in the performance of security and investigative work, but has not developed the administrative capability necessary to support these functions. The need for Mr. Spade to actively participate in the conduct of investigations, and his preference for that role, have retarded his progress as a manager. He has, at times, been accused of failing to provide the direction and control vital to the success of his business enterprises.

Currently employed are Mr. Spade, Gloria Spade (who serves as security personnel manager), a full-time investigator, a part-time investigator, and a part-time receptionist-typist, in addition to the pool of men who service the security and patrol accounts. The organizational arrangement might be represented:

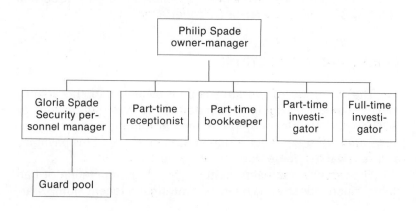

Mr. Spade's span of control is burdensome for a man required to spend much of his time in the field.

On two occasions, men hired to manage the security accounts in Daytona Beach have quit, to go into business for themselves, taking some of the accounts with them. Mr. Spade acknowledges that he did not provide adequate supervision, but still questions the loyalty of his subordinates. Since operations are now centered in Jacksonville, control should be easier to maintain.

MARKETING

1. The product

The services of the Richard Tracy Agency may be identified as security, patrol, and investigations. At present, no such differentiation has been made, although Mr. Spade has expressed keen interest in pursuing such an undertaking through aid from SCORE.

2. The price

Patrol and security accounts are obtained through competitive bidding. Contracts may be obtained for as short a period as one week or for as long as one year. The price quoted by the agency is determined by two factors: the cost of providing the service, and rates charged by competitors. No system of allocating the expense of administrative overhead has been developed. The agency is always willing to revise its prices downward, just to meet competition.

Investigative work is billed on a combination of retainer, hourly charge, and expense basis. The client pays a specified sum in advance, agrees to an hourly rate of ten to fifteen dollars per hour, and also assumes the obligation of all expenses incurred in the course of the investigation. This system has two problems: the "retainer" is not always clearly identified as such in the contractual agreement, and has been the subject of heated disputes; and the method of reporting expenses is so shoddy that Mr. Spade cannot be sure that the amount of expenses for which he reimburses his investigators tallies with the amount for which the clients are billed.

3. The place

All security and patrol accounts, except one, are in the Jacksonville vicinity. Investigative work is pursued throughout the state and beyond, depending upon the willingness of the client to assume costs.

4. The promotion

In addition to advertisements in the Yellow Pages of the telephone directory, which Mr. Spade currently uses, advertisements in various trade association publications are also utilized.

PERSONNEL

Throughout the security industry, the primary personnel problem is turnover. This is usually the result of the low pay scale, which attracts only retired individuals, students, or others unsuited for skilled employment. The fact that most security jobs are dull and of uncertain duration adds to the dissatisfaction of employees.

This agency is in a better position than many companies in the field because it has access to off-duty soliders from Fort Smith. These men work on a part-time basis and are better qualified for security work than the typical civilian applicant. But their relative financial security makes them independent of the agency, and as a consequence, the guard pool is in a state of constant regeneration. The fact that these individuals are paid the minimum wage reduces their dedication, since they can make the same money anywhere else. Nevertheless, the flexibility of schedule offered by Richard Tracy is an advantage to them, and provides some stability in the labor pool.

Of pressing importance is the need to institute a training program for new guards, to comply with a state law that went into effect in January. Compliance has been lax among security services in this area, but the requirement may be enforced more strictly at any time.

FINANCES

The SBA loan received by the Richard Tracy Agency had a dual purpose: to provide $6000 for the purchase of radio equipment, and to furnish $4000 for working capital.

At present the agency is still caught in the trap of inadequate capital investment. The prospects of obtaining further financing are nonexistent, and the possibility of attracting capital through incorporation is almost as slight. The following Exhibits represent the most recent financial data of the agency.

Case exhibit 8–2

RICHARD TRACY DETECTIVE AGENCY

Balance sheet for December 31, 1974

Assets

Cash in bank		$ 1,200
Mobile homes (2):		
Rental unit	$ 6,800	
Other	3,000	9,800
Automobiles (3):		
1973 Pontiac	$ 4,400	
1972 Chevy Nova	1,800	
1973 Chevy Nova	3,000	9,200
Equipment:		
Guns, night sticks, etc.	$ 1,550	
Uniforms	4,200	
Radios	3,000	
Beepers, misc. surveillance equip.	2,650	
Office equipment	1,500	
Personal effects	1,600	14,500
Total assets		$34,700

Liabilities

Notes payable:		
Mobile homes	$ 5,500	
Automobiles:		
1973 Pontiac	4,000	
1972 Chevy Nova	1,400	
1973 Chevy Nova	2,600	
Small Business Administration	7,800	
Total liabilities		$21,300
Net Worth		13,400
Total liabilities and net worth		$34,700

Case exhibit 8-3

RICHARD TRACY DETECTIVE AGENCY

Statement of operations for the year ended December 31, 1974

Income

Security fees	$164,772	
Investigative fees	5,400	
Gross fees		$170,172

Expenses

Gross payroll	96,036	
Telephone	8,520	
Equipment	3,600	
Auto	5,700	
Travel	1,884	
Professional fees	9,876	
Insurance	2,640	
Office	1,848	
Other	132	
Advertising	2,088	
Total expenses		$132,324
Net income		$ 37,848
Personal withdrawals		$ 32,000

Case exhibit 8-4

RICHARD TRACY DETECTIVE AGENCY

Statement of operations for the year ended December 31, 1973

Income:

Security fees	$229,448	
Investigative fees	10,047	
Total income		$239,495

Expenses:

Gross payroll	$169,173	
Equipment	5,203	
Auto	5,464	
Travel	12,331	
Professional fees	8,045	
Insurance	6,233	
Office expenses	8,273	
Other expenses	11,094	
Telephone	10,589	
Taxes	4,284	
Advertising	3,036	
Total expenses		243,725
Net loss		$ 4,230
Personal withdrawals		$ 26,283

Case exhibit 8–5

RICHARD TRACY DETECTIVE AGENCY

Statement of operations for the year ended December 31, 1972

Income

Gross receipts (security and investigations)		$100,112
Deductions		
Depreciation	$ 3,621	
Salaries and wages	58,543	
Insurance	2,520	
Interest on business indebtedness	286	
Telephone	5,134	
Uniform expense and supplies	5,133	
Advertising	1,444	
Automobile expense	974	
Travel	6,529	
Fees paid	3,347	
Office supplies and expense	5,124	
Payroll taxes	1,810	
Miscellaneous expenses	3,382	
Total deductions		97,847
Net profit		$ 2,265

Case exhibit 8–6

RICHARD TRACY DETECTIVE AGENCY

Statement of operations for the year ended December 31, 1971

Income

Security fees	$41,835	
Investigative fees	1,382	
Gross fees:		$43,217
Expenses		
Salaries	$23,048	
Uniform expense and supplies	391	
Telephone expense	2,674	
Advertising	423	
Automobile expense	1,080	
Travel	4,826	
Professional fees	4,511	
Insurance	1,093	
Office supplies and expense	1,786	
Depreciation	525	
Miscellaneous expense	1,347	
Payroll taxes	1,188	
Total expenses:		42,892
Net income:		$ 325

SUGGESTED QUESTIONS FOR DISCUSSION

1. Evaluate the current financial records of the agency. What does this suggest about the agency's management?

2. Assess the present management structure of the firm in terms of future growth.

3. Mr. Spade, in recent years, has made some rather large personal draws against the agency. What is your opinion regarding this practice?

4. Should the agency continue with investigative services?

5. Evaluate the current balance sheet in the context of the goals of the firm.

S.T.'s CHOPPER SHOP

DESCRIPTION OF THE FIRM

In November, 1971, Samuel Thomas Swayne, known as "S.T.," started a motorcycle shop with an initial investment of $11,000. He ran it on a part-time basis and the business grew as an extension of his personal interest in motorcycles as a hobby. The operation of the shop centered around customizing new and used motorcycles into the then popular "choppers." In July, 1972, Mr. Swayne resigned from his full-time job to devote himself entirely to the operation of his new business.

The facilities were expanded the following year with the aid of a $19,000 loan from the Small Business Administration. The loan, taken out in July, 1973, enabled Mr. Swayne to set up a fully equipped machine shop, acquire needed inventory, and enclose his operations in a new building. Later that same year the business was expanded to include an electroplating shop. A partnership was established with John Kelly, a man with 22 years' experience in electroplating, who had been subcontracting the chrome plating for Mr. Swayne's motorcycle parts. Complete electroplating facilities were purchased for $70,000 and placed in the same building as the motorcycle shop. Mr. Swayne acquired a 40 per cent interest in the electroplating unit, which was named Benton Plating Company, through the financial backing of a silent partner, who in turn acquired a 25 per cent interest in the motorcycle shop.

The partnership with Kelly terminated in February, 1975, with the death of Mr. Kelly. Mr. Swayne began to buy control of Mr. Kelly's interest in the electroplating business from Kelly's family and currently has $3000 to pay before assuming complete control of Benton Plating Company. This has caused some cash flow problems, and is a result of an inadequate partnership agreement and a lack of partner insurance.

Both businesses are situated in the same building on Mill Road, in Benton, Arkansas. Benton is approximately 25 miles from Little Rock. Mr. Swayne's home is also located on the same 2.5 acre plot adjacent to the business. A warehouse located within the city limits of Little Rock is rented for storage of used motorcycles and motorcycle parts. The somewhat isolated location of the firm tends to rule out sales to casual walk-ins; however, this has not hampered business, since Mr. Swayne has a reputation for doing quality work. This, coupled with the unique services offered in both electroplating and motorcycle customizing, has attracted enough clients to keep the firm busy. The location is accessible to supply companies and customers by main highways.

PHYSICAL ARRANGEMENT

Both the motorcycle and electroplating operations are housed in the same 40' by 60' by 12' metal-sided building, the floor plan of which is shown in Case exhibit 9–1.

Most of the floor area is used for permanent storage of used motorcycles—kept for parts—and a new parts inventory, with a small area used for temporary storage of motorcycles that are being repaired. Any open floor space tends to become cluttered with various parts and tools. The parts kept on shelves along the wall are neither labeled nor systematically arranged. The electroplating portion of the business requires little storage area for supplies, but a much larger work area for the actual plating operation.

The equipment in the shop has been carefully selected by Mr. Swayne. It allows flexibility and is also capable of handling the high tolerances required in rebuilding high-performance "chopper" engines.

Next to the machine shop is a paint room with all the equipment necessary to do both general motorcycle painting and the popular, highly artistic, fine-detail custom paint work.

The electroplating shop layout is designed for a more repetitive manufacturing process, since the job orders encountered usually involve processing a number of items at one time. The electroplating facilities are roughly subdivided into pre- and post-plating; grinding, polishing, and buffing; and electroplating areas.

In addition to the well-equipped machine shop and electroplating operations, there is a small display room which exhibits chromed motorcycle parts and completed custom motorcycles and serves for temporary storage of incoming motorcycles. Customers are normally served in this room.

Case exhibit 9–1

S.T.'s CHOPPER SHOP

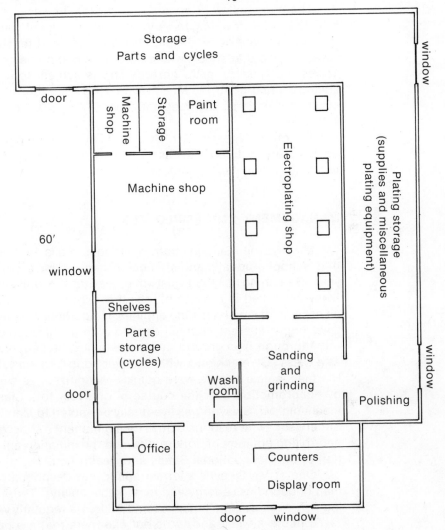

COMPETITION

S.T.'s Chopper Shop offers a range of services unique throughout the entire state. Because of his abilities, his experience with small engines—particularly Harley Davidson—and the capabilities of his shop, Mr. Swayne provides the only work of this nature and quality in the state. He says he has all the work that he can do. He currently turns out ten to twelve custom motorcycles a year, in addition to doing a large number of smaller, specialized, mechanical or painting jobs. He is also virtually the only source of a complete line of used Harley-Davidson parts in Arkansas. Mr. Swayne has a scheduling problem, because he does the jobs he likes to do first. Some jobs may sit in the shop as long as a year because of this type of scheduling.

There are six other platers in Arkansas; however, none appear to be able or willing to handle the wide range of plating jobs that Mr. Swayne does, despite the large demand for them. Mr. Swayne feels that shop owners do not do plating because it involves recognized health hazards and is subject to expensive environmental controls. Mr. Swayne does a number of jobs for large corporations, but does not become too reliant on any one customer.

In both businesses, Mr. Swayne is in a unique competitive position, and although he has more work than he can handle, he is failing to fully tap the potential market.

MANAGEMENT AND EMPLOYEES

Mr. Swayne manages both operations. He is 35 years old, a high school graduate, and attended Arkansas University for one year. Beginning in 1960, just after leaving the university, Mr. Swayne worked in a series of jobs that exposed him to virtually all aspects of small gasoline engines. In addition, he attended at least eight different courses dealing with small engines. With this thorough background in small engines, he began working as a Class "C" mechanic, with Cambell Soup Company, in 1966. His mechanical talents were quickly recognized, as evidenced by his promotion over the course of one year to a Class "AA" mechanic. Mr. Swayne was eventually promoted to Maintenance Supervisor "with responsibilities for maintenance shop, grounds and rolling equipment, fork trucks, and the initiation and operation of the Occupational Safety and Health Act."

One of Mr. Swayne's former employees described him as a man of boundless energy and remarkable ability, "There's nothing S.T. can't do if he puts his mind to it." He regularly works 60 to 70 hours a week and turns out choppers that are generally recognized as the best in Arkansas, if not the Southwest.

Mr. Swayne's wife, Susan, assists her husband in the business by taking care of the financial records and by handling telephone inquiries and walk-in trade. There are two full-time employees, John Rider and Frank Smith, and a part-time painter, Mike Mingo. Rider works as a mechanic in the motorcycle business and Smith works in the plating shop preparing items to be plated. The painter takes care of part of the motorcycle painting load; however, Mr. Swayne still does most of the painting.

Susan Swayne graduated from Benton College with an associate's degree in general business studies. She worked at Campbell Soup Company as a secretary in the Industrial Engineering Department for about six years. In that time, she became secretary to the head of the department, and her duties in this capacity exposed her to many different methods of gathering and utilizing data.

The death of Mr. Kelly has created a severe labor problem. Mr. Swayne has been unable to replace him, and has therefore taken on the chores of the plating shop as well as the machine shop. Mr. Swayne has experienced some difficulty in the past in obtaining reliable and competent help in the plating shop. The long and difficult training of new employees, combined with the ease of doing critical damage to the expensive chemical baths, has forced Mr. Swayne to assume these operations himself, to the detriment of the chopper business.

While competent machinists are available, customizing motorcycles involves so many decisions that Mr. Swayne must oversee and manage every step. He is often the only one who can perform certain functions, and is unable to allow a machinist to work independently. Therefore, Mr. Swayne is attempting to run all aspects of both the motorcycle shop and the electroplating business, personally.

PARTS AND SUPPLIES INVENTORIES

When opportunities arise, Mr. Swayne purchases both wrecked and used motorcycles from insurance companies or individuals. He uses these either for parts or for resale after rebuilding. The items from these purchases are not recorded or catalogued. This is evidenced by the large number of used motorcycles and parts scattered throughout the shop. In addition to used parts, Mr. Swayne keeps a small stock of new parts, items such as spark plugs, and chains. He orders these parts, when needed, from various suppliers. These items are also uncatalogued.

Mr. Swayne has, displayed in his showroom, a number of chromed parts which he bought in bulk a couple of years ago. He feels these items have not sold well and has no plans to reorder when they are depleted. Mr. Swayne's store of used and wrecked motorcycles is the best source of parts for Harley-Davidsons in Arkansas. Harley-Davidson dealers rarely stock many parts, particularly for older models, and therefore used parts are in great demand.

Susan Swayne has attempted to devise a method to record the motorcycles in inventory and assign costs to them; however, she is inexperienced in the techniques for controlling an inventory of this nature. It is obvious to the Swaynes that something must be done, since Mr. Swayne recently engaged in a contract with the Government Employees Insurance Company (GEICO) to buy all the wrecked motorcycles they own in Arkansas.

On the plating end of the business, Mr. Swayne inherited a large amount of the chemicals needed for the plating operation from Mr. Kelly. This stockpile has been nearly depleted. He expects to purchase most of his plating supplies from Allied Kelite, a division of the Richardson Corporation. As in the case of the cycle business, few records are kept.

ADVERTISING

Most of Mr. Swayne's current business has come about through word-of-mouth. He has tried advertising by radio spots, newspapers, Yellow Pages, and a large billboard east of Benton on the Benton Highway. With the exception of newspaper ads, Mr. Swayne has been dissatisfied with the results of advertising expenditures for either business. The shop itself has no real identification, other than an old Shell gasoline sign. Mr. Swayne plans to put up a sign in the near future.

PRICING

The motorcycle shop and electroplating business are both highly specialized and make pricing decisions difficult. At present Mr. Swayne sets prices arbitrarily, based on what he thinks a customer will pay. Often he sets prices that will enable him to pay a current bill, saying, "The fifty dollars in my hand is better than a hundred dollars I don't have. It pays the bills." He has no bad debt loss since he does not extend credit, except to large industrial plating customers.

There seem to be few standards on which Mr. Swayne bases his prices. This can be attributed to the nature of custom work. In some cases, however—particularly for chrome motorcycle parts—he uses a wholesale price list from the Tennessee plater (dated January, 1973), and adds a percentage, usually from 30 to 50 per cent. Currently, there is no attempt at figuring various expenses in a job, to help establish prices, in either the motorcycle shop or the plating operation.

FINANCIAL RECORDS

Mr. Swayne's current accounting system is designed to provide his accountant with information for tax reporting. The ac-

Case exhibit 9–2

S.T.'s CHOPPER SHOP

Income statement for year ending December 31, 1974

Sales		48,951
Rental income		2,055
Total revenue		51,006
Beginning inventory 1/1/74	6,037	
Purchases	34,411	
Ending inventory 12/31/74	16,888	
Less cost of goods sold:		23,560
Gross margin		27,446
Expenses:		
Accounting fee	125	
Advertising	493	
Truck	800	
Contributions	10	
Utilities and telephone	2,820	
Entertainment	262	
Freight	1,446	
Insurance	1,478	
Laundry	710	
Office supplies	151	
Equipment rental	253	
Shop supplies	2,873	
Sales tax	666	
Travel	364	
Repairs	3,320	
Legal expenses	527	
Taxes and license	723	
Salaries and commission	11,917	
Interest	1,322	
Miscellaneous	65	
Depreciation	3,744	
		34,069
Net loss		(6,623)

countant is given these data once a year. The system is also used to provide the SBA with a general balance sheet covering all of Mr. Swayne's financial interests. As a result, the financial records do not separate personal financial information from financial data related to his business. In addition, the records for the motorcycle shop and plating business are integrated. This situation makes it very difficult to get a clear financial picture of either aspect of the business. The financial data are shown in Case exhibits 9–2 and 9–3.

LOANS AND INSURANCE

Mr. Swayne's initial loan of $19,000 was secured in July, 1973, through the SBA. The loan was set for six years at 5.5 per cent interest. On three occasions, the SBA has had to defer

Case exhibit 9–3

S.T.'s CHOPPER SHOP

Balance sheet for October 1, 1974

Assets:		**Liabilities:**		
Cash	3,000	XYO Quip Co.	1,351	
Accounts receivable	9,870	National Bank	5.000	
Merchandise inventory	13,289	John Ivester	700	
Used motorcycles for resale	18,870	W. A. Reynolds Co.	175	
Shop equipment	41,525	Joseph Behr Co.	2,348	
Building and furnishings	88,390	FHA	11,000	
Home and land	20,000	SBA	17,000	
Vehicles	2,600	Total liabilities		37,574
Total assets	$197,544	Net worth		159,970
		Total liabilities and net worth		$197,544

Balance sheet for March 5, 1975

Assets:		**Liabilities:**		
Cash	369	XYO Quip Co.	1,140	
Accounts receivable	3,288	IRS	1,412	
Merchandise inventory	16,889	Tax commission	593	
Used motorcycles for resale	11,895	Hester County	431	
Shop equipment	41,525	Miscellaneous	1,717	
Building and furnishings	88,390	National Bank	3,077	
Home and land	20,000	FHA	10,800	
Vehicles	2,600	SBA	17,000	
Total assets	$184,956	Total liabilities		36,170
		Net worth		148,786
		Total liabilities and net worth		$184,956

monthly payments. The collateral for this loan includes a mortgage on the shop, land, and home; a first mortgage on the lot adjacent to his home; and a first security interest in his machinery, equipment, and inventory. The conditions on the loan include life insurance on Mr. Swayne's life, not less than the amount of the loan.

In 1975, after Mr. Kelly's death, Mr. Swayne requested a loan of $7000 for working capital from the SBA. His request was denied, principally because he would not give the SBA sufficient information regarding his silent partner. The SBA suggested that he ask the silent partner to provide the needed money. Mr. Swayne continues to have cash flow problems but has refused to elaborate on the silent partner.

Mr. Swayne has property insurance on his shop and its contents. The limits are $30,000 on the building and $50,000 on the contents. He also has minimal liability insurance, covering owned automobiles—including one dealer's tag for motorcycle operation—and damage resulting from faulty workmanship. He also has garage-keepers' legal coverage (limit $18,000) which covers damage and destruction to the motorcycles in his care belonging to others.

SUGGESTED QUESTIONS FOR DISCUSSION

1. What type of inventory policy would aid Mr. Swayne in managing his firm?

2. What are some specific controls Mr. Swayne should consider?

3. How can Mr. Swayne establish a realistic pricing system?

4. What is the major problem facing Mr. Swayne?

CASE **10**

REPAIR, RENOVATION, REJUVENATION: AUTO-RESTORATIONS, INCORPORATED

HISTORY OF THE FIRM

Auto-Restorations, Incorporated was founded in November, 1973, by Paul A. Johnson and Joe P. Hardy. Together, Paul and Joe organized the enterprise and officially opened for business in a 5000 square foot warehouse at 1401 Madison Street in Austin, Texas. The business encompasses both complete and partial restoration of antique and classic cars. Cars and parts are also bought, sold, and traded. This venture started as a part-time endeavor for both individuals, since they each already held prominent positions in the Austin area. After several months of operation it became apparent that there existed a larger demand for this type of service than could be fulfilled on a part-time basis. Therefore, Paul took a leave of absence from his job in order to develop a business which could meet this increased demand.

It also became apparent that a larger facility would be needed to house such an operation. Thus, in June, 1974, Auto-Restorations, Incorporated moved to its present location at 2405 Johns Avenue. This new facility is roughly 40,000 square feet in area, including a large garage and showroom on the first floor, as well as second and third floors, used for storage.

In the beginning, the firm was a partnership between Paul and Joe. However, with the expansion of the business it was incorporated in April, 1974, under Subchapter S of the Internal Revenue Code. Paul became president of the firm, and Joe became secretary/treasurer. Because Joe was unable to leave his own business to devote himself full-time to the firm, John Harris became vice-president. Common stock amounting to 10,000 shares was authorized at $10.00 per share, par value. At the present time, the firm's common stock is owned by these individuals in these amounts:

president, Paul Johnson—780 shares;
vice-president, John Harris—120 shares;
secretary/treasurer, Joe Hardy—300 shares.

THE INDUSTRY

Locally:
In Austin, there was another firm engaged in the same business. This firm, named Vintage Coach, has since gone out of business. The only other competition in the area is the Classic Car Corral, in Jonesville, thirty miles away. However, that organization only sells antique and classic cars, doing no repair or restoration work. The closest competitors that offer the same services on the same scale are found in Louisiana and New Mexico.

Nationally:
Collecting antique automobiles is one of America's fastest growing pastimes. People are collecting old cars for two reasons: first, of course, the beauty and luxury of these automobiles; second, their growing value, since most antique and classic cars have doubled in price in the last two years.

A recent surge in old car prices has made many antiques too expensive for the average individual, so many people are turning to what are termed "special interest" autos. These include Model A's, Chrysler Airflows, and the Lincoln-Zephyrs of the 1930s, as well as more recent cars, such as Edsels, Corvairs, and Thunderbirds. This all contributes to the fact that there are more than half a million car collectors in this country. This number is still growing and has a long way to go before it reaches its peak.*

PHYSICAL AND MARKETING ASPECTS OF THE BUSINESS LOCATION

The present location at 2405 Johns Avenue offers all the physical attributes needed in such an operation. On the Johns Avenue side of the building is a large showroom, with room to display five automobiles. A general office is located at the rear of the showroom. The president's office is next to the general office. The parts department is behind these areas, but currently

---

Phillips 66 Magazine, Phillips Petroleum Company, Bartlesville, Oklahoma, October 1975.

Case exhibit 10-1

AUTO-RESTORATIONS, INCORPORATED

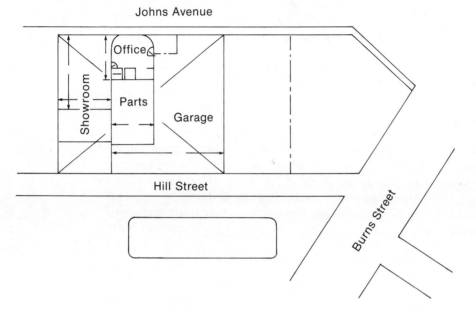

houses only a small amount of inventory. An engine room, dust-free and air-conditioned, is behind the proposed parts department, and next to that is the vice-president's office. The garage can hold forty cars, some of which have been put in storage by their owners, and others of which are being restored. The entire second and third floors are used to store parts which have been removed from cars during restoration. Each car being restored has had a number assigned to it, and its stored parts are numbered accordingly.

The biggest marketing advantage the firm has is its location, since Johns Avenue and Burns Street form one of Austin's major intersections only half a block away. Being located on a main thoroughfare makes the firm readily accessible to established customers, as well as to those who may become interested while passing the large showroom window.

MANAGEMENT

The firm is a closed corporation. The three officers are also the entire board of directors, the only stockholders, and the principal managers. The organization chart is shown in Case exhibit 10-2.

Paul A. Johnson is 29 years old, and holds a Bachelor of

Science degree in mathematics from Austin College. He was previously employed by Oneal Plumbing Company, as vice-president and applications engineer.

John Harris is 30 years old, with a Bachelor of Arts in broadcast journalism. Before coming to work at the firm he was employed by Austin Educational Television for four years.

The secretary/treasurer, Joe P. Hardy, is a prominent veterinarian. At the age of 41, he also holds a degree in business psychology and has experience as a drug sales representative.

Since the start of the firm, no employee has ever been fired. This stems from the nearly complete lack of available metal crafters in the labor market. It seems everyone is a replacer, not a rebuilder. Because of this, each new employee has to be extensively trained, and so becomes a valuable asset to the corporation.

Each individual in the organization is paid a flat-rate salary on a weekly basis. The first week's salary is held back on each new employee. Employee benefits include group life and group hospitalization insurance. Also, each worker gets a ten-day, fully paid vacation each year. As yet, no pension plan is in effect.

Case exhibit 10–2

AUTO-RESTORATIONS, INCORPORATED

Organizational chart

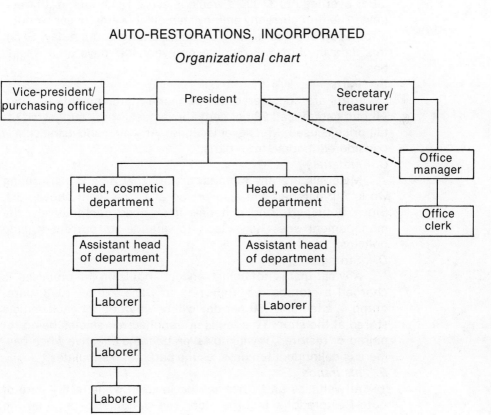

The current main objective of the firm's owners is to make the business self-sustaining. In order to do this, they are working toward making it one of the most complete restoration facilities in the Southwest. The first step has been taken, since the managers now deal mainly with the public and do little or no work in the shop, as they were forced to do initially.

Ultimately, the managers plan extensive travel to car shows throughout the nation, as they try to expand their sales.

SERVICES OFFERED

A. Labor

Labor consists of any work performed on cars either under contract or under non-contract specifics. All contract work is given a number, while non-contract work, encompassing simple service repairs, is not. All labor is supervised by a department head. All labor is priced at $13.00 an hour, whether it is skilled or non-skilled. Since most of the work done by the firm is skilled, the owners feel this is a fair price. The majority of the restoration shops in the country price their labor at $15.00 an hour and up.

This firm's monthly break-even on labor, given the current labor overhead of $1600 a week, is every 123 hours, or thirteen days. The firm currently employs ten billable employees working a four-day week consisting of nine working hours a day. Given this data the firm will break even every 1.37 days on a weekly basis.

B. Parts

Parts are considered any permanent attachments to a car. All parts are priced 20 per cent above cost, or the suggested retail price is used, whichever is higher. Anything above the cost is considered income from parts.

C. Materials

Materials are any material or tool that aids in performing work. All materials are also priced at 20 per cent above cost. Since both parts and materials are priced competitively, the management sees no reason to change its current pricing policies.

D. Storage

Any car that is not being serviced, but is on the premises, is charged a storage fee. Referring to Case exhibit 10–3, paragraph 4, a fee of $1.50 per day will be charged for each vehicle stored at the shop. This fee is not applied to vehicles being repaired or restored. It will, however, become effective when payment is delinquent ten days, as the paragraph stipulates.

E. Insurance

All vehicles and parts will be insured while in the care of Auto-Restorations, Incorporated. The customer determines the

Case exhibit 10-3

AUTO-RESTORATIONS, INCORPORATED

Auto-Restorations, Inc.

2405 JOHNS AVENUE   AUSTIN, TEXAS

Paragraph 1. It is hereby understood that any prices, general estimates, or hourly rates discussed prior to the signing of this contract were for discussion only. All work will be performed on a time and material basis at the prevailing wage and material prices of that period.

Paragraph 2. It is the standard policy of Auto-Restorations, Incorporated to furnish all clients with a monthly projection, which should be paid as soon as possible so as not to delay work on your vehicle.

Paragraph 3. Payment to Auto-Restorations, Incorporated will be on a weekly schedule, payable ten (10) calendar days after date of statement. If payment is not received within the ten day period, no further work will be performed on the vehicle until payment is received. If payment is not received within thirty (30) calendar days from date of statement, a mechanic's lien will be placed against the said vehicle and it shall become the property of Auto-Restorations, Incorporated.

Paragraph 4. A fee of one dollar and fifty cents ($1.50) per day will be charged for each vehicle stored at Auto-Restorations, Incorporated. This paragraph does not apply to vehicles being repaired or restored by Auto-Restorations, Incorporated. It will, however, become effective when payment is delinquent ten calendar days as stipulated in paragraph 3.

Paragraph 5. All vehicles and parts will be insured against collision, fire and lightning, theft or larceny, windstorm, hail or explosion, and malicious mischief or vandalism, while in our care, custody, or control. The insured value shall be determined upon acceptance of the vehicle and increased as work is performed on said vehicle on a monthly basis as determined by the owner, if he so desires, on the first of each calendar month. If the owner does not increase the value of said vehicle on the first of each calendar month, then the original insured value shall stand until

Case exhibit continued on following page.

changed by the owner. Said vehicle as described in paragraph 8 is set at an insured value of $ _____ as of _____, payable to Auto-Restorations, Incorporated at ten cents ($.10) per $1,000.00 per day for a total of $_____ for a minimum of one month's premium.

Paragraph 6. It will be the responsibility of the owner to remove the vehicle when notified by Auto-Restorations, Incorporated that said vehicle is ready to be released. If the vehicle is not removed within five (5) working days, then it shall go into storage as defined in paragraph 4. It is understood that no vehicle or part will be released by Auto-Restorations, Incorporated unless paid for in full.

Paragraph 7. Minimum monthly payment for work described on said vehicle shall be _____ per month (no car will be accepted for restoration with less than $200.00 per month minimum).

Paragraph 8. Description of vehicle or part:
Make _____ Year ____ Body style ____ Motor no. _____
Body no. _____ Title no. _____ State reg. no._____
License plate number, state and year _____

Paragraph 9. Note here if intact car: _____ engine only
_____ body only
_____ other

Paragraph 10. Describe work to be performed by Auto-Restorations, Incorporated. Describe in detail.

Date signed_____Owner's signature_____
Home phone_____Mailing address_____
Bus. phone_____City_____State_____Zip ___
Signature of agent for Auto-Restorations, Inc._____

appropriate amount of insurance. It is priced at ten cents per day per thousand dollars of insurance, for a minimum of one month's premium.

F. *Sale on consignment*

The firm offers this service to the public for a small fee. If the firm itself is not willing to buy the vehicle outright, then the owner may leave it in Auto-Restoration's custody, under the condition that it will be sold only for a specified price. The price that is charged for handling the sales transaction is ten per cent of that price, payable upon sale of the car.

G. *Sale of inventory cars*

The firm offers cars to the public that are purchased by the corporation for resale. While prices vary somewhat depending upon the type of vehicle being sold, normal pricing policies amount to a 40 to 50 per cent mark-up.

H. *Subcontract labor*

The firm performs a great deal of subcontract labor. Because of the size and complexity of the operation, the firm finds this necessary. While all subcontract work is priced 20 per cent above the cost to the firm, this price is competitive.

INVENTORY

The firm's inventory consists of cars, parts, and materials, all listed at current market value. At this time, the value of this inventory is about $1200. The inventory on hand is very small, compared to what is needed. Parts have to be ordered for some cars on a daily basis, when a larger inventory would eliminate this ordering delay. Inventory is a necessity in this type of business as a marketing device. An inventory of about $20,000 would place the firm among the largest antique and classic car parts dealers in the area.

CREDIT POLICIES

Payment to the firm is on a weekly basis, payable ten calendar days after the date of the statement. The firm currently is experiencing a turnover of accounts receivable as long as 98 days.

ADVERTISING

Advertising for the firm has been mainly free publicity. During the past year alone, all the local television stations have

Case exhibit 10–4

AUTO-RESTORATIONS, INCORPORATED

Balance sheet, December 31, 1974

Assets

Current assets		
Cash		$ 2,540.00
Trade accounts receivable		7,599.00
Other receivables		300.00
Inventories		
Parts	$ 9,914.00	
Auto	1,600.00	11,514.00
Prepaid interest		2,151.00
Total current assets		24,104.00
Organization cost (net of amortization)		87.00
Fixed assets		
Leasehold improvements	905.00	
Shop equipment	8,208.00	
Trucks	8,500.00	
Furniture and fixtures	2,329.00	
Less allowance for depreciation	(3,497.00)	16,445.00
Total assets		40,636.00

Liabilities and stockholders' equity

Current liabilities		
Payroll taxes		5,063.00
Accounts payable		1,031.00
Money tree advances		2,337.00
Open note payable		2,566.00
Current portion of installment notes payable		12,348.00
Total current liabilities		23,345.00
Other liabilities		
Stockholders' loan payable		4,330.00
Long-term liabilities		
Notes payable—installment obligations	18,687.00	
less portion shown under current liabilities	(12,349.00)	6,338.00
Total liabilities		34,013.00

Stockholders' equity

Common stock—$10.00 par value		
Authorized 10,000 shares, issued and		
outstanding 1,000 shares	10,000.00	
Paid-in capital	12,318.00	
Retained earnings	(15,695.00)	6,623.00
Total liabilities and stockholders' equity		40,636.00

Case exhibit 10–5

AUTO-RESTORATIONS, INCORPORATED

Statement of income and retained earnings for the period April 1, 1974 through December 31, 1974

Net sales		$87,866.00
Cost of goods sold		
Autos and parts	$49,722.00	
Direct labor costs	27,374.00	77,096.00
Gross profit on sales		10,770.00
Other income		
Commissions	900.00	
Miscellaneous	272.00	1,172.00
Gross profit		11,942.00
Expenses		
Commissions	450.00	
Subcontract work	1,219.00	
Taxes and licenses	3,313.00	
Uniforms	181.00	
Truck repairs	136.00	
Gas and oil	311.00	
Shop supplies	3,876.00	
Shipping and freight	213.00	
Telephone	1,759.00	
Insurance	1,722.00	
Depreciation	2,871.00	
Office supplies	470.00	
Utilities	983.00	
Rent	6,800.00	
Advertising	608.00	
Employee relations	270.00	
Legal and professional	907.00	
Interest expense	1,360.00	
Amortization organization expense	13.00	
Miscellaneous	175.00	27,637.00
Net income (loss)		(15,695.00)

featured the firm on at least one of their news programs. Because of the lack of competition in the Austin area and the free publicity, the management has found no need for an extensive advertising program. Business cards, key chains, and calendars are distributed to let people know of the services offered.

FINANCIAL DATA

The bookkeeping system is made up of journal and ledger records. Each account in the ledger is a record of a particular asset, liability, or corporate item. In practice, an initial record of

Case exhibit 10–6

AUTO-RESTORATIONS, INCORPORATED

Balance sheet, June 30, 1975

Assets

Current assets		
Cash		$ 2,349.00
Trade accounts receivable		17,422.00
Inventories		
Parts	$ 9,914.00	
Auto	1,600.00	11,514.00
Prepaid interest		1,423.00
Total current assets		32,708.00
Organization cost (net of amortization)		80.00
Fixed assets		
Leasehold improvements	985.00	
Shop equipment	8,208.00	
Trucks	8,502.00	
Furniture and fixtures	2,329.00	
Less allowance for depreciation	(5,584.00)	14,440.00
Total assets		47,228.00

Liabilities and stockholders' equity

Current liabilities		
Payroll taxes		1,097.00
Accounts payable		1,717.00
Accrued expenses		1,001.00
Money tree advances		1,814.00
Open note payable		1,500.00
Current portion of installment notes payable		10,580.00
Stockholders' loan payable		3,000.00
Customer deposits		2,106.00
Total current liabilities		22,815.00
Other liabilities		
Stockholders' loan payable—long-term		5,902.00
Long-term liabilities		
Notes payable—installment obligation	12,468.00	
less portion shown under current liabilities	(10,580.00)	1,888.00
Total liabilities		30,605.00

Stockholders' equity

Common stock—$10.00 par value		
Authorized 10,000 shares, issued and outstanding, 1,200 shares	12,000.00	
Paid-in capital	10,318.00	
Retained earnings	(5,695.00)	16,623.00
Total liabilities and stockholders' equity		47,228.00

Case exhibit 10–7

AUTO-RESTORATIONS, INCORPORATED

Statement of income and retained earnings for the period January 1, 1975 through June 30, 1975

Gross income from parts and labor		$63,734.00
Cost of goods sold		
Direct labor	$11,742.00	
Officers' salaries	14,460.00	
Parts	9,247.00	
Sub-contract work	2,559.00	38,008.00
Gross profit from parts and labor		25,726.00
Other income		
Commissions	4,654.00	
Miscellaneous	340.00	4,994.00
Gross profit		30,720.00
Expenses		
Taxes and licenses	2,710.00	
Uniforms	43.00	
Truck repair	379.00	
Gas and oil	726.00	
Shop supplies	3,570.00	
Shipping and freight	21.00	
Telephone	452.00	
Insurance	1,078.00	
Depreciation	2,087.00	
Office supplies	518.00	
Utilities	989.00	
Rent	4,635.00	
Advertising	54.00	
Janitorial services	81.00	
Professional fees	1,695.00	
Interest expense	967.00	
Amortization of organization expense	6.00	
Bad debts	663.00	
Miscellaneous	49.00	20,723.00
Net income — earnings per share = $8.33		9,997.00

each transaction is evidenced by a source document (ticket, invoice, or receipt). On the evidence provided by the documents, transactions are analyzed in terms of their effect on the elements of the accounting equation, and then are recorded in the journal or book of original entry. All entries are recorded in the ledger, which in turn supplies the cumulative data for financial statements and other reports. These statements are presented in Case exhibits 10–4 through 10–7.

SUGGESTED QUESTIONS FOR DISCUSSION

1. Evaluate the qualifications of the three individuals who own and manage the firm.

2.   How do you think the firm can improve its market appeal?

3.   Both balance sheets have the same dollar figures for inventory. What does this mean in terms of inventory control?

4.   Evaluate the general financial condition of this firm.

HARRIS TIRE AND
RETREADING COMPANY

HISTORY OF THE FIRM

The Harris Tire and Retreading Company, Incorporated was started in Cookeville, Tennessee, in 1963, by George Harris (now deceased) and his two brothers. It began as a small, dilapidated service station, dealing mostly in recap tires. The company was not incorporated and only George Harris took an active part in the management. Mr. Harris' two brothers, who lived in North Carolina, quickly grew disinterested in the business, and by 1967 wanted to sell their interests. In 1967, Mr. Harris' son, Parker, who was attending Georgia Southern College, saw an opportunity in the small station and discussed the matter with a friend, Ronnie Gucker, who was also attending Georgia Southern College. These two men bought out the inactive Harris brothers in 1967.

Late in 1967, the owners of Harris Tire and Retreading Company tore down the old station and built a new, much larger, steel structure. Parker Harris and Ronnie Gucker started managing the business. Mr. George Harris, who then worked for Farmer's Ice and Fuel Company, aided them but did not take an active part in managing the Harris Company. During these first years, Parker Harris and Ronnie Gucker had success due to their hard work, the counsel of Mr. George Harris, and the advice of the Goodyear field representative. The company started with little or no capital and all profit was put back into the company except for modest salaries paid to Parker Harris and Ronnie Gucker.

Around 1969 the Harris Tire and Retreading Company decided to expand. A stockroom was added to the existing structure, and a large inventory of tires from Farmer's Ice and Fuel Company and a front-end alignment machine were purchased. The stockroom worked out well, but they found that they had over-extended on their inventory and there was no place to put the front-end alignment machine.

In 1970, the Harris Company appealed to the Small Business Administration for financial assistance. The company was at this time in poor financial condition due to the heavy debt owed Farmer's Ice and Fuel Company. The original loan request was for $100,000. This money was to be used for more expansion, working capital, and to reduce the Farmer's Ice and Fuel Company debt. The expansion was to include additional space for the front-end alignment machine and the paving of the front parking lot.

The original loan request was rejected due to lack of reasonable assurance that the loan could be repaid. In June, 1971, a revised loan proposal was submitted and approved, since the company's ability to repay had been enhanced by several conditions. First, the loan request was reduced by 11.5 per cent. Second, the improvements to be made would increase profits, and the debt to Farmer's Ice and Fuel had been reduced. Finally, the owners of Harris Tire and Retreading Company, George and Parker Harris and Ronnie Gucker, had mortgaged their residences to provide increased equity capital for the business.

DESCRIPTION OF THE FIRM

The Harris Tire and Retreading Company has one location on the Route 121 by-pass at Cookeville. This location is easily accessible to large tractor and pulpwood trucks, which have a difficult time driving the small streets of Cookeville. The company is located two miles out of town.

The Harris Tire and Retreading Company, as the name states, deals mainly in tires and retreads. Their specialty is large truck tires and they have the only complete line of truck tires in the vicinity of Cookeville. Truck tires account for approximately 45 per cent of total sales. This large volume is due directly to their complete line of tires, their tire mounting services, and their road service.

Related to the truck tires and service are the farm tires. The Harris Tire and Retread Company also carries a complete line of tractor tires. It is almost impossible for a tractor owner to bring a tractor with a flat tire to a tire store. Also, the weight of these tires is enormous (tractor tires are filled either with water or some heavier liquid, to maximize traction). The Harris Tire Company has a service truck especially equipped to aid in the mounting of tractor tires. Harris Tire's employees can go to the tractor, pump the liquid out of the tires into a special tank in the truck, remove the old tire, and mount the new tire with the air guns and other necessary equipment. Farm equipment tires account for approximately 20 per cent of the company's business.

At present, Harris Tire and Retreading is expanding its passenger car tire service, which accounts for approximately 20 per cent of its business. The company carries two major brands of passenger tires, Michelin and Goodyear, and provides a recap service for passenger vehicles and small trucks. Goodyear tires are the strongest line, accounting for half of the passenger tire sales. Michelin tires account for one-fourth of these sales, leaving the other fourth to the recap service. The company does not push the last, although the largest margin of profit is in the recap line.

Non-tire services, providing parts such as fan belts and shock absorbers for passenger cars, are relatively new to Harris Tire. The company has also recently purchased a Sun tune-up machine, and has trained an employee in its use and in the use of the wheel alignment machine.

MARKETING

The large-truck tire market in Cookeville County is held almost totally by Harris Tire and Retreading Company. Most local trucks are involved with the pulpwood business. There are several wood dealers along Highway 76, which runs into Route 121, making Harris Tire accessible to wildcat pulpwood workers, whose purchases are billed through the wood companies for which they are working and the amount subtracted from their pay. In addition, the wood companies buy tires from Harris Tire Company, and these tires are billed directly to the companies.

This success is due to three aspects of the Harris Tire Company's operation. First, the complete inventory of truck tires assures the truck drivers they can always find what they need. Second, Harris Tire is conveniently located close to the pulpwood areas. Finally, Harris Tire's services, such as on-the-road tire changes and convenient billing, increase demand for their tires.

The tractor tire market is almost as strong as the truck tire market. Harris Tire carries a more complete line of tractor tires than other dealers in the area, but for the most part, Harris' tractor tires are slightly higher in price. In this market, Harris' drawing-card is its service and the rapport Parker Harris and Ronnie Gucker have with the farmers. The service truck minimizes down-time for farmers. Parker Harris and Ronnie Gucker are constantly visiting farmers in their area. The area around Cookeville is rural, but most of the farming is done on a small scale, the primary reason farm equipment tires account for a smaller percentage of the total sales than truck tires.

Although Harris Tire carries a complete line of passenger vehicle tires, and offers a complete line of services, the passenger vehicle business is more difficult to obtain. It is in this line that the competition most hurts Harris Tire Company. In the passenger line, there are ten major dealers, plus many smaller companies, that offer the same quality service at a lower price, and are more convenient to the Cookeville business district.

PHYSICAL ASPECTS

The Harris Tire and Retreading Company is located in a modern steel warehouse. The parking lot is large, but is often crowded due to the large volume of truck tire sales. An impressive, eye-catching sign stands in the parking lot. On the front of the warehouse is a large shed. The area under the shed stays dry during rain and is not cluttered, offering a dry place to service large truck tires on rainy days. To the left of the shed is a door which leads to the customer waiting area and the office space; these are often dirty and offer few places to sit. Behind the office space a storeroom extends the length of the original building. Passenger vehicle tires are kept in this storeroom. The far left corner of the large work area is separated by a bar extending halfway across the building. It is in this area that finishing touches are put on recap tires. Here, the machines are kept which heat the recaps under pressure to form a secure bond between the tire boot and the new tread.

On the back wall of the main building to the right is a small blocked-in area. In this room, tires that are not radials are put in-round, and rubber is stripped from the tire boots that are to be recapped. This is done by shaving off part of the tire, which gives off a stifling black smoke. The Occupational Safety and Health Administration has recommended ventilation in this room. A very small area to the front of this room is the glue spraying area. Here the glue is sprayed on the tire boots which are to be recapped. This forms a temporary bond between the boot and the retreading rubber until the recap can be taken to the heat and pressure machines. In front of these smaller areas is a large general work area. Although there seems to be an abundance of space here, discarded tires and related waste occupy every corner.

The newest addition to the Harris Tire Company's warehouse is to the far right, and is the most uncluttered area in the building. It was built for passenger vehicle services but is used very little due to the small volume of passenger sales. The front-end alignment machine and the Sun tune-up machine are kept here.

MANAGEMENT

Three people manage the Harris Tire and Retreading Company. In addition to Ronnie Gucker and Parker Harris, Mrs. George Harris also takes an active part in the management. Mrs. Harris is in charge of bookkeeping, billing, and other office duties while Parker Harris and Ronnie Gucker supervise the work and make contacts with customers.

Lawrence Parker Harris was born on March 14, 1944, in Cookeville County, Tennessee. He attended Cookeville High School, and after graduation went to Brevard Junior College, Wingate Junior College, and Georgia Southern College, majoring in physical education. Parker Harris withdrew from Georgia Southern to go into business with his father, George Harris (now deceased). Parker Harris has held no previous jobs, but he is a good worker and amiable, and he is enthusiastic about Harris Tire and Retreading Company.

Ronald L. Gucker was born on June 13, 1943, in Augusta, Georgia. Ronnie Gucker attended Strom Thurmond High School, in Augusta. After finishing his high school education he attended Gordon Military College, also in Georgia, and Georgia Southern College, where he met Parker Harris. Mr. Gucker was also a physical education major and withdrew to go into business with Mr. George Harris.

Mrs. Ruth Harris is Parker Harris' mother. She had worked with her husband, George Harris, as bookkeeper since the conception of the business. After her husband's death, Mrs. Harris continued to work as office manager at Harris Tire and Retreading Company.

ORGANIZATION OF FIRM

The Harris Tire and Retreading Company started out as a family business and to a large degree remains such (see Case exhibit 11–1), although it has been incorporated. Each of the three managers holds fifty shares of stock, and there are one hundred and fifty shares issued. There is a board of directors, consisting of the three managers, Ronnie Gucker's wife, and Parker Harris' wife. The board of directors takes no active part in the business.

Holding equal amounts of stock formally gives each of the managers equal power in the business, as was intended. Informally, Parker Harris makes the final decisions.

The Harris Tire Company employs six workers, who fall directly under the supervision of Parker Harris and Ronnie Gucker. Mrs. George Harris rarely has contact with the workers outside the office. Her duties are limited to writing receipts, collecting money from sales, and other office routines.

Case exhibit 11–1

HARRIS TIRE AND RETREADING COMPANY

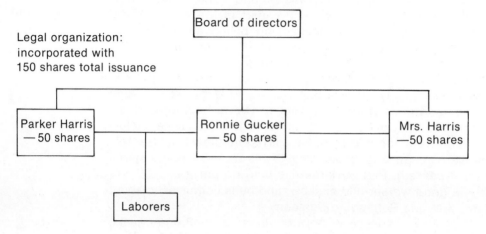

Legal organization: incorporated with 150 shares total issuance

Board of directors

Parker Harris — 50 shares

Ronnie Gucker — 50 shares

Mrs. Harris —50 shares

Laborers

PERSONNEL

The Harris Tire and Retreading Company provides their workers with worker's compensation and a life insurance policy. The company pays minimum wage, with the exception of one man who has been with the company since its beginning, who is paid just above minimum wage. According to Harris and Gucker, the company has fired only one employee since the reorganization in 1969, and he was fired because of laziness. The company has no plans for expanding its personnel.

The managers often allow the personnel a day off from work with pay. This sometimes causes the men who are working to be pushed, and often causes a backlog of work. On the whole, though, the workers are happy and productive. This is due, mostly, to the lack of close worker supervision. The workers know what is to be done, and they do it.

MARKETING POLICIES

Product

Harris Tire is primarily involved in selling new tires and retreading old ones. At least two of every type of car tire are stocked. All Goodyear tires are purchased through Murphy Oil Company in El Dorado, Texas—usually at quantity discounts. Total sales can be broken down according to activity: farm tires and retreads, 20 per cent; truck tires and retreads, 45 per cent; passenger tires and retreads, 20 per cent; and tune-ups and front-end alignment, 15 per cent.

The company is emphasizing its weaker product lines, to counter increased competition from the Goodyear company-owned store in Cookeville, which is beginning to service trucks and offer truck tires. The shift in marketing emphasis, from truck and farm tires to passenger car tires, front-end alignment, batteries, shock absorbers, and accessories, has made Harris Tire a full service garage. This appeals to customers who need more than tires.

In addition, the service truck, added in February, 1974, is a factor that, together with the company's ability to service large trucks and trailers "on the road," has been valuable in maintaining sales.

Price

Higher priced, higher quality tires are emphasized at Harris Tire. New tires are priced 40 per cent above wholesale prices. Discounts are not generally given, except for some discounts on quantities of six to eight tires. Recapping operations are priced at $3.00 for materials and $6.50 for labor, plus a 50 per cent mark-up. Pricing in the front-end alignment shop is competitive with the locale, as is the case with related services. The managers emphasize their policy of selling only necessary products and services to their customers. It is believed that fair prices and good services, especially after the sale, have generated a following of customers.

Promotion

The bulk of advertising is done on Radio Station WKOR in Cookeville. For the past six years, Harris Tire has sponsored, along with other advertisers, football games played by the University of Tennessee and Vanderbilt. These spots have been "cooperative advertising agreements" with both Goodyear and Michelin. In January, 1975, Harris Tire changed its advertising strategy to sponsor the 7:30 A.M. News and Sports on WKOR. Currently, a "fifty–fifty co-op" is arranged with Michelin. Harris Tire plans to switch to Goodyear spots soon with the same cooperative agreement. Management would also like to advertise in the local newspaper.

The advertising stresses passenger car tires and the other car services at Harris Tire. The management feels that Harris Tire is the major dealer in the Cookeville truck and farm tire market and does not need, and cannot practically reach, truckers and farmers by radio. Instead, Mr. Harris and Mr. Gucker visit both new and old farm and truck tire customers, particularly during periods of slow sales. Since truck tires average $1,000 to $4,000 per set, personal selling and promotion are thought to be more effective with this market. Farmers and lumber haulers usually do not work in the rain. This situation causes slow work at Harris Tire, but affords the managers opportunities to make personal contacts.

RECORDS SYSTEM

The basic system is an NCR Systemmedia Company bookkeeping system. An NCR cash register is used for handling daily cash and charge operations in the store, summarizing the daily activities on "proof sheets" and maintaining customer's accounts. The cash register allows sales to be described in nine categories: new car tires, new truck tires, retreads—cars, retreads—trucks, miscellaneous, tubes and batteries, resale, labor, and alignment. The register provides keys to accomplish these functions: cash, charge, cash credit, charge credit, received on account, paid out, amount tendered, credit balance, and previous balance.

The record keeping process begins with the completion of the triplicate form for the job or work order. If the total amount due is not paid in cash, it is posted to the customer's account statement through the register. This account statement is used to maintain and collect customer's accounts. At the end of the day, a "proof sheet," or daily statement of business, is inserted into the machine. The day's transactions in cash and charge, received on account and by department, are recorded on the form. These daily statements are transferred to Mr. B. A. Taylor, the firm's accountant, once a month. Harris Tire maintains two separate checking accounts in two different banks. The checkbooks are switched every two weeks. In the interim two weeks, Mr. Taylor balances and checks the checking account not being used. A logbook of monthly sales has been maintained since October, 1965. The bookkeeping system was installed in 1971. The most recent financial data are shown in Case exhibits 11–2 and 11–3. Financial ratios are shown in Case exhibit 11–4.

INVENTORY POLICIES

The inventory consists primarily of new automobile, truck, and farm equipment tires. The bulk of the new car tires are neatly stored in the rear of the main building. Most of the new truck and farm tires are stored in a rented warehouse, about one mile away from the main store. A few new truck tires are stored at the shop. The next largest inventory item includes pieces of rubber used in the recapping process. Batteries, front-end alignment tools, shock absorbers, and other accessories provide the balance of the inventory.

Case exhibit 11–2

HARRIS TIRE AND RETREADING COMPANY

*Comparative income statement, in dollars**

Item	1970	1971	1972	1973	1974
Net sales	$256889.0	$259817.6	$306503.4	$373478.0	$450795.3
Cost of goods sold					
Beginning inventory	53147.7	79965.4	81992.2	73824.6	94699.4
Purchases (gross)	194030.5	173315.8	172446.2	233626.2	289626.1
Purchases (net)	194030.5	173315.8	172446.2	233626.2	289626.1
Cost of goods available for sale	247178.2	253281.1	254438.4	307450.8	384325.4
Ending inventory	79965.4	81992.2	73824.6	94699.4	115903.9
Total cost of goods sold	167212.8	171289.0	180613.8	212751.4	268421.6
Gross profit	$ 89676.0	$ 88528.6	$125889.6	$160726.6	$182373.7
Operating expenses					
Selling expenses	37167.3	40199.2	50782.2	62402.8	73117.8
Total subcategory operating expenses no. 1	9792.6	9162.8	11546.0	17188.3	21588.3
General plus administrative expense	38780.6	32440.2	42287.2	51951.4	56758.8
Total operating expenses	85740.4	81802.1	104615.3	131542.4	151464.8
Net operating income	3935.6	6726.4	21274.3	29184.1	30908.9
Net profit before taxes and ex inc.	3935.6	6726.4	21274.3	29184.1	30908.9
Federal income tax	865.7	1479.8	5676.0	8572.8	8191.6
Net profit after taxes and ex inc.	$ 3069.3	$ 5246.6	$ 15598.3	$ 20611.3	$ 22717.3

*Totals may be slightly incorrect due to rounding.

Case Exhibit 11–3

HARRIS TIRE AND RETREADING COMPANY

*Comparative balance sheet, in dollars**

Item	1970	1971	1972	1973	1974
Assets					
Current assets					
Cash	$ 4000.8	$ 2792.3	$ 24178.3	$ 21241.0	$ 5692.5
Receivables, trade (net)	35066.6	47497.3	46426.4	50940.2	55934.7
Inventory	79965.0	81992.3	73824.6	94699.4	115903.9
Short-term prepayments	0.0	0.0	0.0	960.0	480.0
Total current assets	119032.4	132281.8	144429.3	167840.6	178011.1
Fixed assets (gross)	104630.0	113493.3	127761.5	127761.5	142053.7
less accumulated depreciation	18562.0	30672.8	45104.4	59983.4	76339.4
Fixed assets (net)	86068.0	82820.5	82657.1	67778.1	65714.3
Organization expense	154.0	154.0	154.0	0.0	0.0
Prepaid income tax	0.0	198.0	0.0	0.0	0.0
Total noncurrent assets	86222.0	83172.5	82811.1	67778.1	65714.3
Total assets	205254.4	215454.3	227240.3	235618.6	243725.3
Liabilities and net worth					
Current liabilities					
Accounts payable	92852.0	103764.2	29734.9	38783.4	33121.0
Notes payable	54000.0	47152.1	36290.3	25767.5	28305.8
Accrued taxes payable	4000.0	4890.1	6522.6	2706.3	3362.9
Accrued income tax payable	0.0	0.0	0.0	3693.9	3041.1
Total current liabilities	150852.0	155806.3	72547.8	70951.1	67830.8
Long-term notes payable (SBA)	0.0	0.0	79446.3	68810.3	57319.7
Loans from stockholders	12638.3	12638.3	12638.3	12638.3	12638.3
Total long-term liabilities	12638.3	12638.3	92084.5	81448.5	69957.9
Total liabilities	163490.3	168444.6	164632.3	152399.6	137788.7
Net worth					
Common stock	15000.0	15000.0	15000.0	15000.0	15000.0
Capital paid-in in excess of par	2416.5	2416.5	2416.5	2416.5	2416.5
Retained earnings	24346.6	29593.2	45191.5	65802.8	88520.1
Total net worth	41763.1	47009.7	62608.0	83219.3	105936.6
Total liabilities and net worth	$205254.4	$215454.3	$227240.3	$235618.6	$243725.3

*Totals may be slightly incorrect due to rounding.

Case Exhibit 11–4

HARRIS TIRE AND RETREADING COMPANY

Financial ratio summary

Item	1970	1971	1972	1973	1974
Net profit after taxes to net sales	1.19%	2.02%	5.09%	5.52%	5.04%
NIAT and before ex inc to net sales	1.2ᴜ	2.02	5.09	5.52	5.04
Net profit before taxes to net sales	1.53	2.59	6.94	7.81	6.86
Net profit after taxes to total assets	1.50	2.44	6.86	8.75	9.32
NIAT and before ex inc to total assets	1.50	2.44	6.86	8.75	9.32
Net profit before taxes to total assets	1.92	3.12	9.36	12.39	12.68
Net profit after taxes to net worth	7.35	11.16	24.91	24.77	21.44
NIAT and before ex inc to net worth	7.35	11.16	24.91	24.77	21.44
Net profit before taxes to net worth	9.42	14.31	33.98	35.07	29.18
NPAT to (REC + INV − PAYABLES)	13.84	20.39	17.23	19.29	16.38
Federal Income Tax to NIBT	22.00	22.00	26.68	29.37	26.50
Operating exp to gross profit	95.61	92.40	83.10	81.84	83.05
Gross profit to sales	34.91	34.07	41.07	43.04	40.46
All expenses to sales	33.38	31.48	34.13	35.22	33.60
Operating exp to sales	33.38	31.48	34.13	35.22	33.60

Inventory control is managed by Mr. Gucker and Mr. Harris. Employees often have trouble locating tires and it is often necessary for an employee to ask the managers where a tire is located. The inventory log has a page for each passenger car tire, with space only for quantities purchased and sold.

SUGGESTED QUESTIONS FOR DISCUSSION

1. Evaluate the attitude of the young men in this case in relation to their chance of success.

2. How effective are yearly financial statements as management tools, particularly for the small-business owner?

3. What suggestions would you make for the inventory policies currently used?

4. Should Harris Tire concentrate on truck and tractor tires, or on passenger car tires?

5. A common problem in small business is over-attention to one functional area, to the exclusion of others. Do you feel this is true at Harris Tire?

SPORTS 1999

BACKGROUND

Sports 1999 is a retail sporting goods outlet located in the Kennett Shopping Center approximately one mile outside of Kennett Square, Pennsylvania. This 1200-square foot retail outlet is the subsidiary of the ABD Corporation, an organization composed of members of the Dunn family of Newark, Delaware. The ABD Corporation was incorporated in 1973 and is organized as follows:

Thomas Dunn, Sr.   President, treasurer, and director
Richard Dunn, III   Vice-president and Director
John Dunn   Vice-president and Director
Dale Dunn   Secretary

A sporting goods store originated from the elder Dunn's two-fold desire to find a profitable occupation for his son Dick and to tap the tremendous recreational potential of the Kennett Square area. Kennett is a small town of ten thousand citizens in southern Pennsylvania with at least fifteen churches and recreational leagues which support numerous teams in need of equipment. Three county high schools in the vicinity provide additional sports-minded people. Nearby lakes provide recreational diversion for ever-increasing numbers of fishers, hunters, and other outdoor enthusiasts, each group having its own equipment demands. Dunn, Sr., manager of a local mill and a highly regarded local resident, was certain that this untapped potential, coupled with his personal rapport with Kennett Square's citizens, would result in a thriving sporting goods business. Prior to initiation, a local consulting firm conducted an extensive marketing survey via questionnaires to further gauge the area. The survey confirmed Dunn's earlier estimates.

In addition to initial capital of approximately $98,000, a $25,000 start-up loan was secured from a local bank in October, 1973. Excerpts from pro forma statements submitted at that time indicated the projected range of activity:

Projected gross sales in 1974	$150,000
Projected net income in 1974	$ 11,074
Projected break-even sales in 1974	$113,083

Unfortunately, the store was unable to begin operations in the fall of 1973 because of failure to complete the leasing arrangement with a firm in Newark, Delaware. In correspondences with his attorney, the elder Dunn indicated he believed the firm to be intentionally delaying him for some unspecified reason. Negotiations were finally closed and Sports 1999 was opened for business on May 20, 1974.

The store was to be managed by Dick Dunn, son of the elder Dunn and a 1964 engineering graduate of The University of Delaware. Although he possessed no formal retailing background, Dick Dunn had previous work experience with IBM and NCR. Dick has experienced a number of emotional problems.

Initial sales objectives focused on the church and recreational leagues and the concept of team sales. The plan called for Dick to personally contact these churches and leagues to solicit orders for equipment, based upon the demands of upcoming seasonal sports. Advertising, in the form of spots on two local radio stations and advertisements in the local newspaper, were intended to mark the opening of the store, generate curiosity and excitement, and supplement personal contacts with the local citizenry. Initial inventory was selected to reflect the results of the marketing survey by providing a broad array of recreational gear. Items for seasonal sports such as tennis, golf, fishing, football, baseball, and basketball were to comprise the major portion of the merchandise. Finally, *high-quality* service was supposed to differentiate Sports 1999 from its principal competitors: Jim's, a large discount house next door, and other nearby retail outlets that had "scrambled" sporting goods into their merchandising scheme, but were not primarily engaged in marketing sporting goods. The Dunns felt that their expertise in the local area, particularly as it applied to hunting and fishing, would further differentiate their store. They also felt that they were the only store in town concerned with, and equipped to handle, the leagues in town. Prior to the establishment of Sports 1999, all leagues had obtained their uniforms and supplies from out of town stores.

The nine college fraternities and sororities in the Newark area each purchase $1000 to $1500 worth of equipment every year. Moreover, the fifteen church leagues make considerable purchases in basketball, softball, and other equipment. Additional purchases are made by the Little League, the Kennett City Athletic Association, Red River Athletic Association, Dixie League, Kennett Academy, and local high schools.

Orders might also come from the Kennett Police Department and the State Police for small-arms ammunition. Mr. Dunn projected that a good deal of money can be made in this area without significant investment by the store. He estimated that $88,000 worth of orders could be secured each year in the ammunition reloading business.

Sports 1999 is a store geared toward a high-price, quality image, appealing to quality- and brand-conscious customers. It offers nationally known brands with a professional "touch," manufactured mainly in the United States. Sports 1999 also offers a personalized relationship with its customers. By comparison, Jim's chain store next door offers lower prices for generally lower quality products, manufactured both in the U.S. and less-developed countries where production costs are lower (Taiwan, South Korea, Hong Kong, and Portugal). Therefore, Jim's has a strong competitive advantage in prices. For instance, a Browning automatic rifle assembled in Portugal from parts manufactured in Mexico is sixty to eighty dollars cheaper than one of similar caliber offered at Sports 1999. In fishing, the simplest fishing rod is offered at under two dollars at Jim's (bamboo, made in Japan) while the cheapest at Sports 1999 is over six dollars.

INVENTORY SYSTEM

Inventory is maintained by individual departments in several three-ring binders. Within each binder is a perpetual system of inventory, composed of forms listing every item carried in the department. These forms include quantities sold and ordered (at retail price), quantities on hand (also at retail), and mark-up on each item. When maintained properly, this system serves to alert the manager to the exact composition of his inventory in addition to pinpointing fast- and slow-moving items. Daily sales are supposed to be promptly posted to these books, to reflect changes commensurate with the daily volume of business. However, for the first five months of 1975, sales were not posted and, according to the elder Dunn, records of sales have not always been maintained on a current basis. Thus, it is not always possible to verify accurately the quantities of merchandise on hand. This is a direct result of Dick's being absent from the store on an average of three days a week.

The store, as shown in Case exhibit 12–2, is well stocked in golf equipment, hiking boots, firearms, reloading equipment, archery equipment, and other seasonal sports items. Fifteen per cent of the floor space is utilized for the display of golf and golf-related equipment, firearms, ammunition, and reloading

Case Exhibit 12–1

SPORTS 1999

*Pro forma income statement for the
year ended December 31, 1974*

Sales	$150,000.00
Cost of goods sold:	
Inventory, January 1, 1974	$ 30,000.00
Purchases	105,000.00
	$135,000.00
Less inventory, December 31, 1974	30,000.00
	105,000.00
Gross profit	$ 45,000.00
Expenses	
Rent	8,568,00
Utilities	1,500.00
Telephone	360.00
Repairs and maintenance	180.00
Office supplies and postage	198.00
Store and general supplies	180.00
Accounting and legal	450.00
Insurance	402.00
Licenses	180.00
Advertising	1,008.00
Freight	525.00
Dues and subscriptions	72.00
Property tax	453.73
Lease and fixtures	3,000.00
Payroll taxes	1,096.44
Salaries	13,200.00
Depreciation	348.00
Miscellaneous	504.00
Interest	1,700.00
	33,925.17
Net income	$ 11,074.83

Projected cash flow

Net income	$ 11,074.83
Add—non-cash expense—depreciation	348.00
Less—payments on loan principal	(4,000.00)
Increase in cash	$ 7,422.83

Break-even analysis

Sales needed to pay expenses	$113,083.90
Sales needed to pay cash requirements	$124,590.57

equipment. There is also a vast array of merchandise that seems only remotely connected to recreational sports. For instance, electric trains and accessories, model aircraft and engines, plastic model kits and paints, craft and decorator kits, electric fishing motors and depth sounders, multicolored rugby shirts, and even a large number of bicycles are evident in the store.

Case exhibit 12–2

SPORTS 1999

Floor Diagram

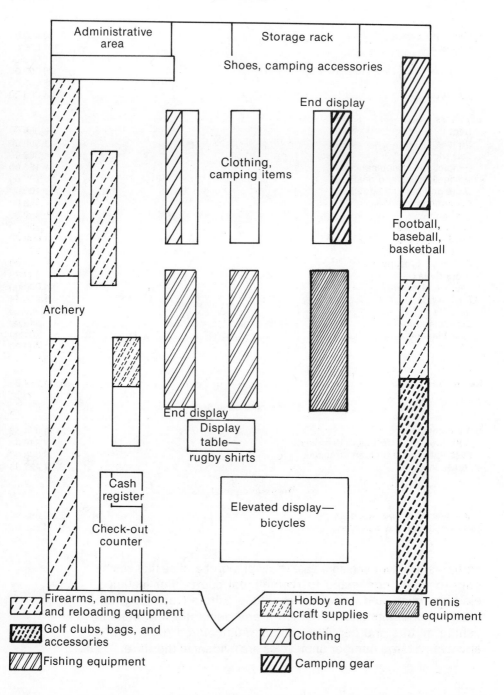

Inventory problems are a result of the pricing policies, all of which were established by Dick Dunn. Mark-up on cost ranges from 10 to 90 per cent with a store-wide average of 30 per cent. These prices are high because of the cost of merchandise. For example, on occasion, Jim's retail prices on bicycles have been less than Sports 1999's wholesale on the same bikes.

Other inventory problems have been caused by late deliveries. For instance, although electric trains were ordered long before Christmas, the shipment of trains arrived at the store too late in the shopping season, December twentieth to be exact, to have a measurable impact on Christmas shoppers. At the present rate of sales, trains will still be on hand for next Christmas.

Rugby shirts were purchased to meet the upsurge in rugby clubs in the Newark-Wilmington area, but no marketing strategy was devised prior to their purchase. At $21.95 they are not selling rapidly: only three have been sold. The appealingly displayed golf clubs and golf bags, in the latest styles and models, also possess high markups, some as high as 90 per cent. Another problem with golf items is that most local golfers purchase golf items at their local pro shop.

MARKETING

A marketing strategy, planned to stimulate sales, is the Sports 1999 Club. For two dollars a customer/member receives a Sports 1999 club card giving a 10 per cent discount on all subsequent purchases. Local schools that sell these cards are also to receive a 10 per cent across-the-board discount. A number of cards have been sold but no follow-up has been done to determine the effects of this policy. Other marketing and credit tools used by the store include BankAmericard and Mastercharge. The impact of these charge systems has not yet been determined, although Dunn, Sr., feels that this credit is particularly useful today, when more and more people are buying leisure now and paying for it later.

MANAGEMENT

Dick Dunn, the intended manager and chief salesman, has been severely hampered by his mental illness. The personal contacts and follow-ups vital to the development of the team sales concept have not been implemented. While he has undergone treatment, the store has been "minded" by the elder Dunn (when he is free from his primary duties at the mills) and two

Case exhibit 12–3

SPORTS 1999

ABD Corporation,
Kennett Square, PA—
Balance sheet, December 31, 1974

Assets:
Current:

Cash on hand and in banks		$ 1,480.52
Security deposit		400.00
Accounts receivable		240.08
Inventory		49,139.21
Total current assets		$ 51,259.81

Fixed: (Note 1)

Equipment and fixtures (Note 4)	$11,130.49	
Buildings (Note 2)	20,600.00	
	$31,730.49	
Less accumulated depreciation	2,149.00	
	$29,581.49	
Land (Note 3)	67,800.00	$ 97,381.49

Other:

Incorporation costs		51.00
Total assets		$148,692.30

Liabilities and Stockholders' Equity
Liabilities:
Current

Accounts payable		$ 29,106.45
Accrued taxes		1,209,37
Current portion of long-term debt		6,586.78
Total current liabilities		$ 36,902.60

Case exhibit 12–3 *(Continued)*

Liabilities and Stockholders' Equity

Long-term

Notes payable—Leasing Co. of Penna. (Note 4)	$ 6,835.24	
Notes payable—Bank notes (Note 5)	23,685.88	
	$30,521.12	
Less portion due within one year	6,586.78	23,934.34
		$ 60,836.94

Stockholders' Equity:

Capital stock (2145 shares @$10. par value)	$21,450.00	
Paid in capital	79,484.92	
Retained earnings	(13,079.56)	87,855.36

Total liabilities and stockholders' equity	$148,692.30

Note 1: The straight line method of depreciation on all fixed assets is used. Estimated life of:
a. equipment and fixtures is 8 to 10 years.
b. buildings is 20 years.
Investment credit is treated as a reduction in income tax liability.

Note 2: Composed of two buildings transferred to the corporation for issuance of stock. Appraised as follows: one at $16,000, one at $4,000.

Note 3: Composed of various parcels of land transferred to the corporation for issuance of stock. Appraised as follows:
a. 92.3 acres @ $46,200
b. 5.79 acres @ $18,400
c. 2 lots @ $2,400
d. 1 lot @ $800

Note 4: Secured by fixtures valued at $9,046.06. Installment loan for 36 months at interest rate of 14 per cent.

Note 5: Secured by fixtures, equipment, and inventory of corporation. Installment loan for 7 years at interest rate of 5.5 per cent.

Case exhibit 12–4

SPORTS 1999

ABD Corporation
Kennett Square, PA—
Statement of income and retained earnings
for the year ending December 31, 1974

			Percentage of sales
Sales		$40,055.71	100.0
Cost of goods sold:			
Inventory, Jan. 1, 1974*	0		0
Purchases	77,389.82		193.2
	$77,389.82		193.2
Less inventory, December 31, 1974	49,139.21	28,250.61	122.7 70.5
Gross profit		$11,805.10	29.5
Other income—received rents		991.01	2.4
Total income		$12,796.11	31.9
Operating expenses			
Salaries	$ 8,341.75		20.8
Rent	4,000.00		10.0
Telephone	411.64		1.0
Utilities	883.71		2.2
Repairs and maintenance	430.00		1.1
Licenses and taxes	1,079.61		2.7
Office supplies and postage	490.00		1.3
Professional fees	175.00		.4
Accounting and legal	475.00		1.2
Insurance	1,129.45		2.8
Store supplies	782.02		2.0
Advertising	1,253.15		3.1
Interest expense	1,379.66		3.4
Depreciation	1,618.00		4.0
Travel	380.89		1.0
Bank charges	37.76		.1
Miscellaneous	128.52		.3
Freight	1,298.97		3.2
Dues and subscriptions	248.23		.6
Uniform rental	42.02		.1
Amortization	17.00	24,602.38	.1 61.4
Net loss		($11,806.27)	29.5
Retained earnings, January 1, 1974		(1,273.29)	
Retained earnings, December 31, 1974		($13,079.56)	

*Retail sporting goods operations began May, 1974.

Case exhibit 12–5

SPORTS 1999

ABD Corporation
Kennett Square, PA—
Schedule of sales and inventory turnover, by department,
for the year ending December 31, 1974

Code	Item	Sales*	Inventory	Annual turnover
01	Archery	$ 1,433.14	$ 1,775.23	1.38
05	Bicycles	1,550.20	1,571.50	1.69
10	Camp and backpacking	1,188.04	2,257.08	.90
15	Crafts	668.36	778.28	1.47
20	Fishing	2,450.53	4,232.59	.99
25	Golf	2,477.53	4,565.88	.93
30	Golf apparel	531.02	1,590.65	.57
35	Guns	6,625.48	7,746.55	1.46
40	Gun accessories	3,592.78	2,957.53	2.08
45	Hobbies	2,379.80	3,850.86	1.06
50	Hunt and fishing apparel	203.76	45.51	7.67
55	Reload and ammunition	2,977.98	2,858.40	1.79
60	Seasonal sports	3,342.45	1,964.84	2.92
65	Shoes	3,166.01	4,857.79	1.12
70	Tennis	2,910.66	1,691.56	2.95
75	Tennis apparel	1,611.40	2,208.32	1.25
80	Miscellaneous	2,198.82	868.90	4.34
53	Outerwear	747.75	3,317.74	.38
	Totals	$40,055.71	$49,139.21	1.40

*Retail sporting goods operations began May, 1974.

part-time men. One of these men, George Davis, a retired Army sergeant major, has expressed a desire to ultimately manage the store, but is concerned with his lack of formal background in retailing. He has also expressed a desire to receive on-the-job training through a program sponsored by the Veteran's Administration at no cost to the store. He intends to make massive changes if he assumes the position of manager. The other part-time worker, Harry Sims, has also expressed misgivings concerning the store's present state of affairs, but feels that his interest in the store is merely temporary. He has made other plans for the future and works at the store only to assist the elder Dunn. Both Davis and Sims, in their respective ways, have indicated that they have been at odds with Dick Dunn for a number of reasons. Recent attempts by the elder Dunn to find a competent, skilled replacement for his son have met with no success. Present management has virtually ground to a halt and the storekeeping tasks are being handled completely by the elder Dunn, Davis, and Sims.

SUGGESTED QUESTIONS FOR DISCUSSION

1. Compare the results of operations with those predicted by the pro forma statements.

2. Evaluate the management of the firm.

3. Referring to Case exhibit 12–5, evaluate the inventory policy of the store.

4. What would you recommend to Dunn, Sr., in terms of management, marketing, and inventory?

LUNDBERG'S SUPERETTE AND PACKAGE STORE

HISTORY OF THE FIRM

Lundberg's Superette and Package Store was established on September 1, 1974, in a building 46' by 24' on U.S. Route 441 in Holopaw, Florida. This building had previously been used as a bait shop, and a tackle and gun shop. The shops had been closed for two months prior to the Lundbergs' acquisition of the facilities. There was not a full-service grocery store in the area. The nearest such stores were in St. Cloud and Melbourne, which are fourteen and thirty miles away, respectively.

Business in the package store was good from the outset. Groceries were slower to catch on, but as local needs were determined, the Lundbergs began carrying the items in highest demand. Business steadily increased.

In December, 1974, the Lundbergs sponsored a trophy banquet for the Little League football and baseball teams of Holopaw. They provided all the food, plates, cups, and furnishings for the banquet. The Lundbergs attended the banquet and met many Holopaw residents for the first time. From that time forward, their business received a considerable boost and this banquet has since been sponsored as an annual event.

Early in the spring of 1975, many requests were received for fishing bait and tackle. Therefore, a limited line of these items was added to their inventory. They have continued to build a good business in bait and tackle from Holopaw and the surrounding area.

After negotiations with the Small Business Administration, the Lundbergs secured a loan of $40,000 to acquire land and construct a new facility. In June 1975, the Lundbergs moved into their new location. Adequate space was available to handle a complete convenience store inventory, ABC Package Store, and a complete bait and tackle store line. A gasoline and diesel fuel service station was also added. After moving into their present building, an additional adjacent lot was acquired that is currently used as a truck park for their diesel fuel operations. The lot has been paid for from earnings of the business.

MANAGEMENT

Lundberg's Superette is owned and managed by William and Anna I. Lundberg. There are no formal management objectives stated nor is there a formal statement of each one's responsibilities. However, Mr. Lundberg is the dominant force, and he assumes responsibility for hiring employees, inventory management, marketing, advertising, and public relations work. Mrs. Lundberg assumes responsibility for all accounting functions and inventory purchases.

The Lundbergs had no previous experience in convenience store operations prior to establishing the company. However, both had extensive experience in business prior to opening the store. Mrs. Lundberg, a native of Augusta, Georgia, is a high school graduate. She has taken a supplementary accounting course at a local business college. Mrs. Lundberg's work experience includes administrative work in a textile plant and serving as an administrative assistant for a finance company.

They attempt to hire people of good character who have a sincere desire to do a "day's work for a day's wages." The seven part-time employees are either young people or retirees. They are paid minimum wage, with no benefits. There are always two employees on duty in addition to either Mr. or Mrs. Lundberg. The Lundbergs' preference is to hire retirees. They believe this is a good source of labor for experience and maturity.

The Superette has received management and marketing assistance from Reitz and Horowitz Wholesalers, the SBA, and the Central Florida Bank on a rather limited basis. Reitz and Horowitz Wholesalers provided the most elaborate assistance by their analysis of the need and marketing variables affecting the opening of the store. Mr. Ron Pierce, vice president of the Central Florida Bank, advises the company on routine management related functions.

No formal planning techniques or forecasting process are currently employed. However, Mr. Lundberg is always searching for ways to improve, expand, or change his business to meet the needs of the community. He seeks information; analyzes it for its relevance or impact on the business; establishes priorities according to profitability; attempts to reach a logical conclusion; estimates a realistic implementation date; secures and allocates necessary resources as they become available to

Case exhibit 13–1

COLLATERAL AVAILABLE TO SECURE LOAN

Lundberg's Superette and Package Store

Item	Cost	Value
Lot, 100' by 230'	$ 4,000.00	$ 9,000.00
Building on above lot 55' by 50'	29,000.00 (approx.)	29,000.00
Inventory	20,000.00	20,000.00
Coca-Cola cooler	75.00	75.00
Two 12' grocery gondolas	400.00	400.00
Cash register	150.00	125.00
Adding machine	60.00	35.00
Two 35' grocery gondolas	768.00	768.00
Belt driven check-out counter	300.00	300.00
Produce scales	175.00	175.00
8' double deck produce counter	1,000.00	1,000.00
52" 2-door commercial refrigerator	1,005.00	1,005.00
119" 2-door commercial freezer, with outside compressor unit	2,800.00	2,800.00
Freezer, ice-cream type, four lids	50.00	25.00

implement his decision; and conducts a continuous audit of his decisions.

FINANCIAL DATA

The Lundbergs obtained a loan in the amount of $40,000 from the SBA to acquire and build their present facility. This loan is secured by the collateral as listed in Case exhibit 13–1. The loan is repayable in the amount of $539.72 per month. Mr. Ron Pierce of Central Florida Bank stated that the Lundbergs' overall credit rating is excellent. Current financial data are shown in Case exhibits 13–2 and 13–3.

The Lundbergs' bookkeeping system is a single entry journal in which sales and expenses are recorded as they are incurred. No formal ledger exists in which assets, liabilities, and equity are listed separately. The only source of assets is depreciable property as outlined on the yearly tax return, the cash balance in the checkbook, and the individual accounts receivable book.

Initially, the Lundbergs had a liberal credit policy. Since moving into their new location, they are reluctant to accept new credit accounts. Their current accounts are, for the most part, carryovers from their old location. For those credit accounts retained, their payment policy and procedure is:

1. Accounts must be paid in full at the end of each week or end of the month (most by the end of each week).
2. Failure to pay on time results in the person's name being

Case exhibit 13–2

LUNDBERG's SUPERETTE AND PACKAGE STORE

Profit and loss statement, January 1, 1975 to December 31, 1975

Net sales	$108,828.16	
Beginning inventory	9,116.22	
Merchandise purchased	83,865.15	
Ending inventory	14,831.82	
Gross profit	30,678.61	28.2%
Expenses		
Rent	1,200.00	1.1%
Electricity	1,324.32	1.2%
Telephone	291.60	.3%
Heat	110.81	.1%
Advertising	502.50	.5%
Uncollectable checks	221.62	.2%
Federal and state licenses	758.00	.7%
State sales taxes	3,314.27	.3%
Net profit	$ 22,955.49	21.1%

Case exhibit 13–3

LUNDBERG'S SUPERETTE AND PACKAGE STORE

Financial statement, March 26, 1976

Assets:	
Cash on hand in banks	$ 3,899.10
Accounts receivable	1,836.84
Store building and lot	41,500.00
House and lot, Lakeview Acres	45,000.00
Lots 6, 7, 8, 9, and 10, Bellaire	3,000.00
1974 Glassmaster boat, motor and trailer	3,500.00
1973 Monte Carlo Landau	2,600.00
1969 Ford F-100 pickup	1,200.00
Business inventory	32,689.00
Business equipment	9,500.00
Personal property, (appliances, furniture)	3,000.00
Coin collection	1,150.00
Total assets	$148,874.94
Liabilities	
Loan on building and lot	38,750.69
Loan on home and lot	27,350.00
Loan on lots 6, 7, 8, 9, and 10, Bellaire	2,275.00
Loan on boat	2,500.00
Auto loan—1973 Monte Carlo	1,286.73
Auto loan—1969 Ford Truck	348.92
Personal accts. payable	650.00
Business accts. payable	2,922.85
Total liabilities	$ 76,084.19
Surplus, or net worth	72,790.75
Total	$148,874.94

posted on a delinquent list. This list is publicly displayed where all patrons using the store can see it.
3. After 30 days, a claim is filed with the local magistrate to secure payment.
4. If warranted, individuals can negotiate other credit arrangements with the Lundbergs.

The Lundbergs state they have very few bad debts.

INITIAL INVESTMENT DECISION

The Lundbergs decided to enter the convenience store business because of the opportunity for economic growth it offers. There was no competition in the Holopaw area at the time of their decision. In the Holopaw area, there is a population of about 5000 people. The decision to invest became final once the results of the Reitz and Horowitz analysis were available. The Lundbergs' decision was based on the facts that they wished to reside in Holopaw, and that there was a need for a business of this nature in the community.

MARKET AREA

The market area is the Holopaw community. Mrs. Lundberg states that they are trying only to provide this market area with "convenience" goods and that they do not attempt to provide the area with a "full line" grocery operation with which the population could fulfill all of its grocery demands. The residents can visit either St. Cloud or Melbourne for this weekly shopping need. The primary objective of the Superette is to supplement the needs of the public between visits to the major shopping areas. This statement can be substantiated by the fact that 90 per cent of their customers' purchases have seven or less items in them.

The package store operation is primarily intended to satisfy local demand. Therefore, it is competing directly with another package store located a quarter mile down the road. Additionally, a limited amount of revenue is generated from through traffic on U.S. Route 441.

The gasoline operation satisfies both a local need and also is directed at the market generated by traffic on U.S. Route 441. This through traffic is a major source of revenue.

ADVERTISING

Lundberg's Superette concentrates on six methods of advertising: support of community activities, pamphlets, signs, the Yellow Pages, informal or cost-free publicity, and word-of-mouth.

At a cost of $100, Lundberg's Superette, in conjunction with two other local merchants, sponsors a Little League baseball and football team. The contribution entitles the Superette to have its name listed in the program available at the games. The Superette also contributes $40 for an ad in the high school annual, $25 for five spots on a nearby radio station to inform the public of the Shriner's Children Hospital campaign, and $50 to a nearby Little Theater. This support of community activities illustrates to the community the desire of the Lundbergs to become an integral part of its development.

A second method of advertising has been a pamphlet, specifying each week's T.V. shows, that the Superette makes available to its customers. The annual cost for this is $310. The pamphlet is popular because of its convenient listing of television programs, the humorous anecdotes it offers on the back page, the unavailability of a local newspaper, and the simple crossword puzzle included in it. The most direct advertising methods are the various signs at the site of the business. These signs make a distinct impression from the highway. Approximately $150 has been spent on these signs. A fourth method of advertising is the telephone directory, in which Lundberg's Superette has a listing in the Yellow Pages.

Lundberg's Superette has been the beneficiary of numerous public interest stories in the Melbourne newspaper. The "great shark" story, involving a shark supposedly caught in a nearby freshwater pond, listed "a customer at Lundberg's Superette" as the source of the article. Needless to say, this free advertising created a substantial influx of customers into the store for several weeks. An article about Mr. Lundberg changing a flat tire for a Tennessee man passing through was printed in the National Lions Club publication and in the local newspapers. Numerous individuals congratulated Mr. Lundberg on his good deed and the publicity it showered on the people of Holopaw.

PRICING POLICY

The Superette has a simple pricing policy. A comparative analysis indicates that the Lundbergs' prices are similar in their grocery, liquor, and bait and tackle operations; but are lower in the gasoline operation. All grocery items are marked up one third from the wholesale price. Bait and tackle receive a 40 to

60 per cent mark-up unless they are prepriced. If items are prepriced, that price is maintained. Liquor items are sold at the suggested retail price. This is basically a 25 per cent mark-up. Recently, increased competition in liquor sales has led to a decrease in Lundberg's liquor sales. Gasoline, kerosene, and diesel fuel are supplied on a consignment basis from the petroleum distributor. The margins are four cents per gallon for gasoline, four cents per gallon for kerosene, and two cents per gallon for diesel fuel. Currently, these margins are maintained without regard to market price fluctuations. Lundberg's price structure is lower than any competing stations within thirty miles in either direction on U.S. 441. All the fuels are placed by the distributor, who receives payment once the fuel has been sold.

INVENTORY POLICY

Lundberg's policy is to maintain the smallest inventory level that is economically practical. All inventory is on the shelves, except for some liquor. Inventory levels are estimated weekly by visual checks. Reorders are placed to maintain the initial inventory level. Purchases are made weekly with terms being either cash on delivery or net seven days. Suppliers of milk and bread are paid monthly; however, no cash discounts are received.

The most popular items, such as milk, soda, and bread, are displayed at the back and sides of the store furthest from the door, making it necessary for the customer to walk through the store. It is hoped that impulse items will be brought to the customer's attention, and subsequently purchased as he or she walks through the store.

Security of inventory in this type of business is a problem because of the large amount of inventory that is inaccessible to the view of store employees, and the abundance of small items. Furthermore, due to the lack of formal counting, inventory losses are difficult to measure.

SUGGESTED QUESTIONS FOR DISCUSSION

1. What are the goals of the Lundbergs? Would you classify them as small-business people or entrepreneurs? Why?

2. What particular actions did the Lundbergs take that would aid any new business in terms of advertising?

3. What suggestions would you make to improve the present controls utilized by the Lundbergs?

THE SPORTS CENTER

DESCRIPTION OF THE FIRM

In February, 1975, two individuals began the planning believed necessary to enter the retail sporting goods business. Kip Deutsch, age 27, attended Virginia Military Institute and graduated from the University of Virginia in 1972 with a B.S. in business administration. He received an M.B.A., with a major in finance, in 1974. After completing the work for his M.B.A., Kip worked in the office of the Governor of the State of Virginia. While at V.M.I., he played both freshman and varsity football. John Belew, age 27, is a 1971 graduate of V.M.I., where he also played freshman and varsity football. John worked as a sales agent, first in real estate, and then with the Georgia Pacific Corporation. In August, 1975, both Kip and John quit their jobs to begin their final preparations for opening The Sports Center in October, 1975.

Prior to opening the business, Kip and John intensively researched twenty other sporting goods businesses in the state, used potential suppliers as sources of information, obtained expense information, and prepared projections of sales, operating expenses, and the capital required. In addition, each of the two partners in The Sports Center agreed not to take a salary for the first year of operation. This was made possible by the partners' wives agreeing to support them, and by a careful projection of capital needed.

LOCATION

The partners decided to lease a location within one block of a large shopping mall in Charlottesville, Virginia. This general area of Charlottesville is characterized by many upper-middle income residential areas. The daily traffic count in front of the proposed store was 23,000 automobiles. The site has 1050 square feet in a corner unit of a four unit retail building. This area of Charlottesville offers no direct competition from full line sporting goods stores. A specialty tennis shop is located within three blocks of The Sports Center location. Most of the floorspace is allocated to selling area, which eliminates space for storage. The owners decided to use a 1942 food tractor trailer for a warehouse, placing it behind the store.

PRELIMINARY ANALYSIS

Two well-established major full line sporting goods stores exist in the Greater Charlottesville area. Both of these stores can be classified as primarily institutional sellers; that is, their predominant sales are to athletic teams, including university, high school, middle school, and private school teams, and organized leagues, such as Little League or Pony League. Sales include football, baseball, basketball, and soccer equipment.

In view of the competitive situation, The Sports Center owners decided to find a specific market niche. Their basic objective was to be consumer oriented rather than institution oriented. Emphasis was to be placed on women's sporting goods which, surprisingly, compose 25 per cent of retail sporting goods sales. An attempt was to be made to make it "easy" for women to shop at The Sports Center, since women purchase about 70 per cent of sporting goods merchandise for themselves, their children, and their spouses. Generally, competition in the Charlottesville area has neglected the women's market.

Golf clubs were not to be carried owing to their slow turnover, the large capital investment required to provide adequate depth, and heavy competition from discount stores and golf course pro shops. Fishing equipment was not to be carried because of competition from discount and specialty stores. Firearms were not to be sold because of their slow turnover, high unit value, the high risk of burglary, and problems of supply — particularly with handguns.

The partners decided that the dollar volume of inventory composition would be as:

Athletic shoes	40%
Athletic clothing	30%
Tennis racquets and accessories	10%
Inflatables	5%
Miscellaneous	15%

It was felt that a small proportion of inflatables (footballs, basketballs, and soccer balls) could be carried because supplier service and delivery in these products are extremely fast.

PERSONNEL, ADVERTISING, PRICING

Deutsch and Belew decided that they would not employ any person other than themselves for the first year.

All advertising for the first year was to be handled by an advertising agency. The first year budget for advertising was to be $6000. The funds were to be allocated among three radio stations, two newspapers (during the Christmas season), and six billboards in the area of the store.

Manufacturers' suggested retail prices would be generally adhered to. This is consistent with competition, with the exception of discount stores. The partners felt that slight discounts from recommended retail prices go unnoticed by consumers.

Funding to begin operations was secured:

$35,000 from a Small Business Administration participating loan. 6.5 year term; 10.5 per cent interest; monthly payments to begin on March 21, 1976;
$20,000 from relatives and other personal sources.

According to industry averages, gross profit averages about 35 per cent of sales. The partners projected $23,000 of fixed costs for the first twelve months of operation. As previously stated, the owners elected not to receive a salary for the first year. Estimated sales for the first year were $100,000. As noted in Case exhibit 14–1, this is well above the break-even point.

Mr. Deutsch and Mr. Belew opened The Sports Center for business on October 20, 1975. The first year objectives of the new company were to make a profit in the first year's operations, to establish a foothold in the Charlottesville retail sporting goods market, to establish good relations with suppliers, and to consider opening a second location at the opposite end of town once the first store became profitable.

Case exhibit 14–1

THE SPORTS CENTER

Schedule to compute break-even point

Fixed operating expenses $23,590*
Mark-up   35% of sales
Let X equal the amount of sales needed to break even.

$$(.35)(X) = \$23,590$$
$$(X) = (\$23,590)/(.35)$$
$$(X) = \$67,400 \text{ needed to break even}$$

---

*This amount includes a variable element: $2000 for salaries and wages.

Case exhibit 14–2

THE SPORTS CENTER

*Projected income statement for the
year ending December 31, 1976*

Sales			
	Jan.	$11475	
	Feb.	16258	
	Mar.	22684	
	Apr.	20000	
	May	20000	
	June	15000	
	July	15000	
	Aug.	22000	
	Sept.	20000	
	Oct.	15000	
	Nov.	20000	
	Dec.	40000	$237417
Less sales tax (4%) (Sales ÷ 1.04)			9131
			$228286
Less cost of merchandise sold (.65 × 228286)			148386
Gross profit			$ 79900

Less operating expenses

Salaries and wages	$ 2000	
Rent	6000	
Advertising	3600	
Electricity (110 × 112)	1210	
Telephone (incl. Yellow Pages)	2000	
Travel and entertainment	1200	
Interest expense	2640	
Accounting fees	1000	
Insurance	1200	
Burglar alarm	240	
Licenses	300	
Depreciation	360	
Supplies and postage	120	
Dues and subscriptions	360	
Donations	120	
Collection expense	120	
Repairs and maintenance	120	
Other	1000	$23590
Net income		$56310

SUGGESTED QUESTIONS FOR DISCUSSION

1. Are the two owners realistic in their outlook?

2. Do you think that they have selected a reasonable market niche?

3. As an epilogue, the men have now opened another store across town. They did make a profit the first year, they established a foothold in the retail market, and they established good relationships with suppliers. Enumerate the reasons you think are responsible for their success.

THE LAST DINOSAUR: A CRAFTSMAN IN THOUGHT AND DEED

INTRODUCTION

Edward Hollan's Cabinet Shop is located at 1190 South Pike Street in Albany, Georgia. The business is in a strategically located commercial area, with a new K-Mart department store and a soon-to-be-opened Winn Dixie food store adjacent to Mr. Hollan's shop. Although the shop is not on a main highway, heavily traveled Highways 878 and 125 intersect within sight of the business (Case exhibit 15–1). However, prospective customers unfamiliar with the area will probably miss the shop: no signs announce the shop and the view from the main highway is blocked by debris and weeds.

The facility used by Mr. Hollan is a Butler, steel-framed, metal building erected adjacent to his residence (Case exhibit 15–2). It was built in January, 1968, following a fire that destroyed his old, wooden building. An addition, 30' by 80', was built in March, 1974, in which the finishing process of the cabinets is done. The actual construction is done in the main building which measures 50' by 80'. The shop has some parking facilities on the lawn adjacent to the building.

Prior to opening the present facility, Mr. Hollan had erected a building on his property, adjacent to his present house, and was in business there until a fire completely destroyed the building Thanksgiving Eve, 1967. He was able to salvage a very limited amount of equipment. His losses were severe due to a complete lack of insurance on the structure and its contents. He did have insurance on some of the personal belongings that were consumed by the fire, but in clearing the smoldering debris from the site, Mr. Hollan unintentionally eliminated any proof of his losses. Consequently, he was not reimbursed for them and has acquired a mis-trust of the insurance company. Total losses

Case exhibit 15–1

THE LAST DINOSAUR

Location map

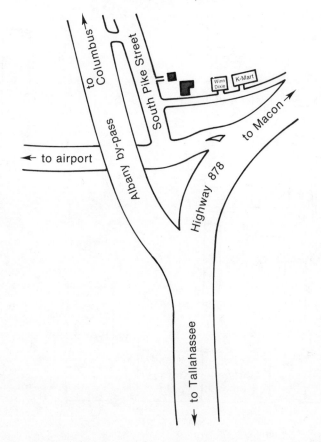

were estimated at $45,000. Securing a loan for this amount, Mr. Hollan began operations in his present facility.

No insurance was taken on the original building because of the insurance company's refusal to assume the risk, since Mr. Hollan's finishing and paint area was in the same building as the cabinet construction. This hazard is eliminated in the present facility since the finishing shed is not located in the main building. If a fire should break out, Mr. Hollan feels it can be restricted to the immediate area.

DESCRIPTION OF OPERATIONS

Mr. Hollan considers himself a woodcrafter, not a carpenter, who specializes in "top of the line" kitchen cabinets. He will not

Case exhibit 15–2

THE LAST DINOSAUR

Floor plan

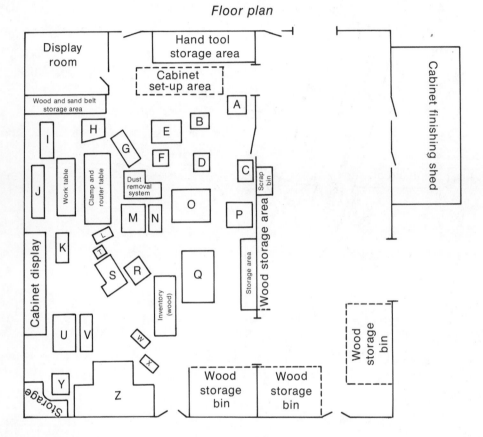

Driveway

Machinery Code

A. Mortise
B. Surfacer
C. Hollow chisel mortise
D. Pin router
E. Molding air stapler
F. Single end tenoner
G. Band saw
H. Wide belt sander
I. Frame clamp
J. Belt sander
K. Stationary hinge router
L. 3 inch belt sander
M. Shaper

N. Shaper
O. Sliding table handle saw
P. Cross-cut saw
Q. Rip saw with automatic feeder
R. Shaper
S. 10 inch bench saw and 4 inch joint
T. 1 inch belt sander
U. Pinch roller
V. Drill press and chop saw
W. Unit plane
X. 6 inch joiner
Y. Picture frame stapler
Z. Panel saw

agree to build bathroom cabinets or other small jobs unless he is also paid to do the kitchen. He feels the installation and other costs would not be worth his time and effort. He uses a job order procedure in which no inventories are produced for stock, but are produced solely for individual customer orders.

Various styles and designs such as "inlaid" and "raised-panel" cabinets can be produced with Mr. Hollan's talents and the sophisticated machinery he has acquired. A "big" kitchen job is worth anywhere from $6000 to $8000—the type of work which is usually done in $70,000 to $100,000 homes.

Mr. Hollan's business is unique to this particular area, since there are no cabinet makers who are capable of producing the same type of work, simply because they do not have the necessary machinery to do so. In fact, the nearest competitor, another woodcrafter, is presently operating in Atlanta, Georgia, and the distance between the two eliminates any direct competition. There is, however, quite a bit of competition around Albany. His chief rivals are the local carpenters who are able to build cabinets faster and less expensively, but these are of lesser quality and fewer styles. There are also a number of building supply stores that sell pre-assembled mass-produced cabinets. Mr. Hollan's main advantage is his ability to manufacture his cabinets to fit different ceiling heights for different homes. The supply stores do not produce a variety of cabinet sizes. Instead, they stock only for the standard eight-foot ceiling.

MANAGEMENT

Edward Hollan is the owner and only full-time employee of Hollan's Cabinet Shop. He was born in Albany, Georgia, in October, 1931, and has lived there ever since. Mr. Hollan's father was a contractor, and it was his influence that interested Mr. Hollan in his trade. Ed Hollan graduated from Albany High School where he took five years of shop. His interests in building and construction projects, however, ran deeper than either the class or his instructor was willing to go. Mr. Hollan spent much of his time helping his classmates work on their projects, knowing they would never make proficient carpenters or the type of woodcrafter he desired to be. Consequently, his grades were not very good.

In April, 1961, Ed Hollan began his own business, operating out of his garage. He started with a few essentials, unable to do the very sophisticated type of work he does now. One of his brothers worked in the shop part-time until his death in 1965. Other than this, and a few periods when some full-time help was employed, Mr. Hollan has not hired any permanent help since 1966. His reasons for this practice are varied: primarily, because he considers himself a woodcrafter, he requires two things from his work — customer satisfaction and self-satisfaction. Whenever he has employed others, he has felt that the quality of cabinets has suffered. Delegation is not Mr. Hollan's forte.

He does not think that the people who worked for him were really concerned about the quality of work they did, but were primarily interested in wages. Mr. Hollan realizes that the job lacks status, and therefore any hired help tend to become dissatisfied. Based on this assumption, Mr. Hollan has not had any full-time help since 1966.

Instead of paying for labor, Mr. Hollan has re-invested in the business by purchasing machinery. He feels that if he decided to hire full-time help, he would need at least two people: one person to perform menial jobs and assist the other person in more difficult tasks, while he himself concentrates on the very technical and involved work. Mr. Hollan stresses, however, that it would take a very versatile and dedicated individual to do all of the things expected of him, since Hollan's Cabinet Shop is such a small enterprise.

Presently, Mr. Hollan has two individuals who help him part-time. Kenneth Harris, an employee of Ace Industries in Albany, does all of the finishing work for the shop. He is proficient at his job, since he does the same kind of work for Ace Industries. He likes to earn some money on the side and comes in whenever there is some finishing work to be done. The second part-time employee is used only after the cabinets are fully constructed and the finishing job is completed. Since Mr. Hollan does all the installation work after building the cabinets, he needs a second worker to help him lift and hold the cabinets while installing them.

Mr. Hollan has two young sons whom he hopes will one day assume the responsibilities of the business. He hopes that his sons will take business courses in high school and college to develop a proficiency in business he has never had the opportunity to achieve.

Mr. Hollan is not a profit oriented business owner, but is in business for the enjoyment of his craft. As he puts it, "Money is necessary in every business, but I am doing something I have always wanted to do."

PRICING AND CREDIT POLICIES

When a customer decides to hire Mr. Hollan to build cabinets, the first thing required is the plan of the room in which Mr. Hollan will be working. This is necessary to evaluate the required dimensions. After estimating the amount of materials needed, Mr. Hollan discusses with the customer the types of wood available. Once the variety of wood is selected, the customer chooses any desired special features, such as raised panel doors, inlaid designs, three-inch chopping blocks set in the counter top, and lazy susans built into the cabinets. In arriving at a final cost figure for the customer, Mr. Hollan estimates the difficulty in construction and costs for use of equipment.

Before beginning the actual construction, the shop requires 40 per cent of the bill in advance. The remainder is collected immediately after completion of the job. He does not require the customer to sign any type of contractual agreement and he has never checked on any customer's credit standing before beginning a job. The only bad debt Mr. Hollan has had was a fifteen dollar bad check. He feels that the experience he has gained in the cabinet business enables him to judge prospective customers effectively.

Mr. Hollan feels strongly that the prices he charges are competitive for the type of work he does, especially since his machine costs are so high. But he often feels it necessary to lower his prices in order to keep a customer—sometimes to the point of failing to make any profit. Also, he finds it difficult to refuse to do favors for church members or friends. Consequently, he fails to make as much as he should for his work.

ADVERTISING

Hollan's Cabinet Shop uses three forms of advertising. The first is a sign attached to his building. Since the building is nondescript, the sign is the only means of recognizing the business. The present sign is placed flat against the front of the shop, making it impossible to read when approaching the building from the main highway. A customer cannot distinguish the words on the sign until he reaches the driveway.

Mr. Hollan's second type of advertising is ads placed in the local weekly newspaper. This form of advertising is limited, since it has failed to bring in the kind of patron Mr. Hollan desires. Because the ads fail to stress the importance of the high quality of work performed by Mr. Hollan, quite a few people have called the shop asking to have work done that Mr. Hollan is not prepared to do. For instance, many people have called or come by the shop asking to have old or damaged furniture repaired, to buy pieces of lumber, or to have such simple items as bookcases built. These types of customers take time and the costs involved in doing these small jobs are not worth his effort. For this reason, Mr. Hollan has discontinued this advertising.

The last type of advertising presently used by Mr. Hollan is word-of-mouth. He feels this is the best form of advertising. He is confident that the customers who have purchased his cabinets are satisfied with the quality of the product and the work, and they would not hesitate to tell other people who could become future customers. This is how he expects to obtain most of his job orders. It is generally agreed that word-of-mouth advertising is effective, but there are some drawbacks. It concentrates only on the local market; and since Mr. Holland does not like to work outside a fifty to sixty mile radius of the shop, he has never actively sought to expand his market.

No matter what forms of advertising are decided upon, it is clear, as Mr. Hollan says, "The important thing is trying to get the right people in the shop."

INVENTORY POLICIES

The main supplier of the wood for Mr. Hollan's cabinet shop is Wood Products, Incorporated, located in Atlanta, Georgia. There is a lumber company in Albany, but Mr. Hollan found the cost to be higher without any additional service to offset the difference. U.S. Plywood has a sales representative who calls on the business once a week. The pricing policy offers a cash discount of 2/10 net 30, but Mr. Hollan does not take advantage of the discount. There is no minimum order on the quantity of wood the shop is required to purchase. He does, however, try to order in large quantities when he places an order, to reduce the work on the lumber company. If the lumber is of poor quality and cannot be used in a cabinet, Wood Products, Incorporated will not allow Mr. Hollan to trade the wood for nondefective wood, but will make a price adjustment.

The wood is stocked in a central area in the building, with each wood-type separate. There is no formal method, except visual inspection, to control the inventory level. Because no formal inventory system is maintained, the inventory level is often very large.

FINANCIAL RECORDS

Mr. Hollan uses no formal bookkeeping system. The only papers kept are invoices of goods received. His wife helps with the limited system and stores the invoices in a desk drawer. His financial statements are prepared at the end of each year by a local CPA. The accountant prepares his financial statements by reviewing his checkbook and invoice receipts. Inventory levels given to the accountant are Mr. Hollan's visual estimate of inventory on hand.

The statements in Case exhibits 15–3 through 15–5 reflect the financial status of the shop.

Case exhibit 15-3

THE LAST DINOSAUR

Statement of income and expense,
December 31, 1970–74

	1970	1971	1972	1973	1974
Income	$43,237.92	43,596.17	52,488.62	47,541.92	49,532.74
Less: cost of goods sold					
Beginning inventory	750.00	1,150.00	3,000.00	1,500.00	3,000.00
Labor	4,421.70	1,815.20	1,501.76	1,196.00	1,294.25
Materials and freight	11,428.58	13,374.81	13,697.64	12,390.76	10,936.75
Total	16,600.28	16,340.01	18,199.40	15,086.76	15,231.00
Less: ending inventory	<1,150.00>	<3,000.00>	<1,500.00>	<3,000.00>	<800.00>
Gross profit on sales	27,787.64	30,256.16	35,789.22	35,455.16	35,101.74
Less expenses					
Auto and truck	-0-	-0-	-0-	-0-	234.44
Accounting	-0-	275.00	120.00	120.00	140.00
Advertising	378.00	389.80	437.41	371.45	268.00
Bank charge	23.77	-0-	-0-	-0-	-0-
Depreciation	2,611.45	2,852.40	3,533.19	3,221.57	3,677.24
Dues and subscription	104.45	129.00	98.00	81.94	-0-
Freight	153.95	-0-	-0-	-0-	-0-
Insurance	345.33	867.75	861.64	739.91	720.89
Interest	2,373.52	2,117.93	2,225.05	2,382.08	3,015.26
Lights and power	1,202.52	1,064.00	1,159.95	1,329.26	1,859.14
Mileage	1,440.00	1,200.00	1,200.00	1,200.00	-0-
Miscellaneous expenses	88.50	111.84	128.53	29.00	259.89
Repairs	228.36	64.10	127.52	195.08	66.79
Taxes	2,889.30	2,677.84	2,798.54	2,793.72	2,883.59
Telephone	530.67	375.55	451.03	544.37	559.33
Net income:	15,417.82	18,130.95	22,648.36	22,446.78	21,417.17

LOAN HISTORY

After the fire in 1967, Mr. Hollan requested a loan of $45,000. He intended to divide the money:

1. $18,000 for construction of building;
2. $21,000 for equipment;
3. $2,800 for payment to bank; and
4. the balance for working capital

An SBA participation loan was granted on January 24, 1968, by the Citizens and Southern Bank. It was a ten year (120 months) loan, to be paid at a rate of $375 a month, plus interest. The interest rate was 7 per cent. In 1973, the C & S loan became an SBA direct loan.

Mr. Hollan became three months delinquent on his loan payments by November 24, 1970, in the amount of $1,125 plus interest. He was having trouble meeting payments and requested that the bank defer the principal payment. By April 21, 1971, he was no longer behind in his payments and had lowered the balance owed on the loan to $32,825. Exactly four years

Case exhibit 15–4

THE LAST DINOSAUR

Statement of assets, December 31, 1970–74

Assets:	1970	1971	1972	1973	1974
Cash	37.77	334.08	2,098.13	1650.00	67.00
Accounts receivable	–0–	50.00	–0–	–0–	–0–
Inventory	1150.00	3000.00	1,500.00	3000.00	800.00
Life insurance: cash surrender value	2366.44	2797.04	3,382.76	3978.08	4,582.56
Real estate:					
Land	15,500.00	15,500.00	15,500.00	15,500.00	15,500.00
Residence	15,000.00	15,000.00	15,000.00	15,000.00	15,000.00
Frame house	7,500.00	7,500.00	7,500.00	7,500.00	7,500.00
Building	16,000.00	16,450.00	16,450.00	16,450.00	16,450.00
Spray building	2,200.00	2,200.00	2,200.00	2,200.00	2,200.00
Building addition	–0–	–0–	–0–	–0–	–0–
Total	56,200.00	56,650.00	56,650.00	56,650.00	56,650.00
Less: allowance for depreciation	<2,743.96>	<3,533.62>	<4,330.78>	<5,127.94>	<6,236.09>
Auto and trucks	1,000.00	1,000.00	1,000.00	1,000.00	4,975.85
Machinery and equipment	28,067.24	35,022.24	37,333.34	37,922.24	40,700.39
Less: allowance for depreciation	<6,752.57>	<8,815.31>	<11,551.34>	<14,056.75>	<16,625.84>
Furniture and fixtures	3,000.00	3,000.00	3,000.00	3,000.00	3,000.00
Work in process	2,200.00	4,600.00	1,000.00	6,000.00	8,255.03
Total assets	84,524.92	94,104.43	90,082.01	94,015.63	96,168.90

Case exhibit 15–5

THE LAST DINOSAUR

Statement of liabilities and net worth,
December 31, 1970–74

Liabilities and net worth:	1970	1971	1972	1973	1974
Accounts payable	6,534.84	3,797.07	3,003.13	1,066.72	1,283.72
Notes payable	1,216.55	1,701.28	7,288.39	9,500.00	11,703.02
Sales tax payable	86.58	72.34	138.36	183.88	100.84
Payroll taxes payable	31.01	28.39	–0–	–0–	–0–
Mortgage payable					
C & S National Bank	33,565.74	26,750.00	22,250.00	–0–	–0–
First Federal S & L	–0–	13,485.94	12,476.66	11,658.00	11,214.20
Sander	–0–	5,333.52	–0–	–0–	–0–
Southland Insurance Co.	4,116.77	–0–	–0–	–0–	–0–
Pilot Life Ins.	700.00	713.25	793.72	793.72	2,147.57
Southland Life Ins.	–0–	451.53	478.41	478.41	478.41
SBA	–0–	–0–	–0–	17,792.37	13,672.84
Carolina Life Ins.	–0–	–0–	–0–	–0–	–0–
E. C. Brown	–0–	–0–	–0–	–0–	7,200.00
Net worth	38,273.13	41,771.11	43,653.34	52,542.53	48,368.30
Total liabilities and N.W.	84,524.92	94,104.43	90,082.01	94,015.63	96,168.90

later. Mr. Hollan has again found himself three months delinquent and has been granted a deferment for a period of six months. The balance owed on the loan is $12,945.34.

THE FUTURE

In light of a current lull in business, Mr. Hollan has recognized the growing importance of forecasting future demand for his products. His main method of forecasting demand has been reading trade magazines, which keeps him abreast of the housing industry and new designs in cabinets.

He is also considering building cabinets of colonial design, such as dry sinks, to tie in with the current popular interest in Americana. He feels that this might be a large market, but the cost of the goods produced may be too high for the public to purchase.

Mr. Hollan has considered selling the equipment of his business and selling pre-assembled cabinets. This idea was quickly discarded because the cabinet building is more than a business to Mr. Hollan — it is a way of life.

In forecasting demand for cabinets, Mr. Hollan has also determined that he may be better able to accommodate the customers by adding a showroom to the front of his building. This would give the customers a more relaxed feeling than walking through the shop.

In earlier years, Mr. Hollan did sub-contracting work, but he has ceased to do so because he felt that the contractors were trying to squeeze him out of profits. He is now strictly his own boss.

SUGGESTED QUESTIONS FOR DISCUSSION

1. Evaluate the present management in this case.

2. What are the major strong points of this business; the weak ones?

3. Evaluate Mr. Hollan's investment in machinery.

4. What suggestions would you make regarding Mr. Hollan's present approach to advertising?

5. What suggestions would you make to Mr. Hollan regarding his long range plans (one to five years)?

SUNNY DAYS NURSING HOME

INDUSTRY BACKGROUND

American society is in general agreement that health care must be provided for the elderly. The nursing home is one facility developed to provide necessary care for the long-term patient, and plays a significant role in the total medical care program, being itself a product of the tremendous achievements in medicine over the past sixty years.

The licensing program for nursing homes began around 1945. Since that time, the American Nursing Home Association has encouraged state licensing agencies to strengthen their regulation, and state authorities have responded by establishing regulations governing the operation and maintenance of such facilities.

At the federal level, legislation is helping to improve quality of care. The Community Health Services and Facilities Act of 1961 provided substantial financial aid, and, more recently, the Kerr-Mills program for medical services to the aged mentioned "skilled nursing home services" as one of the types of medical assistance to be provided. Proprietary nursing homes are eligible for federal aid on construction loans made through the Small Business Administration.

The American Nursing Home Association announced, in 1962, a "crash program" for accrediting homes under which each State Association was directed to establish an accreditation board. Subsequent negotiations between the Association and the Joint Commission on Accreditation of Hospitals studied the possibllity of establishing an accreditation program. Had the Commission undertaken such a program then, the Association's program would have served as a screening plan. However, as announced in April, 1963, by the President of the American Hospital Association, the program of the Joint Commission was halted by the refusal of the American Medical Association to concur in its establishment. In the same month, the American

Medical Association and the American Nursing Home Association jointly announced a plan to establish a national accreditation program for nursing homes. In the same year, the South Carolina Hospital Association voted to revise its bylaws to allow the acceptance of nursing homes to membership.

At the beginning of 1963, the American Hospital Association had registered more than 600 nursing homes. The listing requirements include:

1. The facility shall be licensed by the State and must comply with local governmental regulations.
2. Each patient must be under the care of a doctor who must see the patient as the patient's need indicates.
3. A doctor of medicine must supervise the clinical actions of the institution and advise on medical administrative problems.
4. A medical record must be maintained for each patient.
5. The nursing service must be under the supervision of a registered nurse, or a licensed practical nurse, with a registered nurse regularly serving in a consulting capacity.
6. Food must meet the nutritional and dietary requirements of patients.
7. Care must be provided for patients on a 24-hour per day basis and arrangements must be made to provide diagnostic service on a regular and convenient basis.

The nursing home of today is more and more regarded as a medical facility that provides skilled nursing care under medical supervision for the chronically ill.

The administrator should have knowledge of, and experience with, the care of the sick; this administrator must recruit, supervise, and educate the staff, and should set up and coordinate medical, nursing, dietary, housekeeping, and other necessary departments. It is seen, therefore, that proper staffing of the nursing home has become one of the most important tasks of the administrator.

In addition, a physician is necessary, to supervise and be responsible for all medical care. The M.D. in charge should visit the nursing home at least twice a week. If any changes in treatment are necessary, they should be discussed with the chief nurse.

Other necessary personnel include a physical therapist, an occupational therapist, a speech therapist, and social workers. A professionally trained dietician should be employed by each nursing home.

Sufficient nursing time must be made available to assure that each patient receives treatments, medications, and diets as prescribed. In addition, each patient must receive proper care to prevent bedsores, and to be kept comfortable, clean, and well-groomed. The patient must be protected from accident by the adoption of all indicated safety measures, and each patient must be treated with kindness and respect.

The work load in a nursing home must be considered carefully in planning for its coverage. On certain wards, the demand for more personnel is increased in order to meet the heavier work load. The heaviest nursing peaks are usually experienced between 7:00 A.M. and 3:00 P.M. Many hospitals utilize part-time personnel satisfactorily to meet the peaks of nursing needs. Usually the hours of work can be scheduled at a satisfactory time. Patient activity and the atmosphere of hospital units change markedly during the 24-hour day, day of the week, and season of the year. Nursing activities differ on the day shift from those on the evening or night shifts, as does patient behavior.

The ratio of nurses to patients is very important. Many factors affect staffing, and it is axiomatic that quality and quantity of nursing care are influenced by knowledge, judgment, and skills of those participating in the care. If a patient is acutely ill, then that patient requires more professional nursing care. A less acute, or intermediate, patient can be entrusted to the care of less skilled personnel. The degree of the patient's illness and the kinds of total care required determine who will care for the patient.

Good nursing home staffing requires at least one licensed person, either R.N. or L.P.N., on each shift.

HISTORY OF SUNNY DAYS NURSING HOME

Sunny Days Nursing Home is located on a 4.1 acre plot of land in Butler County, about twenty miles north of Millville, South Carolina. Most of the home is contained in one building, with the laundry in a separate building (see Case exhibit 16–1). Sunny Days Nursing Home has had a sole proprietor since it was founded in 1948 — Mrs. Betsy Breger. Mrs. Breger and her husband are both natives of Butler County. Mrs. Breger, now 62 years old, has been a registered nurse since 1932. She was a private duty nurse until 1935, when she became head nurse at a clinic in Millville. In 1936, Mrs. Breger became head nurse at Haven Emergency Hospital in Pisgan. She became a resident nurse at Warren Hospital in Middletown, in 1940. From 1941 to 1948, Mrs. Breger was engaged as a private duty nurse.

Mrs. Breger founded Sunny Days Nursing Home in 1948 when she took a patient into her own home. By the end of 1948, she expanded her home in order to accommodate nineteen

Case exhibit 16–1

GENERAL LAYOUT

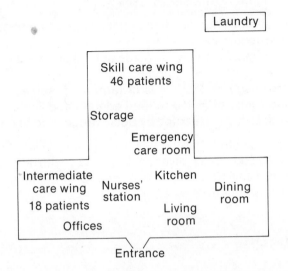

patients. In 1952 and 1953, the home was enlarged a second time to add seven more patients. In 1958 the home was expanded to thirty beds, and remained that size until 1964, when a new facility was built.

In 1963, when Mrs. Breger decided to build a new nursing home facility, she gave two reasons: first, the old home was too small, as shown by a seventeen patient waiting list; in addition, she had a Class III state license for the home and she was about to lose it due to the age of the old wood frame facility.

When a loan was rejected by a bank in Hamilton, Mrs. Breger went to the Small Business Administration and arranged a direct loan for a new 64-bed facility. The structure was to be built adjacent to the old structure on land owned by Mrs. Breger. The total contract price for the new home was $127,313, broken down:

Building costs	$106,953
Architect and engineer	3,000
Attorney fees	2,000
Interim financing	1,000
Landscaping	1,800
Fencing	458
Kitchen equipment	7,000
Room equipment	5,102
Total	$127,313

After negotiating with the SBA, Mrs. Breger's loan was authorized on September 20, 1963 in the amount of $128,000.

The loan was disbursed on August 25, 1964 with a maturity date of August 25, 1974. The ten-year note was to be repaid in monthly installments of $1321, including principal and interest, commencing on November 25, 1964. Collateral for the note was:

1. First mortgage on all material and equipment, furniture, and fixtures;
2. First mortgage on 4.1 acres of land and the building on the site of nursing home;
3. Mortgage on 202 acres of farm land, subject to a prior mortgage of $5850 to the Federal Land Bank;
4. A note to be executed by Betsy Breger and her husband.

It was estimated that the new 64-bed facility would be capable of $100,000 gross revenues per year, with an estimated net profit of $49,619, according to the pro forma income statements made at the time of the loan.

MANAGEMENT

Sunny Days Nursing Home is a family operation. Four Breger households receive income from it. Mrs. Breger's stepson, W. D. Showalter, is the Administrator of the home. Showalter took the position in 1964, when the home moved into the new building. He is a graduate of the University of South Carolina with a major in psychology. According to Showalter, Mrs. Breger lets him run the business as he wishes. Showalter's sister, Christy Breger, who is married to Mrs. Betsy Breger's son, is the Administrative Assistant. She is responsible for secretarial duties in the office. Showalter's wife, Kitty Showalter, is in charge of the kitchen, all housekeeping, and maintenance for the building. Mrs. Breger is also on the payroll. Showalter said that Mrs. Breger helps out with some of the nursing duties at the home.

Showalter indicates that he has had little formal training in management, only seminars provided by the state nursing home association. However, the SBA file has an entry which states that the South Carolina Nursing Home Association has used the Sunny Days Nursing Home as a model for other homes in the state to follow. All top personnel selection is handled by Showalter. The various department heads subsequently hire employees for the lower job positions. The control of performance is also the department head's responsibility. Showalter does all planning and forecasting for the home, but he admits little emphasis is currently put on this area of management.

There are also two Directors of Nursing, one for each wing, Intermediate and Skill. The Intermediate Care wing requires only one nurse, the Director of Nursing for that wing. In the Skill Care wing, there is a registered nurse on each of the three shifts, plus various L.P.N.s and nurse's aides. The home employs a social worker—a full-time employee. Her main duty is to try to keep the patients busy, if they are capable of doing some kind of work or recreation. All financial transactions are taken care of by an accountant in Pisgan, who pays all bills and credits all receipts. The home serves three meals a day, seven days a week, and has a full kitchen staff. Also, all laundry is done at the home and requires several full-time employees.

MARKETING

There is no marketing process, per se, for Sunny Days Nursing Home. As a result of the close contractual agreements between the state and the nursing home, there is not much flexibility on management's part for pricing or for other market-related decisions. Sixty-three of the 64 patients are welfare cases. The Department of Social Services classifies each patient, and the monthly payments are determined by the nature of the patient's physical, mental, and financial condition. The patients are between 65 and 95 years old and 75 per cent are black. Prior to 1971, Sunny Days offered only "skilled care" services. A "skilled care" patient requires more attention in terms of feeding, bathing, and medications, than does an "intermediate" patient. However, in 1971 a new 100-bed nursing home opened in Oxford, and as a result, Sunny Days' occupancy began to fall. In an attempt to remedy this decline in revenue, Sunny Days converted one wing into an intermediate care facility. Compounding this problem is the fact that classification of the patient is done by the Department of Social Services, and this classification determines the monthly payments made to the nursing home. Mr. Showalter states that some of the "intermediate" patients may require more service (cost) than many of the "skilled" care patients; yet the corresponding payments to the nursing home are considerably less for the intermediate care patient than for the skilled patient. In effect, the contractual agreement system between the state and the nursing homes needs to be revamped, and conflicts resulting from the method of payment, classification of patients, and adjustments for services need to be resolved. Now, a nursing home can negotiate the fees, basing its argument on last year's costs. As a result, there is no incentive for the nursing home to cut costs.

The occupancy rate for Sunny Days Nursing Home has typically been near 100 per cent, with a waiting list at most times. Sunny Days receives calls from the local hospital inquiring about possible vacancies. However, many of their patients come from all over the state, as a result of the Department of Social Services' placement bureau in Columbia. The facilities are well maintained, clean, and competently staffed. The home must meet all county, state, and federal requirements for health, sanitation, food, and safety. These requirements are enforced by periodic inspections from the appropriate authority.

Although there is no advertising, Sunny Days does release articles for the county paper about the social activities of the home, such as birthday parties, holiday events, religious activities, and any other information about the patients. These activities are planned by a Director of Social Activities. Church meetings are held at the home every Sunday morning, and visits by the churches, friends, and families of the patients are encouraged. Volunteer help is accepted, although not actively solicited.

FINANCES

The Nursing Home remained in good standing with its loan repayment schedule until 1970. W. D. Showalter, administrator of the home, said that the reason for their troubles has been a lack of working capital due to contract problems with the South Carolina Department of Social Services. Sunny Days Nursing Home has always had a majority of their patients who are welfare recipients; currently 63 of their 64 beds are filled by welfare patients. At this time, the home has eighteen Intermediate Care patients and forty-six Skill Care patients. Intermediate Care patients, a service the home was forced to add four years ago, are patients who do not require round-the-clock nursing care, as a Skill Care patient does. The Sunny Days Nursing Home was forced to add the Intermediate Care service owing to state regulations and competition from the nursing home in Oxford.

In 1970 the South Carolina Department of Social Services changed its method of reimbursement. Showalter indicated that instead of getting full reimbursement, all nursing homes, as of 1970, are paid according to the preceding year's costs, which reduced reimbursement greatly. Currently, Sunny Days Nursing Home is reimbursed $340 a month for Intermediate Care patients and $16.23 a day for Skill Care patients. The Home charges $380 a month for Intermediate Care, which leaves $40 a month that must be paid by the patient.

As of August, 1974, 29 principal payments on the Home's SBA loan have been deferred. The mortgage on the 202 acres of farm land has been subordinated three times. The only payments made on the loan since June 1971 were two token $300

Case exhibit 16–2

SUNNY DAYS NURSING HOME

Balance sheet, September 30, 1972

Assets

Accounts receivable		36,064.64
Accounts receivable emp.		80.59
Prepaid expense		600.00

Long term assets

	Cost	Depreciation	Balance		
Land	9,250.00		9,250.00		
Buildings	131,650.00	58,024.00	73,626.00		
Lake house	7,339.68	366.00	6,973.68		
Equipment	64,990.59	47,287.00	17,703.59		
	213,230.27	105,677.00	107,553.27	107,553.27	
Total assets				144,298.50	

Liabilities

Accrued expense	2,000.00		
Accounts payable	31,814.27		
Withholdings US	9,392.81		
Accrued payroll	6,849.30		
National Bank overdraft	856.09		
Withholdings S.C.	1,370.94		
Note payable equipment	3,147.76		
Note payable Bank of Claredon	296.34		
Mortgage mobile unit	6,728.04		
Note payable National Bank of S.C.	33,200.00		
SBA	39,419.05		
	135,074.60	135,074.60	

Capital	27,317.13		
Loss	(17,508.88)		
	9,808.25		

B. Breger withdrawal	584.35		
	9,223.90	9,223.90	
		144,298.50	144,298.50

payments in 1972. In August the SBA extended the maturity date on the loan from August 25, 1974 to August 25, 1982, so the monthly installments were reduced from $1321 to $549. The new payments started on August 25, 1974. The balance due on the note as of August 19, 1974, was $42,517.

The financial difficulties of the Sunny Days Nursing Home started when the federal government enacted the Medicaid program. The Medicaid program was not designed with "for profit" institutions in mind. The program provided for the reimbursement of cost plus a return on equity capital; it also paid

Case exhibit 16–3

SUNNY DAYS NURSING HOME

*Profit and loss statement for the
year ended September 30, 1972*

Income			256,922.47
Expenses			
Food		26,764.48	
LHWT		7,828.44	
Drugs		4,429.07	
Nursing supplies		9,128.40	
Salaries		168,030.71	
Employees group insurance		1,307.21	
Repairs		3,521.47	
Auto		1,012.90	
Insurance		5,925.43	
Interest		4,493.56	
Taxes*		12,377.74	
Miscellaneous expense		13,093.94	
Miscellaneous expense		5,000.00	
		262,913.35	262,913.35
			(5,990.88)
Depreciation			
Buildings		6,329.00	
Equipment		5,189.00	
		11,518.00	11,518.00
Loss			(17,508.88)

*Licenses and taxes

State Board of Health	27.50
Property tax	1,024.88
Unemployment tax	2,650.52
Social Security tax	8,674.84
	12,377.74

depreciation. The Medicaid program is aimed at "non-profit" institutions, which of course only worry about covering their costs. The fact that the Sunny Days Nursing Home was, and is, under-capitalized caused the Home to be unable to receive an adequate return. Another cause for difficulty was that the cost reimbursement was based on the previous year's costs; the rising costs of everything could not be paid with the same amount of money as in the previous years.

The federal government not only resitricted the amount that nursing homes could receive, but also ordered them to upgrade their facilities and personnel or lose their nursing home license. Homes which had previously restricted their facilities to skilled

Case exhibit 16–4

SUNNY DAYS NURSING HOME

Balance sheet, September 30, 1973

Current assets

Cash in bank	(1007.94)
Accounts receivable	32,042.23
Prepaid expense	600.00

Long term assets

	Cost	Depreciation	Balance	
Land	9,250.00		9,250.00	
Lake house	7,339.68	732.00	6,607.68	
Building	131,650.00	63,986.86	67,663.14	
Equipment	64,990.59	52,137.69	12,852.90	
	213,230.27	116,856.55	96,373.72	96,373.72
				128,008.01

Liabilities

Accounts payable	29,705.70	
Notes payable—oper.	24,450.00	
Withholdings	6,449.16	
Accrued withholdings	6,253.95	
Accrued payroll	5,008.31	
Loans payable	1,910.33	
Accrued expense	2,400.00	
Note payable—Lake	4,485.36	
Note payable—SBA	40,092.63	
Total liabilities	120,755.44	120,755.44
Capital	9,224.00	
Loss, September 30, 1973	(1,971.43)	
	7,252.57	7,252.57
		128,008.01

patients only were forced to convert a number of beds to intermediate care. The individual patient income for intermediate care dropped from $13.50 per day reimbursable income per bed down to $8.50 per day. The operating costs and the fixed costs could not be reduced to offset the required upgrading of facilities or the reduced patient income under the intermediate care program.

In 1973, the Nursing Home Association negotiated a new contract with the state, whereby the cost reimbursement has a built-in adjustment for inflation and other factors. The net result of the new contract has been that Sunny Days Nursing Home is now showing a profit.

Case exhibit 16–5

SUNNY DAYS NURSING HOME

*Profit and loss statement for the year
ended September 30, 1973*

Income

ICF—gov't	73958.71	
ICF—private	14601.77	
Skilled—government	146033.04	
Skilled—private	39278.71	
Total Income	273872.23	273,872.23

Expenses

Food	35582.96	
LHWT	8719.90	
Drugs	4402.52	
Nursing supplies	5826.42	
Salaries	167141.01	
Unemployment tax	1403.16	
Social Security tax	9767.80	
Repair	1096.57	
Bank charge	414.73	
Auto expense	1642.13	
Insurance	1508.46	
Supplies—linen	206.72	
housekeeping	2334.51	
laundry	669.75	
administration	319.01	
dietary	103.56	
Kitchen consultant	4263.38	
Donation	20.00	
Medical records consultant	100.00	
Leased equipment	231.18	
UR meetings	1000.00	
Social consultant	2910.00	
Dues and subscriptions	838.00	
Advertising	361.80	
Legal and audit	1092.05	
Maint. Yard	12.50	
Pest control	485.00	
Conventions	1383.33	
Bookkeeper	300.00	
Leased auto	1938.00	
Interest	4124.76	
Health insurance	571.56	
Refund ICF	11.60	
Taxes	620.43	
Licenses	22.00	
Patient activities	92.66	
Gifts	129.70	
Depreciation expense,		
bldg	6328.86	
equipment	4850.69	
Total expenses		272826.71
Net profit		1045.52
B. Breger, drawing		(3016.95)
Loss		(1971.43)

Case exhibit 16–6

SUNNY DAYS NURSING HOME

BALANCE SHEET
September 30, 1974

Assets

Cash		100.00	
Cash in bank		(1700.12)	
Accounts receivable		29501.49	27901.37

Long term assets

Land		9250.00	
Buildings	138989.68		
Accounts dep. bldgs.	64718.86*	74270.82	
Equipment	65757.73		
Accounts dep. equip.	52137.69*	13620.04	97140.86
			125042.23

Liabilities

Salaries payable		6566.14	
Accts payable		31557.35	
Installment note payable		1698.25	
Notes payable—SBA		41627.07	
—NBSC		17900.00	
Employee W/H		5054.13	104402.94
Capital—October, 1973	7252.57		
Add current period earnings	16448.82	23701.39	
Deduct draw—B. Breger		3062.10	20639.29
			125042.23

*Depreciation has not been accumulated since October 1, 1973.

Case exhibit 16–7

SUNNY DAYS NURSING HOME

*Profit and loss statement
for the year ended September 30, 1974*

Income

ICF		67512.69
Skilled		125123.84
Private		57526.34
Total Income		250162.87

Expense

Admin & General

Salaries	18268.64	
Auto expense	3308.52	
FICA expense	7246.98	
Insurance	3762.36	
Office supplies	1099.87	
Interest	1794.28	
Legal	2850.00	
Conventions	700.00	
Taxes	2302.18	
Dues and subscriptions	310.00	
Advertising	100.00	41742.83

Dietary

Salaries	19236.27	
R/M kitchen		
Food	30022.17	
Other supplies	96.63	49355.07

Medical

Salaries—Nurses	35874.46	
—Aides	53897.95	
—Orderlies	5677.75	
—Medical Records	700.00	
—Social Worker	2257.68	
Supplies	9950.47	108358.31

Housekeeping

Salaries	5043.39	
R/M	790.18	
Supplies	2359.90	8193.47

Laundry

Salaries	5859.45	
R/M	324.04	
Supplies	989.69	7173.18

Case exhibit 16–7 *Continued*

Operation and Maintenance of Plant

Utilities	9593.21	
R/M	1536.20	
Pest control	800.00	
Salaries	994.44	
		12923.85

Other

Purchased services	5617.20	
Miscellaneous	350.14	5967.34
Total expense		233714.05

Net income 16448.82

SUGGESTED QUESTIONS FOR DISCUSSION

1. Many firms face problems with cost-reimbursement programs initiated by governmental agencies. What specific problems were encountered by Sunny Days Nursing Home?

2. How can firms protect themselves from the changes made by governmental agencies that affect their revenues?

3. A common failing of health institutions in this country is a lack of marketing. How does this criticism apply to Sunny Days?

4. What effect do you feel national health insurance will have on small businesses in the health care field?

INDUSTRIAL DOOR INC.

INTRODUCTION

Industrial Door was originally incorporated on June 2, 1961, under the name of Bostick Door Sales Company and on January 1, 1974, changed its name to Industrial Door, Incorporated. The firm was incorporated under the laws of Delaware. Its principal business is the sale and installation of commercial and residential doors. The company operates from leased facilities in Lansing, Michigan. There are 300 shares of common stock authorized at a par value of $100 per share. There are presently 172 shares issued and outstanding. Harry Bostick is president and treasurer, and M. C. Glenn is vice-president and secretary. Both are on the Board of Directors.

Mr. Bostick feels that the objectives of the company are basic and well-defined: orderly growth and increased profits, and maintenance of a reputation for quality work upon which the first objective depends. As far as his personal objectives are concerned, Mr. Bostick plans to retire from the business at age 55 (a period of twelve years) after having hired and trained employees who can carry on without his active direction while maintaining the Company's profits.

The main concern of the business is commercial doors. A wide variety of doors and enclosures are handled by the firm. These enclosures include automatic opening doors, metal guards for store windows, and overhead and swing doors, including rolling steel doors. A number of the different kinds of door offered by the firm are kept in inventory, while others are ordered directly from the manufacturers and can normally be obtained in about two weeks. The firm is capable of modifying doors that are in inventory to fit odd-sized openings. This modification is done on the premises and then delivered to the job site.

Most of the door sales and installations take place within a fifty mile radius of four major cities in central Michigan—

Lansing, Flint, Grand Rapids, and Kalamazoo. With these towns as focal points, the firm's sales agents work the areas, soliciting contracts with building contractors and sub-contractors. A close association is maintained with the contractors in each of these areas, to insure that the firm is aware of any and all opportunities to bid on new installation contracts. Because of this working relationship and reputation built up over the years, much of the firm's business consists of repeat orders from satisfied customers.

Approximately 75 per cent of the company's work is negotiated: that is, because of the company's close contact and good working relationship with contractors, it is asked to bid on certain jobs in competition with other door companies. At times it is asked to re-bid on a project and cut the price if the bids are at all close and the contractor desires Industrial Door for the job because of its reputation.

Industrial Door maintains two "in" WATS lines and one "out" WATS line for the convenience and close, informal communication they offer contractors. These lines are available to the firm and the majority of sales are transacted over them.

The main office of Industrial Doors, Incorporated is in Lansing, Michigan. This location puts it in a central position, with access to major traffic routes. Industrial Doors also maintains three satellite warehouses, one each in Flint, Grand Rapids, and Kalamazoo. These satellite warehouses are primarily holding warehouses, since only materials ordered for a specific job are maintained in them. All other inventories are maintained in Lansing. The positioning of these warehouses allows rapid customer service to these areas, while also allowing the company to establish and maintain good relations with contractors. The staff at each of these satellite warehouses is composed of:

Flint—One residential sales agent and three service trucks, each with a crew of two installers
One industrial sales agent
Grand Rapids—One industrial sales agent
One service truck, with a crew of two installers
Kalamazoo—One residential sales agent
One industrial sales agent
Two service trucks, each with a crew of two installers

The central office and grounds in Lansing are located on a 3.4 acre site. The building itself is divided into three connecting warehouses and an office. Case exhibit 17–1 shows the layout of the Lansing office. There are fourteen crews in the Lansing office, and five residential and industrial sales agents.

Case exhibit 17–1

INDUSTRIAL DOOR, INC.
Diagramatic description

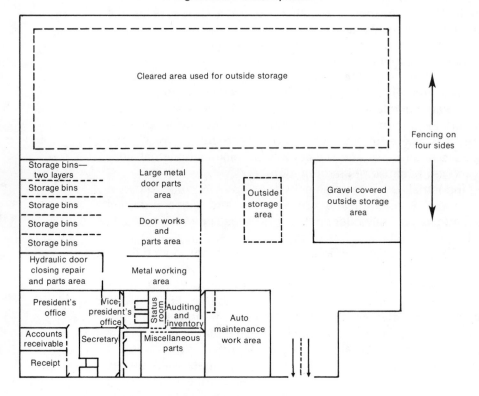

THE MANAGEMENT

Harry Bostick began Bostick Door Sales Company in 1961, after working four years in the overhead door business as a mechanic and installer. Mr. Bostick has a high school education, and most of his business ability has been either self-taught or gained through experience. He is proud of his business competence, and the growth and profits of his company attest to his ability. At present Mr. Bostick owns 70.9 per cent of issued and outstanding stock.

Mr. Bostick assumes the major portion of directing the administrative activities of the firm, in addition to specializing in price estimation and promoting the overhead door segment of the product lines. In addition, he maintains close supervision of all the firm's activities.

M. C. Glenn was hired to assist Mr. Bostick in the operation of the firm. Mr. Glenn now owns 29.1 per cent of the capital stock and is the vice-president and secretary of Industrial Door.

Mr. Glenn assists Mr. Bostick in bids and job price estimation, is responsible for maintaining company records (in which he is assisted by a CPA firm), and acts as overall manager. He is in his mid-thirties, a high school graduate with extensive and very successful product related sales experience acquired prior to joining the firm in 1968. Mr. Glenn assumes a portion of the responsibility of the firm's activities by concentrating on the automatic door and hollow metals product lines. He also assists in other administrative activities and is capable of running the firm in Mr. Bostick's absence.

Mr. Harris, the service manager, is the third key manager in the organization. His major duties involve the operational management of the firm, and he is responsible for all activities outside the firm's office area. These duties include directing the installation crews, in addition to overseeing the shop and warehouse activities. Mr. Harris supervises approximately fifty individuals, including fourteen installation crews. He is a high school graduate with seven years experience with the firm.

The company employs 54 individuals in Lansing: 2 officials and managers, 5 sales agents, 12 metal crafters, 4 office and clerical workers, and 31 semi-skilled laborers.

EMPLOYEE RELATIONS

Industrial Door's philosophy, as reflected by Mr. Bostick, is to hire people who want to work and then pay them a salary that is commensurate with their efforts, while exceeding that offered for comparable work in the area. By adhering to this plan, the firm has been able to keep turnover to an absolute minimum. No opportunity exists to obtain a comparable job for a higher salary in the area. Another factor that keeps turnover low is that the firm is run as if it were a family business, giving a pleasant and close-knit atmosphere. The principal stockholders of the firm, Mr. Bostick and Mr. Glenn, are also the hardest workers of the firm, thereby setting work performance standards by example. This sense of purpose and of zeal for getting the job done can be noted throughout the work force.

Another factor that affects the low turnover rate is the existence of an early retirement plan. The employee contributes 3 per cent of his wages, which is matched by the firm. The retirement fund is invested in government securities for maximum safety and a reasonable return on investment. The aim of the retirement plan is to allow retirement by age fifty-five, after twenty years' service.

Because of the small turnover, an elaborate system of hiring and firing is not required. Hiring decisions are based heavily on interviews with the individual in question, plus a review of references and past experience. If the job opening requires a particular skill, such as welding, then the applicant is given a shop test to demonstrate his capabilities. The main factor looked for is a strong desire for hard work on the individual's part. Keeping the job is primarily based on honesty and performance. A serious lack of either of these two qualities has, in the past, led to agreed-upon separations.

LOCAL COMPETITION

The door industry primarily functions through the franchise system. Large door manufacturers, such as Northeastern Door, Incorporated and Lock Door Company have established franchises in lucrative areas, primarily for the advertisement and sales of their product lines. The franchise does not avoid handling other products, but encourages maximum use of the company's lines. The competition is significant, and locally, several companies are in direct competition with Industrial Door, the largest competitor being the local franchise of the Lock Door Company.

Unlike Industrial Door, the Lock Door Company competes on a coast-to-coast basis and has additional outlets in Canada. Unlike Industrial, Lock Door Company is listed on the American Stock Exchange. It has 25 plants and 400 distributors. It employs 2990 persons and has 2068 shareholders. Sales for the six months ending in June 1974 were up 14 per cent. Net income gain was 4.2 per cent; share earnings increased from $.74 to $.78. Overhead assets stand at $40.3 million, liabilities at $10.4 million, and net working capital is $29.9 million. Return on common equity is 20.8 per cent. Total sales for 1974 are estimated to exceed $100 million.

A POSSIBLE MERGER

Industrial Door, Incorporated is presently being considered by the J. M. Corporation as a possible addition to its extensive holdings. J. M. Corporation produces the nation's broadest line of building materials, and is also engaged in coal mining, oil and gas production, sugar cane growing and refining, other mining activities, and the production of shell homes and various industrial products.

J. M. Corporation showed net sales of $1,291.92 million in 1974, with a net income of $63.33 million. Estimated profits per share were $3.65, up from $3.01 in 1973. It is reporting current assets of $825.01 million, and current liabilities of $672.57 million. Working capital is $152.44 million and current ratio is 1.2. With this capital backing and the advantage of associating with related industries, Industrial Door, Incorporated may be able to benefit as a subsidiary of J. M. Corporation, in relation to its national competitors.

MARKETING POLICIES

The main method for advertising the firm's products and service is through the continual customer contacts maintained by the sales force. Sales agents have a minimum of two years on the job training. The agent keeps in close contact with the contractors and keeps them aware of the firm's large and diverse product lines, plus its ability to expertly install and service the products. This frequent contact has established a large clientele of satisfied customers and a valuable source of repeat business, as well as a further means of passing work to their potential customers. As noted previously, this repeat business represents approximately 75 per cent of the firm's orders.

Another type of advertising the firm engages in is putting a label with the firm's name and phone contacts on each installation. This particular segment of the advertising program has also proved highly effective. Not only does it identify the product and installation with the firm so that other potential customers can make judgments, it is also a reminder later, if the doors should require some type of servicing. The label not only reminds the customer which firm installed the door, it also provides the correct phone number so that prompt action can be taken to call Industrial Door, rather than searching through the Yellow Pages.

The third type of advertising used by the firm is the classified ad section in the telephone directory Yellow Pages. This particular form of advertising accounts for a significant amount of new business, though not in high volume. These Yellow Page advertisements are used to make contact with potential businesses and are in several sections of the listing, covering marketable items of the company throughout.

Other advertising can be grouped into less measurable areas, such as attractively painted trucks, company signs, and a subtle reminder to new customers of other product lines the firm carries. Residential door sales' advertising is played down to allow the firm's resources to be more profitably directed to the higher profit area of commercial doors.

A cost/benefit analysis of the firm's advertising expenditures reveals an inverse relationship. From 1973 to 1974 the firm reduced its advertising budget by 30 per cent and at the same time increased sales by 44 per cent. In 1974, advertising costs represented 0.2 per cent of sales. The low advertising budget and the inverse relationship were possible due to an unusually economically active year in 1974. This reduction in advertising expenditure points out the often overlooked fact that less advertising is needed when business is good.

Another part of the systematic marketing plan is the use of the state-wide WATS line service of the telephone network. Sales agents continually report any new customers, or hints of contracts to be issued, as well as receive contracts they are to make. Bostick, the primary owner, stresses the importance of WATS lines and uses them constantly in regard to new and old customers. These WATS lines reach to the major areas of business: Grand Rapids, Flint, and Kalamazoo.

Pressure is continually applied to the sales force to be more productive and persistent. A good reputation with the public is appreciated, and Industrial Door's standing in business and public communities is a crucial point of concern for Mr. Bostick. He credits much of his sales to word-of-mouth, and he estimates that 50 per cent of repeat business is from previous relationships with contractors. Seventy per cent of the company's contracts come from non-industrial areas and 30 per cent from industrial areas. Mr. Bostick stays in contact with new developments in business by reading, research, and personal contact. He has sole responsibility as sales manager.

Sales agents are salaried employees and do not make commissions as a result of sales. These agents receive no specific list of contacts and work primarily through Mr. Bostick and his contacts. Mr. Bostick informs the sales agent of a bid quotation on each contracted job and can use this, along with WATS line contact, to follow up in the job's area. The sales cost is known before auditing, since sales agents receive a straight salary.

As sales manager, Mr. Bostick does not use a timetable as a guideline for any given course of action. The only device used is the monthly profit and loss statement. If a new product isn't produced in a desired time, a new approach is considered. The schedule for each product, division, or service depends solely on the demand. Day-to-day execution of any plans are also Mr. Bostick's responsibility. The marketing efforts of Industrial Door are carried out under his supervision and are delegated sufficient money for their purpose. Evaluations of cost versus results are sporadically attempted. WATS lines are evaluated at regular intervals to determine their effectiveness in contacting new business for sales. Survey evaluations on the divisions have shown the profitability of each WATS line. When a WATS line does prove to be too expensive, the sales agent and service workers are reassigned to more profitable locales and the unprofitable locale abandoned.

The current fluctuation in sales is a result of a market that is presently unstable. Accurately assigning each product an individual cost is not possible since the wide variance in products forces all profits to be simply lumped together. Each product's selling price cannot be accurately compared with its contribution to sales, since all sales are combined into one sum without regard to which product accounted for what volume of those sales. Costs are not classified according to either the service, product, or the division that uses the product.

PRICING POLICIES

The price Industrial Door offers a customer is usually based on bids submitted for the specific job. The competition tends to price services lower than Industrial Door. Competitive prices reflect approximately 12 to 15 per cent profit after material cost, while Industrial Door, Incorporated charges 23 to 25 per cent for profit.

This practice of pricing 10 to 15 per cent above competition is not across-the-board. The firm's prices are based on costs, plus a profit margin. Depending on the circumstances, this could be as high as 15 per cent above competition. This is due mainly to the firm's higher labor costs and will affect jobs that require a great deal of labor. Bids for jobs are usually set with between 23 per cent and 25 per cent profit after material cost, depending on job site, job specifications, and the job itself. A sales price consists of sales tax, material cost, mark-up, and installation price.

Material is acquired "freight on board" from supplier plants. These plants will sell to Industrial Door on a fixed price or volume discount. The fixed price arrangement is based on a four dollars per hundred-weight of material which includes material, freight, and support steel needed in the shipping. The volume discount arrangement is based on truckloads of material and includes a basic discount for material plus freight.

CREDIT POLICIES

The credit policies are the same for all customers: one per cent in ten days and net in thirty days. Fifty per cent of the business is with larger companies, while the remainder is with smaller, self-employed contractors and individuals. These smaller concerns usually create more bad debts, being not well-established, and business is "cash on delivery" with these concerns.

Bad debts are a problem and the company is now employing a part-time credit manager whose responsibility it is to screen potential customers for reliability of payment. To collect bad debts, the company has its lawyer issue a summons and complaint against the customer. Even the credit extended long-time reputable customers is becoming unstable with the ever-increasing frequency of bankruptcy.

As a sub-contractor called in by a primary contractor, Industrial Door's legal claim is subordinate to both the prime contractor and the mortgagee in most situations. If the builder (owner) cannot pay the contractors and mortgagee, the property is put up for sale and the first chance of purchase goes to the first mortgage holder, who normally bids the amount of the mortgage and gains title. This leaves sub-contractors like Industrial Door unable to collect.

FINANCIAL AND LOAN DATA

The continuing increase in sales for Industrial Door, Incorporated, over the last eight years, has been accomplished through hard work on the part of all members of the firm. Even with slowing business trends, Industrial Door had a total sales volume of $987,671 for the first five months of 1974–75. These sales figures show the increasing trend:

Sales (000)

1967	1968	1969	1970	1971	1972	1973	1974
492.3	496.8	651.6	748.5	836.4	896	1,464	2,102

The increase in sales has been the result of a number of changes in the firm. Specifically, Mr. Glenn, a sales oriented individual, was taken on as a partner. He has been very effective, because of his prior sales experience, in reorienting the firm toward goals that increase sales. Also, facilities have been expanded to meet this higher demand, product lines have been expanded to cover almost all types of enclosures, a leasing section was added to the business, which has added to revenues, and the reputation of the firm has constantly been increasing along with increased demand for quality work. With additional installations come additional servicing which also adds to revenues; repeat business is a large contributor to increases over the years. Sales increases have been a product of all of these factors.

At present (1975), $138,000 is the fixed overhead amount

which must be covered to break even each month. Dollar volume decreased in January and February of 1975 and was not enough to reach the break-even figure. Dollar volume is expected to fluctuate during the year because of the instability of money markets. The total sales increase is expected to be approximately 20 per cent. An expected dollar volume for 1975 is 2.5 million in sales. The approximate volume will break down by products:

a.	Sectional doors	25% of Dollar Volume
b.	Rolling steel doors	35%
c.	Special doors	10%
d.	Hollow metal and hardware	10%
e.	Automatic door entrance	10%
f.	Service	8%
g.	Residential	2%

The gross profit on this expected dollar volume for June, 1974, through May, 1975, will be 4 to 5 per cent; and for June, 1975, to May, 1976, 2 to 3 per cent. Forecasting accuracy and manageability are adversely affected due to the lack of breakdown by product sales and profit goals for each product.

Certain products are expected to increase their proportion of sales volume. Hollow metal products will increase substantially owing to new product lines and development of products with their related services. This line is expected to increase from its present 10 per cent of dollar volume to 30 per cent. Residential sales are decreasing, but will be kept in the product line for the sake of service and product reputation.

RECORDS

Industrial Door, Incorporated uses a modern, innovative approach which serves to simplify everyday business operations. The records system is the Safeguard system, which has a "pegboard" for making entries in duplicate. The bookkeeping under this system is broken down into three divisions: accounts receivable, invoicing, and general bookkeeping—the last of which handles the sales journal, cash disbursements journal, cash receipts journal, and the purchase journal. Each of the three segments is handled by a different individual and in this manner they are able to verify each other's figures. The Safeguard company itself, with headquarters in Ft. Washington, Pennsylvania, receives copies of all entries and transactions and compiles statements on a monthly basis for Industrial Door. Charge for the service is based on the number of transactions per month. A cost/benefit analysis has not been undertaken.

Payroll for Industrial Door is handled on an automated basis by Michigan Bankers' Trust Company which handles all of Industrial Door's banking needs. Hours for each hourly worker are submitted on Monday for the prior week, checks are received on Wednesday, and are disbursed on each Friday at noon. The average monthly charge for this service is $110. Bankers' Trust also prepares all W-2 forms for the workers, along with quarterly reports for the company. Every indication points to the fact that this method of payroll justifies itself on a cost-benefit basis.

FURTHER OBJECTIVES

Mr. Bostick feels that the goals of this firm should include a feasibility study of expanding the operation; in particular, expansion to the Jackson and Saginaw areas. As part of this study, managerial problems in communication and in span of control must be assessed. His personal attention to all facets of the operation will no longer be possible in an expanded firm.

He feels that a study of managerial practices can best be initiated if it is considered in definite steps. Step 1 should involve top management defining its goals and objectives. These goals should be as specific as possible and as measurable as practical. These goals should also be realistic, feasible, and set up on a priority basis.

Step 2 would involve breaking up the firm's goals and objectives into sub-groups as they apply to different sections of the firm. These objectives would inform subordinates of what to do, when, and with what authority. In this step, top management should directly involve lower managers in the information gathering for decision making.

Step 3 should involve manager and subordinate agreement on a performance contract. This is the most important step, since it involves specific objective definition, functions, tasks, responsibilities, authorities, and resources over a specified time period. Communication is extremely important in this step because both parties must be frank about desires and capabilities. Management should not ask for what cannot be delivered, and the subordinates should not accept what they cannot produce. A mismatch at this point will only cause future conflict.

Step 4 is the implementation phase of the plan. It is during this phase that the manager and subordinates work in concert to insure that the program does not get lost in implementation and that the proper coordination and mutual cooperation are given any new problems. Often, very meaningful programs get a good launching, but little or no steering later on.

Step 5, the last step, evaluates results. During this stage of

Case exhibit 17–2

INDUSTRIAL DOOR, INC.

Balance sheet,
May 31, 1974 and 1973

Assets

Current assets		1974	1973
Accounts receivable	$457,184.88		
Less allowance for bad debt	41,578.95	$415,605.93	$337,242.19
Other		67,195.53	46,817.05
Inventory		379,873.89	261,999.99
Pre-paid expenses			637.33
Total current assets		$862,675.35	$646,696.56

Fixed assets	1974	1973
Cost	$221,161.18	$203,378.32
Less accumulated depreciation	106,578.66	82,510.18
Book value	$114,582.52	$120.868.14
Other assets	$ 7,124.68	$ 9,665.57
Total assets	$984,382.55	$777,230.27

Liabilities

Current liabilities	1974	1973
Accounts payable	$256,545.83	$373,740.28
Notes payable	391,987.32	111,629.76
Accrued expenses	87,140.00	7,294.62
Taxes payable	34,238.00	23,520.99
	$769,911.15	$516,185.65

Long-term liabilities	1974	1973
Notes payable	82,235.15	162,545.76

Stockholders' equity

Common stock

	1974	1973
Par value $100	$ 17,200.00	$ 15,000.00
Paid-in capital	25,000.00	12,200.00
Retained earnings	90,036.25	71,298.86
Total stockholders' equity	$132,236.25	$ 98,498.86
Total liabilities and stockholders' equity	$984,382.55	$777,230.27

the program there should be no surprises for either the manager or the subordinate. The subordinate should be checking personal performance as the contract time period progresses, and so, at this point, should be well aware of how the manager will judge that performance in relation to the contract. Also, the manager will be kept informed through variance reports. A very important factor that must be realized is that if at any time

Case exhibit 17–3

INDUSTRIAL DOOR, INC.

Statement of income and return,
Years ended May 31, 1974 and 1973

Income		1974	1973
Sales—materials and labor		$2,101,624.41	$1,463,593.05
Deduct, cost of sales		1,554,151.14	1,198,279.90
Gross profit on sales		$ 547,473.27	$ 265,313.15
Other income		4,979.61	4,896.07
Total income		$ 552,452.88	$ 270,209.22
Deduct expenses			
Selling expenses	$ 98,305.02		
General and administrative	423,718.37	522,023.39	252,313.56
Net income before taxes		$ 30,429.49	$ 17,895.66
Deduct income taxes		11,692.10	2,907.49
Net income		$ 18,737.39	$ 14,988.17
Add retained earnings—beginning		71,298.86	56,310.69
Retained earnings—ending		$ 90,036.25	$ 71,298.86
Net earnings per share		$ 108.94	$ 99.92

(172 shares 5/31/74; 150 shares 5/31/73)

during the contract period there are any unavoidable changes, a new contract should be negotiated. Again, as stated earlier, clear communication between manager and subordinate is essential.

Finally, Mr. Bostick states that the complexity, uselessness, and time involved in computing break-even points for all the products that Industrial Door sells and services are not worth the effort and cost. The monthly break-even point for all products has been computed at $138,000. Residential sales are considered to be the least profitable aspect of Industrial Door's business, but the capacity for this type of work is maintained in order to offer a complete line of service, and to maintain a competitive position.

He concluded by stating that whether the company would become part of J. M. Corporation is still under consideration.

SUGGESTED QUESTIONS FOR DISCUSSION

1. What does the case illustrate about industrial advertising?

2. What are the strong points of the firm? weak points?

3. Evaluate the present management set-up.

4. How can the firm handle its bad debts problem?

5. Given Mr. Bostick's objectives at the end of the case, would you recommend a merger with the J. M. Corporation? Why? Why not?

MAX'S EXXON SERVICE STATION

DESCRIPTION OF THE FIRM

Max's Exxon station is located at 3321 Main Street at the intersection of North Main Street and Sunset Drive in Albany, New York. The location affords easy access for traffic in either the north- and south-bound lanes of Main Street or the east- and west-bound lanes of Sunset Drive. Max's Exxon is designated as a dealer managed station. Max owns all of the inventory, but leases the premises from Exxon Corporation on a yearly basis.

The business is set up according to standard Exxon service station design. This includes two service pump islands and one self-service island. In addition, the station has two restrooms, and a concession area and a small office area located inside the station. Three service bays are located adjacent to the main building of the station. A public telephone booth is present on the far side of the service area. Tires, tire racks, and displays are set up around the outside of the station, and a lighted Exxon sign is situated at the intersection of the two streets.

As a result of the three gas pump islands, the station has sufficient equipment and ample space to service rush periods of the day. Customers want quick service, which is feasible with the three islands. Mr. Max indicates that he can service up to seven cars at one time. Customer waiting time is an important consideration in the service station business. The self-service island sells gas at a lower price than those serviced by attendants. This permits Max's to compete with independent stations such as the Spur Station across the street, which sells gas at a discount, under the posted price of the major oil companies.

The three service bays are equipped with the material and tools to perform everything but major car repairs like a complete overhaul of the engine, the rebuilding of an engine, or automatic transmission work.

On clear days, Mr. Max has a tire display set outside the station. A display of this sort often arouses a customer's curiosity about the price of tires, particularly when a sale is going on. The positioning of the lighted Exxon sign at the intersection allows for maximum customer viewing because it can be seen from all directions and for a distance of several hundred yards. The Exxon name generally means dependable service and credit card acceptance. The Exxon name itself undoubtedly accounts for a large share of Max's initial business. However, Mr. Max estimates that 80 per cent of his present business is repeat business.

MANAGEMENT

The lessee and manager of Max's Exxon is Charles R. Max. Mr. Max is thirty years of age, and married. He is a high school graduate and had five years of active duty and four years of reserve duty in the armed forces. In June, 1974, he entered the Exxon Retail Training School for its six week training program. Upon completion of this program, he went to work for Mr. Panschar, the then lessee and manager of the station, in September of 1974. In December of 1974, Mr. Max purchased the dealership from Mr. Panschar. Mr. Max does not consider himself an "authorized mechanic." However, he does feel that he can do most mechanical work, except for air conditioning. In fact, Mr. Max took over his mechanic's duties on one occasion for a three month period when the mechanic quit.

Mr. Max employs two full-time people who work 54 hours per week each. The mechanic receives $3.70 per hour and the driveway attendant receives $3.00 per hour. In addition, Mr. Max employs another driveway attendant, who works from 40 to 42 hours per week for $2.90 per hour, and a young woman, who keeps the station's daily records. She works on Monday, Tuesday, Wednesday, and Thursday afternoons and receives $40 per week.

When a mechanic is hired, that mechanic must own a basic set of tools, which includes small tools such as wrenches, pliers, and screwdrivers. Any major tools used are supplied by the business. Also, all employees are told by Mr. Max that, upon request and consent, they may be asked to take a polygraph test at any time deemed appropriate by Mr. Max. Mr. Max fires any employee who does not show initiative and/or productive work. Needless to say, any employee caught stealing merchandise or embezzling money is dismissed.

Most of Mr. Max's employees either receive on the job training or already possess the necessary skills for the job. However, Mr. Max does send his employees to the Exxon training center for training in areas such as "driveway sales techniques." This program teaches the employee the skills, knowledge, and tactics needed for efficient and effective service station operations, primarily, when dealing with the customer at the service island.

ADVERTISING

The business purchases cooperative advertising from Exxon at a cost of approximately $300 per year. Included in this package are visual displays and "gift of the month" mailers. Max feels that the "gift of the month" advertising (Mr. Max sends customer names and addresses to Exxon, and Exxon sends these customers a small gift and advertisements of the month's specials) is successful. Max's Exxon also uses leaflets to advertise certain specials that he is running for a particular month. When a customer pulls in for gas or service, that customer is given a leaflet that can be read while the car is being serviced. Max found that if the leaflets were distributed after the customer's car had been serviced, the customer did not read them. Because of telephone inquiries that he has received concerning the specials, Max believes that this advertising technique is very effective. The cost of printing a hundred leaflets is $3.00. Consequently, if one or two customers take advantage of the special offerings, this initial cost is justified.

MERCHANDISE

At all times, the station has the facilities and capable workers to perform "usual" mechanical repair work. In addition to selling gasoline, the station has a wide variety of motor oils and lubricants, tires, batteries, and windshield wiper blades. The station also serves as an official New York Vehicle Inspection Center. Exxon Corporation offers to its dealers a TBA Program (Tires, Batteries, and Accessories), which allows quantity discounts. For example, if a dealer buys ten tires, the eleventh will be free. Obviously, the TBA program offered by Exxon Corporation to its dealers is one of the ways Exxon is assisting the dealers in stocking their inventory. Mr. Max explained that when the stock is received, it is paid for immediately. Also, Mr. Max explained that, in his opinion, Exxon tires, batteries, and accessories are superior to those offered by Sears, Firestone, and the discount chains. However, because of the massive purchases made by these competitors, and the subsequent reduction in overall prices of their products to the consumer, Max is unable to compete effectively, unless he buys in volume. Because he has to keep working capital available for his gasoline purchases, Max has not been able to utilize effectively the volume discount purchase offered by Exxon.

THE INDUSTRY

Most major oil company service station dealers are highly dependent upon the policies established by the respective oil companies. The independent dealer, in effect, must manage his station according to the major oil company's policies and prices. Locally, Mr. Max faces intense competition in gasoline sales from such stations as Spur, Mobil, and Hess. The Spur station located at the same intersection as Max's Exxon usually keeps its regular gasoline priced one cent below Mr. Max. The Mobil station also located at this intersection generally keeps its regular gas priced one cent above Max's price. The competition obviously is keen at this particular intersection and Mr. Max must rely on regular customers and the convenience of credit cards to stabilize his sales. In regard to tires, batteries, and accessories, Max's prices are being undercut by Western Auto, Sears, and those discount stores located relatively close to his station. The discount stores often sell tires at the same price that Max pays for a similar Exxon tire.

FINANCIAL RECORDS

Max's Exxon uses a single entry bookkeeping system for daily records. All cash receipts and disbursements, credit card sales and receivables, dealer withdrawals, and vending machine receipts are recorded daily and submitted to an accountant on a monthly basis. In addition, daily pump readings are recorded on a checkout sheet. This is done to determine the number of gallons of each kind of gasoline sold.

This bookkeeping system affords Mr. Max a method to observe which products are selling well and which are not. Mr. Max is able to balance all cash disbursements and receipts each day. At the end of each day, he is able to account for all transactions that have taken place. Consequently, any mistake on his or his employees' part may be remedied immediately. By taking both meter readings and a "stick check" of the tanks at the end of each day, Max is able to account for all gasoline sales.

The Small Business Administration granted Max a loan of

$9000 in December of 1974 to purchase the business from Mr. Panschar. This loan, which has a 7.4 per cent interest rate, is to be paid in monthly installments of $158 for seven years. In addition, Mr. Max has a separate note with Mr. Panschar, for $4500, which is being paid in monthly installments of $65.08. In April, 1976, Max obtained a bank note for $5000 to pay 1975 Federal Income Tax. This note is being paid in monthly installments of $454 and will be paid in full by April, 1979. The taxes for which Mr. Max was liable were, in his opinion, a direct result of faulty quarterly tax predictions by his accountant. Specifically, for the first and second quarters of 1975, Mr. Max paid from $500 to $600 in estimated taxes. In the third and fourth quarters, after

Case exhibit 18–1

MAX'S EXXON SERVICE STATION

Yearly income statement, December 1975

Sales:		Costs:	Gross Profit:
Gasoline	$354,806	$280,197	$74,609
Oil and ATF	8,484	4,714	3,770
Vending	4,597	3,148	1,449
Tires and tubes	8,599	6,839	1,760
Batteries	2,281	1,653	628
Accessories	16,342	8,954	7,388
Labor	9,930	–	9,930
Totals	$405,039	$305,505	$99,534

Gross profit	$99,534.00
Operating expenses:	
Wages	34,928.00
Payroll tax	2,983.00
Insurance	446.00
Depreciation	1,476.00
Supplies, tools, and station use	3,451.00
Professional service	666.00
Stamps–premiums	75.00
Advertising and Promotion	651.00
Rent	12,188.00
Laundry–Uniforms	247.00
Station car	1,093.00
Maintenance and repair	
Utilities	2,427.00
License and taxes	407.00
Discounts and refunds	528.00
Outside services	553.00
Interest	643.00
Bad debts	575.00
Cash shortage	3,746.00
Total expenses	$67,083.00
Net profit	32,451.00
Withdrawal: Mr. Max	$17,094.00

revising the income projections, his accountant suggested that Max pay $2500 for each of these quarters.

Mr. Max's current financial data are displayed in Case exhibits 18–1 through 18–4.

PLANNING

Forecasting is a problem for Mr. Max. Prices of petroleum products are constantly fluctuating. Consequently, the service station manager is left with little or no control or knowledge of sudden cost increases. Exxon currently does not honor credit card receivables toward purchases of petroleum products. Since it takes approximately ten to fourteen days to receive payment from Exxon for credit card sales, Max often incurs working capital shortages. Mr. Max estimates that he has about

Case exhibit 18–2

MAX'S EXXON SERVICE STATION

Balance sheet, December 31, 1975

Assets

Cash on hand	$ 1,732.00
Bank—commercial	3,409.00
Bank—petroleum	
Credit cards	10,991.00
Depository receipts	1,767.00
Inventory—gas	6,060.00
Inventory—other	13,434.00
Equipment	6,821.00
Accounts receivable	2,423.00
Deposits	200.00
Capitalized S/T and supplies	94.00
Other—interest	2,084.00
Total assets	$49,015.00

Liabilities

Sales tax	$ 126.00
Federal withholding tax	1,389.00
Social Security	1,167.00
State and local withholding tax	288.00
Unemployment	270.00
#1 notes payable—on company	9,638.00
#2 notes payable	465.00
#3 notes payable	4,174.00
Accounts payable	2,857.00
#1 accounts payable	2,932.00
Owners equity	25,709.00
Total liabilities and owners equity	$49,015.00

Case exhibit 18–3

MAX'S EXXON SERVICE STATION

Year-to-date income statement, June 30, 1976

Sales:		Costs:	Gross Profits:
Gasoline	$214,296.00	$179,661.00	$34,635.00
Oil and ATF	4,818.00	2,842.00	1,976.00
Vending	3,457.00	2,722.00	735.00
Tires and tubes	6,579.00	6,153.00	426.00
Batteries	1,696.00	1,333.00	363.00
Accessories	12,959.00	6,758.00	6,201.00
Labor	7,210.00	—	7,210.00
Totals	$251,015.00	$199,469.00	$51,546.00

Gross profit		$51,546.00
Operating expenses:		
Wages	20,558.00	
Payroll tax	1,759.00	
Insurance	885.00	
Depreciation	743.00	
Supplies, tools, and station use	2,139.00	
Professional service	150.00	
Stamps–premiums	129.00	
Advertising and promotion	1,968.00	
Rent	5,734.00	
Laundry–uniforms	153.00	
Station car	474.00	
Maintenance and repair	188.00	
Utilities	1,755.00	
License and taxes	580.00	
Discounts and refunds	519.00	
Outside services	726.00	
Interest	327.00	
Bad debts	1,228.00	
Cash shortage	2,183.00	
Total expenses		$42,198.00
Net profit		$ 9,348.00
Withdrawal: Mr. Max		$19,188.00

$4000 tied up in his credit card accounts receivable at any given time.

PRICING

Retail prices of petroleum products are regulated by governmental mandates. Dealers are allowed to raise and lower prices on their gasoline only within a given range. For example, the maximum amount that Mr. Max can charge for premium gasoline (Extra) is 69.0 cents. This is based on a 1972 price of 34.9 cents, plus an increase of 34.1 cents. He is presently charg-

Case exhibit 18-4

MAX'S EXXON SERVICE STATION

Balance sheet, June 30, 1976

Assets

Cash on hand	$ 671.00
Bank—commercial	1,132.00
Bank—petroleum	–
Credit cards	14,770.00
Depositary receipts	1,456.00
Inventory—gas	465.00
Inventory—other	21,856.00
Equipment	6,171.00
Accounts receivable	2,246.00
Deposits	200.00
Capitalized S/T and Supplies	–
Other—interest	1,886.00
Total assets	$50,853.00

Liabilities

Sales tax	150.00
Federal withholding tax	1,019.00
Social Security	1,044.00
State and local withholding tax	258.00
Unemployment	241.00
#1 Notes payable—on Co.	8,696.00
#2 Notes payable	4,192.00
#3 Notes payable	4,547.00
Accounts payable	6,628.00
#1 accounts payable	3,420.00
Owner's equity	20,658.00
Total liabilities and owner's equity	$50,853.00

ing 66.0 cents per gallon for Extra. In addition, in this area, the law currently states that unleaded gasoline cannot be sold for more than 1.0 cent per gallon above the price of regular gasoline. Any prices in violation of these standards subject the violator to criminal charges.

Suggested retail prices for the complete line of TBA are established by the Atlas company, an Exxon subsidiary. Mr. Max feels that the prices set by Atlas are competitive with those set by other wholesalers. However, as noted earlier, discount stores are able to purchase in much larger quantities.

Labor costs are difficult to determine in the service station business. Certain regular service station jobs, such as tune-ups, oil changes, lubrications, and brake jobs, have a fixed cost. For example, labor charges on a tune-up on a V-8 American car are $15.00. This is the standard labor charge, and the brand of parts used determines the complete cost. However, labor costs for jobs that are not done as frequently are computed through the use of a flat rate table, which specifies the job to be done and the estimated labor time involved. Consequently, the cost of labor on repairs is computed by multiplying the estimated time for a job by the flat fee of $11.00 per hour. For example, if Mr. Max were to replace disc pads on a car, and it took him thirty minutes, the labor charge would be $5.50. Max feels that the use of the flat rate table prevents arbitrary price setting and gives the customer an accurate cost estimate before the job is done.

Mr. Max's credit policy is stringent. He exhibits a sign on his cash register that states "no credit." However, he does allow the area post office trucks, the Commission for the Blind, and the Coca-Cola Company credit on a monthly basis. Max states that these accounts are always paid in full, and should he need the money from these accounts earlier than the end of the month, he can collect it from them.

SUGGESTED QUESTIONS FOR DISCUSSION

1. After managing the station for less than three years, Mr. Max went out of business. Why do you feel this happened?

2. Evaluate Mr. Max's qualifications for operating a service station.

3. Evaluate Mr. Max's planning process prior to purchasing the station; after purchasing.

4. Evaluate the controls that Mr. Max utilized in his firm. What controls should he have utilized?

5. Evaluate Mr. Max's withdrawal of $19,188 in 1976. What effect can this have on a firm?

AMERICAN HYDRAULIC PAPER CUTTER, INCORPORATED

HARRY MARCOWITZ—ENTREPRENEUR

Harry Marcowitz is president of American Hydraulic Paper Cutter, Incorporated, but he doesn't like to use the title. "Does a corporation president dress like this?" he asks, gesturing at his plaid shirt and grease-smudged work pants in his rented machine shop in this Chicago suburb of Elk Group Village, Illinois. "I'll call myself a president when I can come to work in a suit and tie and spend my time dictating letters to a secretary."

That day might come fairly soon, or not at all. Right now, American Hydraulic Paper Cutter, Incoporated consists mostly of Mr. Marcowitz, his employee Sigmund "Ziggy" Janiszewski, and a 6000-pound industrial paper-cutting machine he built with his own hands at a personal cost of more than $25,000. The company, incorporated just last April (1974), has yet to make a delivery.

A good indication of how things might turn out should come within three months, about the middle of February, 1975. Mr. Marcowitz is negotiating for a $10,000 bank loan that would help enable him to build three machines he will offer for sale before the year is out. He already has a commitment—and a $4000 down payment—on one of those three. "When I get the loan and make those other two sales, I'll have the money to go into serious production." he says. "Once people realize how good my machine is, I'll be in good shape."

And what if the loan and the sales aren't forthcoming? "I don't think negatively," declares Mr. Marcowitz, an energetic, strongly built man of 49 years who at various times in his life has

---

been an Army aircraft mechanic, coal-truck driver, baby photographer, and life-insurance sales representative. "Starting this business has been my dream. If I got discouraged easily, I'd never have come this far."

PROBABILITY OF SUCCESS

Going into business for oneself requires more than dreams and an optimistic nature, however. Being a fledgling entrepreneur isn't easy in the best of times, and these aren't the best of times. Besides the usual difficulties that go with turning out a product and beating entrenched competitors to sales, the new business owner, perhaps more than most, must wrestle the twin bullies of tight and expensive money, and high and rising costs.

"In more normal times, a guy going into the manufacturing business has about a 60-40 chance of succeeding for, say, at least a half-dozen years," says an official of the federal Small Business Administration in Chicago. "With the economy off the way it is, I'd estimate the odds at no better than 50-50. For other types of new businesses, the risk is even greater."

Those who follow the field say that the apparent reasons most new businesses fail are a lack of sales, capital, or both, or an inability to control costs. But a further search almost always points to the inexperience or ineptitude of management.

"Typically, the person starting the business is a salesman who doesn't know much about production or an engineer who doesn't know much about sales," says Rowena Wyatt, manager of the business economics department of Dun and Bradstreet, the credit reporting firm. She continues that the current high costs and interest rates have put an added premium on management expertise, noting that her company's statistics show business failures to be on the rise this year for the first time since 1970.

THE ENTREPRENEUR AS A SALESMAN

Harry Marcowitz knows first-hand about costly money and materials. The bank he's trying to borrow from is asking interest of 11.5 per cent, up from about 10 per cent a year ago, and he says that everything he buys "gets more expensive every time I place an order." As a result, he's had to increase the base price he plans to charge for his machine to about $14,000, from about $13,000 last year.

Yet he professes to be fatalistic about such matters. "When's the right time to go into business? I could die waiting for the right time," he says. "My machine is ready and I have to make a living. Now's as good a time as any."

Harry Marcowitz's background of skills and experience would seem to give his endeavor a better chance of succeeding than most. Foremost among these is a mechanical aptitude that amazes those who know him, considering that his formal training in the area consists of a few shop courses in high school and his World War II instruction in fixing aircraft engines (he dropped out of junior college after a year).

His sales ability is attested to by his record as an agent and district manager for Equitable Life Assurance Society of the U.S. in Chicago; in two of his eight years with that company his sales of life insurance topped the one million dollar mark.

He has a good knowledge of the printing and bindery industries—his main targets for sales—because he spent four years traveling around the country selling and servicing paper cutters for Schimanck-Universal Company, a now-defunct German firm whose machine his is patterned after. His reputation in those industries is good. "When I need a new cutter, Harry will get the order," asserts Charles Soukup, president of Repro Incorporated, a Chicago printing firm that has two Schimanck machines. "Getting service is a big thing with our equipment, and Harry never let us down."

Finally—but not incidentally—people who have done business with Mr. Marcowitz say he is a very nice fellow. "People do things for him because they like him," says David Kayner, his attorney. Mr. Kayner should know. Earlier this year he was approached by Mr. Marcowitz to handle his incorporation; he wound up donating his legal services and investing $1000 in the business in return for a small ownership share.

All this might not be enough, however. "Harry has an excellent machine and he's selling it at a good price, but the market might not be there," says one large Chicago distributor of printing gear. "Things in the business have been pretty tight lately. They might not loosen up in time to get him off the ground."

Mr. Marcowitz came to his present vocation by a circuitous route. After leaving college shortly after the war ("It wasn't my bag, as the kids today might say") he spent several years helping out around his father's retail coal business. Then came five years as a baby photographer; he says the business prospered but folded because of "partner trouble."

His eight-year stint as an insurance representative was remunerative (he earned as much as $20,000 a year) but unsatisfying. "I've got this thing about machinery—I'm happiest when I'm taking something apart and putting it back together so it runs right," he says. "I can't explain this ability; it must be a gift from God. Gloria, my wife, has perfect musical pitch. She can play the piano by ear. She can't explain how she does it, either.''

THE RIGHT PLACE AT THE RIGHT TIME

He got into paper-cutting machinery by chance. "In 1966, I went to a printing-equipment show with a friend who was in the cutter business," he relates. "When I got there, the thing wouldn't work for them. I'd never seen one before, but I took off my jacket, sat down on the floor and fixed it." The company offered him a job on the spot and he took it, even though it meant less income than he was making selling insurance.

The firm—Schimanck-Universal—"made a marvelous machine, but had problems," Mr. Marcowitz goes on. "It was mostly with the parts—they were slow in coming from Germany. On top of that, some of the owners didn't get along well with each other. They closed down in 1969.''

That left Mr. Marcowitz without a job and with a decision to make. "I could have gone back to selling insurance, but I really loved that machine," he says. "It was hydraulic, so it didn't have all those gears, clutches, and brakes and things that mechanical machines have. I know how it worked and I figured I could make one myself, or even make it better. Gloria, who's a teacher, said she'd support us both until I get going.''

So Mr. Marcowitz moved into a friend's vacant storefront and went to work—from memory, without any drawings or specifications. "The German thing was so fouled up I couldn't get their plans, but I asked a patent lawyer about it and he told me I could go ahead," he says. He made a wooden model of the machine's big parts and contracted with a foundry to cast them. Then he went to another friend's machine shop and spent a year making the small parts himself.

In January 1971, the prototype was ready for testing. "The big moment came, and a lot of the guys from the shop gathered around," he says, gesturing for dramatic effect. "I went into the men's room and got a piece of two-ply toilet paper. I separated the layers, put one of them under the blade and pushed the buttons. When the blade came back up, it looked like the paper hadn't been cut and the guys thought I'd blown it. But I wet one finger and peeled back that piece of toilet paper along the cut the blade made. It was as clean a cut as you'll ever see.''

A year of more testing and alterations followed, and when 1972 began, Mr. Marcowitz was ready to go into production, but problems intervened. One prospective partner—who had a substantial amount of cash to invest—mulled things over for a year before deciding against it. Mr. Marcowitz then took his cutter to a machine shop owner who had expressed an interest in making many of its parts, but the shop got so busy with other work that this owner had to decline, too.

Late last year Mr. Marcowitz took a trip to Spain with an eye toward going into manufacture there, but he wound up deciding to set up shop around Chicago. "I might have saved a few dollars by having the machine built in Spain, but it would have meant lots of traveling, a language barrier, and all sorts of shipping problems, and I wouldn't have had a good handle on quality control," he says.

"Also, I got to thinking that there are enough Volkswagens and Toyotas on the road. America used to make good, competitive products, and there's no reason we can't again. My parents were immigrants and this country was good to them. Maybe I can pay some of it back by setting up a business that employs people and makes something useful."

FINANCING THE NEW BUSINESS

The past five years have been expensive ones for Mr. Marcowitz. He has continued to work part-time servicing Schimanck machines, earning about $7000 a year, and he has put almost all of that into his business. The remainder of the $60,000 or so the company has used to date has come from investments by a relative, by employee Janiszewski, by Mr. Kayner, and by Mr. Marcowitz's accountant.

Expenses have been particularly heavy since June, when the company moved into its 3700-square-foot shop here. Mr. Marcowitz has purchased—for cash—a lathe, drill press, steel-cutting saw, and forklift truck, costing about $8000 in all. A milling machine, costing another $4800, has been ordered.

The equipment would have been more expensive if not for Harry's resourcefulness. "I got a terrific bargain on the forklift," he points out. "On the lot, it sounded terrible, but I put in a $25 water pump and now it works great."

And he had some help from his friends. One gave him a welding machine; another sold him the almost-new drill press for $125, one-third its original cost.

The company has kept up with its bills so far, but not without some difficulty; when Mr. Marcowitz's application for a $20,000 bank loan recently fell through, he had to turn to a relative for $10,000 in operating capital. He still needs $10,000 more, but he thinks he can get it without too many strings as a result of the $4000 down payment he has collected for his first sale.

THE FUTURE: A QUESTION

He and Mr. Janiszewski, an expert machinist, are already making parts for the three machines. There have been enough nibbles to make him confident he will get those sales. He plans to produce twelve machines in 1975, "and after that, who knows?"

Mr. Marcowitz asserts, and people in the business agree, that his paper cutter has some competitive advantages over others. Most paper cutters used in the U.S. are made in Europe, and recent devaluations of the dollar have pushed up their price so Harry's cutter will sell for about $2000 less than those models. Its hydraulic operation should cut down on parts and maintenance costs for users, and its safety features are said to be excellent; the cutter's 42-inch blade won't drop unless two widely separated buttons are held down, keeping operators' fingers out of danger.

Automation is the wave of the future and Mr. Marcowitz is providing for that. He's designed a cartridge program that can be attached to his present machine and automatically move the paper to be cut into different positions. That won't be ready until next year, though.

"The main thing will be for Harry to get some machines into commercial operation. That way customers can see how they do," says the printing machinery distributor. "It's kind of a vicious circle—you can't sell many machines unless you've proved they work, and you can't prove they work until you sell some."

A YEAR LATER: ACTUAL VERSUS FORECASTED RESULTS

A year ago Mr. Markowitz had not forecasted taking the industry by storm, but he had expected to sell at least twelve of his paper cutters.

Today, the 50-year-old Mr. Marcowitz is still wearing work clothes. Instead of selling twelve machines, he has sold two. He remains confident of eventual success, but he admits that getting started in business has been much tougher than he expected.

"The water is up to here and I'm yelling 'don't make waves,'" he laughs, placing his hand, palm down, just under his nose. "The machine is as good as I knew it would be, but selling it is something else. It's awfully hard to get people to part with their money these days."

PROBLEMS CONFRONTING THE NEW FIRM

Those who follow the subject say that the first three years of a business' life are critical; according to Dun and Bradstreet, the credit reporting concern, about 30 per cent of the corporations that fail do so within that period. That figure could well be higher this year. Dun and Bradstreet says 10,755 companies bit the dust this year through November 20, a 17 per cent increase from the same 1974 period.

Mr. Markowitz's costs have risen about 15 per cent, forcing him to increase the price of his basic cutter to about $17,000 from $14,500 a year ago and reducing his price advantage over some competitors.

Raising money proved to be more difficult than he had imagined—a $10,000 bank loan he had been negotiating fell through. And he underestimated his prospective customers' desire for an attachment to his machine that would automatically position the paper to be cut. He has spent most of the past six months working with a nearby electronics firm on such a device.

Most importantly, the many inquiries he has received—including some spurred by the *Wall Street Journal's* story about him—have yet to turn into many sales.

"A company in Cincinnati that read about me is talking about distributing my cutter," he says, "That would set me up pretty good, but they're waiting to see how my automatic spacer works. Other guys say they'll buy my machine when the one they've got breaks down. Others say they'd buy it now if they had the cash. God willing, if I can hang in long enough for these things to work out, I should be all right."

ATTEMPTS TO RESOLVE PROBLEMS

Harry is scraping along, trying to keep his shop running at the lowest possible cost. For six years, he has kept his project afloat partly by doing repair work on paper cutters made by Schimanck-Universal Co. He has earned about $8000 repairing Schimancks this year, and he has put all of it back into his business. He has never drawn a paycheck, from his company; he lives on the earnings of his wife, Gloria, a schoolteacher.

Besides the profit from the two new machines he has sold, he has taken to dealing in used paper cutters; the sale of one he took in trade netted him about $800. When a friend's machine shop failed earlier this year, he let the man move into his shop in return for paying one-third of his rent and utility bills.

He has also used his self-taught mechanical skills to acquire bargains in some needed equipment. In this category is his current prized possession—a sparkling, 1973 Chevrolet van that carries his firm's name and the slogan "Buy American" in red, white, and blue.

"I used to haul parts around in my old Buick, but it broke down last summer," he explains. "A guy I knew had the van in his lot, but he thought the motor was shot so he let me have it for $800. Turns out, all it needed was a part, which I picked up for $35. The painting and lettering cost me $250. When you take out the 500 bucks I got for my Buick, I got a beautiful van with only 25,000 miles on it for $600."

The former coal-truck driver, baby photographer, and life-insurance sales representative's first year in business had other, more substantial, bright spots. "You can't imagine the feeling of elation I had when those two new machines I sold went out my door," he exclaims. "It's what I've been working for all these years."

Better yet, the two cutters have performed very well. "It's an excellent heavy-duty machine. I'm very satisfied," says Charles Soukup, president of Repro Incorporated, a Chicago printing concern that purchased one.

"It's a fine machine—extremely well built," says Bruce Hansen, vice president of Kinney Printing Company, also of Chicago, which bought the other. He adds: "We had a few minor problems at first, but Harry straightened them right out. It's nice having a machine you can get fixed quickly if anything goes wrong"—a reference to the fact that most paper cutters used in the U.S. are foreign-made.

AN ENTREPRENEUR'S DILEMMA: SPREADING HIS TIME OVER TOO MANY ACTIVITIES

Both of Mr. Marcowitz's initial customers knew him from his Schimanck days, and he realizes that such contacts won't be enough to sustain his enterprise indefinitely. His operation still consists of just himself and one employee, the machinist who owns a small share of the business. This leaves Harry precious little time for the crucial job of selling.

He has rejected the idea of hiring a manufacturers' representative to do that work. "I'd take on a rep if I could find one who'd work on straight commission, but they all want a salary, too, and I can't afford that," he says.

So he must find a distributor of printing equipment to handle his product. That's a difficult task for any new manufacturer because distributors typically have long-standing connections with established lines.

Two distributors have talked to Mr. Marcowitz about selling his cutter. He is furthest along in his talks with Nessler and Wagner Company, a 56-year-old Cincinnati concern that recently ended its ties with a foreign maker.

George Wagner, president of Nessler and Wagner, has seen Harry's machine and likes it but he adds that "a lot of details have to be worked out" before an agreement can be reached. "There's the matter of price, of course, and there's the spacer, which we'll have to have," Mr. Wagner says. "Also, we sell only in Ohio, Indiana, Kentucky, and West Virginia, and that's not a big enough territory to handle profitably a product as expensive as Harry's. We're trying to put together a network of six or eight independent distributors who would sell the cutter nationally. If we can do it we would buy twelve or fifteen cutters from Harry the first year and as many as forty a year after that, but it's a pretty big 'if.' "

FUTURE PROSPECTS: REVISITED

The mere prospect of such a break-through sustains Mr. Marcowitz's natural enthusiasm; he is full of plans to convert his one-room shop into an honest-to-goodness production line.

"Ziggy and I have made enough parts to turn out the first dozen machines ourselves, but after that we'll need more employees," he says, eyes aglow. "We've got the process down pat, so that's no problem. The money we'll get in down payments will give us all the capital we'd need. Of course, to turn out forty machines, we'll need more space, but there's a building right across the street that would be perfect."

He quickly comes back down to earth, however. "If, God forbid, we don't get a big order right away, we'll still get by. If I haven't learned anything these past six years, I've learned how to skimp and scrounge, and I can do that some more."

"The important thing for me is to build a solid company that isn't at the mercy of creditors," he continues. "I could have had that $10,000 bank loan, but I walked right out when they asked my wife to co-sign the note for me. What kind of business is that? She has nothing to do with the company!"

"After the article in the *Wall Street Journal* appeared, a couple of people offered me money. One woman even came down here with a check for $11,000 she wanted to give me. But I don't need that kind of responsibility. I've got enough worries without worrying about a poor woman's life savings. I'm not built that way. We'll make it because people will realize we have a superior machine. It's inevitable. I won't be defeated."

SUGGESTED QUESTIONS FOR DISCUSSION

1. Is Harry Marcowitz personally prepared to start and manage his own firm?

2. Evaluate Mr. Marcowitz's market research.

3. Has Mr. Marcowitz realistically forecasted his cash needs for his first three years of operation?

4. Evaluate Mr. Marcowitz's comment stating that his wife is not part of the firm in light of the fact that her income supports them.

5. What steps would you recommend that Harry Marcowitz take at this time?

BARNES LUMBER COMPANY

Raw material, equipment, and financing problems of a small lumber company

INTRODUCTION

Jack Barnes, age 55, is one of three owners of the closely held Barnes Lumber Company. Jack formed the company, and watched it grow from a small sawmill, producing five thousand board feet of lumber per day in 1946, to its present capacity of sixty thousand board feet per day. In order for him to expand to that level, however, he took in two partners, Jim Lewis and Harold Thompson, to provide expertise in forest management and engineering, and office management and sales. Jim Lewis graduated from a forestry school in the Pacific Northwest with a degree in forest engineering. He supervises the raw materials side of the company and is responsible for acquisition, harvest, and transportation of all raw materials. Harold Thompson attended a business school and has primary responsibility for the office procedures as well as sales management. His job includes everything from preparing the balance sheet to closing orders for lumber in distant markets. The company went public in 1946. Jack Barnes owns most of the stock, so he oversees the other managers. However, he manages the mill himself.

This case is reproduced with the permission of its author, Dr. Stuart U. Rich, Professor of Marketing and Director, Forest Industries Management Center, College of Business Administration, University of Oregon, Eugene, Oregon. It was prepared by Graduate Assistant Bill Blankenship, under the supervision of Professor Rich, and was designed for class discussion rather than to illustrate either effective or ineffective handling of an administrative situation. Copyright, 1974, by Professor Stuart U. Rich. Distributed by the Intercollegiate Case Clearing House, Soldiers Field, Boston, Mass. 02163.

BACKGROUND

The company mill is located in Gladewater, a town of about two hundred people on the east slopes of the Coast Range in Oregon. The primary species used in manufacture is Douglas fir, which accounts for 95 per cent of the mill volume produced annually. The western hemlock, white fir, incense cedar, and western red cedar which the company obtains in its timber sales are sold primarily as logs to other mills. Barnes Lumber Company produces a wide range of lumber products in its mill, most of which require old-growth, clear Douglas fir logs as primary raw materials. Jim Lewis has developed a "trade" policy with other mills whereby he trades the logs of the species other than Douglas fir to these mills for high-quality, old-growth Douglas fir.

The mill produces lumber ranging from 1" by 3" boards to 10" by 12" mine timbers. The mill also produces a wide variety of specialty products including stadium seats, lumber for boats, and truck body stock. These specialty items account for 6 per cent of present production. Additionally, 10 per cent of dimension lumber production is exported to Holland and Germany. The export market requires rough, very clear lumber because the lumber is remanufactured in Europe. This export market pays a premium over domestic markets and is free of many of the export restrictions which plague the export of logs (in contrast to lumber). The other lumber produced by the company is sold primarily in Northwest markets, except for a small amount of utility grade, which is shipped to Southern California. All lumber sales are "freight on board" at the mill.

The company owns three thousand acres of old-growth Douglas fir with a total volume of approximately ten million board feet. Company policy dictates holding this timber in reserve, and purchasing all timber from government and private timber sales. The company is surrounded by Bureau of Land Management (BLM) land. In the past, Jim Lewis has been able to purchase most of the required timber from the BLM sales, which were generally held in May and June. Sometimes he purchased logs on the open market in addition to trading for them.

The company does all its own logging, hauling, and road building. Jim Lewis feels that as long as the company can log and haul as cheaply as it can subcontract, the company will continue to do its own logging and hauling. The company has never purchased a timber sale farther than 49 miles from the mill and does not plan to do so in the immediate future.

The company's logging equipment consists of a recently purchased, reconditioned, 1966 M-2 Berger tow-truck and yarder, a 1961 M-3 Marion heel-boom log loader, a 1966 C-6

Euclid crawler with U-shaped blade, and a 1968 D–6c Caterpillar crawler with straight blade. The C–6 Euclid is used primarily for road building, and the D–6c is used to log timber sales, which are on relatively flat ground and do not require the use of tower and yarder. The company owns three logging trucks: a 1961 Peterbilt, and two recently purchased 1972 Peterbilts. Originally, the 1961 Peterbilt was kept as a spare truck when the other, older Peterbilts were traded for the new, 1972 trucks. It also owns two late-model International dump trucks which are used for road building. One of the trucks is also fitted with a water tank for use as fire truck during the summer.

The mill contains a seven-foot headrig. Recent investments in the mill improved efficiency to the point at which a 35 per cent overrun was realized. Jack Barnes is upset, however, at the requirements the ecology movement has placed on him. Oregon has passed a law outlawing wigwam burners, and small mills like Jack's are among the hardest hit by this legislation. To continue operations, Jack has been forced to install a $50,000 machine for converting the bark waste to hog fuel, since he can no longer burn it. The hog fuel nets no return; he simply gives it away to the fuel companies in the local area. He figures he is better off than some companies, who have to pay the fuel companies to truck the bark away. Additionally, he has been forced to install a hopper to hold the shavings made by the planer. These shavings are sold to companies for use in manufacturing flakeboard, and the mill's sawdust is sold to a pulp mill for use in manufacturing tissue paper. His net return from these by-products, however, does not pay for the operating costs and initial investment of the equipment he purchased to convert the waste materials. He figures he is losing $5000 per year converting the waste, instead of burning it.

COMPETITION AND SOURCES OF TIMBER

Since the Barnes Lumber Company is surrounded by BLM land containing fine-quality, old-growth timber, the firm has experienced increasing competition in bidding for the timber sales near their mill. United States Papers borders the company to the north, and Lebanon Lumber Company borders them to the south. Jack Barnes feels that he deserves consideration from the other companies in keeping the stumpage bid within his grasp because he built his mill and established his area of raw material supply before the other two companies became competitors. U. S. Papers is a very large, international company that could be extremely competitive because they could use much of the timber presently being logged by Barnes. However, their chief forester is a good friend of Jim Lewis, and they manage to carry this friendship forward in timber bidding.

Lebanon Lumber Company is a cutthroat operation. It is a regional multi-product company, which buys much of the old growth Barnes seeks, logs the sales, and sells the logs to many of the plywood companies in the local area. The plywood peeler logs characteristically sell for more than Barnes can afford to pay for them. Lebanon requires 15.75 million board feet of logs per year, of which it usually seeks 15 percent from Barnes' area. Lebanon lost an export lumber contract to Barnes and intends to get revenge in future timber sales (see case exhibit 20–1). Lebanon needs 30 percent hemlock in its annual production. Lebanon management knows it can probably bid Jim Lewis up on sales to his maximum bid, then subsequently buy the hemlock, white fir, and cedar from him for the appraised price because Barnes has little use for these species. Also, Lebanon management knows they can trade clear Douglas fir logs for Barnes' hemlock at an even better exchange rate. Jim Lewis knows he needs to calculate an exact price he can afford to bid for each upcoming sale. He will also have to bid on every upcoming sale in order to secure his supply of old-growth logs, even though some sales do not contain as much Douglas fir as he would like. And he knows that he will have to sell or trade most of the unusable species to Lebanon (see Case exhibit 20–2).

Recently the BLM was starting to place more thinning sales on the market. In addition, many small private land owners, interested because of the high stumpage prices presently being paid, approached Jim Lewis and asked him to buy their timber. Jim has turned these sales down in the past because he needed old-growth timber to manufacture his current products, and the present mill cannot saw a log smaller than fourteen inches in diameter. Logs smaller than fourteen inches in diameter, which Barnes obtained on timber sales in the past, were either sorted at the mill and sold to other mill operators, sold at the landing, or left in the woods. These logs account for 20 percent of present logged volume. Jim wonders whether the addition of a small mill to handle logs down to five inches in diameter would be a worthwhile investment. He talked to mill-equipment sales representatives and determined that a mill which would produce 32 thousand board feet (Mb.f.) of lumber (mostly utility grade) per shift would require an investment of $750,000, including the purchase of a log stacker to move the logs around from the cold deck to the feed ramp of the mill. The small mill, according to the salesmen, should produce a 50 percent overrun on small logs. Jim believes he could obtain 4.5 million board feet of these small logs per year with no difficulty, and these logs probably will not cost more than $150 per Mb.f. Milling costs on the old

Case exhibit 20-1

BARNES LUMBER COMPANY

Upcoming timber sales, May 24, 1973,
Bureau of Land Management

Parcel #	Species	Estimated volume (thousand board feet)	Appraised price/Mb.f.	Estimated volume times app. price
14	Douglas fir	3,599	$160.35	$577,099.65
	Hemlock	724	82.55	59,766.20
	Western red cedar	179	83.55	14,955.45
	Total	4,502		$651,821.30
	Log export volume allowed: 360 Mb.f.			
16	Douglas fir	908	144.50	$131,206.00
	White fir	3	86.00	258.00
	Hemlock	46	81.35	3,742.10
	Western red cedar	53	77.20	4,091.60
	Total	1,010		$139,297.70
	No logs shall be exported			
17	Douglas fir	885	146.75	$129,873.75
	White fir	15	85.55	1,283.25
	Hemlock	10	83.85	838.50
	Incense cedar	103	74.05	7,627.15
	Western red cedar	37	74.35	2,750.95
	Total	1,050		$142,373.60
	No logs shall be exported			
18	Douglas fir	3,697	145.25	$536,989.25
	White fir	22	91.00	2,002.00
	Incense cedar	33	80.85	2,668.05
	Total	3,752		$541,659.30
	Log export volume allowed: 300 Mb.f.			
19	Douglas fir	2,742	137.30	$376,476.60
	Hemlock	36	75.00	2,700.00
	Western red cedar	209	65.00	13,585.00
	Total	2,987		$392,761.60
	Log export volume allowed: 239 Mb.f.			

mill are $29.50 per Mb.f., log scale, and would be $17.50 per Mb.f., log scale, in the new mill.

Jim knows that if his company does not add the new mill, they will have to change their method of scaling these small logs. The logs are presently sold on a lump sum basis; that is, a prospective buyer offers a total price for a deck of logs. Jim is sure the company loses 35 percent of the scale volume of these logs by selling them in this fashion. The reason for this 35 per-

Case exhibit 20-2

BARNES LUMBER COMPANY

Selling price and anticipated sales, 1973

Product	% of Company Sales	Average price 1972	Anticipated price 1973
Export clear lumber (European markets)	10	$397/Mb.f.	$489/Mb.f.
Crossarms and mine timbers	18	$257/Mb.f.	$389/Mb.f.
Large planks	29	$227/Mb.f.	$327/Mb.f.
Timbers	12	$314/Mb.f.	$425/Mb.f.
Utility	25	$167/Mb.f.	$207/Mb.f.
Stadium seats; other specialty products	6	$460/Mb.f.	$555/Mb.f.

cent loss is that the scaler does not have time to properly scale the many small logs in these decks. The scaler who presently works for them is swamped with work. Adding a new scaler would mean a cost of $17,500 a year, including industrial safety insurance and employer taxes. Other options include weight scaling of the trucks, but this requires an investment of $17,500 in scales, and requires an additional worker to operate the scales, and to maintain the scales and the area around them. Jim estimates this man would cost the company $11,500 per year. An electronic log scaler costs $75,000 and would require the logs to be run through one at a time, which means many handling problems, so Jim dropped the electronic scaler from consideration.

EQUIPMENT CONSIDERATIONS

Some of the company's logging equipment is rapidly becoming a maintenance headache. Jim thought the purchase of the new tower and yarder would solve many of the company's logging shutdown problems, but recently the loader was causing as many delays as the old yarder had caused. The 1956 model loader is in need of extensive maintenance. Normally, Jim can rely on logging 160 days of the year, but a look at 1972 trucking days showed that only 151 days of logging occurred. All but one of the extra down days was caused by the loader. Jim has talked with some of the equipment dealers and found that he likes the newer Link-Belt loaders best of all, but he feels the company is not in a financial position to buy a new one. He compared specifications of the new loaders with two used models and found:

Brand	Model year	Purchase price	Annual scheduled maintenance cost[1]	Annual allow. for unscheduled maint.[2]	Useful life	Salvage value
Link-Belt	1973	$121,740	1.458%	$4,500	10 years	$5,500
Lorain	1973	$127,100	1.65%	$4,300	10	$6,000
Link-Belt	1968	$ 66,500	3.1%	$4,900	6	$5,600
Bucyrus-Erie	1967	$ 51,200	4.7%	$6,100	5	$5,400

[1]Annual scheduled maintenance cost is a percentage of purchase price. These figures were supplied by the equipment dealers.

[2]Both new machines carry two-year warranties covering *all* unscheduled maintenance not caused by operator negligence or abuse. These figures were obtained from owners of similar loaders.

The decision of which loader to buy is an important one, because he does not want to be shut down for maintenance because of the old loader this year. The winter has been an unusually dry one, so he expects an unusually dry summer with more logging days shut down for lower humidity than normal. All dealers offered him $6000 trade-in allowance for his old loader. Another alternative is that of leasing the loader at 4 percent of the purchase price per month with no maintenance expenses by the Barnes Lumber Company.

Compounding the equipment issue is that of the truck. Jim Lewis was reluctant to keep the 1961 Peterbilt truck when the other two Peterbilts were traded in last year on the two new trucks. Although he had originally planned to use one truck as a spare, he found that the 1961 Peterbilt is being used every day, because the logging operation requires three trucks to keep up with the new tower and yarder. Jim figures hauling costs average $7.25 per thousand board feet on his average haul of 25 miles. Unscheduled maintenance on the 1961 Peterbilt pushed this rate to $7.50 for the last six months. Jim used the $7.25 rate for devising his timber-bidding strategy and is convinced keeping the old truck will change his hauling rate to $7.50. He knows the trucks average four loads of logs per day, and figures 25 miles is the average length of haul. After a good deal of debate with Jack Barnes and Harold Thompson over the investment in a new truck, Jim obtained the following facts on which truck to purchase, if the company decided to purchase (all trucks listed are new):

Brand	Purchase price	1961 Peterbilt trade-in allow.	Useful life	Salvage value
Peterbilt	$31,089	$5,500	12 years	$5,500
Diamond Reo	$26,564	$4,100	10	$3,500
Mack	$36,500	$5,500	12	$5,950
Kenworth	$31,197	$5,000	12	$5,700

Jim did not compare prices of the lighter trucks, such as Ford, Chevrolet, and International, because he prefers the ruggedness of the trucks listed above. He prefers Peterbilts because of the dependability of these trucks in the past. The Mack dealer pointed out, however, that the Mack truck, coupled with the Mack engine, offers these advantages over the other trucks in his field of consideration:

1. only six forward gear speeds, instead of twenty as in other trucks. This results in 30 to 40 percent less gearshifting, or an estimated 10 to 15 percent less maintenance than his current Peterbilts,
2. 10 percent better fuel economy.
3. 10 percent higher trade-in value.
4. only Mack trucks currently meet 1975 emission standards, so no modifications would be necessary in the next two years to meet emission standards.

Jim estimates that all trucks, except the Mack, would get five miles per gallon fuel mileage, and diesel fuel will cost 25¢ per gallon. Maintenance and upkeep average $2100 per year on the Peterbilts, so he decided to use this base for computing maintenance costs.

Jim is also considering leasing the trucks through a leasing agency. The agency will supply any one of the trucks he desired, at a rate of 1.8 percent of the purchase price per month. These payments would be paid only during the months the trucks are in use, so that no payments would be due from November through February when the trucks are inoperative. The leasing agency would perform all maintenance and upkeep. Barnes Lumber Company would just supply the fuel and driver. At any rate, the truck decision needs to be made in the very near future because the drivers have just informed him that the old Peterbilt needs an engine overhaul.

Jim looks to a new loader as a means of reducing logging costs from the present $28 per thousand board feet to about $26 per thousand board feet. He believes a new truck can effectively reduce average hauling costs by up to $7.00 per thousand board feet. But he is not sure what to buy and whether the company can afford to buy this equipment.

OTHER CONSIDERATIONS

One of the mill workers pointed out that the headsaw has to saw cants into smaller pieces before they go to the resaw. This results in a 30 percent loss of production at the headrig. Jack Barnes toyed with the idea of installing a "pony" headrig in the main sawmill in order to relieve the load on the headrig. The pony headrig would cost $41,000 to install, have a twenty year useful life, and cost $1000 annually to maintain. Jack is aware that the remainder of the present mill is not able to handle the entire output of the headsaw, if the headsaw does not saw up the cants. Bottlenecks in the manufacturing process would allow only 67 percent of the increase in production to pass through the mill without stopping the headrig, if the pony headrig were installed. The installation of the pony headrig would also require the hiring of another sawyer. The union wage for sawyers is currently $6.26 per hour.

Mr. Thompson, the office manager, is reluctant to change any of the financing policy the company has been following. His logic is that since the operation is relatively small, the company cannot afford to go heavily into debt and rely on monthly payments to creditors. Several times in the past, a large company produced an excess of one of Barnes' main products. This company subsequently dumped these products on the market at a very low price, causing Barnes to stockpile its products until the price went up. Sometimes this waiting period consumed three to four months. Barnes would not have met its monthly payments had it a large number of investments. Barnes therefore acquires financing on three-year contracts with one-third down, and the balance due in three years on all investments greater than $10,000 and less than $50,000. The company uses a three-year payback criterion for all small investments. All single investments greater than $150,000 use appropriate long-term financing. The penalty for following this procedure is that interest rates on the three-year contracts average 9.5 percent. The Gladewater bank has informed Jack Barnes that they will provide interest rates of 8.25 percent on these same contracts, if paid back in monthly installments. Currently, the company has $75,000 financed in three-year borrowings, and any purchases of new equipment would raise this figure radically. Mr. Thompson continued, to point out that the corporation paid income taxes on $28,000 worth of earnings last year and the higher interest rate gave them a good tax break. Jack Barnes does not know whether to believe him or not.

Other companies in the local area have been forming so-called export companies, and Jack Barnes considered doing likewise. The company does not export any logs because it harvests its timber from federal lands, which have an export quota, and Barnes feels the amount of timber allowed for export from any one sale is generally too small to worry about. The 10 percent profit (after harvesting costs and hauling costs to the port) obtained from exporting logs is less than the return to be made on manufacturing and selling the lumber. The company nonetheless does export lumber. The advantage of forming an export company is that one can leave one half of the year's profits as retained earnings in the export company and not pay income tax on those earnings until the earnings are taken out. Thus the company can hold money until a less profitable year before taking the money out. Forming the company would cost up to $5000. Jack is not sure he wants to invest that money, even if the tax break is good.

CONCLUSION

Barnes Lumber Company is left with many issues to be resolved. Jack Barnes wonders if the installation of the small mill is a worthwhile venture and if he should install a pony head-rig in the main mill. Jim Lewis knows that he will have to buy some of the upcoming timber sales, but he has not calculated how much he can afford to pay for the timber. He wants to replace the old equipment, but does not know which of each to buy. Financial considerations plague the company. More important, all three owners are worried that they cannot afford to pay the high prices for raw materials in the future that some of their competitors are already paying. Once a sale is purchased, the company would have to wait a year before it could harvest the sale, since it has a backlog of previously purchased sales to log. Thus management is afraid the price of lumber will drop drastically at any time, leaving them holding a lot of high-priced stumpage.

SUGGESTED QUESTIONS FOR DISCUSSION

1. What are the factors to be considered by Barnes in deciding whether to invest in a small mill to handle logs down to 5 inches in diameter?

2. Advise Jim Lewis regarding:
    a. purchase of new equipment
    b. purchase or lease of new trucks.

3. Establish a concise decision model to evaluate the situation in the conclusion of the case.

J. W. ADAMS COMPANY

ENVIRONMENTAL FACTORS AND OVERVIEW

The J. W. Adams Company, Incorporated, was founded in April, 1953, by J. W. Adams in an industrialized midwest town of 235,000 population. The company is engaged in the service and installation of heating and air conditioning units and is a closed corporation operating in the one to two million dollar sales range.

In 1967, the company divided into three departments: Service, Negotiated Sales, and New Construction. This system functioned well through 1970, taking in contracts ranging from $30,000 to $200,000.

Tom Adams, 45 years of age, has been with the company since 1955, and assumed the presidency in 1970. He holds a degree in electrical engineering from Cleveland State University.

Mike Deder is the executive vice president in charge of the shop and installation. Deder is 36.

Joe Doakes is the service manager. Doakes is 38.

Al Fern is the sales manager, and is responsible for generating sales for both the Adams Service Company and the J. W. Adams Company. Fern is 47.

John Thom is the manager of the parts department. Thom is 27.

Bernice Pete is the bookkeeper–payroll clerk.

The secretary is Janice Bert.

This case was prepared by Drs. Joseph C. Latona and Jonathon S. Rakich of The University of Akron as a basis for class discussion rather than to illustrate either effective or ineffective handling of an administrative situation. Presented at the Intercollegiate Case Clearing House and Southern Case Research Association Workshop of the Intercollegiate Case Clearing House, Atlanta, Georgia, November 11–13, 1974. Copyright 1974 by The University of Akron.

The remaining personnel are distributed: five in installation, five in the shop, one in parts, twelve in service, and one in the office. Also, the sole sales person is currently concentrating in residential sales for the Adams Service Company, due to an inability to sell industrial accounts. The average age of non-salary personnel is 34.8 years, with ages ranging from 18–56. Only two employees are scheduled for retirement in the next ten years. No current management personnel are due for retirement within the next 10 years.

In 1970 and 1971, the profit margin declined because of three major jobs that proved to be financial losses. These jobs were two university buildings and one building for a local service organization. The firm eliminated bidding on new construction in October of 1972. The company has not recovered from these losses and at the end of fiscal 1973, both Service and Sales, and New Construction were deeply in the red.

MARKETING

The J. W. Adams Company is at present suffering from the effects of several problems, the most pronounced of which, according to Tom Adams, is the company's poor profitability position. Mr. Adams believes that one of the most important, if not "the" most important, reasons for the profit problem is that the company has no viable financial feedback system. Actual and estimated job cost comparisons suffer because of this feedback deficiency. Adams has all but given up on establishing a system by which he may receive this critical information on cash flow.

From a marketing viewpoint, however, an even more critical problem exists for the company, affecting not only its short-term operations, but its long-term operations and, quite possibly, its very survival in the industry. Projected sales for this year (1974) indicate a $300,000 drop from the previous year's sales of $1,000,000. Ninety per cent of these projected sales are estimated to be primarily repeat business. The service department is expected to produce $600,000 in revenue, which represents a very slight increase from last year.

The type of work the company handles is confined generally to the designing, remodeling, and servicing of small commercial and industrial structures. The residential operations have been turned over entirely to the newly incorporated Adams Service Company. Adams Service does only remodeling work in the residential markets.

Nearly all sales, aside from service, are negotiated sales. Bidding new construction proved disastrous for the company and contributed much to the company's present predicament. According to Adams, "if we can't get the mark-up, then we don't take the job." The company, however, now operates to break even.

With regard to sales, Mr. Adams is apparently aware of the problem, but at the same time believes in a low-key kind of promotion:

> We are limited in sales at the present time. The company has no sales program as such. In fact, we've never had a marketing program; we're not even sure what marketing is. Overall, we've been guilty of some wishy-washy thinking in the sales department in the last two years. I don't like the local newspaper. Newspaper advertising never got us any notice. Radio promotion always got us attention, but no business. Homebuilder shows have value, but take too much time, although we have received thirty to forty bona fide leads. Pen and pencil sets with our name on them used to be popular, but if I'd consider anything now, it would be handout material, such as brochures. Right now, the best advertising we have is our name painted on the sides of our trucks.

Judging from Mr. Adams' statement above, it seems apparent that the lack of sales is a direct result of the company's perfunctory marketing program. In addition to the ineffective promotional campaign, the advertising budget for the 1974–1975 period has allotted $8,000 to sales and $2,000 to service—a drop from the previous year's total of $20,000. This budget figure appears to have been arbitrarily set and the dollar deduction from the previous year seems to be based primarily on Mr. Adams' opinion that advertising is ineffectual for the industry.

Mr. Adams characterizes his sales staff, consisting of a sales manager and one new sales person:

> Al Fern, the sales manager, has been with us ten years. Although he lacks polish, he gets sales. Right now, Al can only devote twenty to twenty'five per cent of his time to actual sales managing. Tim Bach, the new salesman, has potential, but needs to settle down. He's working primarily in the residential section now, since he doesn't know how to get an in with the commercial market yet.

Al Fern, in turn, states his views on the company and its promotional activities:

> The bulk of our business is in new construction for small office and manufacturing buildings. We'll negotiate sales for both large and small jobs in the commercial and industrial field.
>
> Advertising for us is a sore point. The brochure we had made up, we didn't use, because it doesn't reflect our real image. It might appeal to someone who's very artistic, but it wouldn't appeal to our clientele. Our newspaper advertising has been sporadic and home shows don't pay off. We have no way of tying any sale to a show.

The radio promotions once used by the company had been assigned to an FM radio station operating from a suburb. Though Mr. Fern was unaware of any research involved in choosing the morning hour promo-coverage, he feels certain that the radio station itself made the time-slot decision.

The company issued a new commission policy in March, 1974, with regard to wages and salaries for the sales personnel. Some of the more important points are:

1. maximum commission on each sale shall be established at the time of quote;
2. commission paid, in dollars, will depend on the actual results of the installation when compared to estimate (a reduction, equal to the percentage over estimate, will result, except that no commission will be paid for jobs with a gross profit of less than 23 percent, unless previously authorized by the sales manager or company officer);
3. for sales-estimators who do not receive fringe benefits, other than transportation, a split of fifty–fifty on profit over 30 percent will be paid (these people will not be eligible for company profit sharing);
4. sales personnel receiving fringe benefits will be eligible for the company profit sharing program;
5. weekly draw of sales person will be set at approximately $250, depending on sales record.

Mr. Fern feels that competition has not been a significant factor for the company. When asked, however, why the residential segment of the company had failed, Mr. Fern remarked, "Our advertising for residential was a complete flop all the way." The main reason for the failure, though, he attributes to the fact that J. W. Adams is known primarily for its commercial and industrial work. "Other companies who specialize in residential got the jobs because a lot of people didn't know we even did residential. We still receive calls on the residential jobs, but refer them immediately to Adams Service." Mr. Fern sums up the company's line of thought in deciding to shift residential work to Adams Service by saying, "We finally came to the conclusion that you just can't sell commercial and residential out of one operation."

Neither Mr. Adams nor Mr. Fern has indicated any plans to introduce the new company to the public via a promotional campaign. Business at present is generated solely by word-of-mouth and the efforts of Tim Bach.

Mr. Fern comments, too, on the company's present operations and what he feels are the sales department's major problems:

I don't want to go back to bidding new construction. We should stay away from those large jobs in order to maintain our reputation. Sales are slow in coming because of economic conditions. People are price buyers right now rather than quality buyers.

Our immediate problem is a lack of orders, but the real problem is the lack of personnel. I think we need one or two dedicated people who could bring in the business. We already have 40 per cent of the good customers in the area through repeat business. Eventually, the company could support four good men, but right now we just don't have the money.

INDUSTRY TRENDS

The following is a brief review of industry background, trends, and projections. For the building industry as a whole, privately financed housing starts in 1973 amounted to 2.04 million dwelling units, down from 2.36 million in 1972. Total investment in all types of new construction for 1973 was reported at $135.5 billion, or 9.4 percent greater than in 1972. Privately financed residential construction amounted to $58 billion and industrial construction reached $6 billion in 1973. The dollar figure for commercial projects amounted to $15.5 billion and all publicly financed construction last year totaled $32.6 billion. However,

the 9.4 percent rise in dollar volume of construction last year is quite misleading . . . the figure is inflation-logged. But, even more significant, the overall data mask the reversal in the direction of construction activity that occurred last year. The rate of new investment in residential building peaked in February-March. By year-end, the tempo of residential construction had slipped 11 percent, if measured in current dollars, and 18 percent, if measured in dollars of constant value. The highest rate of public works spending occurred in January, 1973. By year-end, government investment in new construction had dropped 4 percent in current dollars and 11 percent in constant dollars. The peak in all types of new construction came in July, when a seasonally adjusted annual rate of $138.4 billion was reached. But, by the end of the year, the overall pace had declined 3 percent in current dollars and 6 percent in constant dollars from the July level.[1]

With respect to projections for 1974 and the building industry, first half ". . . housing starts will probably be 30 percent fewer than a year ago. Earnings comparisons of most companies dependent on the residential market will be unfavorable. . . ."[2] Residential construction however, will probably begin to recover by July.

An improved flow of savings into thrift institutions presages a higher rate of housing starts in the second half . . . privately financed housing starts should total 1.73 million, or 15 percent less than the 2.04 million of 1973 and 27 percent below the record 2.36 million starts of 1972. Whenever housing volume drops below 2.0 million for very long building materials and components come into easy supply since the building materials industry has the capacity to support two million starts a year. This year's estimated starts total will be almost as far below the two million dividing line as 1972's bumper starts crop was above. Thus, the pinch of shortages will end this year unless the energy emergency seriously impairs production of building supplies.[3]

---

[1]"Building Industry," *Value Line Investment Survey,* February 15, 1974, p. 851.

[2]Ibid., p. 851.

[3]Ibid., p. 851.

Presently, industrial construction is doing quite well due to new capital investment and commercial construction is flattening out due to general economic conditions and the energy crisis.

Expectations for the air conditioning and heating market in particular are provided by some of the leaders in the industry.

Mr. N. S. Stake, vice president and general manager of the commercial division of Honeywell, Incorporated, in Minneapolis, Minnesota, states that traditional business indicators ". . . give a mixed outlook. Hospital and industrial building activity would appear to be heading up; schools, colleges, and officies should stay about the same; and apartments, shopping centers, and stores will probably be drifting downward."[4] With regard to the energy shortage and its effects, Mr. Stake feels that by its very nature, ". . . the energy crisis should benefit the controls industry. For all types of buildings—schools and skyscrapers, hotels and hospitals—will be looking for more sophisticated systems to wring maximum performance from every operating BTU."[5]

Mr. Mathew G. Bolin, president of the Airtemp division of the Chrysler Corporation, in Dayton, Ohio, feels that "high capacity, applied air conditioning equipment should continue to enjoy increased sales for 1974 in spite of the energy crisis talk. Airtemp Division, Chrysler Corporation, is projecting an increase of almost 20 per cent for the coming year . . . all in all, we see 1974 as a good year for the applied systems and commercial unitary portions of the air conditioning industry."[6]

Mr. A. Whittell, Jr., the president of Raypak, Incorporated, in Westlake Village, California, believes that indicators for 1974 ". . . point to an increase in the amount of industrial heating. Manufacturing capabilities are running at peak capacity, with lead times running to six months in many areas. In terms of total dollars to be spent this year in heating, we expect an increase of 10 per cent. Unit volume will be down, however. If we look to commercial and industrial heating requirements, the possibility of a new construction market of 85 per cent and a replacement market of 15 per cent is very real."[7]

Mr. H. J. Baker, president of the Mechanical Contractors Association of America, Inc., Indianapolis, Indiana, thinks that

"the year 1974 should be a year of continued growth for the heating, piping, and air conditioning industry. In general, I expect an increase of approximately 14 per cent over 1973. The average mechanical contractor finds his volume of work leaning heaviest toward the heating,

[4]"Air conditioning market for 1974: repeat of 1973," *Heating/Piping/Air Conditioning*, January 1974, pp. 100–101.

[5]Ibid., p. 100.

[6]Ibid., p. 100.

[7]Ibid., p. 102.

Case exhibit 21-1

$3.45 billion market: estimated installed value of air conditioning equipment in 1974

Market	Total (mill.)	Change from 1973	Unitary pkgd. sys.	Central Built-up
Schools	$ 344	−3.4%	59%	41%
Hotels/motels	293	0.0	67	33
Stores, supermarkets, and shopping centers	497	+1.2	74	26
Hospitals	466	±2.6	28	72
Industrial plants	499	+5.5	55	45
Multiple dwellings	585	−4.7	68	32
Office buildings	765	−0.7	32	68
Total market	$3449	0.0	52	48

ventilation, and air conditioning sides. Statistically speaking, approximately 60 per cent of the work installed by the mechanical contractor is in this area. There are a couple of items, however, that could have a negative effect on our industry. One would be material supply. We are substantial users of metal products of all types—from the structural, piping, and sheet steel standpoints. Some circles feel that pricing controls do not favor the types of materials our industry consumes in large volumes and that basic raw materials have been diverted to other more profitable areas. The materials situation is serious; if it continues in the same direction, it will have a very definite adverse effect. The mechanical contractor's favorable position will continue for several years because he installs the systems that are a direct result of our technological advances and ecological problems. The primary challenge to the entire construction industry will be the requirement for manpower, both in the craft and management areas. Effectively employing the unskilled worker is one means of combating this expected craft shortage."[8]

An HPAC Survey of a $3.45 billion market shows installed values by building and system type in Case exhibit 21-1. Overall, this table shows a no-growth situation for the industry. Industrial plants, however, as indicated, are expected to experience the greatest increase while multiple dwellings are expected to suffer the greatest decrease.

ACCOUNTING-FINANCE

In the past five years the J. W. Adams Company has spent a total of $78,103 in legal and auditing fees. This averages $15,620 per year and would be an adequate salary for an accountant or financial administrator.

---

[8]"Air Conditioning Market for 1974: repeat of 1973," p. 102.

The company has never employed an accountant or finance manager. Financial records were handled by a Mrs. Rule who was more a bookkeeper with experience than an accountant with knowledge to analyze. As for her system, Tom Adams states that she was the only one who knew how it worked. She retired in 1972 and Adams presently oversees the accounting function.

Adams states that he has no faith in a statement. Since the Adams Company is a closed corporation, it does not normally require audited statements, although they were required for some of the loans the company has received.

When asked why he does not hire an accountant, Mr. Adams stated, "No money."

The company employs a production manager, a sales manager, a man to take care of inventory, and a president, but no accounting or finance manager. Adams also handles the firm's financial matters along with being a general manager. There was no mention of time sheets being placed in the folders. Cost sheets, a summary of time and material, are kept. Partial billings are completed at the end of the month with production supplying job summaries to insure proper billing. When the job is completed, the cost sheets are summarized and a final bill is sent out. No analysis of the job is performed other than for billing purposes.

Since 1968, nearly $100,000 in unapplied labor costs have been recorded in the sales department alone. The service department has recorded almost $4000 in the same period. The cost for unapplied materials for the same period was nearly $60,000 (see Case exhibit 21–2). Since this does not include 1972, the average per year was $16,963 for labor and $9912 for materials. These figures indicate a need for improving the collection and assisgnment of material and labor costs.

Case exhibit 21–2

J. W. ADAMS COMPANY

Excerpt from financial statement

	Service Department	Sales Department
1969 unproductive labor	22,933	2,867
unproductive materials	2,046	–
1970 unproductive labor	27,596	4,212
unproductive materials	307	7,622
1971 unapplied labor	20,995	9,232
unapplied materials	419	–
1972 unapplied labor	18,437	30,920
unapplied materials	542	419
1973 (not recorded in financial statements)		
1974 unapplied labor	8,000	4,000
unapplied materials	500	200

Case exhibit 21-3

J. W. ADAMS COMPANY

Statement of sources and uses of funds, 1974

Use	Amount	Percentage
Increase cash	8,979	6.0%
Increase notes and A/R—employees	2,776	1.9
Increase inventories	12,182	8.2
Increase prepaid expenses	2,878	1.9
Increase deposits	7,292	4.9
Increase cash value of insurance	1,231	0.8
Increase leased equipment	8,202	5.4
Increase unamortized lease costs	10,425	7.0
Decrease notes and mortgages S/T	56,455	37.7
Decrease officer advances	118	0.1
Decrease customer advances	925	0.6
Decrease union dues and funds	7,461	5.0
Decrease accrued payroll	19,654	13.2
Decreased accrued payroll taxes	7,617	5.1
Decrease accrued sales taxes	3,063	2.1
Decrease retained earnings	125	0.1
	149,383	100.0%

Sources	Amount	Percentage
Decrease trade A/R	47,144	31.6%
Decreased fed. income tax refund	7,486	5.0
Decrease property and equipment	2,410	1.6
Decrease land contract	7,436	4.9
Decrease Worker's Comp. premium	9,856	6.6
Decrease stock subscription rec.	983	0.7
Increase trade A/P	53,319	35.7
Increase accrued interest	1,613	1.1
Increase accrued property taxes	3,000	2.0
Increase accrued welfare, pension, and industry funds	1,933	1.3
Increase deposits on leased equipment	4,636	3.1
Increase long term notes and mort.	100,786	67.5
Decrease of profit to date	(91,219)	(61.1)
	149,383	100.0%

Sixty-seven per cent of Adam's funds in 1973–1974 came from decreasing trade receivables and increasing trade payables (see Case exhibit 21–3).

Considering the importance of budgeting and cash flows, and the time necessary to do them properly, an accountant or finance person is a necessity.

Adams' present collection procedure is:

1. list accounts over 30 days;
2. person who deals with particular customer call each account;
3. repeat the calls;
4. turn (reluctantly) accounts over to collection agency (charge of 25 per cent on all collected accounts).

Adams has also indicated a policy of finance charges. This was a very good idea because it induced customers to pay on time and avoid the extra charge. The only problem is that the present bookkeeping machine cannot compute the charge. Therefore, it must be done by hand. Recent bills sent out did not contain the charges, since there was no time to compute them. He indicated this will be corrected.

Tom Adams indicated he plans to reduce inventories to around $20,000, yet in the 1973–1974 fiscal year they increased by $12,182 (see Case exhibit 21–4). There is presently no system of inventory control.

Case exhibit 21–4

J. W. ADAMS COMPANY

Comparative balance sheets

Assets	1973	1974
Cash	3,157	12,136
Trade A/R	281,576	234,432
Current installments land contract	7,337	7,337
Notes and A/R employees	11,948	14,724
Fed. income tax refund receivable	7,486	
Inventories	89,068	101,250
Prepaid expenses	5,226	8,104
Deposits	264	7,556
Marketable securities	5,888	5,888
Property and equipment	38,716	36,306
Cash value—officer life insurance	6,525	7,756
Leased equipment	6,401	14,603
Land contract	86,233	78,797
Worker's Compensation premium	9,856	
Stock subscription receivable	4,035	3,052
Unamortized lease costs		10,425
Total assets	563,716	542,366

Liabilities		
Notes and mortgages payable	141,693	85,238
Trade A/P	163,273	216,592
Customer advanced payments	925	
Officer advance	118	
Union dues and funds	13,462	6,001
Accrued interest	1,612	3,225
Accrued payroll	19,654	
Accrued payroll taxes	15,791	8,174
Accrued sales taxes	2,489	(574)
Accrued property taxes		3,000
Accrued welfare, pension, and industry funds		1,933
Deposits on leased equipment	500	5,136
Notes and mortgages payable	61,139	161,925
Capital stock	136,934	136,934
Retained earnings	6,126	6,001
Profit to date		(91,219)
Total liabilities	563,716	542,366

Case exhibit 21-5

J. W. ADAMS COMPANY

Operating ratios

Ratio	Adams 1970	Adams 1971	Industry 1971	Adams 1972	Industry 1972
Quick	1.2	1.2	1.2	1.1	1.2
Current	1.7	1.5	1.4	1.6	1.5
Fixed/worth	.4	.5	.4	.6	.4
Debt/worth	2.5	3.2	1.3	2.5	1.3
Sales/rec.	7.1	5.4	5.9	7.7	6.5
Rec. coll. per.	51.0	68.0	51.0	47.0	55.0
Cost of work in progress/inv.	12.9	16.7	——	17.3	——
Days in inv.	28.0	22.0	——	21.0	——
Sales/W.C.	12.1	12.1	6.6	14.0	8.2
Sales/worth	8.5	10.9	5.4	8.9	6.1
% net income before tax/worth	15.5	(9.8)	18.8	1.9	18.1
% net income before tax/total assets	6.3	(3.0)	8.7	.8	6.2

According to Adams, the lag between payments and receipts is an industry-wide problem. Materials for a job must be purchased in advance and payment is not received until the job is completed. A job may last as long as a year or more and consequently, needed cash is tied up for extended periods of time. This problem is somewhat alleviated by escalation clauses in the contracts, which provide for partial billing of delivered materials. With all sales being negotiated, more emphasis could be placed on percentage of completion contracts.

SUGGESTED QUESTIONS FOR DISCUSSION

1. How can the company improve its marketing efforts?

2. Evaluate Mr. Adams' reason for not hiring an accountant, "no money."

3. What do you think of the changes in the company's cash account from 1973 to 1974?

4. Review Case exhibit 21-5 and determine the type of actions indicated by the ratios.

HARTEN HOUSE MOTOR INN
AND RESTAURANT

INTRODUCTION

The Harten House motor inn and restaurant is located in West Chester, Pennsylvania. Harten House has been operated by H & H, Incorporated for three years.

HISTORY OF THE FIRM

1951. A. T. Jordan and H. L. Pearce formed a partnership for the purpose of constructing, owning, and operating an Esso service station in West Chester.

1951. Service station sold to the Pennsylvania State Highway Department to allow for highway construction.

1954. Jordan and Pearce constructed a twelve unit motel in West Chester.

1960. West Chester Motel sold to Mr. Gene Jents and Associates for $40,000.

1963. First National Bank and Toggs Savings and Loan Association, both located in West Chester, granted a loan of $400,000 to Jordan and Pearce, to construct a thirty-one unit motel and restaurant on a site approximately fourteen acres in area, located at the junction of Highway 202 and the 202 bypass in West Chester.

1969. The restaurant was extensively damaged by fire. A new loan was negotiated through Toggs Savings and Loan Association and First National Bank for $430,000. The proceeds of this loan were used to liquidate the debt remaining from the previous loan, to repair and enlarge the restaurant facilities, and to add a forty unit expansion to the motel.

However, because of certain problems Jordan and Pearce revoked the lease of "USA Hosts" within six months. Jordan and

Pearce then leased motel and restaurant to Mr. B. C. Kanaught, who held this lease until March 1, 1972.

March 1, 1972. Motel and restaurant leased to Mr. D. Q. Hanson under the auspices of "Talley-ho Motor Inn." This lease expired March 1, 1973, and was not renewed.

April 1, 1973. A corporation was organized by ten West Chester citizens, each with an equal investment of $5000. The corporation, registered as H & H, Incorporated, purchased Harten House Motor Inn and Restaurant from Jordan and Pearce for $50,000 cash and a second mortgage. No formal notice for a loan application was made by H & H, Incorporated. Thus, Jordan and Pearce were not granted releases by the lenders, and the loan documents in force are those that were originated in 1969, which are not officially those of H & H, Incorporated. Payments on this loan are now being made by H & H, Incorporated.

July 1973. Mr. Gordan Roberts, one of the original investors of H & H, Incorporated, died. His share of the corporation was absorbed by the remaining members.

January 1976. Harten House Motor Inn caters primarily to commercial travelers, although some business is derived from family travelers. The motel is open 24 hours a day, 7 days a week. The amounts charged per night by the motel are:

single (1 bed) — $12.00
single (2 beds) — $16.00
double (2 beds) — $18.00

The restaurant observes these hours:

Monday–Friday 6:00 A.M. — 10:00 P.M.
Saturday   6:00 A.M. — 11:00 P.M.
Sunday   7:00 A.M. — 2:00 P.M.

The restaurant caters to motel guests and to the population of West Chester and the surrounding area. Located in the same building are a ballroom and lounge. The ballroom is used for the Sunday buffet and is rented for special occasions and private parties. It is used seven or eight times a month.

MANAGEMENT OF THE FIRM

In April, 1973, when H & H, Incorporated purchased Harten House Motor Inn and Restaurant, H. L. Pearce was asked to stay on as manager of the motel. Mr. Pearce agreed, and is currently in this position. Due to poor health, Mr. Jordan is no longer actively engaged in any facet of the motel and restaurant operation.

As manager of the Motor Inn, Mr. Pearce has responsibility for all phases of operation at the motel, and exercises direct control over ten employees, consisting of four desk clerks, five maids, and one housekeeper. Mr. Pearce also assists with the management of the restaurant, supposedly on a very limited basis.

Since February, 1973, Mrs. Jean Harris has been the day manager of the restaurant. She is responsible for all phases of operation at the restaurant, including hiring and firing, and supervising and purchasing. Mrs. Harris works from 8:00 A.M. until 4:00 P.M. or later. She exercises direct authority over eleven employees, including five waitresses, three dishwashers, two cooks, and one part-time waitress.

In addition to Mrs. Harris, there is a morning hostess who works from 6:00 A.M. to 2:00 P.M. Another hostess is employed from 2:00 P.M. until closing time.

CREDIT

The management of the motel-restaurant has tried to enforce a stringent credit policy without harming business operations. Credit cards and personal checks in the amount due, payable to the motel-restaurant, are honored. These credit cards include: American Express, with a five per cent service charge to be paid by the motel-restaurant; Mastercharge, with a four per cent service charge; and BankAmericard, with a three per cent service charge. A folio system is used whereby the customer may charge the price of the room, the telephone, and the meals on one check. This system is built into the cash registers. The main source of problems for management is bad checks. Even though thorough identification forms are maintained, these bad accounts persist. Adjustment for these accounts is not made immediately.

The restaurant offers an open account policy to a few individuals and companies in the area, who are reputable customers of long standing. Payments are sent to the restaurant either weekly or monthly. Occasionally, the restaurant will cash a check in excess of the amount of the meal but only for individuals who are known well by the management.

EMPLOYEES

The motel-restaurant employs 32 people on a full or part-time basis. The majority of the employees are unskilled. The only skilled personnel are the night auditor for the motel, the cooks, and restaurant managers.

All hiring is done by personal interview and by application. All applications are kept on file in compliance with federal law, and hiring is nondiscriminatory. Attrition takes care of most undesirable employees, and if Mr. Pearce is forced to let someone go, he confronts them personally and privately. Under the original ownership of Pearce and Jordan, employee benefits included medical insurance for all, a small amount of life insurance on the management personnel, a pension plan, and workers compensation. Under the present management there are no employee benefits other than workers compensation.

Repairs and maintenance are handled by Mr. Pearce. If he is unable to do the work himself, he contracts it to others. The manager of the lounge adjacent to the restaurant is responsible for the inventory of liquor.

LEGAL STRUCTURE

Although H & H, Incorporated has legal title to all property and equipment of the Harten House Motor Inn and Restaurant, Jordan and Pearce are still responsible for the loan as specified in 1969. They are protected by a second mortgage on the property, and a personal note of $10,000, from each individual in H & H, Incorporated. Togg Savings and Loan Association and the First National Bank hold the first mortgage.

When H & H, Incorporated originally took control of the motel and restaurant, the intention of the members was to lease the restaurant because the motel was very profitable and the restaurant was not. They intended to have income from the restaurant lease and from the motel. However, the corporation was unable to lease the restaurant. Consequently, at the end of the 1974 fiscal year, the accountants for H & H, Incorporated advised the members to reorganize their ownership of the motel and restaurant under subchapter S of the Internal Revenue Code to take advantage of the losses in their taxes.

MARKETING

There are no specific monies allocated to advertising or other forms of sales promotion. All advertising is presently directed to the motel and none to the restaurant. Newspaper ads specify the motel's accommodations, the lounge, and ballroom dances. The local newspapers are published three times a week. Some radio and direct mail advertising is utilized. In the latter, a select group in West Chester receives a leaflet, which announces a function or dance to be held at the facilities. Specialty advertising has been employed, usually at Christmas, in which pens and car cup-holders, displaying the name, address, and telephone number of the motel-restaurant, have been distributed.

In the past, the motel leased ten billboards from the 3M

Company, which were effective. These billboards are located on the main roads approaching West Chester.

CURRENT PLANNING TECHNIQUES

There are some repairs going on at both the restaurant and the motel; the trim and several rooms are being repainted.

There are plans to actively promote the ballroom. As mentioned before, the ballroom is presently used only seven or eight times a month, despite being not only the largest facility of its kind in West Chester, but the best, with a dance floor, a band area and stage, air conditioning, and a separate entrance from the restaurant. It is not actively promoted for bridal receptions, and only occasionally promoted for dances and special functions.

A night auditor is also needed. Since this is the most difficult position in the whole operation to fill, it is estimated that some time will be required to replace the man now in the position. The present night auditor is a retiree who is not up to the job any longer.

PRICING

As stated before, the nightly room rental at the motel is:
        Single (1 bed) — $12.00
        Single (2 beds) — $16.00
        Double (2 beds) — $18.00
The motel caters extensively to working people and travelers in the area. State highway workers, surveyors, and sales representatives, who come into town on Monday night and stay through Thursday night, are given a weekly rate that is slightly lower than the normal, daily rate. Harten House being one of only three motels in West Chester, this traffic more than compensates for the usual midweek slowdown, and accounts for the almost eighty-five percent occupancy rate in the seventy unit motel. The motel's rates are reasonable for the area.

The breakfast menu has an acceptable variety and is competitively priced; this is true for the lunch buffet. This is corroborated by the fact that the restaurant has a good breakfast and lunch trade.

The dinner menu, on the other hand, is both over-ambitious and over-priced, so the dinner trade is "poor." The management feels the restaurant is the cause of the losses incurred — specifically, the dinner meal. In an attempt to rectify this, the restaurant has held "special" nights for families and to feature certain entrees. Recently, these specials have been advertised on the radio and in the newspaper. This has not been done on a regular basis, however, and does not appear successful.

The lounge is attached to the restaurant, has a separate entrance, and is competitively priced with mixed drinks selling for $1.25 and up, and beer selling for fifty cents.

The ballroom price is negotiable. When an organization wants to rent the facilities, the price is either a percentage of the receipts or a set fee, depending on the services rendered.

INVENTORY

The only inventoried items in the motel, other than the furniture, are the items most likely to be stolen: ashtrays, washcloths, and towels. These items are stored in the office and replaced as needed. Other linens are supplied by a linen service and the loss on all other items is negligible.

The facilities at the restaurant are excellent. There are walk-in coolers and walk-in freezers. There is also a chiller for high turnover items such as eggs and salads. There is, however, no inventory control. When an item is needed in the kitchen, the person who needs it simply gets it. There is free access to all food, no locks on any of the storage areas, and no formal reorder policy. When an item runs low, it is reordered (some items are replenished on a regular basis). There is no way of knowing whether the lobster tails in the freezer are six days or six months old.

Recently, a consultant suggested the inventory system described in Case exhibit 22–1.

COMPETITION

Harten House is one of three motels in West Chester. There are, however, a number of competing motels within twenty miles, in nearby towns. There is only one restaurant in town of a similar nature, "The Carriage." The Carriage is "the place" to eat in town. There is no other competition, except small grills. There are no franchises near either of these restaurants.

FINANCIAL INFORMATION

The financial data on the H & H, Incorporated portion of ownership is included as Case exhibit 22–2.

Under the direction of H & H, Incorporated all financial data are handled by a public accounting firm. The firm follows

Text continued on page 434

Case exhibit 22–1

HARTEN HOUSE MOTOR INN AND RESTAURANT

Proposed Inventory Control System

Assign two individuals to handle the different functions of the system. One person will be in charge of all the receiving, while the other will take responsibility for all breakout and issue. These functions must be kept separate and be staffed by different personnel, for internal control. This approach will maintain checks on the personnel performing the inventory tasks.

The present storage facilities of the restaurant are very good, but the security needs to be upgraded. All spaces should be kept locked unless issuing and receiving functions are being performed. The present open-door policy can lead to the unauthorized issue of goods.

The proposed system is a basic, manually operated, first-in, first-out system. The system for selecting what food supplies will be used for any meal is presently a random one, employed by the person charged with breakout for that meal. Under the proposed system each item will be stamped with the date of receipt of that item. The person charged with issuing must breakout the items with the oldest date stamp. This will eliminate shelf spoilage.

Documenting the flow of goods under this system is simple. An inventory control card is prepared for each item in stock. There should be enough columns on the control card to post the date of receipt, date of issue, number received, number issued, cost of the item received and issued, and the initials of the individual making the transaction. The date of receipt and date of issue columns will help management determine the rate of turnover for each stock item. Using the turnover rate, management can determine order size and possible shelf spoilages. The number received and number issued columns allow management to take a spot inventory at any time. The cost column allows management to value the inventory and determine meal cost without referring to purchase orders. The column for initials helps determine responsibility for any given transaction.

The importance of who is assigned the tasks of this inventory system cannot be overemphasized. If the people do not see the benefits of the system they cannot be expected to operate the system as it is designed, and management will not have gained control over food storage and cost.

Case exhibit 22–2

HARTEN HOUSE MOTOR INN AND RESTAURANT

Income statement, November 1, 1973 to October 30, 1974

Sales		%
Gross sales	$420,168.47	
Admissions	1,076.26	
Miscellaneous	15,940.58	
Total sales	$437,185.31	100.0
Expenses		
Food	$ 95,973.27	22.0
Alcoholic beverages	13,226.86	3.0
Utilities	26,913.88	6.2
Sales tax	15,808.01	3.6
Repairs	3,365.62	.8
Bank charges	153.09	.0
Credit card discounts	661.12	.2
Returned checks and refunds	1,941.77	.4
Supplies	26,206.51	6.0
Linen and laundry	3,130.26	.7
Music and bands	2,415.60	.6
Advertising	2,023.94	.5
Exterminating	624.00	.1
Officers' salaries	.00	.0
Payroll	126,201.10	28.9
Payroll tax expense	11,820.17	2.7
Interest	36,793.69	8.4
Miscellaneous	6,533.31	1.5
License and permits	.00	.0
Insurance	6,204.00	1.4
Heating and air conditioning	3,622.91	.8
Legal and professional	1,800.00	.4
Maintenance and upkeep	3,561.23	.8
Dues and subscriptions	.00	.0
Office expense	496.81	.1
Depreciation	71,624.00	16.4
Contributions	.00	.0
Contract labor	2,335.20	.5
City and county tax	5,742.89	1.3
Other taxes	1,356.03	.3
Moving expense	371.09	.1
Travel	878.12	.2
Entertainment	.00	.0
Postage	78.54	.0
Lease	20.60	.0
Restaurant	4,610.75	1.1
Directors' fees	.00	.0
Total expenses	$476,494.37	109.0
Net loss	$39,309.06–	9.0–

Case exhibit 22–2 (*Continued*)

HARTEN HOUSE MOTOR INN AND RESTAURANT

Balance sheet, October 31, 1974

Assets

Current assets

Cash	$ 3,398
Bank	13,950
Merchandise inventory	4,530
Accounts receivable	2,740
Accounts receivable employees	140
Prepaid interest	177
Prepaid federal unemployment tax	320
Other receivable	15,000
Other current assets	5,050
Total current assets	$ 45,305

Fixed assets

Land	$ 25,000
Building	375,000
Building improvements	5,200
Furniture and fixtures	230,080
Mobile home	1,900
Other assets	1,680
Total reserve for depreciation	117,358–
Total fixed assets	$521,502
Total assets	$566,807

Liabilities

Current liabilities

Accounts payable	$ 11,750
Accounts payable other	800
Accrued fed. and S.S. taxes	2,140
Accrued W/H taxes	260
Sales tax payable	1,370
Income tax payable, state	50
Notes payable, bank	21,570
National cash register	565
Notes payable, FNB of St. Louis	400
Notes payable, Coca-Cola	1,560
Notes payable, stockholders	35,200
Mortgages payable, bank	241,400
Mortgages payable, Pearce and Jordan	249,220
Other payables	0
Total liabilities	$566,285

Capital

Net worth

Common stock	50,000
Treasury stock	5,000–
Paid-in capital	0
Retained earnings	44,478–
Total net worth	522
Total liabilities and net worth	$566,807

Case exhibit 22–2 *(Continued)*

HARTEN HOUSE MOTOR INN AND RESTAURANT

Income statement, November 1, 1974 to October 30, 1975

		%
Sales	$ 344,087.57	
Gross sales	777.25	
Admissions miscellaneous	29,159.38	
Total sales	$ 374,024.20	100.0
Expenses		
Food	$ 93,933.49	25.1
Alcoholic beverages	12,860.78	3.4
Utilities	23,744.63	6.3
Sales tax	14,032.97	3.8
Repairs	3,234.81	.9
Bank charges	129.07	.0
Credit card discounts	601.28	.2
Returned checks and refunds	985.08	.3
Supplies	13,685.26	3.7
Linen and laundry	1,459.18	.4
Music and bands	3,294.60	.9
Advertising	1,512.79	.4
Exterminating	654.00	.2
Officers' salaries	.00	.0
Payroll	107,094.94	28.6
Payroll tax expense	8,317.53	2.2
Interest	30,139.02	8.1
Miscellaneous	815.24	.2
License and permits	.00	.0
Insurance	5,705.87	1.5
Heating and air conditioning	4,773.05	1.3
Legal and professional	2,090.00	.6
Maintenance and upkeep	2,829.22	.8
Dues and subscriptions	70.00	.0
Office expense	405.22	.1
Depreciation	65,849.94	17.6
Contributions	.00	.0
Contract labor	1,728.80	.5
City and county tax	6,331.68	1.7
Other taxes	794.97	.2
Moving expense	.00	.0
Travel	562.30	.2
Entertainment	.00	.0
Postage	.00	.0
Lease	.00	.0
Restaurant	3,437.43	.9
Directors' fees	.00	.0
Total expenses	$411,073.15	109.9
Net loss	$ 37,048.95—	9.9—

Case exhibit 22–2 (*Continued*)

HARTEN HOUSE MOTOR INN AND RESTAURANT
Balance sheet, October 30, 1975

Assets

Current assets		
Cash	$ 1,225	
Bank	20,000	
Merchandise inventory	4,731	
Accounts receivable	3,500	
Accounts receivable employees	40	
Prepaid Federal Unemployment Tax	300	
Prepaid, other taxes	430	
Prepaid insurance	715	
Other receivable	15,000	
Other current assets	5,050	
Total current assets		$ 50,991
Fixed assets		
Land	$ 25,000	
Building	375,000	
Building improvements	5,800	
Furniture and fixtures	230,500	
Mobile home	1,900	
Other assets	2,200	
Total reserve for depreciation	183,208−	
Total fixed assets		457,192
Total assets		$508,183

Liabilities

Current liabilities		
Accounts payable	$ 10,300	
Accounts payable other	0	
Accrued fed. and S.S. taxes	1,800	
Accrued W/H taxes	700	
Sales tax payable	1,300	
Income tax payable federal	0	
Income tax payable state	50	
Notes payable, bank	11,700	
National cash register	0	
Notes payable, FNB of St. Louis	0	
Notes payable, Coca-Cola	1,560	
Notes payable, stockholders	44,000	
Mortgages payable, bank	223,350	
Mortgages payable, Pearce and Jordan	249,220	
Other payables	730	
Total liabilities		$544,710

Capital

Net worth		
Common stock	$50,000	
Treasury stock	5,000−	
Paid-in capital	0	
Retained earnings	81,527−	
Total net worth		$ 36,527−
Total liabilities and net worth		$508,183

standard accounting procedures, and, as previously noted, the only recent change was the reorganization of H & H, Incorporated under subchapter S to take advantage of the firm's losses from a tax standpoint. Therefore, the only changes since the advent of H & H, Incorporated is the way data are handled. The bookkeeping system used in the motel is the general one used in most motels. The motel employs a night auditor who records all check-ins and check-outs for each twenty-four hour period. This auditor also acts as night clerk for the motel. Each day the proceeds of the previous twenty-four hours are deposited and the records are sent to the accountants on a weekly basis. The restaurant operates on the same procedure.

The company receives monthly financial statements from its accountants. The data on account operation contained therein is detailed, and the motel and restaurant have cash flow reported separately. With these reports, the owners are aware of what operations are not profitable and what expenses are not under control.

SUGGESTED QUESTIONS FOR DISCUSSION

1. How should the owners establish a price structure for the ballroom?

2. Evaluate the present and the proposed inventory systems.

3. How can the ballroom be more fully utilized?

4. How can the evening meal trade be increased?

5. What type of advertising would you recommend?

6. Cite, define, and offer a solution to the major problem in the case.

7. What can be done to turn this organization into a profitable, viable firm?

INDEX

Page numbers in *italics* refer to illustrations and to sample material.

ABC classification inventory, 130–132, *131*
  and inventory control systems, 139
Abstract, in business plan, 39
Accessibility, in location analysis, 69–71
Account, budget, 61–62
  installment, 62
  open credit, 61
Accountant, Certified Public. See *Certified Public Accountant.*
Accounting, machine shop, 256–257
  standardized, and advertising, 58
Accounting classifications, and management by objectives, 132–133
  setting up, 130–132, *131*
Accounting practitioner, as record-keeper, 129
Accounts receivable. Also see *Balance sheet.*
  periodic check of, 64
Accreditation. See *Licensing.*
Accrual method, of income reporting, 133
Acquisition of ownership, to protect investment, 41
Actions, reassessment of, 15
Activities, delegation of, 118–119
Actual sales less allowance, and accounting classifications, 130
Address, specific, for a business, 67
Administration, legal adaptability of, 176
Administrative expenses, bookstore, *235*
Administrator-operator, characteristics of, 15–17
Ads, classified, as source of applicants, 124
Advertising, 56–57. Also see *Marketing.*
  auto repair shop, 307–309
  cabinet shop, 351–352
  cooperative, 57
  convenience store, 340
  dry goods store, 103–104
  effectiveness of, 56–57
  evaluating a franchise, 160
  for restaurant, 279
  institutional, 56
  motorcycle shop, 296
  service station, 385

Advertising (*Continued*)
  short-term methods, 56
  specific item, 57
  sports shop, 325–326, 344
  witholding, 57
  word-of-mouth, 57
Advice, legal, in choosing legal structure, 174
Aesthetic factors, in location analysis, 70
Agents, in electronics firm by-laws, *194–196*
Aggressiveness, of competition, 36
Agreement, assembly, *221*
  promoter's, electronics firm, *214*
  purchase and sales, electronics firm, *211–213*
Air conditioning company, case involving, 412–422
Allowances, role in pricing, 58
Alterations, to building, in lease for electronics firm, *207*
American Institute of Certified Public Accounts, in special service companies, 5
Analysis, job evaluation, 116
  location, example of, 79–82
    for wholesalers, 71–72
    retail, 67–71
  of pro forma statements, 39
  projected break-even, bookstore, *234*
  self, entrepreneurial potential, 17
Annual Statement Studies. See *Robert Morris Associates.*
"Annual Survey of Buying Power," and census information, 35
Appearance, in location analysis, 70
Applicant sources, in personnel function, 124
Application, consumer credit, 62–63
Application form, in personnel function, 124
Appraisal, land, volatility of, 46
Area, reputation of, 70
  residential, proximity to, 70
  trading, 67–68
Area map, in assessing competition, 36
Area newspapers, information from, in location analysis, 77

Articles of Organization, electronics company, *180*
  general laws, Massachusetts, *183*
  role in by-laws, electronics firm, *190*
Assembly line, in case, *219, 220*
Assets, financial, protection of, 38
  fixed, purchase of, 46
  statement of, cabinet shop, *354*
Assigns, in lease for electronics firm, 210
Athletic toy, manufacture of, case involving, 216–224
Attitudes, political, in location analysis, 72
Attorney, handling accounts, 64
Attraction, cumulative, in location analysis, 69
Authority, delegation of, 14
Auto repair shop, case involving, 300–312
Average family income, computation, 36
Average gross margin, in cost control, 108

Bad debt losses, dry goods store, 104–105, 107
Bait pricing, 59
Balance sheet, 37, 135–136
  as pro forma statement, 87
  auto repair shop, *308, 310*
  bicycle shop, *270*
  detective agency, *287*
  door sales company, *381*
  drugstore, *88*
  heating and air conditioning company, *421*
  machine shop, *258–261*
  motor inn and restaurant, *431, 433*
  motorcycle shop, *298*
  nursing home, *363, 365, 367*
  projected, in drugstore, *92*
  service station, *388, 390*
  sports shop, *330–331*
  tire company, *322*
Bank loan, in case, 228
Bank of America, as information source, 85
  brochures from, 85, 86
Banks, as information sources, 8
  as source of debt financing, 45–46
  commercial loan officers in, 8
  information from, in location analysis, 78
  sales financing departments in, 47
Base rent, bookstore, *233*
Believability, in checklist for newspaper advertising, 170
Bicycle shop, case involving, 263–273
Bid pricing, 59
Billboards, 56
Billing, cycle, 61
Billing terms, extended, 47
Bills, dry goods store, 108
  reducing, 102
Bin cards, 138
Board of directors, electronics firm by-laws, *192–194*
  vacancies in, electronics firm by-laws, *197*
Bonus, in profit sharing plan, in case, *223*
Bookkeeping. Also see *Records.*
  door sales company, 379–380
  single *versus* double entry, 134

Bookstore, case involving, 225–238
  location of, 226
Boundaries, natural, effect of, 81
Brand preference, 52
Breakage, guarding against, in dry goods store, 104
Break-even schedule, sports shop, *344*
Budget, advertising, evaluating a franchise, 160
  existing business, 86
  new business, 85–86
  on-going business, 87
  purposes of, 84
Budget accounts, consumer credit and, 61–62
Budget statement. See *Pro forma statement.*
Building materials, case involving, 245–250
Bureau, credit, 63
Business, "mix" of, in location analysis, 69
Business, on-going, and choosing a business, 148
Business climate, 68
Business loan, support from franchise, bookstore, *237*
Business plan, 33–40
  complete, preparation of, 26–27
  components of, 34
  in checklist for choosing a business, 152
Business strips, in location analysis, 69
Buyer behavior, 54
Buyer needs, fulfilling, 56
Buying expense, 102
By-laws, electronics firm, *190–200*
  amendments, *200*
  articles of organization, *190*
  board of directors, 192–194
  capital stock, *197–198*
  officers and agents, 194–196
  resignations and removals, *196–197*
  stockholders, *190–192*
  transfer of stock, *198–199*
  vacancies, *197*

Cabinet shop, case involving, 346–355
Capacity, credit investigation and, 63
Capital, acquisition of, 41–50
  debt. See *Debt capital.*
  equity. See *Equity capital.*
  legal methods for acquisition, 177
  starting, and choosing a business, 147
  withdrawal of, 26, 42
  working, bookstore, *232*
    consumer and, 60
Capital gains rate, 44
Capital loans, working, 45–46
Capital needs, industry averages and, 60
Capital stock, in electronics firm by-laws, *197–198*
Carrying costs, inventory, 138
Case analysis, self-analysis and, 22
Cash, control of, 8
Cash budgeting, 84
Cash flow, in control process, 115
Cash investment, minimum, bookstore, *230–231*

Cash method, and income reporting, 133
Cash position statement, as pro forma statement, 87
Cash receipts and disbursements, 137
Cash statement, 37
Census data, availability of, 35
    in starting business, 85
    to determine demand, in management, 114
Census tracts, in estimating population, 79
    in location analysis, 74
Certified Public Accountant, and buying a business, 86
    as record-keeper, 129
Chamber of commerce, information from, in location analysis, 73, 77, 81
Character, credit investigation and, 63
Character of city, in checklist for location analysis, 166
Chattel mortgage, 62
Check, credit, 63
    periodic, of accounts receivable, 64
Checklist, buying an on-going business, 162–163
    evaluating a franchise, 154–162
    interior layout, 171–172
    location analysis, 163–165
    marketing analysis, 167–169
    newspaper advertising, 169–170
    site analysis, 165–167
    starting a new business, 145–154
Chinese restaurant, case involving, 274–279
City planning boards, information from, 77
City reclamation projects, effect of, 77
Civil Rights Act of 1964, in personnel function, 123
Classified ads, as source of applicants, 124
Climate, business, 68
Collateral, credit investigation and, 63
    owner's property as, 45
Collection agency, turning accounts over to, 64
Collection period, in dry goods store, 106
Collections, in cost control, 108
Collections schedule, for drugstore, 89
    and record-keeping, 136
Commercial banks. See Banks.
Commercial finance companies, as source of debt financing, 48
Commercial land appraisal, volatility of, 46
Commercial loan officers, as information sources, 8
Commitment, need for, 11, 22
Common area charge, bookstore, 233
Community advertising, 103
Comparison shopping, 53
Competition, assessment of, 35–38
    bicycle shop, 268
    checklist for location analysis, 164–165
    checklist for market analysis, 168
    checklist for site analysis, 165–166
    door sales company, 374
    in location analysis, 68–69
    large corporations as, 5
    location near, 53

Competition (Continued)
    lumber yard, 404–407
    managerial capability, 36–37
    motorcycle shop, 293–294
    nature of, 35
    source of job applicants, 124–125
Competitive niche, 141
    loss of, minimizing risk from, 142–143
Competitors, promotion methods of, and choosing a business, 150
Construction, dry goods store, 98
    wood products for, case involving, 245–250
Contract, auto repair shop, 305–306
    for limited partnership, 174
Control, cash and inventory, 8
    purchasing and inventory, bicycle shop, 266
Control process, in management, 115
Control systems, inventory, 138–139
Convenience goods, 52–53
Convenience store, case involving, 335–341
Cooperative advertising, 57, 103
Corporate seal, electronics firm by-laws, 199–200
Corporation, acquisition of capital, 178
    as legal structure, 174
    costs and procedures for starting, 175
    effect of laws on, 177
    legal adaptability of, 176
    Subchapter S, 178–179
Cost, calculation of, 5
    credit card system, 61
    inventory carrying, 138
    of doing business, in location analysis, 78
    records of quality and, 139–140
Cost management, in dry goods store, 98
Cost method, of inventory valuation, 135
Cost of goods sold, and accounting classifications, 131
    bookstore, 235
Cost of merchandise sold, for drugstore, 88
Costs, bookstore, 230–232
    in starting a business, 174
    overhead, and pricing, 59
    variable, and pricing, 59
Counsel, legal, in choosing legal structure, 174
County planning boards, information from, 77
Coupons, as advertising, 57
Covenants, in lease for electronics firm, 206–207
Craftsmen, 6
Credit, as method for capital acquisition, 177
    auto repair shop, 307
    business and consumer, considerations, 60–61
    cabinet shop, 350–351
    consumer, procedures for extending, 62–64
        varieties of, 60–62
    door sales company, 377–378
    follow-up, 64
    informing applicant for, 64
    motor inn and restaurant, 425
    new accounts, in cost control, 108
    trade, terms of sale, 137
Credit account, open, 61

Credit application, 62–63
Credit and collections, detective agency, 283–284
Credit bureau, consumer credit and, 63
Credit cards, 61
Credit check, 63
Credit department, establishing, 61–62
Credit function, 47
Credit investigation, 63
Credit risk, 61
Credit terms, extension, 46
Creditors, liability to, in starting business, 175
    trade, as source of debt financing, 46–47
Crime, minimizing risk from, 143
    risk to business, 142
Crime control, in management, 115
Cumulative attraction, in location analysis, 69
Current assets to current debt, 135–136
Current debt to tangible net worth, 136
Customer relations, 57
Customers, as sources of capital, 44
    familiarization with product, 55
    list of, 39
    potential, finding, 67
Cycle billing, 61

Damage to business, as risk, 142
    in lease for electronics firm, 208
    minimizing risk from, 143
Death of key personnel, 142–143
Debt capital, definition of, 41
    forms of, 41–42
Debt financing, sources of, 45–50
Debt repayment, source of, 82
Decision making, and management by objectives, 109
Decisions, ability to make, 14
Deed transfers, 55
Default, in lease for electronics firm, 208–209
Delegation, of activities, 118–119
Delegation of authority, need for, 14
Delinquency notices, 64
Demand, changes in, as risk, 141–143
Depreciation, dry goods store, 104
    in projected income statements, 90
Depreciation schedules, 133–134
Detective agency, case involving, 280–290
Developer-implementer, characteristics, 15–17
Direct investments, by owner, 42
Direct loans, Small Business Administration, 49
Direct mail, 56
Direct promotion methods, 54
Directors, board of. See Board of directors.
Directory, telephone, in location analysis, 78
Disaster, natural, in lease for electronics firm, 208
Disaster relief loans, Small Business Administration, 49
Discounts, earning of, in cost control, 108
    role in pricing, 58
    trade, and pricing, 59
        obtaining, 137

Display, advertising by, 57
    in checklist for interior layout, 171
Distribution, in checklist for market analysis, 168
Diversified industry, areas with, 68
Door sales company, case involving, 370–382
Down payment, consumer credit and, 62
Dun and Bradstreet, 79
    operating ratios, dry goods, 107

Economic considerations, in checklist for location analysis, 163
Economic opportunity loans, Small Business Administration, 49
Economy, influence on business, 36
Electricity, cost control, 102
Electronics company, legal documents for, 180–214
Electroplating shop, case involving, 291–299
Eminent domain, in lease for electronics firm, 207
Employee theft, 8
Employees. Also see Personnel.
    availability of, and choosing a business, 148
    dishonest, control of, 115–116
    pay policy, for drugstore, 89
Employees' wages, dry goods store, 99, 101
Employment, stability of, 63
Employment agencies, as source of job applicants, 124
Employment agreement, electronics firm, 202–204
Employment history, in personnel function, 124
Entrepreneur, technological, 3–4
Entrepreneurial potential, self-evaluation for, 17
Equal Employment Opportunity Commission, in personnel function, 123
Equipment, loans of, 57
Equipment bids, restaurant, 276
Equity, acquisition of, 42–45
Equity capital, definition of, 41
Equity shares, acquisition of, 27
Equity statement, heating and air conditioning company, 420
Estimate, sales, need for, 81
Estimates, for new business, 85–86
Ethics, in management, 120
Evaluation. Also see Checklist.
    of competition, 36–38
    of information, importance at outset, 29
    self-. Also see Self-evaluation.
        as preparation for opening business, 21–22
Expense information, operating, in location analysis, 78
Expenses, administrative, bookstore, 235
"Expenses in retail businesses," 64
Experience, and choosing a business, 146
    and success, 8–9, 23
    as qualification for business, 8–9
Expertise, need for, 16
External funds, obtaining, 27

Factoring companies, 47
Failure, past, in site analysis, 71
  small-business, rate of, 18
Fair-trade laws, in location analysis, 68
Family, as suppliers of equity, 43–44
Family support, need for, 11
Feasibility study, restaurant, 278–279
Federal Income Tax. Also see *Income Tax.*
  "Circular E," 138
  forms for, 138
Feedback, ability to evaluate, 14
  in management, 120
Fees, payment to franchisor, 7
Field support, in evaluating a franchise, 162
FIFO, and inventory valuation, 135
Finance companies, as source of debt financing, 48
Finances, personal, 39
Financial assets, protection of, 38
Financial condition, future, importance of estimating, 25
Financial data. Also see *Balance sheet.*
  bicycle shop, 269–273
  convenience store, 337–339
  door sales company, 378–379
  machine shop, 257, *259–261*
  pro forma, 38. Also see *Pro forma analysis.*
Financial information, timing of, 132
Financial plan, in management, 111
Financial planning, and risks to business, 142, 143
Financial ratios, tire company, *323*
Financial records, cabinet shop, 352
  detective agency, 282–283, *283, 287, 288, 289*
  motorcycle shop, 296–297
  service station, 386–388
Financial statement, 38–39
  and buying a business, 86
  and choosing a business, 149
  convenience store, *338*
  heating and air conditioning company, *419*
  motor inn and restaurant, *430, 432*
Financing, in evaluating a franchise, 158
  paper cutter, 396–397
  role of financial statement in securing, 38
  securing of, 27
  times needed, 33
Financing alternatives, 42–50, *43*
Financing schedule, bookstore, *230*
"Fire-fighting," 10
  in management, 110
Firm, objectives of, 39
First in-first out, and inventory valuation, 135
Fixed payment levels, 63
Fixtures, cost of, bookstore, *232*
Floor planning, as function of finance companies, 47
Forecasted income levels, and expectations, 25–26
Forecasting, in managment, 111–114
  paper cutter, 393
  service station, 388–389
Foreclosure, to protect investment, 41

"Four 'C's," 63
Franchise, and choosing a business, 149
  case involving, 225–238, 383–391
  checklist for evaluating, 154–162
Franchise agreement, 7
Franchising, opportunities in, 7
Freight absorption pricing, 59
Full line pricing, 59
Funds, external, obtaining, 27
Furniture, cost of, bookstore, *232*
Future financial condition, importance of estimating, 25

Gas station, case involving, 383–391
General partnership. Also see *Partnership.*
  costs and procedures for starting, 174
General records. Also see *Records.*
  types of, 128
Generalist, specialist *versus,* 16–17
Generated sales, 51
Goals. Also see *Management by Objectives.*
  personal, in checklist for choosing a business, 152
Goods, familiarizing customers with, 55
  types of, 51–54
Goodwill charge, bookstore, *231*
Grocery store, inventory in, 138
Gross margin, dry goods store, 99–100
Gross profit, and accounting classifications, 131
Growth figures, projected, in location analysis, 78
Growth potential of an area, 68

Headline, in checklist for newspaper advertising, 169
Health, and chances for success, 22
  necessity for good, 10–11
  of an area, 68
Heating, reducing cost of, dry goods store, 102
Heating bills, controlling, 102
Heating company, case involving, 412–422
Highway department, information from, in location analysis, 77
History, site, 70–71
Home office support, in evaluating a franchise, 161
Hours of operation, 71
Hydraulic paper cutter, case involving, 392–401

Illustration, in checklist for newspaper advertising, 170
Immigrants, cases involving, 251–262, 274–279
Improvements, cost of, bookstore, *232*
Improvements to building, in lease for electronics firm, 207
Income and expense reporting, 133
Income levels, 63

Income statement, 37. Also see *Financial statement.*
  as pro forma statement, 87
  auto repair shop, *309, 311*
  bicycle shop, *271*
  cabinet shop, *353*
  door sales company, *382*
  drugstore, *90*
  dry goods store, *99, 105*
  in cost management, 98–110
  in record-keeping, 137
  motorcycle shop, *297*
  restaurant, *278*
  service station, *387, 389*
  sports shop, *327, 332, 345*
  tire company, *321*
Income Tax, Federal, and equity acquisition, 44
  forms for, 138
Indemnity, in electronics firm by-laws, *199*
Indirect promotion methods, 54
Individual attention, small businesses that provide, 5
Individualized services, opportunities in, 5
Industrial goods, 54
Industrial land appraisal, volatility of, 46
Industries, diversified, fields with, 68
Industry, local, and location analysis, 68
Industry trends, heating and air conditioning company, 416–418
In-file report, credit bureau, 63
Information, census, availability of, 35
  evaluation of, importance at outset, 29
  inconsistencies in, 81–82
  local sources, in location analysis, 77
  operating expense, in location analysis, 78
  sources of, 85–86
    in location analysis, 74
Installation, with specialty goods, 52
Installment accounts, 62
Installment plan, for small-business credit, 47
Institutional advertising, 56
Insurance, and choosing a business, 151–152
  and minimizing business risk, 143
  in lease for electronics firm, 208
  in projected income statements, 90
  motorcycle shop, 297–299
  on merchandise, dry goods store, 104
Interest, inclusion in projected income statements, 90
Interest rates, consumer credit and, 62
Internal Revenue Code, Section 1244, 44
  Subchapter S corporation, 178–179
Internal Revenue Service, and depreciation schedules, 133–134
Interviewing, in personnel function, 123
Introductory pricing, 59
Inventory, auto repair shop, 307
  bicycle shop, *266, 269*
  bookstore, *231*
  cabinet shop, 352
  convenience store, 341
  cost of, bookstore, *232*
  motor inn and restaurant, 428

Inventory (*Continued*)
  motorcycle shop, 295–296
  perpetual, 138–139
  sports shop, 326–329
  time utilization, 118–119, *119*
  tire company, 320–323
  valuation of, 134–135
Inventory control, 8
  bicycle shop, 266
  standardized, and advertising, 58
Inventory control system, 138–139
  motor inn and restaurant, *429*
Inventory policy, of drugstore, 88
Inventory records, 138–139
Inventory turnover, schedule of, sports shop, *333*
Investigation, credit, 63
Investment, by owner, as method for capital acquisition, 177
  return on, and choosing a business, 146–147
Investment letter, for sample electronics firm, 201–202
Investors, as sources of equity, 44

Job description, in case, *222*
  in management, 121
  need for, 34
Job evaluation, *117*
Job evaluation analysis, 116

Key people, information on, in business plan, 34

Labor. Also see *Personnel.*
  availability of, 72
Labor market, local, and job evaluation, 117
Land appraisal, volatility of, 46
Last in-first out, and inventory valuation, 135
Laws, and choosing a business, 151
  effects on business structure, 177
  fair trade, in location analysis, 68
Layout. Also see *Site* and *Site layout.*
  auto repair shop, *302*
  cabinet shop, *348*
  door sales company, *372*
  in checklist for newspaper advertising, 170
  machine shop, *255*
  motorcycle shop, *292, 293*
  nursing home, *359*
  tire company, 316
Leader pricing, 59
Leadership function, in management, 120
Lease, for electronics form, *205–211*
Lease information, bookstore, *233*
Leasing, as source of debt financing, 48
Ledger, and inventory control systems, 139
Legal counsel, in choosing legal structure, 174
Legal form, statements of, 38

Legal structure, and continuity of business, 175–176
  motor inn and restaurant, 426
  types of, 173
Legislation, state and local, in location analysis, 68
Levels, income, 63
Liability, as risk to business, 142
  legal, in starting business, 175
  minimizing, 143–144
  protection from, 38
  statement of, cabinet shop, 354
License, nursing home, 356–358
  purchase of, in case, 230
License fee, bookstore, 231
Licensing, and choosing a business, 151
Licensing policies, in location analysis, 68
Lien, and choosing a business, 149
  mechanics', in lease for electronics firm, 207
Life, quality of, in location analysis, 72
LIFO, and inventory valuation, 135
Lighting, cost control, 102
Limited market, 6–7
Limited partnership. Also see Partnership.
  costs and procedures for starting, 174
Lined pricing, 60
Liquor store, case involving, 335–341
Loan, bank, in case, 228
  business, support from franchise, bookstore, 237
  collateral for, convenience store, 337
  difficulty with, detective agency, 281
  door sales company, 378–379
  immigrants and, 252
  in location analysis, 68
  motorcycle shop, 297–299
  nursing home, 359–360, 362–365
  Small Business Administration, 48–50
  term, 45–46
  working capital, 45–46
    drugstore, 90
Loan history, cabinet shop, 352–353
Local industry, and location analysis, 68
Local labor market, and job evaluation, 117
Local legislation, in location analysis, 68
Local market, need to evaluate, 15
  opportunities in, 6
Local ordinances, and choosing a business, 151
Local sources of information, in location analysis, 77
Location, and choosing a business, 148
  bicycle shop, 264
  bookstore, 226
  definition of, 66–67
  in newspaper, in checklist for advertising, 169
  near competitors, 53
  sports shop, 342–343
Location analysis, example, 79–82
  information sources, 74
  retail, 67–71
  wholesalers, 71–72

Location information, bookstore, 233
Lower of cost or market method, inventory valuation, 135
Lumber company, case involving, 245–250, 402–411

Machine shop, case involving, 251–262
Mail, direct, 56
Management, auto repair shop, 302–304
  bicycle shop, 264–265
  cabinet shop, 349–350
  convenience store, 336–337
  door sales company, 372–373, 380–382
  good, traits of, 120
  heating and air conditioning company, 412–413
  lumber company, 402
  machine shop, 253–255
  motor inn and restaurant, 424–425
  motorcycle shop, 294–295
  nursing home, 360–361
  service station, 384
  sports shop, 329–333
  tire company, 317
"Management by crisis," 10
Management by Objectives (MBO), 109–110
  self-evaluation for, 126
Management problems, and choosing a business, 150–151
Managerial capabilities, of competition, 36–37
Managerial obsolescence, as risk to business, 142–143
Managerial roles, 9–17, 9
Managerial skills, need for, 22
Manufacturers, location analysis for, 72
Manufacturers of special equipment, as sources of debt financing, 48
Market, bicycle shop, 268–269
  characteristics, 35, 36
  convenience store, 339
  determining existence of, 35
  lack of, as reason for failure, 37
  local. See Local market.
  proximity to, for manufacturers, 72
  seasonal components, 36
  share of, and choosing a business, 149
  small, 6–7
Market niche, definition, 7. Also see Niche.
Market potential, in checklist for market analysis, 168
Market size, 35, 36
Market survey, 23–25
  and location analysis, 66
  as factor in residual sales, 51
  assumptions underlying, 25
  components of, 35–38
  conducting, 23–24
  in business plan, 39
  success and, 24–25
Marketing, auto repair shop, 301–302
  bicycle shop, 267–268

Marketing (*Continued*)
  detective agency, 285–286
  door sales company, 375–377
  heating and air conditioning company, 413–416
  in evaluating a franchise, 160
  machine shop, 255–256
  motor inn and restaurant, 426–427
  nursing home, 361–362
  restaurant, 278
  sports shop, 329
  tire company, 315–316, 318–320
Markup pricing, 59
Mass distribution, large business geared to, 6
Mass production, large business geared to, 6
Materials, raw, availibility and adequacy of, 72
Media, coverage of, 56
  in promotion, 52
Merchandise, familiarizing customers with, 55
  in checklist for newspaper advertising, 169
  model assortment, and choosing a business, 150
  size of, and accounting classifications, 130
  types of, 51–54
Merchandise emphasis, in checklist for interior layout, 171
Merchandise information, in checklist for newspaper advertising, 170
Merger, door sales company, 374–375
Minimum cash investment, bookstore, *230–231*
"Mix" of businesses, in location analysis, 69–70
Money. See *Capital*.
Mortgage, chattel, 62
Motivation, in management, 119–120
  need for, 9–10, 22
Motor inn, case involving, 423–434
Motorcycle shop, case involving, 291–299

National boundaries, effect of, 81
National Cash Register Corporation, 64
  in location analysis, 78
Net profit to tangible net worth, 136
Net sales, in dry goods store, 99–100
Net sales to net working capital, 136
Net sales to tangible net worth, 136
Net worth, statement of, cabinet shop, *354*
Newspaper advertising, 57
Newspapers, in promotion, 52
  information from, in location analysis, 77
Niche, competitive, 141
  competitive, and minimizing business risk, 142–143
  market, 7
Notice, delinquency, 64
  in lease for electronics firm, 210
Novelties, 56
Nursing home, case involving, 356–369

Objectives, 111
  need for personal, 14
  of firm, 39
  worksheet for, *112–113*
Occupancy expense, 102
  in dry goods store, 102
Officers, in electronics firm by-laws, *194–196*
On-going business, and choosing a business, 148
Open credit account, 61
Opening cost, for bookstore, *230*
Operating expense, variable, in cost control, 108
Operating expense information, in location analysis, 78
Operating ratios, analysis of, dry goods store, 98–110, *99*
  heating and air conditioning company, *422*
Operation, hours of, in site analysis, 71
Opportunities, criteria for evaluating, in management, 116
  fields with, 3–17
Ordinances, and choosing a business, 151
  local, in location analysis, 68, 73
Organization, Articles of, 180. Also see *Articles of Organization*.
  detective agency, 284–285, *284*
Organization chart, auto repair shop, *303*
  in case, *221*
  in management, 116
  in personnel function, 121
  of dry goods store, *117*
  printing company, *240*
  tire company, *318*
Orientation to results, *15*
Originator-inventor, characteristics, 12–14
Overhead, and accounting classifications, 131
  in cost calculation, 5
Overhead costs, and pricing, 59
Owner, as source of debt financing, 45
  as supplier of equity, 42
  information on, in business plan, 34
Owner investment, as method for capital acquisition, 177
Ownership, acquisition of, to protect investment, 41
  sharing of, and choosing a business, 147–148

Package store, case involving, 335–341
Paperback Booksmith, case involving, 225–238
Parking facilities, in checklist for site analysis, 166
Participation loans, Small Business Administration, 49
Partners' compensation, in dry goods store, 99, 101
Partnership, acquisition of capital, 178
  as legal structure, 173
  costs and procedures for starting, 174

Partnership (*Continued*)
  effect of laws on, 177
  legal adaptability of, 176
Payment, down, consumer credit and, 62
Payment dates, in control process, 115
Payment levels, fixed, 63
Performance appraisal, in personnel function, 122
Perpetual inventory, 138–139
Personal finances, 38–39
Personal goals, and checklist for choosing a business, 152
Personal objectives, need for, 14
Personal preparation, 21–22
Personal qualifications, 21–23
  and choosing a business, 146
Personal selling, 55
Personalized service, opportunities in, 5
Personnel. Also see *Employees.*
  availability of, and choosing a business, 148
  college students as, 218
  detective agency, 286, *284*
  developing, 15–16
  door sales company, 373–374
  employee theft, 8
  heating and air conditioning company, 412–413, 418–422
  machine shop, 253–254
  motivating, 15–16
  motor inn and restaurant, 425–426
  motorcycle shop, 294–295
  nursing home, 357–358
  of competition, abilities of, 69
  paper cutter, 399
  qualifications of, 39
  selecting, 15–16
  selection and training, and choosing a business, 150
  sports shop, 344
  tire company, 318
Personnel function, 121–125
  and Civil Rights Act of 1964, 123
  applicant screening in, 123–124
  interviewing and, 123, 125
  job description, 121
  organization charts in, 121
  performance appraisal in, 122
  selection of personnel, 122
  sources of applicants, 124
  training in, 122
Pilferage, as risk to business, 142
  guarding against, in dry goods store, 104
Plan, business, 33–40. Also see *Business plan.*
Planner-organizer, characteristics, 14–15.
Planning, in management, 110–115
Planning boards, information from, 77
Policy formulation, and type of company, 176
Political attitudes, in location analysis, 72
Population, and location analysis, 73
  estimation of, 79
  in location analysis, 164
Potential, growth, of an area, 68
Potential sales, 79
Premises. See *Site.*

Preparation, personal, 21–22
Prestige pricing, 60
Price. Also see *Marketing.*
  and choosing a business, 148–149
Price-cutting, ineffectiveness with specialty goods, 52
Price lining, 60
Price range, and choosing a business, 150
Price skimming, 60
Pricing, bicycle shop, 267–268
  cabinet shop, 350–351
  convenience store, 340–341
  door sales company, 377
  methods of, 58–60
  motor inn and restaurant, 427–428
  motorcycle shop, 296
  service station, 389–391
  sports shop, 344
Pricing structure, of competition, 36
Printing plant, case involving, 239–244
Pro forma statement. Also see *Income statement.*
  conditions affecting, 85–87
  definition of, 83
  in business plan, 39
  machine shop, 257, *258*
  preparation of, 87–91
  process of small business, 25
  product coverage, 37
  role in location analysis, 82
Problems, defining, 21
Process, small business as a, 19–29, *20*
Product, familiarizing customers with, 55
  in checklist for market analysis, 169
  types of, 51–54
Product classifications, 132. Also see *Accounting classifications.*
Product knowledge, need for 55, 64
Production, team, in case, 221
Professionals, in checklist for site analysis, 167
Profit, and accounting classifications, 131
  calculation of, *135*
  pricing and, 59
Profit and loss statement, nursing home, *364, 366, 368–369*
Profit sharing plan, in case, *223*
Profits, projected, and choosing a business, 149
  withdrawal of, 42
Projected growth figures, in location analysis, 78
Projected income statement, in drugstore, analysis of, 91
Projected sales, lumber yard, *406, 407*
Promoter's agreement, electronics firm, 214
Promotion. See *Advertising* and *Marketing.*
Promotion techniques, 54–64
  short-term, 56
Proprietorship, 173
  acquisition of capital, 177
  costs and procedures for starting, 174
  effect of laws on, 177
  legal adaptability of, 176
Prospecting, definition, 55

Prospectus, bookstore, *229–236*
Proximity to market, for manufacturers, 72
Public accountant, as record-keeper, 129
Public utility companies, information from, 77
Purchase and sales agreement, electronics firm, 211–213
Purchase schedule, and record-keeping, 136–137
  drugstore, *89*
Purchases, payment for, to suppliers, for drugstore, 89
Purchasing agents, as source of information, 54
Purchasing control, bicycle shop, 266
Purchasing power, total, of an area, 67

Qualifications, of personnel, 39
  personal, 21–23
    and choosing a business, 146
Quality, records of, 139–140
Quality control, 217
  in management, 115
Quality of life, in location analysis, 72
Questionnaire, advertising effectiveness, 57

Radio, in promotion, 52
Rates, interest, consumer credit and, 62
Ratios, and records for MBO, 135–136
  financial, tire company, *323*
  operating, heating and air conditioning company, *422*
Raw materials, availability and adequacy of, 72
Real estate loans, 45–46
Reality testing, need for, 15
Receipts, sales, bicycle shop, *270*
Receivables, excessive, in dry goods store, 107
Reclamation projects, city, effect of, 77
Recommendations, for dealing with problems, 21
Record-keeping, and choosing a business, 151
Records. Also see *Bookkeeping, Pro forma statement, Balance sheet, Financial statement.*
  and Management by Objectives, 135–138
  bookkeeping methods, 134
  in cost control, 108
  inventory, 138–139
  maintenance of, 128–130
  tire company, 320
References, for immigrants, 252
  in personnel function, 124
Region, business, 67
Regional planning boards, information from, 77
Regional Planning Center, in location analysis, 81
Regulations, and choosing a business, 151
  local, and location analysis, 73
  zoning, compliance with, 71–72

Relatives and friends, as suppliers of equity, 43–44
Remodeling, in location analysis, 70
Renovation, in lease for electronics firm, *207*
Rent, in lease for electronics firm, *205–206*
  in projected income statements, 90
Repayment, debt, source of, 82
Repossession, 64
Reputation, as a factor in residual sales, 51
  of an area, in location analysis, 70
  of competition, 36
Residential areas, proximity to, 70
Residual sales, definition of, 51
Resignations and removals, in electronics firm by-laws, *196–197*
Responsibility, delegation of, 118–119
Restaurant, case involving, 274–279, 423–434
Results, orientation to, 15
Retail location analysis, 67–71
Retreading company, case involving, 313–323
Return on investment, and choosing a business, 146–147
Revenue, inadequate sales, 79
Revenues, total, estimating, 81
Risks, credit, 61
  for small business, minimizing, 142–144
    types of, 141–142
  legal, in starting business, 175
  willingness to take, 13
Robbery, control of, 115
Robert Morris Associates, 60, 78
  and buying an existing business, 86
  as information source, 85
Roles, managerial, 9–17, *9*
Royalties, cost of, bookstore, *235*

Salaries, in projected income statements, 90
Sale, terms of, bookstore, *230*
Sales, for bicycle shop, *272–273*
  effect of quality and cost on, 139
  estimation of, in pro forma statement, 87
  generated, definition, 51
  lumber yard, *406, 407*
  paper cutter, 393–395
  potential, 79
  residual, definition, 51
  schedule of, sports shop, *333*
Sales agents. See *Marketing.*
Sales agreement, electronics firm, 211–213
Sales and Marketing Management, in location analysis, 74
Sales department, lumber yard, 246
Sales estimate, need for, 81
Sales finance companies, 47
Sales forecast, for drugstore, 88
Sales less allowance, actual, and accounting classifications, 130
Sales Management Magazine, and census information, 35
Sales program, and adequate income, 26

Sales projections, bookstore, *234*
  by month, and record-keeping, 136
  need for, 87
Sales promotion, and choosing a business, 150
  techniques, 54–64
Sales ratios, in acquiring existing business, 86
Sales receipts, bicycle shop, *270*
Sales representatives, as advertising, 57
Sales revenue, inadequate, 79
Sales schedule, for drugstore, *89*
Sales tickets, 139
Saturated market, 6
SBA. See *Small Business Administration.*
Schedule, collections, 136
  for drugstore, *89*
  purchase, 136–137
Schools, as source of job applicants, 124
Seasonal market, 36
Security industry, case involving, 280–290
Self-analysis, entrepreneurial potential, 17
Self-confidence, 13
Self-discipline, need for, 11
Self-evaluation, as preparation for opening business, 21–22
  entrepreneurial potential, 17
  in management, 126
Seller's warranty, and choosing a business, 149
Selling methods, and choosing a business, 150
Service, opportunities in, 4–5
Service business, and chances for success, 141
Service firms, location analysis, 73–74
Service station, case involving, 383–391
Services, auto repair shop, 304–307
  bicycle shop, 265–266
Shoplifting, as risk to business, 142
Shopping centers, in location analysis, 69
Shopping goods, 53–54
Site, auto repair shop, 301–302
  definition, 66–67
  in checklist for market analysis, 168
  in lease for electronics firm, *205*
Site analysis, example, 79–82
  sports shop, 343
Site availability, for manufacturers, 72
Site history, 70–71
Site layout, cabinet shop, *348*
  door sales company, *372*
  lumber yard, *247*
  machine shop, *255*
  motorcycle shop, 292, *293*
  sports shop, *326*
Site location, as factor in residual sales, 51
Skills, managerial, need for, 22
Skimming, price, 60
Small business, as process, 19–29, *20*
  failure rate of, 18
  financing, 41–50
  opportunities, 3–17
  sales programs for, 51–65

Small Business Administration, as information source, 85–86
  as source of financing, 48–50
  information from, in location analysis, 77
  population estimation, 80
Small market, opportunities in, 6–7
Small-business owner, characteristics of, 9–17
Solvency, definition of, 41
Special service, small businesses providing, 4–5
  with specialty goods, 52
Special service companies, American Institute of Certified Public Accountants in, 5
Specialists, generalists *versus,* 16–17
Specialties, 56
Specialty goods, 51, 52
Specialty items, and accounting classifications, 130
Specific item advertising, 57
Spoilage, in dry goods store, 104
Sports shop, case involving, 324–334, 342–345
Stability, of an area, 68
  of employment, 63
Standard Metropolitan Statistical Area (SMSA), in location analysis, 74
Starting a business, costs and procedures, 174–175
Starting capital, and choosing a business, 147
State legislation, in location analysis, 68
State tax, forms of, 138
Statements. Also see *Financial statement.*
  cash, 37
  financial, 38–39
  income, 37
  of legal form, 38
  personal financial, 38
Statement of assets, cabinet shop, *354*
Statement of liabilities and net worth, cabinet shop, *354*
Statement of operations, detective agency, *288, 289*
Statement of profit and loss, nursing home, *364, 366, 368–369*
Stock, capital, in electronics firm by-laws, *197–198*
  transfer of, in electronics firm by-laws, *198*
Stockholder. Also see *Corporation.*
  role of, in by-laws, *190–192*
Storage area, and accounting classifications, 130
Strategy formulation, 114–115
Student-run business, case involving, 216–224
Subchapter S corporation, 178–179
Success, chances for, 141
  and choosing a business, 146
  personal qualifications and, 22–23
  market survey and, 24–25
Suppliers, and choosing a business, 149
  as information sources, 8–9
  as source of job applicants, 124
  availability of, for manufacturers, 72
  in estimating seasonal markets, 36
  need for list of, 39

Support, familial, need for, 11
  field, in evaluating a franchise, 162
  home office, in evaluating a franchise, 161
Survey, market. See *Market survey*.
"Survey of buying power," in location analysis, 74

Tax, Federal, forms of, 138. Also see *Income tax*.
  forms for, 138
  state, 138
Taxation, legislation on, in location analysis, 68
Taxes, and choosing a business, 151–152
Team production, in case, 221
Technical assistance, as advertising, 57
Technical skills, need for, 22
Technological innovator, 3–4
Telephone company, information from, in location analysis, 77–78
Teletype, printing company and, 243
Television, in promotion, 52
Tenant mix, in location analysis, 69
Term loans, 45–46
Terms, credit, extension, 46
  extended billing, 47
Terms of sale, bookstore, *230*
  in trade credit, 137
Timetable, pre-opening, bookstore, *236*
Tire and retreading company, case involving, 313–323
Tool shop, case involving, 251–262
Total opening cost, bookstore, *230*
Total purchasing power, of an area, 67
Total revenues, estimating, 81
Trade credit, terms of sale, 137
Trade creditors, as source of debt financing, 46–47
Trade discounts, and pricing, 59
  obtaining, 137
Trade-in allowances, role in pricing, 58
Trading area, 67–68
  in location analysis, 73
Trade-practice acts, in location analysis, 68
Traffic flow, in checklist for site analysis, 166
Training, from franchise, in case, 227
  in evaluating a franchise, 159

Training (*Continued*)
  in personnel function, 122
  personnel, lumber yard, 246
Training program, in obtaining a franchise, bookstore, *236*
Transportation, for raw materials and finished goods, 72
  in checklist for site analysis, 166

Unfair trade-practice acts, in location analysis, 68
Uniform Limited Partnership Act, 174
Utilities, availibility of, for manufacturers, 72
Utility companies, information from, 77

Visibility, in location analysis, 69–70
Vocational schools, as source of applicants, 124

Wages, employee, in dry goods store, 99, 101
Waiver, in lease for electronics firm, 209–210
Warehouse, locating, 71–72
Warranty, seller's, and choosing a business, 149
Woodworking, case involving, 346–355
Word-of-mouth advertising, 57
Working capital, bookstore, *232*
  consumer credit and, 60
  withdrawal of, 26
Working capital loan, 45–46
  in drugstore, 90–91
Working space, expenses, in case, 218
Worksheet. Also see *Analysis, Checklist* and *Evaluation*.
  for starting a business, *153, 154*

Yellow Pages, 56

Zoning regulations, compliance with, 71–72